CW01081586

Rose Croix
Essays

John Mandleberg

Lewis Masonic

Acknowledgements

I owe a considerable debt of gratitude to many people who have assisted me in compiling this account of the Ancient and Accepted Rite under the Supreme Council for England, etc. The Staff of the Library of The Museum and Library of the United Grand Lodge of England, in particular the Librarian, then Rebecca Combes, and her Assistants, Katrina Jowitt and Martin Cherry now Librarian, have dealt with all my importunate requests with the utmost patience, as, indeed, has Nigel Banks at No.10 Duke Street. My especial thanks go to Jim Daniel who has eliminated some grammatical idiosyncrasies (and corrected one or two blunders!), but the responsibility for any that remain is mine alone. Others, in particular M. Pierre Mollier, who have drawn my attention to various matters, and to all of whom I am equally grateful, are acknowledged in the text.

Finally, I must thank the Sovereign Grand Commander and the Members of the Supreme Council for England and Wales and its Districts and Chapters Overseas for entrusting me with this task.

John Mandleberg
Old Pusey Dale
Shavington
April 2004

First published 2005

ISBN (10) — spiral-bound edition 0 85318 246 9
ISBN (13) — spiral-bound edition 978 0 85318 246 7
ISBN (10) — case-bound edition 0 85318 257 4
ISBN (13) — case-bound edition 978 0 85318 246 3

All rights reserved. No part of this book may be reproduced or transmitted in any form or by any means, electronic or mechanical, including photocopying, recording or by any information storage and retrieval system, without permission from the Publisher in writing.

© John Mandleberg 2005

Published by Lewis Masonic

an imprint of Ian Allan Publishing Ltd, Hersham, Surrey KT12 4RG.
Printed in England by Ian Allan Printing Ltd, Hersham, Surrey KT12 4RG.

Contents

PART ONE

The establishment of the Supreme Council of the 33rd Degree of the Ancient and Accepted Rite for England and Wales

PART TWO

The Eighteenth or 'Rose Croix' Degree

PART THREE

The Ancient and Accepted Rite in England – Selected Topics

Note re References

References are set out in full, other than:

A & A – John Mandleberg, *Ancient and Accepted*, QCCC Ltd, 1995

AQC – *Ars Quatuor Coronatorum*. Transactions of Quatuor Coronati Lodge No. 2076
(with Volume Number, Page and Date of Volume)

R C – A.C.F. Jackson, *Rose Croix*, Revised and Enlarged Edition, Lewis Masonic, 1987

Instant history [that is, letters and records contemporary with the events described] *can tell us how events appeared before they became obscured in the fog of hindsight. For hindsight is the great enemy of the historian. We forget, all too easily, that what is now in the past once lay in the future.* – Victor Bogdanor

History is like a nymph glimpsed between leaves: the more you shift perspective, the more is revealed. If you want to see the whole you have to dodge and slip between many different viewpoints. – Felipe Fernández-Armesto.

Many errors, I doubt not, will be found in the following Oration: But as the Subject is important and as yet but little trodden; my aim truth, and the time allowed me to compose it, and prepare it for the press, was short, I hope they will be excused. I have placed my spes et solatium *in the candour and indulgence of my brethren.*
'Orations of the Illustrious Brother Frederick Dalcho M.D.' – Appendix to Second Oration (Reprinted, John King, Dublin, 1808. See page xxx.)

Introduction

On behalf of all members of the Supreme Council for England and Wales I welcome this collection of Essays which fulfills in every regard the twin aims of the author, namely to update aspects of the standard work "Rose Croix" by ACF Jackson and to provide suitable material for delivery in Rose Croix chapters. Recent years have seen a continued interest in history and background to our wonderful order and a growth in Higher Degree chapters for which this new collection is particularly apposite.

We are also pleased to see, in the Author's introduction, his caution to brethren regarding the all too frequent propagation of "truths" which have no basis of fact. Myths must always be regarded as such. The Supreme Council is, therefore, particularly indebted to John Mandleberg for the depth and care of his research and his diligence in the pursuit of fact across centuries and countries. The learning sits lightly in a text which can be both read and delivered with pleasure.

Our sincere thanks therefore go to V. Ill. Bro. John Mandleberg 33° for contributing a major work of scholarship in a form which will be widely used and appreciated by all members of the Ancient & Accepted Rite as well as by the wider public both Masonic and non-Masonic

GL Tedder 33°
Sovereign Grand Commander

August 2005

About the Author

John Mandleberg was born in Manchester in 1922. Educated at Harrow and Oxford (MA and BSc) he joined the Royal Artillery and served as a Captain in North Africa, Italy and Greece. After the war he became a Senior Scientific Officer at the Harwell Atomic Energy Research Establishment. More recently he was the Director of the Distributive Industry Training Board before becoming Chairman of Reads Limited of which he had formerly been Managing Director. A Fellow of the Royal Society of Chemistry he has written many scientific papers and is author of "Topics in Modern Chemistry".

John Mandleberg was initiated in Apollo University Lodge No. 357 in 1942. Perfected in the Ancient and Accepted Rite in Oxford University Chapter No.40 in 1948 and promoted to 33° in 1995. Brother Mandleberg is a PGSwdB in the Craft and currently W.M. of Quatuor Coronati Lodge No. 2076 and a PAGSoj in the Royal Arch; beyond 'pure antient masonry' he hold Grand Rank in several Masonic Orders, including Knights Templar (KCT), the Mark and Royal Ark Mariners, the Royal and Select Masters (Past Deputy GM), the Allied Masonic Degrees, Red Cross of Constantine, Order of the Secret Monitor and Knighs Templar Priests. He is a Past Deputy Provincial Grand Master in the Royal Order of Scotland. He is the author of "Ancient and Accepted" (1995) and (with L W Davies) "Royal Arch Masons and Knights Templar at Redruth, Cornwall 1791-1829" QCCC Limited 2005.

Author's Foreword

Anyone who reads these Essays and fails to accuse me of plagiarism cannot have read A.C.F. Jackson's *Rose Croix* with sufficient attention. In many respects *Rose Croix* will be, for many years to come, the standard work on the development in England of *The Ancient and Accepted Rite of Thirty-Three Degrees*. However, since Jackson himself revised *Rose Croix* in 1987, much new material about this Order has come to light.

It was originally suggested that on this account a further revision should now be made. Before he died Jackson approved this project – on condition that he himself should not be involved, being already then over ninety years of age! It soon became apparent that there would be considerable practical difficulties in producing such a revision. At the same time it would not meet a need of which The Supreme Council was well aware – that of providing material which could be presented from time to time in open Chapter.

J.K. Galbraith coined the phrase 'the collective wisdom of the Tribe' to describe widely held concepts which had a dubious basis in ascertainable fact. 'Josh Billings'[1] put it another way – "The trouble with people is not that they don't know but that they know so much that ain't so". There is nothing to which this applies more than to Masonic history. For self-evident reasons, much has never been committed to paper, and imagination and invention have often been given free rein. Unfortunately this has resulted in many things for which no evidence can be produced becoming well known as established facts. Not only this, but too often such matters continue to be passed on as 'facts' even when valid evidence of their falsity has been produced. This is something of which even the most senior and experienced of us may have unconsciously been guilty from time to time.

For this reason The Supreme Council has ever displayed that caution in which we have all been instructed about allowing historical statements to be made in open Chapter. However, there are evident benefits in Brethren being given accurate information about the history and evolution of the Ancient and Accepted Rite either as part of the specific Agenda for a Meeting, or at a Meeting when fortuitously there is no Candidate for Perfection. I was therefore commissioned to provide a sequence of 'Essays' or 'Papers', generally based on Jackson's work, but incorporating such further relevant facts which may have been established since his last revision of *Rose Croix*. Each such Essay had to be of no greater length than could be delivered at a single Meeting, and before publication each would be approved by The Supreme Council for such a delivery. The necessity for this careful approval has been a factor in the considerable time taken in bringing these Essays from manuscript to publication

I make no apology for the considerable repetition which is apparent if these Essays are read in sequence. This is inevitable if each is to stand alone for delivery at a single Meeting. There is, in addition, a considerable number of end-notes to each 'Essay'. Although each 'Essay' is sufficiently complete in itself, the 'End-Notes' are included for four reasons:

- • To quote authority for various statements (in particular for those which may be at considerable variance from 'the collective wisdom of the tribe'), and to enable readers to refer to sources if they wish to obtain further information on the topic.
- • To give credit to the various authorities whose works are quoted.
- • To include material which, while not essential to the narrative, may be of interest to a reader, but the inclusion of which in the text would have made the 'Essay' too long for listeners to endure.
- • To provide additional detail which may assist someone who receives questions from his audience after delivering the 'Paper'.

In addition there are Appendices to some of the Essays. These contain material which is unsuitable for verbal delivery, but which is of value to support the preceding text, and which, in many cases, is not otherwise easily available.

John Mandleberg

---

1   Henry Wheeler Shaw.

Part One

The establishment of the Supreme Council of the 33rd Degree of the Ancient and Accepted Rite for England and Wales

Essay 1
The Birth of Higher Degrees

In the seventeenth century in many parts of England there were men, for the most part unconnected with the building trade, who were accustomed to meet in Lodges of Speculative Freemasons to which new entrants received a ceremonial admission. Whatever may have motivated them to meet in this way, in 1717, at least according to Anderson writing 21 years after the event, some of those in London, members of 'four old lodges', decided to amalgamate to 'revive' a Grand Lodge, to which no earlier reference has ever been found.

There is still no consensus about the origin of the Speculative Lodges, nor about the reasons for forming a Grand Lodge. Whatever these may have been, events had progressed sufficiently by 24th June 1721 for John, 2nd Duke of Montagu, then thirty-three years of age, to be installed as the first Noble Grand Master of the new Grand Lodge. He followed the somewhat shadowy figures of Anthony Sayer and George Payne, and the considerably more substantial one of Dr. John Theophilus Desaguliers.

Throughout the seventeenth century, there are many English references to the Society of Freemasons as a 'Fellowship'. There is no doubt that, during this period, those in England who were admitted to its ranks at once became 'Fellows', no more and no less. Indeed, many later writers have seen an analogy with the Royal Society, founded in the second half of the century, whose members were also 'Fellows', and at least one of whom, Elias Ashmole, was also certainly a Freemason. However, by the 1720s English Freemasons appear to have recognised two grades of membership. This differentiation was almost certainly due to the influence of the Scottish operative Gilds, in which stonemasons progressed from Enter'd 'Printices to Fellows of Craft, which were anglicised as Entered Apprentices and Fellow Crafts, terms absent from earlier references to English Freemasonry.[2] Thus, at about the time of the erection of the first Grand Lodge, English Freemasons were acquiring two ceremonies, although it was to be some years before the material contained in each of these was clearly separated.

The publication of Samuel Prichard's *Masonry Dissected* in 1730 marks a defining moment in the development of Speculative Freemasonry. We shall probably never know how much of this exposure of the Craft ritual is a fabrication, or how accurate an account it is of the actual working in English Lodges of three distinct Degrees, culminating in that of 'The Master'. Its most important contribution is to put on to a firm narrative basis the Hiramic legend, the centre-piece from which almost every subsequent Order in Freemasonry is constructed or developed[3]. Hiram may not, however, have been the only character whose dramatic raising was being re-enacted in early Lodges. For example, the Graham manuscript of 1726 refers to the raising of Noah, otherwise using wording identical to that used by Prichard in relation to Hiram[4].

Masonry Dissected is no more than a catechism directed to a Brother who has passed through the ceremonies. It contains neither rubric nor stage directions, and gives no other indication of what actually went on in the Lodge[5]. But for all that, there is considerable evidence that it was seized on by many Brethren as an authoritative guide. It rapidly passed through several editions, both authorised and pirated[6]. A French translation was published in Paris in 1737[7], and reprinted in Brussels in the same year, and a German translation was published in 1738.[8] The influence of *Masonry Dissected* on the development of Craft ritual, both in the British Isles and overseas, can hardly be over-estimated.

In England in the 1730s the Craft was becoming well established. The Grand Mastership of the Duke of Montagu demonstrates that its membership was being drawn from all levels of society. However, the unanswered question posed by the Substituted Secrets in the third or Master's Degree as set out in *Masonry Dissected* soon failed to satisfy those Brethren who had proceeded to it, although it was to be many years before this Degree was universally conferred. As Eric Ward put it:

> 'The loss of the genuine and the finding of substitute secrets can hardly be regarded as a satisfying transaction. The fact that time or circumstance could ... by some means or other restore the genuine secrets[9] suggested that they were ... only temporarily lost and might just as well be looked for right away.'[10]

It was therefore almost inevitable that there would be attempts to provide a more satisfactory conclusion to the *Hiramic* story. For example, in England in the 1730s and for perhaps thirty years afterwards, the additional Degree of 'Scots' or 'Scotch Master' was conferred on several occasions on English Brethren who were already Master Masons, and who had, in some cases, even passed the Chair of their Lodge. The only thing known with any certainty about this Degree is that it had nothing to do with Scotland or with Scottish Freemasonry. It may well have been the precursor of the Degree of *The Holy Royal Arch*, the subsequent development of which seems to have been sufficient for the next quarter of a century or so to have satisfied the majority of English Freemasons who had ambitions outside the three Degrees of the Craft.

By this time Freemasonry was also well established in France. Some authors have claimed that there were Lodges of Speculative Freemasons in France even before the formation of the Premier Grand Lodge in England, but no acceptable evidence of this has yet been found[11]. Traditionally it is said to have been Charles Radcliffe, 'Earl of Derwentwater'[12], who opened the first Lodge in Paris in about 1725, and this was certainly followed by several others in the course of the next few years. At first, the English-speaking element predominated in these Lodges. The greater part of their membership consisted of Englishmen, but many Scotsmen were also included. Thus the word *Ecossais*, for whatever type of Masonry was being worked, would not have been wholly misplaced; it would certainly have been popular with the Jacobites in the service of the Stuart Pretenders. There was at first no official interference with Freemasons' Lodges in France. All clandestine activities were, however, viewed with suspicion by the authorities, spies and informers were encouraged, and it is not surprising that the Police kept the Lodges under surveillance. In many cases the surviving Police Reports provide valuable information about contemporary Masonic activities.

The first 'Book of Constitutions' had been published in England in 1723. It was largely the work of James Anderson, though he certainly received assistance from several others in compiling it. It was prefaced by a long 'Traditional History' of Masonry in the style of the records in the 'Old Manuscript Charges'. Anderson made it clear in this history that while Kings and Princes had been patrons of the Craft, the Masons themselves were workmen, commoners, and it was they from whom Anderson considered that the Speculative Freemasons of his day derived their origins. There was nothing in this pedigree which ran contrary to the character of English society. The English nobility did not consider themselves a race apart from the rest of the population. They saw nothing amiss in taking part in the work of Lodges in the company of those of lower social rank, as was demonstrated by the election of the Duke of Montagu as Grand Master. Indeed, it was not to be too long before there were Royal Brethren. The statement in the present Charge to the Initiate that Monarchs themselves "have not thought it derogatory to their dignity to exchange the Sceptre for the Trowel, have patronised our Mysteries, and joined our Assemblies" would have been perfectly acceptable to most eighteenth century Englishmen, noblemen and commoners alike.

It was otherwise in France. As Jackson puts it, in France "in its early days, masonry, unlike in England, was often an entirely upper class affair ... patronised by the nobility, those around the royal court and their hangers-on"[13]. In 1737 the Police Reports record that among the Masters of Lodges in France were a Prince (Conti), two Dukes (Aumont, and Villeroy who had succeeded to the Mastership of the Lodge founded by John Coustos), and Count Schapsky, a cousin of Maria Leszczynska, then Queen of France. But things were changing. Within a few years several inn-keepers, particularly in the City of Paris, set up Lodges in their own taverns, presumably with an eye to the financial advantages of so doing. They then gave themselves Warrants which conferred on each the perpetual Mastership of his Lodge. Further, by 1744 the lists in the Police Reports include a wine-merchant and a candle-maker as Masters of Lodges. The aristocratic Freemasons had no wish to associate with such people and looked for means of distancing themselves from them.[14]

It was not only Anderson's 'Traditional History' which was not in accord with the fastidious tastes of the French Aristocracy. That Speculative Freemasons were the heirs of Mediaeval operatives was bad enough, but this was accentuated by the Hiramic legend to which Prichard had given currency. The 'Secret of the Temple' was in the joint possession not only of Solomon, King of Israel, and of Hiram, King of Tyre, but also of one of their employees; the legend envisaged a common workman (for it is only as such that Hiram Abif is described in Holy Scripture) being on terms of equality with two Kings. Such a concept was wholly contrary to French aristocratic *mores*[15]; the 'Aristos' had no wish to be considered the heirs of common workmen.

The evident response with which to resolve this dilemma was to invent new Degrees, within which the Nobility and the Court could feel comfortably insulated from the *hoi polloi*. Possibly the earliest reference to this occurs in a Parisian broadsheet. Under the dateline of 'March 1737' it records:

Our Lords of the Court have quite recently invented (*inventé*) an Order called 'Frimassons' following the example of England where there are also different orders of persons, and we are not behind in imitating these foreign irrelevances. Several of our Ministers, Dukes and Lords have been initiated in this Order. It is not known what are the Statutes, Regulations and Objects of this new Order. They have been meeting together and receiving new Chevaliers and the first rule is that of inviolable secrecy concerning everything that happens. As such secret assemblies, being composed of influential persons, are very dangerous in the State, especially during a time of change, which has just been the case in the Ministry, Cardinal de Fleury has felt it his duty to stifle this Order of Chivalry (*Ordre de Chevalerie*) at its birth and he has forbidden all men to meet and hold such Chapters (*Chapitres*)[16].

This may have been the reason why, in the following week, Coustos' Lodge, over which the Duc de Villeroy was presiding, attempted to protect itself by recording "the Brethren added that the Order is not an Order of chivalry ...", thus providing indirect confirmation of Barbier's statement.

By this time there had appeared on the French Masonic scene a remarkable character, Andrew Michael Ramsay[17]. Ramsay was a complex, not to say enigmatic, character. He was

a Scottish expatriate, yet he was welcomed home from France by the English government. He was a Roman Catholic and a Jacobite, but he was awarded an honorary degree from Oxford[18] and made a Fellow of the Royal Society[19]. He was tutor to the eldest son of James Stewart, the Old Pretender, and [was] offered the same position by George II to tutor his son, the Duke of Cumberland ... At different times of his life, he was a Presbyterian, a Roman Catholic, and a Freemason, but he remained a Quietist[20] all his life. His life is a study of dichotomies[21].

In 1709, at the age of 23, Ramsay had left his native Scotland for France having first spent some time in London and afterwards in Holland. Living then in Paris, he was well-received both by the Jacobite followers of the 'Old Pretender' and also by many in the upper reaches of French Society. In 1723 the Scottish baker's son received a Patent of Nobility from the 'Old Pretender', Prince James Edward Stuart[22]. Seven years later, in March 1730, towards the end of a year-long visit to England, Ramsay was initiated into Freemasonry in the Horn Lodge, of which Dr. Desaguliers was also a member[23]. Shortly afterwards, Ramsay returned to Paris where he soon became deeply involved in Masonic affairs, rapidly becoming Grand Orator in the Grand Lodge of France.

Ramsay evidently did not feel at ease with the 'Traditional History' which Anderson had included in his 1723 *Book of Constitutions*[24]. By 1736 Ramsay had written his own very different 'Traditional History', an account which is inaccurately but universally referred to as his '*Oration*'[25]. It is probable that Ramsay delivered the original version of this at "the St. John's Lodge on 26th December 1736"; this "may well have been the Grand Master's Lodge, St. Thomas's No.1" meeting at Epernay[26]. He intended to repeat a modified version of the *Oration* at the Meeting of the Grand Lodge of France on 24th March 1737[27]. Before doing so, Ramsay, who was temporarily absent from Paris, considered it prudent to submit the text to Cardinal Fleury[28], the principal Minister of King Louis XV. Ramsay returned to Paris before receiving a reply from the Cardinal, but on 17th March he learnt of the prohibition which had been briefly reported in *Le Journal de l'Avocat Barbier*, and, moreover, that on that day Fleury had instructed Hérault, the Lieutenant-General of Police, 'that no further meetings of Freemasons were to be held'. Ramsay therefore hurriedly wrote to Fleury[29] on 22nd March to assure the Cardinal that he was now aware 'that Assemblies of Freemasons displease Your Excellency', and went on to say 'I pray you to inform me whether I should return to those Assemblies'. Fleury returned Ramsay's letter endorsed with the terse comment "The King does not wish it"[30]. After Fleury's prohibition, the Grand Lodge Meeting scheduled for 24th March 1737 evidently could no longer take place, and, contrary to what has often been asserted, it appears probable that in 1737 Ramsay did not deliver his *Oration* anywhere in France.[31]

Indeed, after receiving Fleury's curt response, Ramsay appears to have severed his official connection with the French Grand Lodge. This did not, however, prevent him circulating copies of his *Oration*. On 16th April he wrote to the Marquis de Caumont enclosing a shortened version[32]. On 2nd August he wrote (in English) to Carte, an English Jacobite, to say that he had delivered the *Oration* at various times at the aception of eight dukes and peers, and two hundred officers of the first rank and highest nobility. He concludes by saying that had not the Cardinal interfered, he was to have had the opportunity to attempt to persuade the King himself to be initiated[33]. It is impossible to say whether this was true, but in spite of Fleury's comment, it is possible that the King was less opposed to Freemasonry than was his Cardinal-Minister[34].

Hérault had himself published an exposure of Freemasonry at about this time; it is said that Hérault had obtained the manuscript from a dancer at the Paris Opera named Madame Carton[35]. This elicited a response, *Relation apologique et historique de la Société des F.M.*, which was published in Dublin early in 1738. However, on 28th April of that year Freemasonry was pontifically condemned by Pope Clement XII in the Bull *In Eminenti*, a pronouncement which, curiously, was never promulgated in France. But one of the consequences of the Papal condemnation was that the *Relation Apologique* was anathematised by the Holy Office. It was formally burnt in the Piazza de Santa Maria Minerva in Rome on 25th February 1739[36].

Ramsay's widely circulated *Oration* was almost certainly a major influence on the development of Freemasonry in France. The first of its three sections sets out the nature of the Craft and the duties expected of its Members. The second part envisages how Freemasonry might develop in France to the advantage of the world in general and of the French Nation in particular. But it is the third part, a traditional history as fanciful as that of Anderson, which provided the French nobility with what they were looking for. The earliest manuscript version, that believed to have been delivered at Epernay, was 'Andersonian' in the sense that it asserts that Freemasonry could be traced back to the Hebrew Patriarchs and their contemporaries – "Noah, Abraham, the Patriarchs, Moses, Solomon and Cyrus were the early Grand Masters in our ancient order". Ramsay had significantly revised this version of events in preparation for the delivery at the Grand Lodge which he was fated never to give. In this, and in other later versions, Ramsay discounts the attribution of the origins of the Craft to King Solomon, still less to Adam. While he acknowledges the debt which Freemasonry owes to the ancient Mysteries, he looks for a specific origin in a revival which, he asserts, took place during the Western campaigns to recover the Holy Land from the Infidel:

> At the time of the Crusades in Palestine many princes, lords and citizens banded together and vowed to restore the Temple of the Christians in the Holy Land, to employ themselves in bringing back their architecture to its first institution.

> Our ancestors, the Crusaders, who were gathered together in the Holy Land from all parts of Christendom, desired in this manner to reunite the individuals of all nations into one sole Fraternity ...

> Our Order, therefore, must not be considered a revival of the Bacchanals, but as an order founded in remote antiquity, renewed in the Holy Land by our ancestors in order to recall the memory of the most sublime truths amidst the pleasures of society ...

> Our Order formed an intimate union with the Knights of St. John of Jerusalem[37]. From that time our lodges took the name of Lodges of St. John. This union was made after the example of the Israelites when they erected the second Temple who, whilst they handled the trowel and mortar with one hand, in the other held the sword and buckler ...

Then, having given contemporary French Freemasons suitably noble forebears – the Crusaders and the Knights of St. John of Jerusalem – Ramsay goes on to explain from whence the traditional Scottish connection was derived, and also why the Lodges in France were derived from those in England:

> The Kings, princes and lords returned from Palestine to their own lands and there established divers lodges. At the time of the last Crusades many lodges were already erected in Germany, Italy, Spain, France and, from thence, in Scotland because of the close alliance between the French and the Scots. James, Lord Steward of Scotland, was Grand Master of a Lodge established at Kilwinning in the West of Scotland MCCLXXXVI [*1286*], shortly after the death of Alexander III, King of Scotland, and one year before John Baliol mounted the Throne. This lord received as Freemasons into his Lodge, the Earls of Gloucester and Ulster, the one English, the other Irish. By degrees, the solemn proceedings in our Lodges were neglected in most places. That is why, of so many historians, only those of Great Britain speak of our Order. Nevertheless it preserved its splendour amongst those Scotsmen to whom the Kings of France confided during many centuries the safeguard of their royal persons.

This completely fictitious story was well calculated to satisfy every Freemason in France. Not only was the Craft given a suitably aristocratic background without involving ignoble artificers, but its renewal in the Holy Land put even King Solomon and his operative builder into the background. It removed England, with whom relations were strained, from the important role conferred upon it by the erection of the premier Grand Lodge. It elevated Scotland, the country of the 'auld alliance', as the custodian of the Craft, but with no reference to the 'Meason Word' (thereby avoiding the intrusion of the unmentionable operatives and their Gilds) – the 'secret words' of Freemasons were clearly stated, in the later version of the *Oration*, to be those exchanged by the Crusaders 'to guarantee them from the surprises of the Saracens'[38]. That Freemasons had a noble ancestry justified the adoption of terms such as *chevalier* and *chevalerie* as marks of distinction from the common herd. Finally, by the derivation from the Crusades and the alliance with the Knights of St. John of Jerusalem it avoided the Deism with which Anderson had infected the English Craft[39] and it might even have been hoped that this Christian basis would disarm clerical critics such as Cardinal Fleury, although his preoccupation was more probably with conspiracy rather than heresy.

Whether these were the effects which Ramsay intended is very doubtful. On the contrary, he himself placed the emphasis not so much on the aristocratic background as upon the desire which he attributed to the Crusaders "to reunite the individuals of all nations into one sole fraternity". "The whole world," he said "is nothing but a huge republic, of which each nation is a family, and each individual a child". The 'Higher Degrees' had already been born; there is no doubt that the *Oration* provided an impetus for their development, but Ramsay had neither invented them, nor even suggested that they would be desirable.

While there is substantial evidence for the embryonic existence by 1740 of 'Higher Degrees', the evidence concerning their development is very flimsy. In England, apart from 14 Editions of *Masonry Dissected*, little else was published between 1730 and 1760, and nothing that extended the Craft beyond the Third Degree[40]. In France, 12 exposures (several based on Prichard) were published between 1737 and 1751, and have been reproduced in translation by Harry Carr[41]. Some of these appear to be fantastic inventions, while others may contain a substratum of fact; but it is hard to say which is which. But without placing too great reliance on any one of these publications, the earliest development seems to involve material similar to that which appears today in the *Royal Arch* Ceremony. The Degree was specifically known as '*Ecossais*'. By the end of the 1740s a Christian element had appeared, introducing not only St. John, but also "the Blood which the Saviour shed for the human race"[42]. Before 1750 these concepts were extended further into more than one 'Rite', or sequence of several Degrees, following on from the three Degrees of the Craft itself.

There has been much controversy about why the word *Ecossais*, 'Scottish', became attached to these Degrees. It is tempting to derive it from the English Lodges of 'Scots Masters' which may well have been developing similar material, but there is no shred of evidence connecting the English 'Scots' and the French '*Ecossais*' Lodges[43]. That the word *Ecossais* had any connection with the followers of 'the Young Pretender', Charles Edward Stuart, is generally discounted today, although the Jacobites may have used some Lodges to further their plans before their influence in France dwindled after the failure of the 'Forty-Five' and the expulsion of the 'Young Pretender' from France[44]. Certainly the 'Higher Degrees' can claim no descent from the Masonry practised under the Grand Lodge of Scotland[45]. It is considered more probable that '*Ecossais*' and (in England) 'Scots' were simply terms used to differentiate this new 'Higher' Masonry from the Three Degrees practised under the Grand Lodge of England.

But, be all that as it may, in France the Maîtres Ecossais esteemed themselves to be superior to three-degree Craft Masons and they "were assuming privileges in private lodges". Article 20 of new General Regulations approved by the French Grand Lodge on 11th December 1743 forbade them to do this, or, in private lodges, to dress differently from the remaining Brethren[46]. If nothing else, this prohibition is adequate confirmation of the existence of so-called *Ecossais* Brethren. However, within two years, this Article was rescinded, and in new General Regulations the '*Ecossais*' were recognised as Superintendents of the work[47].

By 1750 Degrees providing Masonic ceremonies beyond the three Degrees of the 'Craft' were well established in France. They provided both a more satisfactory conclusion to the Craft legends than the bare facts of the interment of Hiram Abif, and the consequent adoption of 'Substituted Secrets' and also the hierarchic gradation which the upper French social classes desired. Anyone, commoner or gentleman, could become a Master Mason and attain the Mastership of a Lodge, but further 'promotion' was not automatic; those who became Maîtres Ecossais, and thereby assumed a supervisory role, could prevent others whom they considered to be socially undesirable becoming added to their numbers and thus preserve the exclusivity of the aristocrats.

Invention, however, tends to feed upon itself. The fabrication of new Degrees was not only a legitimate intellectual occupation for those genuinely interested in raising further moral lessons on the substrate of Freemasonry. It could also be a financially rewarding one for less scrupulous practitioners who professed to reveal ever more arcane 'secrets' and to confer further splendiferous titles on those gullible enough to pay for the privilege. It was to be another thirty years before order was imposed upon the chaos into which such practitioners were about to plunge the 'High Degrees'.

---

2   All the exposures, catechisms and fragments of ritual prior to c.1710 which refer to a preliminary grade of Apprentice or its equivalent are of Scottish or Irish, apparently Operative, origin. See C.J. Mandleberg, *The Secrets of the Craft*, AQC CXIII, 35-36, 2000, and D. Knoop, G.P. Jones & D.Hamer, *Early Masonic Catechisms* pp. 31-70, QCCC, Revd. Edition, 1963.

3   The 'Three Degree system' was certainly not invented by Prichard. For example, the Graham Manuscript of 1726 refers to 'entering', 'passing' and 'raising'. In his speech at York in December 1727 Drake refers to a division into 'E.P., F.C., and M.M.' Furthermore, a skit in the form of an Advertisement for 'Antediluvian Masonry' had appeared as early as 1726, referring to ' the whole history of the Widow's son killed by the Blow of a Beetle, afterwards found three Foot East, three Foot West and three Foot perpendicular'. D. Knoop, G.P. Jones and D. Hamer, *Early Masonic Pamphlets*, pp. 192-194, QCCC Reprint, 1975.

4   *Early Masonic Catechisms* (v.s.) pp.92/3

5   For a fuller discussion, see *Early Masonic Catechisms* (v.s.) passim.

6   The later Editions contain a list of 67 Lodges, several of which still exist today.

7   *Reception d'un Frey-Mason*

8   Harry Carr, *The Early French Exposures,* p.3 *et seq.*, QCCC, 1971.

9   While this assumption is justifiable, even so eminent an authority as Bro. Eric Ward may have been getting ahead of himself. There is no mention of time or circumstance enabling such a recovery to be made in 'Prichard'.

10   AQC, LXXV, p.158, 1962.

11   See, for example, John Hamill, *The Jacobite Conspiracy*, AQC 113, p.98, 2000.

12   The 'Earl of Derwentwater' was an attainted title to which Charles Radcliffe had no right, for his brother, from whom he claimed to have inherited it, had been executed for his part in the 'Rebellion' of 1715. Charles Radcliffe himself was beheaded after the failure of the abortive 1745 Rising.

13   RC p.8 In his text Jackson inserts the parenthesis '*particularly outside Paris*' , but Bernheim considers that this is inaccurate. (Alain Bernheim, Private Communication, Note 4, 4 March 2000).

14   It has been said facetiously, but with an element of truth, that there might have been no French Revolution if the French Aristocrats had played cricket with their tenantry as their English counterparts did.

15   "De ce chef il détient, suivant ce nouveau mythe, collectivement avec le Roi Salomon et Hiram Roi de Tyr, son ancien employeur, le véritable secret du Temple. Indépendamment de cette implication sociale remarquable: un ouvrier devenu l'égal de deux rois, voilà la base qui va servir de support à tous les soi-disant hauts *[sic]* grades de la Franc-maçonnerie inventés depuis lors." Michel Brodsky, *Les mythes et les légendes de la Grande Loge Unie d'Angleterre*, Renaissance Traditionelle, No.129, p.133, January 2002

16   *Le Journal de l'Avocat Barbier*, Vol. II, pp.148/9, 1737. But see C.N Batham, *Chevalier Ramsay, A new appreciation*, AQC, LXXXI, p.294 1968, for an assessment of whether Barbier, a non-Mason, was really writing of a new development. But in spite of Batham's caution, since Free Masonry had been established in France for more than ten years by 1737, and since the authorities were already well aware of its existence, Barbier could hardly have written as he did if he were not referring to a new facet of it.

17   "He was probably born on 9th June,1686, it was probably in the town of Ayr in Scotland and he was probably christened Andrew Ramsay, but we cannot be certain as there is no mention of his birth, even though the *Records of Baptism* at Ayr from 1684 are extant. He came of a humble family and may well have been the son of Andrew Ramsay, a local baker, and his wife Susanna. If so, he may have been born in Ireland, as his father was in trouble with the authorities in 1684, a time of political and religious strife, and found it necessary to leave Ayr, taking his wife with him, and to live in Ireland until some time in 1686." *Ibidem*, p.280

18   "On 10th April, 1730 Ramsay received the Degree of Doctor of Civil Law at Oxford being the first Catholic to receive a Degree there since the Reformation". *ibidem*, p.285.

19   In 1729

20   Quietism was a profession of the worship of God in spirit and in truth without ceremony, credal professions or ritual, which had been formulated by Madame Guyon, as whose Secretary Ramsay acted 1714–1716.

21   Lisa Kahler *Andrew Michael Ramsay and his Masonic*

Oration, Heredom, 1, p.19, 1992.

22 The Title of 'Chevalier', by which Ramsay is generally known, was derived not from this Patent, but from his admittance, some years earlier, as a 'Chevalier of the Royal and Military Order of St. Lazarus of Jerusalem' by its Grand Master, the duc d'Orléans, to whose grandson Ramsay was Tutor. Batham, *loc. cit.*, p.282.

23 Ramsay was elected to the Royal Society and also initiated into Freemasonry at about the same time as was the noted French philosopher Charles-Louis Montesquieu. Paul Tunbridge, *The Climate of European Freemasonry 1730 to 1750,* AQC LXXXI, p.96, 1968.

24 "TO BE READ At the Admission of a NEW BROTHER, when the *Master* or *Warden* shall begin, or order some other Brother to read."

25 The correct title of the so-called 'Oration' is, in translation, *Discourse pronounced at the reception of Freemasons. Ibidem,* p.102.

26 Batham, *loc. cit.*, p.287.

27 Tunbridge is almost certainly in error in writing that the *Discourse* "was first delivered in the form of a speech in March, 1737". Tunbridge, *loc. cit.*, p.102.

28 "André Hercule de Fleury, Bishop of Fréjus (b. 1653, d. 1743), Cardinal-Minister to Louis XV, 1726/43" Batham *loc. cit.* p.290.f/n 1.

29 The letter bears the date '20th March' in a different hand, 'possibly added by the Cardinal's Secretary when the letter was delivered'. Bernheim, *op. cit.*, Note 7, p.13.

30 Batham, *loc. cit.*, p.290.

31 That no Meeting of Grand Lodge took place on 24th March1737 is confirmed by the Minute-book of John Coustos' Lodge which records that, on that date, a letter was read from the Grand Master (the self-styled 'Earl of Derwentwater') indicating that because of the circumstances which had arisen, the Grand Lodge Meeting would have to be postponed.

32 Whereas in his earlier version Ramsay asserted that the secrets of Masonry were communicated by Noah, through the Jewish Patriarchs, to King Solomon, each successively the Grand Master of the Order, in the version which he sent to Caumont, Ramsay said that this transmission was no more than legendary. Bernheim, Heredom 5, p.10, 1996.

33 Bodleian Library MS No.226, folio 398, quoted by Tunbridge, *loc. cit.* p.103, and Bernheim, *op. cit.*, p.12.

34 If the King himself was opposed to Freemasonry it is difficult to believe that both the duc de Villeroy and the King's *valet de chambre*, Bontemps, would have risked the Royal displeasure by being Initiated in the 'Coustos' Lodge in 1737, or that the duc d'Antin in 1738, and, five years later, the comte de Clermont, himself a member of the Royal family, would have accepted the Grand Mastership.

35 Batham, *loc. cit.*, p.296. In 1730 Mademoiselle Carton had been described as young and pretty and the mistress of the Comte de Saxe. Tunbridge, *loc. cit.* p.111. For a detailed account of the events leading to the publication of Hérault's pamphlet, see 'Henri Amblaine', *Masonic Catechisms and Exposures*, AQC CVI, p.143, 1993.

36 Fr. José A. Ferrer Benimeli, *Masoneria Inglesia e Illustracion*, Vol.i, p.233, Madrid, 1982. It has frequently been stated that it was a copy of the 'Oration' itself which was burnt, but there is no evidence that this was ever done.

37 That is, 'St. John the Almsgiver' to whose protection the Hospital at Jerusalem had originally been confided. It was only later that the Hospitallers sought a more powerful protector in St. John the Evangelist.

38 It is of some interest to read this in conjunction with the Opening of the *Baldwyn* Rite of Knight Templar in Bristol, England.

39 "But though in ancient Times Masons were charged to be of the Religion of that Country or Nation, whatever it was, yet 'tis now thought more expedient only to oblige them to that Religion in which all Men agree, leaving their particular Opinions to themselves". James Anderson *The Charges of a Freemason*, Article 1, in *The Constitutions of Freemasonry*, 1723.

40 Two rejoinders to *Masonry Dissected* were published shortly after its original appearance.

41 *Loc. cit.; v.supra.*

42 RC, p.20

43 This dogmatic statement, which is customarily made, may have to be modified in the light of a document, looted from the Grand Orient of France by the Germans in 1940, subsequently taken to Moscow by the Russians, and recently returned to Paris. This is a hard-back manuscript volume of 140 pages containing the Regulations and the Minutes of 141 Meetings between 1742 and 1752 of the 'Scottish Union Lodge' in Paris. Several entries suggest English influence, although these may have been deliberate contemporary insertions to pretend an English origin for the Degree conferred. Pierre Mollier, News from the "Russian Archives" about the Early History of the High Degrees, *The Chain of Union* (English language edition), No.2, p.59 (2004)

44 See, for example, John Hamill, *The Jacobite Conspiracy*, *loc. cit.*,for an examination of Jacobite involvement in the development of French Masonry, which Bro. Hamill considers was minimal.

45 In 1757, Thomas Manningham, D.G.M. of the Grand Lodge of England, consulted by the Grand Lodge at The Hague about 'Scottish Masonry', replied "Lord Aberdour & all the Scotch Masons (or rather Scotch gentlemen who are Masons) that I have conversed with & I have made it my business to consult many, are entirely unacquainted with the Forms and Titles you mention". E.A.Boerenbeker, *The relations between Dutch and English Freemasonry from 1734 to 1771*, AQC, LXXXIII, Appendix C, p.164, 1970.

46 RC, pp.10/11,'One Article condemned high degree masonry'. This, perhaps, goes too far. The article recognises that there are Ecossais Masters, and does no more than forbid them to assume privileges and powers when attending Craft Lodges.

47 The supervisory role of the Maîtres Ecossais was recognised in France for many years. The position which was restored to them in 1745 was confirmed in new Statutes promulgated in 1755, again recognising them as Superintendents (but only to correct mistakes), who were entitled to speak whenever they wanted, and who would always wear their swords and their hats in Lodge, and making clear that one Ecossais could only be corrected by another.

Essay 2
The Early High Degrees

During the twenty years following 1735, English Freemasons became sharply divided. On the one side were those who considered that the three Craft Degrees – Entered Apprentice, Fellow Craft and Master Mason, together with an embryonic Installation ceremony - were the be-all and end-all of Freemasonry. On the other were those who believed that Freemasonry could offer something further. To the latter, the Degree of the *Holy Royal Arch* gradually emerged to provide a more satisfactory conclusion than the abrupt interment of Hiram Abif[48] and the adoption of a substituted word, which was all that Prichard had to offer in his 1730 exposure, *Masonry Dissected*. By 1751 those who considered that the 'Royal Arch' was the 'Root, Heart and Marrow of Free-Masonry'[49] had set up the 'Grand Lodge of the Antients', the Lodges on its Register being allowed to work this Degree (and also, later, others). Its members scornfully dubbed those who adhered to the more conservative Premier Grand Lodge as the 'Moderns'.

Masonry Dissected had been adopted by many Brethren, both in England and in France, as a guide to Masonic ritual, but the failure to recover the genuine Master-word was not the only omission that an enquiring mind could discover within it. Prichard's exposé recorded nothing about the apprehension and subsequent fate of the assassins – that one of them, at least, must have been interrogated is evident from the description of Hiram's murder and of the first disposal of his body, the details of which, as set out in Prichard's Ritual, only they could know. Furthermore, although the First Temple was certainly completed after Hiram's murder, the death of the principal builder must have required considerable administrative re-arrangements. Prichard had recorded nothing of this, nor, indeed, of the appointment of a successor to Hiram Abif which was an evident necessity.

There is reliable evidence that by 1735 some English Freemasons were looking beyond the Craft. A few 'Scots Masters' Lodges' were working a ceremony which may have already contained the seeds of the 'Royal Arch'. Furthermore, in the early 1740s there were certainly Lodges in the London area owing allegiance to a Provincial Grand Lodge of what is now known as 'The Royal Order of Scotland'. After 1752 these Lodges faded away in England where there does not seem to have been any widespread desire to introduce chivalric Degrees. For several years thereafter English Freemasons with enquiring minds appear to have been satisfied with the discoveries in the 'Royal Arch', a Degree which is solely concerned with the building of the Second Temple[50]. It was otherwise in France. In its early days French Freemasonry had drawn its members almost exclusively from the ranks of the nobility. Within a very few years the Craft became spread widely among small tradesmen and the like from whom the nobility were accustomed to receive considerable deference in the course of their everyday dealings with them. Egalitarian 'English' Symbolic Masonry gave no opportunity for those who frequented the Royal Court to attain a superior Masonic status which would entitle them to receive within the Lodge the social deference which they customarily received outside it. The senior aristocratic Masons therefore had a considerable inducement to develop 'Higher Degrees', the membership of which they would be in a position to restrict.

There was, however, no authoritarian control of how any such developments should take place. Indeed, Masonic governance in France was in a confused state. The French Grand Lodge exercised little influence outside the City of Paris, and was unrepresentative of Lodges in the French Provinces. Before, say, 1750, the greater part of its membership, apart from the Masters of the Lodges in Paris itself, consisted of noble appointees of the Grand Master. Several 'Provincial' Masonic centres considered themselves virtually autonomous and for the most part ignored the undistinguished Deputies whom the noble Grand Officers generally appointed to perform their own duties[51].

Bordeaux was prominent among those towns which housed semi-autonomous Masonic centres. Its Lodges became particularly influential in the development of the 'Higher Degrees'. In 1732 a Lodge had been founded there by English wine-merchants[52]; initially it took the name of *'Loge L'Anglaise'*[53], and owed allegiance to the Grand Lodge in London, not to that in Paris. Towards the end of 1740[54] *Loge L'Anglaise* warranted a daughter-Lodge in Bordeaux, *Loge La Française* and, in May 1744, the two Lodges jointly acknowledged a third, *Parfaite Harmonie,* in order to resolve a disagreement which had broken out among some of the Brethren. In May 1744, a fourth Lodge, *L'Amitié,* was added to the group at Bordeaux. In the following years *Loge La Française* was active in warranting further Lodges not only in its own immediate vicinity, but also overseas, and even in Paris within the jurisdiction of the French Grand Lodge itself.

Before 1737 there had been no official restraint upon Masonic activities in France, although Police spies and informers kept a close eye upon the activities of the lodges, particularly within the City of Paris. However, in that year, Cardinal Fleury, for many years the Chief Minister to King Louis XV of France, heard rumours that aristocratic French Masons were developing a Freemasonry with chivalric overtones. The Cardinal considered that this might be subversive, and, on 17th March, he had instructed Hérault, the Lieutenant-General of Police, that no further meetings of these were to be held[55].

The Cardinal-Minister Fleury died in 1743, and the King appointed no single successor to him. The authority which Fleury had exercised was divided between several Secretaries of State, of whom at least two, the Comte de Saint-Florentin and the Comte de Maurepas, were Freemasons.[56] The repression of Freemasonry instituted by Cardinal Fleury then ceased[57]. It is perhaps no coincidence that it was in the following year that references to the proceedings in 'Higher Degree Lodges' first began to appear in the exposures published in France. These claimed to set out the working of those Degrees which presumably allowed the aristocratic Brethren to detach themselves from their social inferiors. At an early date in the development of these Degrees, those who obtained such promotion were known as 'Maîtres Ecossais', 'Scotch Masters', not because there was any connection between these Degrees and the Masonry practised in Scotland, but almost certainly to do no more than differentiate them from the three Craft Degrees of 'English' Freemasonry[58].

During the life-time of the duc d'Antin, these '*Ecossais*' Masons began to assume privileges when they attended private '3-Degree' Lodges. The duc himself died some months after the death of Fleury, and two weeks later, on 11th December 1743, the comte de Clermont[59] was elected to succeed him as Grand Master. On the day of his election the Grand Master's Lodge promulgated new Regulations forbidding *Ecossais* when attending Craft Lodges to set themselves up as superior to other Brethren by demanding special powers and wearing distinctive clothing[60]. That such a Regulation was seen to be necessary is conclusive evidence that the *Ecossais* were claiming such superiority. Indeed, within two years a further set of Regulations re-instated the *Ecossais* as Superintendents of the Work, a position in French Masonry which they continued to occupy for many years.

The earliest exposure to purport to give any details of the *Ecossais* Degrees was *Le Parfait Maçon,* published anonymously in Paris in 1744. How far this can be relied upon it is impossible to say. Its description of the Craft Ceremonies differs considerably from that in earlier such works, while conveying a familiar Masonic 'flavour'. Harry Carr took the view that

> "it was deliberately designed to put people off the scent, so that the publication of a whole new collection of signs, tokens, words and floor-cloths, so different from earlier texts, might sow doubt in the minds of non-Masons who had acquired a knowledge of Masonic matters from more or less dubious sources"[61].

Whether this applies to the Section on *Ecossais* Masonry it is impossible to say. This part of the text is so much in line with later evidence that it probably contains at least a substratum of truth about the proceedings of the *Ecossais*. There is a flavour of authenticity whatever may be the provenance of the extraordinary and unique Passwords, to which Harry Carr's caution almost certainly applies[62]. The underlying narrative is not necessarily a fabrication, and its contents are those which would have given the *Ecossais* grounds for wearing their swords in Lodge, and for claiming supervisory rights, each of which the 1743 Regulations forbade them to do.

The next exposé in which there is a reference to *Ecossais* Masons is *Les Francs-Maçons Ecrasés,* the title-page of which bears the date 1747[63]. But here the Ecossais Masons are not the armed supervisors of the construction of the Second Temple, as in *Le Parfait Macon,* but are designated 'Architects', who are deemed to have received sufficient preparation in the three Craft Degrees to be capable of understanding the fundamental principles of the Order which have hitherto been veiled in symbolism. The *Ecrasés* is, however, dismissed by many writers as a worthless invention[64].

According to Jackson[65] the earliest manuscript setting out the detailed Ritual of a Rite extending the three Degrees of Symbolic (that is, Craft) Masonry contains six Degrees, and can be dated just prior to 1750. The first three of these additional Degrees are 'Perfect Master', 'Perfect Illustrious Irish Master, Judge of the Workmen' (the word 'Irish' may well have been introduced to do no more than differentiate the degree from both the 'Scottish' and the 'English' Masters), and 'English Master'. The fourth of the Higher Degrees, perhaps significantly in view of the paragraphs noted above in *Les Francs-Maçons Ecrasés,* is 'Ecossais Great Architect'. In the Ritual to which Jackson refers, it was, however, a 'Zerubbabel' Degree, but with considerable Christian overtones.

At about this time things began to become seriously out of control. It might be considered legitimate for sincere Freemasons to invent Degrees that filled in the gaps in the Hiramic story, extending it to the completion of the First Temple, and even to the building of the Second. But for all too many fertile minds, the curiosity and gullibility of their Brethren was too great a temptation to resist. Towards the end of the 1740s it became 'Open Season' for the invention of 'Degrees'. The great majority of these had little relevance to what had gone before, but gave their neophytes the opportunity to acquire more splendid titles and regalia, and the belief that they were being admitted to ever more arcane and valuable secrets. More than a thousand Degrees have been identified as having come to light in the second half of the eighteenth century. In most cases these Degrees disappeared as rapidly as they had arrived. Each had, of course, been conferred for a fee, and their inventors had profited accordingly[66].

It is not easy to navigate through this sea of ceremonies. However, among those which may be considered 'legitimate', it is possible to detect a threefold set of main currents. The first of these is concerned with the re-organisation of the work-force after the death of Hiram Abif, and which, by conferring Judicial or Inspectorial roles on their recipients, provided the recognition of the superiority sought by the aristocratic *Ecossais.* Secondly there were the 'Zerubbabel' Degrees, those in which Secrets, lost during the building or the destruction of the First Temple, were sought among the rubble during the erection of the Second. Neither of these as such provided the chivalrous overtones which the courtiers and nobility wanted. The latter series was therefore initially extended by a distortion of Scripture, and a mis-reading of the Third and Fourth Chapters of the Apocryphal First Book of Esdras. Zerubbabel was made to journey to Babylon from the building-site in Jerusalem, there so to acquit himself as to receive a Knighthood from King Darius. This was known as the *Degree of Knight of the Sword and of the Rose Croix* – but it had nothing to do with the Degree of 'Rose Croix', the 18th in the *Ancient and Accepted Rite of 33°* today. Rather did it resemble the present-day *Red Cross of Babylon*, the 15th and 16th Degrees of today's 33-Degree Rite.

There was a further set of Higher or *Ecossais* Degrees, in itself a legitimate development, but from which it is difficult to derive any moral lessons. These form the so-called *'Elu'* or *'Elect'* Degrees, sometimes known as the 'vengeance' group. In these, the murderers of Hiram are discovered in their various refuges, and one way or another they receive that punishment 'which the heinousness of their crimes so richly deserved', and the trusty Fellow Crafts who apprehend them are appropriately rewarded. However unfortunate the morality (or lack of it) presented in these *Elu* Degrees may appear to present-day eyes, they were adopted not only in Paris[67], but also in many Provincial centres.

For example, in October 1997 a manuscript of 13 Folios was discovered at Quimper in Brittany[68]. This appears to show "beyond doubt that the degree of *Chevalier Elu* was practiced (*sic*) in 1750 in a local Chapter founded by the Count de la Tour du Pin"[69]. The 7th (untitled) Section of the Quimper document[70] sets out what is apparently a Lecture to be delivered to those who had just taken the Degree – a 'Traditional History' the latter part of which may well owe much to Ramsay's *Oration*. It recounts how seven Brethren were chosen by King Solomon to exact vengeance on the Fellow Craft who had struck the fatal blow on Hiram Abif. When the seven Brethren brought back the murderer's head, they were honoured by King Solomon, and were given principal roles during the completion of the Temple. They afterwards referred to themselves as *Elect [Elu] Masters*. They and their descendants aspired to be zealous followers of the Mosaic Law, but in time the latter fell away from these high standards, until the earlier virtuous living was revived by a small nucleus who took the Hebrew name of *Kadoch* (*sic*), meaning 'Saintly' or 'Separated'. These 'Kadoch' accepted the New Gospel after the Coming of Christ, and many became hermits in the Egyptian desert[71]. Eventually St. John the Almoner became their best-known leader. Under the guidance of Hugues de Paens and Geoffrey de Bouillon the 'Kadoch' became Knights Templar. When the Templar Order was dissolved, Jacques de Molay burnt at the stake[72], and the extensive property of the Order transferred to the Hospitallers, those Templars who escaped took refuge in Scotland and resumed the name of '*Elect*'.

There is nothing in the Lecture or in the accompanying Catechism[73] which refers to 'vengeance' being directed against those who were responsible for the Templar Order's destruction and impoverishment, but it is a 'Kadosh' Degree in the modern sense of the word. The questions in the Catechism call not only for a description of the 'Kadosh' ladder, but for the words of its seven staves[74], very similar to those familiar to us today.

During the 1740s *Ecossais* Degrees also underwent considerable development in Bordeaux. This appears to have been stimulated by the arrival in the city in 1744 of a merchant[75], Etienne, or, as he is better known to English readers, Stephen, Morin. Little is known with any certainty about his early life, which is extraordinary in view of his considerable importance in the development of what later became known as the *Ancient and Accepted (Scottish) Rite*. It is probable that he was born in Martinique in the West Indies[76]. There is no certain evidence about his Mother-Lodge, nor even about which of the Bordeaux lodges he initially joined. However, it seems reasonably certain that in 1745 he founded *Loge d'Ecosse ou des Elus parfaits*[77] in Bordeaux where some form of *Ecossais* Degrees may already have been worked for four or five years[78]. He is certainly one of the signatories of the 'Reglemens' or By-Laws of the Lodge which are dated 1746[79], and which are also signed, as 'Grand Master', by Lamolère de Feuillas[80], a member of the *Loge La Française*. What is less certain is where Morin himself had obtained the *Ecosse* or *Elu* Degrees.

Such evidence as there is suggests that Morin had received these in the West Indies before coming to Europe. Lieutenant-General William Matthews, formerly Colonel of the Coldstream Guards, had been appointed Governor of the Leeward Islands in 1732. As commander of the Armed Forces based on the Islands, he was also accorded the Honorary rank of Vice-Admiral. He was a Freemason whom in 1739 the Premier Grand Lodge of England (the 'Moderns', as they were afterwards known) appointed as Provincial Grand Master of the Leeward Islands, in which capacity he exercised the normal powers of a PGM, Warranting, for example, a new Lodge in Santa Eustatia in 1747[81]. Several contemporary records claim that not only was it from General[82] Matthews that Morin received the Degree of *Parfait Elu Ecossais* in Antigua in 1744, but that several others had also done so[83]. Nowhere is there any indication of why Matthews, as a Provincial Grand Master under the Premier Grand Lodge, which disapproved of innovations in Masonry, considered himself entitled to confer such Degrees, or how he himself had acquired them. There were many Frenchmen in the West Indies, and it is not inconceivable that by 1744 one of them had brought the Degree to the Leeward Islands but there is no evidence to support this[84].

Stephen Morin became Master of the Bordeaux Lodge *Parfait Harmonie* in 1747, and shortly afterwards returned to the West Indies where he founded an *Ecossais* Lodge in Dominique. He returned briefly to France in 1750, by this time claiming the title of 'Deputy Inspector'. On his subsequent voyage home, his ship was intercepted and he had to make a brief stay in England before being allowed to continue his journey.[85] On reaching the West Indies he lived thereafter in Martinique and Dominique until 1759, thus avoiding the disruption taking place among the Parisian Lodges during this period.

Although in 1747 'Higher Degree' bodies already existed in Paris, this had not inhibited the Bordeaux 'Mother-Lodge' from authorising Lamolère de Feuillas to establish a Lodge of '*Parfaits Elus*' there, although this was not working 'Vengeance Degrees' as they did not form part of the Bordeaux system. Then, in the course of the next ten years the Lodge at Bordeaux either Warranted or was in amity with half a dozen *Ecossais* Lodges in the New World. Specifically, in 1752, apparently ignoring the presence of Stephen Morin in the Islands, the Brethren of St. Marc in Dominique petitioned the Bordeaux 'Mother-Lodge' for permission to form a Lodge "*D'Elus parfaits ou anciens Maîtres Ecossais*". As a result, Lamolère de Feuillas was empowered to constitute Lodges at Port de Paix as well as at St. Marc[86].

While this expansion was taking place in the New World, several of the other French Provincial centres seem to have accepted the leading role of the 'Mother-Lodge' at Bordeaux, which they consulted from time to time about the *Ecossais* Degrees. Its predominance was such that it took it upon itself to provide Rules and Regulations for all *Ecossais* Lodges. By this time the High Degree Lodges derived from the Lodge at Bordeaux (of whatever this consisted) were using the term 'Rite of Perfection'[87] to describe their sequence of Degrees which included first those concerned with setting things to rights after the death of Hiram, and second the 'Arch' Degrees describing the discovery during the re-building[88].

During the 1750s the Grand Lodge in Paris was failing adequately to regulate the Craft Lodges, let alone those conferring *Ecossais* Degrees. The extent to which the Grand Master, the comte de Clermont, exercised his authority is uncertain. In Paris, Lodge Warrants were sold, and their purchasers thereafter became irremovable from their Masterships. A principal source of information about events at this time is a document, *Mémoire Justificatif*, written by Brest de La Chaussée in 1773. His account is undoubtedly biased, but he records that when Clermont was nominated as Grand Master, the choice "honoured French Masonry, but the Prince did not take an active interest in it. Soon after his nomination, the noblemen who filled the Offices in the Grand Lodge abandoned their duties to their deputies. The Banker, Brother Baur, whom the Grand Master had nominated as his deputy, ceased to summon the Grand Lodge".

La Chaussée went on to say

"Our mysteries and warrants became pure merchandise, anarchy was at its height with three Masters of lodges able to constitute another. One soon saw taverns with indecent orgies in our lodges[89], and candidates and our secrets were defiled by the lowest type of tradesmen, artisans, workmen, common labourers, or even servants."

Jacques Lacorne, a dancing master[90], was Master of one of the Lodges in Paris, and in 1758 he announced that the Grand Master had appointed him *Substitut Particulier*, or a Deputy with limited powers[91]. His claim was not disputed and meetings of the Grand Lodge once more took place. Lacorne was able to restore some order into the proceedings until his authority was challenged by a feather merchant, Martin Pény, who led a schismatic group of Masters of Paris Lodges. Pény issued new regulations which were particularly directed to reforming the way in which the Grand Officers were appointed. In effect, the Grand Lodge split into two factions. Clermont then appointed another Brother, Chaillon de Jonville[92], with full authority as his *Substitut General*, and, working with Lacorne, de Jonville restored a measure of harmony, although Pény and his supporters were far from reconciled with the other Grand Lodge Brethren[93].

Meanwhile, somewhat similar problems were being experienced in the West Indies. While promulgating the Higher Degrees in the West Indian Islands, Morin had become involved in a personal controversy. Lamolère de Feuillas now held an official appointment in the French West Indies. The 'Mother-Lodge' in Bordeaux then appointed de Feuillas also as a 'Deputy Inspector', and, not only this, considered him to be senior to his fellow Inspector Morin. It then refused to recognise the Lodge which Morin had established at Port-au-Prince until Feuillas had authorised it. The reason for this apparent supersession of Morin has never been satisfactorily explained, but the Bordeaux Masons may have disapproved of the substantial changes and additions to the Higher Degrees which Morin was almost certainly making.

Morin again made a temporary return to France in 1759. Evidently disheartened by the action of the Bordeaux Masons in recognising de Feuillas as his superior, he transferred his loyalty to those in Paris. Either in 1759 or in 1760[94] Morin joined the Parisian Lodge *La Sainte Trinité* of which Lacorne was Master. At Lacorne's request, the Parisian Grand Lodge gave Morin a Patent conferring on him wide powers overseas, although, it must be said, not as wide as those which he was subsequently to claim[95]. This gave the Grand Lodge in Paris, as well as the 'Mother-Lodge' in Bordeaux, a foothold in the supervision of the Higher Degrees in the New World.

The truce between the rival parties in Paris did not long survive the death of Lacorne in 1762. Events became even more complex. A Degree, *Knight of the East*, probably not dissimilar to the earlier *Knight of the Sword*, had emerged. It had its own ruling body, or Council, which was accepted as legitimate by the French Grand Lodge[96]. De Jonville, on the other hand, became interested in the Degree of 'Kadosh', the culmination of the vengeance-type *Elu* Degrees, which became established in Paris in the summer of 1761.

There is considerable doubt about how this 'Kadosh' Degree came to Paris. Some writers have considered that it was a development of the German *Rite of Strict Observance*[97], and to have been introduced to France by Meunier de Précourt, the Master of a Lodge in the Provincial Centre of Metz[98], "having apparently arrived from Sweden through the Master of a French military Lodge"[99] and then being taken to Paris. Other authors have regarded Lyons as a more probable source. However, since evidence is accumulating that prior to 1761 the Degree of Kadosh was evidently established in several French Provincial centres, Poitiers, for example, as well as Quimper, there are clearly many routes along which the Degree might have travelled.

The Council of *Knights of the East* condemned the 'Kadosh' Degree as barbarous, as did the Grand Lodge of France. In spite of this it seems almost certain that Stephen Morin took the Degree in 1761 or 1762. At about the same time, Pirlet, the Master of a Paris Lodge, began to confer the Degree of '*Grand Emperor*' which he deemed to be superior to a mere *Knight of the East*. Pény was among those on whom he conferred the Degree. Pirlet then set up a governing body for his Degree, the '*Emperors of the East and West*' on, according to his own account, 22nd July 1762. Confused as events had now become, the stage was in fact set for the next major development in the history of the Higher Degrees. This took place not in Paris, but in the West Indies.

Appendix A

Geoffrey Whitney. *A choice of Emblemes and other divises, for the moste parte gathered out of sundrie writers, Englished and Moralized. And divers newly divised by Geoffrey Whitney Leyden 1586.*

Whitney illustrates several dozen 'emblemes', attaching to each a set of verses, without indicating whether these are his own work, or whether they were originally attached to the 'embleme' which he has 'gathered'.

The 'embleme' which illustrates a forearm, the hand waving a sword, emerging from a cloud, has the following verses:

> When SANABAL Hierusalem distrest
> With sharpe assaultes in NEHEMIAS tyme
> To Warre, and worke, the Jewes them selves addrest,
> And did repair their Walles, with stone, and lime:
> One hand the Sworde, against the foe did shake,
> The other hand, the trowell up did take.
>
> Of valiant mindes, loe here, a worthie parte,
> That quailed not, with ruine of theire wall:
> But Captains boulde, did proove the masons arte.
> Which doth infer this lesson unto all;
> That to defende, our country deare from harme,
> For warre, or worke, we eyther hande should arme.

---

48 It is curious that while modern Rituals state that the trusty Fellow Craft discovered their Master 'very indecently interred', in 'Prichard' the 'Fifteen Loving Brothers' "pursuing their Search found him decently buried in a handsome Grave 6 Foot East, 6 West, and 6 Foot perpendicular" in which his assassins had buried him at "High 12 at Night". The body was then taken up and again 'decently buried'. It is anomalies of this sort which cast doubt on the accuracy of Prichard.

49 Laurence Dermott, *Ahiman Rezon*, p.47 (1756 Edition).

50 Current Rituals do not make clear how the 'Royal Arch' is the completion of the Third Degree, a statement which has mystified many brethren. This is made clearer in, for example, the 'Royal Arch' Ritual of the Druids Chapter held at Redruth. This written Ritual dates, at the latest, from 1809, but the material it contains is significantly older. In the Question and Answer in the Opening occurs – Q.From whence came Joshua? A. From Babylon. Q. Where going? A. To Jerusalem. Q What sho'd induce him to leave Babylon and go to Jerusalem?. A.To Assist in clearing away the Rubish from the Building of the First Temple in hopes of finding the S.W. of Masonry? Q.Was that S.W.Lost? A. It was. Q. How came it to be Lost? A. By the D. of our Gd. M...r H.A.B. [N.B.Much of the original is encrypted.]

51 Provincial centres existed at, for example, Marseilles, Lyons, Toulouse, Narbonne and Metz. At none of these was it considered necessary to obtain authorisation from the Grand Lodge in Paris before, for example, Warranting a new Lodge.

52 The first meeting of the Lodge was held on Sunday, 27th April, 1732 with Martin Kelly in the Chair. The Lodge did not at first prosper until it was virtually

refounded on 26 February 1737 with an influx of new members, after which it flourished. G.W.Speth AQC Vol XII, p.2 (1899)

53 "Although constituted in 1732 the Lodge was not in the [English] Lists until 1766. Its last payment was in 1788. Joined the Grand Orient of France in 1803, but was retained on the English Register until 1813. It still preserves, as part of its title, its last English number. Now named Lodge "Anglaise No. 204" on registers of the Grand Orient of France. Date of Warrant – 8th March 1766, Constituted 27th April 1732. 1755 – No.363, 1770 – No.298, 1780 – No.239, 1781 – No.240, 1792 – No.204". Lane, *Masonic Records*, p.148, 2nd ed. 1895.

54 The exact date is uncertain – it has been quoted both as 29 August and as 13 December. Alain Bernheim, *Notes on Early Freemasonry in Bordeaux (1732 –1769)* AQC CI, p.61 (1988)

55 Fleury further instructed Hérault "that inn-keepers and the like were forbidden to entertain such persons on their premises".(Paul Tunbridge, *The Climate of European Freemasonry 1730 to 1750*, AQC LXXXI, p.102, 1968) This prohibition would therefore have had little effect on the noble Brethren who held Lodges in their own houses, and it is probable that this prohibition was enforced only upon Lodges held in Taverns frequented by those of the lower social orders who were committing the "crime" of aping their social superiors. The Lodges attended by the influential aristocracy continued to meet in their private houses, and to develop Degrees 'beyond the Craft'. Certainly no proceedings were taken against Louis de Pardaillan, duc d'Antin, who was Grand Master from 1738 to 1743. It has even been said that he may have acquiesced in the suppression of some Lodges presided over by Parisian inn-keepers. In an exposé published in 1747, *La Désolation des Entrepreneurs Modernes,* there is inserted, under *Pièces Mêlées*, an account of proceedings against two Parisian tavern-keepers for permitting Masonic Meetings to be held on their premises and catering for them, Chapelot who was fined 1,000 Livres in September 1737, and his Tavern closed for 6 months, and Le Roy who was fined 3,000 Livres in June 1745.

56 Jacques Litvine, *Anti-Masonry: A Neglected Source.* AQC CIV, p.125 (1991)

57 During the reign of King Louis XV there was never a law forbidding Freemasons to meet. *Ibidem*; Note by Alain Bernheim, p.135.

58 It is tempting to speculate that the French Maîtres Ecossais owed both their name and their Degrees to the English Lodges of 'Scotch Masters' which appeared in the 1730s, but there is not the least evidence to support this contention.

59 Prince Louis de Bourbon, Comte de Clermont, was Grand Master of the Grand Lodge of France 1743-1770. "Clermont was both a friend and a blood relation of Louis XV. His mother, Mademoiselle de Nantes, was a daughter of Louis XIV by Madame de Montespan. The bastard children of Louis XIV were legitimized shortly before that king's death, from which act was derived Clermont's royal status." Alain Bernheim, *The Mémoire Justificatif of La Chaussée, and Freemasonry in Paris until 1773.* AQC CIV, p.98 (1991)

60 RC, pp.9/10

61 Harry Carr, *Early French Exposures*, p.159 (QCCC, London, 1971)

62 The anonymous author of *Le Parfait Maçon* states that he has heard that there are six or seven Degrees above that of Master, and that the *Ecossais* formed the fourth grade of these. He goes on to say "Instead of weeping over the ruins of the Temple of Solomon, the *Ecossais* are concerned with rebuilding it". Zerubbabel is in charge of the work, and he is said to have created "a fourth grade of Masons, whose number he limited to 753, chosen from among the most excellent artists". (No reason is given for this curious number, which is, of course, 3-5-7 backwards.) This fourth grade not only supervised the others, but they were also charged with "watching the security of the workmen". The 'Question and Answer' introduces the instruction given by Nehemiah that those rebuilding the Temple should always have their swords by their sides. Harry Carr, *op. cit.*, p194.

The Biblical reference is in Nehemiah, IV, vv. 18-21. The event had been allegorised and moralised in England many years before, for example in "A choice of Emblemes and other divises, for the moste parte gathered out of Sundrie writers, Englished and Moralized. And divers newly divised by Geoffrey Whitney Leyden 1586". See **Appendix A.**

63 Harry Carr, *loc. cit.*, p.278 *et seq.*

64 For example "The *Ecrasés* is a rather lengthy hoax which might have been written by a freemason. It seems to have abused the credulity of a few scholars, though it is unlikely to include any genuine masonic ritual at all." 'Henri Amblaine', AQC CVI, p.142 (1993). This does not necessarily mean that the 'hoax' had no factual basis. The later sequences of 'Higher Degrees' generally include that of *'Architect'* in one form or another, and some part of the description of the *Architect's* Degree in *Ecrasés* is at least reminiscent of one of the Degrees beyond the Eighteenth conferred in today's *Ancient and Accepted Rite*.

65 RC., p.19

66 It is by no means the universal view that all these Degrees were 'fond things, vainly invented'. J.E.S.Tuckett was one of the first of the 'authentic' School seriously to put forward the thesis that before 1717 "Freemasonry possessed a store of Legend, Tradition and Symbolism of wide extent. That from 1717 the Grand Lodge *selected a portion only* of this store". AQC XXXII, p.4 (1919)

67 In Paris in 1747 the Grand Master's Lodge, *Loge Saint-Jean de Jerusalem*, set out the dates on which members of the various *Elu* Degrees should meet. RC, p.35

68 André Kervalla and Philippe Lestienne, *Un haut-grade templier dans les milieux jacobites en 1750: l'Ordre Sublime des Chevaliers Elus aux Sources de la Stricte Observance*, Renaissance Traditionelle, No.112, p.229 *et seq.,*October 1997. This Manuscript document was also analysed in detail by Alain Bernheim in Heredom No.6, *Avatars of the Knight Kadosh in France and in Charleston*, p.162 *et seq.*,1997.

69 Alain Bernheim *ibidem*.

70 The last of the 13 Folios of the Manuscript.

71 That is, they became 'the Desert Fathers'.

72 On 19th March 1314.

73 Folios 6-11.

74 The Catechism also reveals that the ladder has seven staves because originally there were seven 'Elect'.

75 In French, 'négociant'.

76 Alain Bernheim, The Mémoire Justificatif, etc, loc.cit., p.93 and comments on his Paper by F.W.Seal-Coon, ibidem p.123. Morin is described as a 'Creole', that is, that he was born of white parents in the West Indian Colonies.

77 For a full discussion of this strong probability, see ibidem, pp.90/91 and 96.

78 RC., p.32, "There is, however, no doubt that Bordeaux was a centre of elementary high degree masonry from about as early as 1740." Jackson gives no evidence for this except to state that this is the deduction of some other writers. See, for example, J.Fairbairn Smith, The Rise of the Ecossais Degrees. Chapter of Research of the Grand Chapter of R.A. Masons, Ohio, Vol.10, 1965.

79 Alain Bernheim, The Mémoire Justificatif etc., loc. cit., pp.110–113.

80 Alain Bernheim points out that the name of de Feuillas has been wrongly transcribed on several occasions as 'de Feuillard', ibidem p.58.

81 In a copy of the Patent for St Eustatius Lodge (26th June 1747), Mathew (sic) is described as 'General, Governor in Chief ... Grand Chancellor, Vice Admiral and Ordinary of the same, Provincial Grand Master.' Th. G. G. Valette AQC XLIV p.59 (1921)

82 In some accounts he is referred to as 'Admiral' Matthews. This has led to considerable confusion among commentators until it was realised that in his capacity as Governor he held this honorary rank.

83 Sharp Document No.4 "De laneufville (sic) will have handed to you a letter written to me by Bro. Dutillet from Versailles, which will show you that he is E[cossais]... . He told me that he had been admitted to the G. light by some officers who had been received by Admiral Matthews. If that is so it seems to me that this W.Bro.Admiral receives a good many people."

84 A slightly garbled claim has been made that Morin afterwards received authority to establish Lodges of Perfection from the Grand Lodge of England, authority which the Premier Grand Lodge would certainly never have given him. It is however just possible that in the manuscript in which this statement occurs, the reference is not to the Premier Grand Lodge. It could possibly be that when Morin refers to a 'W.Mother L_' in London, it is the governing body of what is now known as The Royal Order of Scotland (but then as Heredom of Kilwinning) to which he is alluding. (According to the 'Records of the H.R.D.M.' for 1750 kept by the Scottish Grand Secretary there were then 6 such bodies in London, 4 recorded as 'Time Immemorial', and 2 as dating from 1743 & 1744 respectively. Robert S. Lindsay, The Royal Order of Scotland, 1971). One of the 'T.I.' bodies was known as the 'Grand Lodge'.

85 If Morin's claim to have received authorisation from a 'W. Mother L_' had any foundation in fact, it could have occurred during this involuntary detention.

86 Lionel Vibert, AQC XLIV p.172 (1921)

87 Not to be confused with later usages of the term of 'Rite of Perfection'.

88 The dominant position which Bordeaux had assumed did not succeed in dispelling the general confusion about these ceremonies. This is illustrated by a letter quoted by Jackson (RC, p.34, but he gives no reference to the source of the letter) written, he says, from Paris to Bordeaux, and which states, inter alia, "......Ecossism is nothing less than the Old Mastership which was changed at the death of H and which was confided by Solomon to a very small number of Elus Parfaits ... I have only one remark to make and that is, to become a Knight of the East, one must be an Elu Parfait, and to be Parfait one must have passed the 9 degrees of Freemasonry ... There is a Council of Knights of the East at Paris, but in addition to not having our Ecossism, they are in error as regards their Knights of the East."

89 This reference to 'orgies' is generally dismissed as extravagant hyperbole. It is, however, curious that in the anti-Masonic pamphlet Examen de la Société des Francs-Maçons, which is dated 1744, the accusation is made that the fraternity take part in debauchery involving 'pleasure filled banquets presided over by a goddess'. Jacques Litvine, loc. cit, p.127.

90 'Dancing master' is the appellation almost universally attached to Lacorne in the literature.Today it has perhaps an unfortunate sound. 'Ballet Master', or even 'Choreographer' might better describe his occupation, or, in early twenty-first century idiom, even 'Dancing Coach' at a time when it was demanded of every young courtier that he be proficient in the formal dance routines.

91 "La Chaussée writes of Lacorne that he was 'a socially pleasant man' who happened to meet Clermont on casual masonic occasions and took that opportunity 'of availing himself of the title of Substitut particulier'... Lacorne was a dancing-master. Clermont was famous for his young mistresses, who were mostly ballet-dancers, which might explain why he and Lacorne happened to know each other." Alain Bernheim, The Mémoire Justificatif of a Chaussée and Freemasonry in Paris until 1773. AQC, CIV pp.98/99.

92 This did not involve the dismissal of Lacorne, as some authorities have alleged, but the appointment of de Jonville as his superior while he himself remained in post as Substitut particulier. ibidem, p.99

93 More detailed information about the Masonic disputes in Paris can be found in Alain Bernheim's Paper on the Mémoire Justificatif, (loc. cit.) to which these paragraphs are considerably indebted.

94 'Choumitzky on Morin.' Reputed transcription presented to Grand Lodge Library by Quatuor Coronati Lodge No.2076 of 'Etienne Morin' Bulletin de la Grande Loge Nationale et Regulière Loge Saint Claudius, No.21 (1927) (Original not available)

95 On several occasions doubts have been cast on the existence of the Patent given to Stephen Morin, and, if it existed, what authority was possessed by the Grand Lodge in Paris which entitled it to delegate to Morin powers to preside over the 14-Degree Rite of Perfection in the West Indies. This is a matter of some importance because on this document rests the legitimacy of the Ancient and Accepted Rite. The whole matter has recently been exhaustively analysed

by Pierre Mollier who definitively concludes that Morin received the document from a body entitled to give it. "La Patente Morin est donc authentique; elle a été délivrée par la Première Grande Loge de France en son Grand Conseil des Grands Inspecteurs Grands Élus Chevaliers Kadosh". P.Mollier, *Nouvelles lumières sur la Patente Morin et le Rite de Perfection* (*Deux Siècles de Rite Écossais Ancien Accepté en France*, pp. 31-58, Éditions Dervy, Paris, 2004)

96 RC., p.39

97 *The Order of Strict Observance* was founded in Germany in 1754 by Karl Gotthelf, Baron von Hund von Altengrotkau. It was based on the wholly unsubstantiated legend that after the dissolution of the Knights Templar Order in 1313, certain of its Knights took refuge in Scotland, and that it was to these that Scottish Freemasonry owed its origin. The *Strict Observance* was one of the Rites in which the obedience of the members was claimed to be owed to anonymous superiors of whose identity they were never made aware. See Frederick Smyth, *Brethren in Chivalry*, pp.14-16 Lewis Masonic, London (1991)

98 Metz had formerly been within the Germanic 'Holy Roman Empire', but had been gained by France on 24 October 1648 by the Peace of Westphalia at the conclusion of the Thirty Years War.

99 Alain Bernheim, *Avatars of the Knight Kadosh etc.. loc. cit.* p.150

Essay 3
Stephen Morin, Henry Francken and the Constitutions of 1762

The foundations of the Ancient and Accepted Rite were laid in the quarter century before 1762. During these years there evolved in France[100] various sequences of Degrees, many of which the Rite later incorporated. The first three Degrees of each sequence were invariably the familiar ones of Entered Apprentice, Fellow Craft and Master Mason. What followed differed in each of these emergent systems. Perhaps the earliest and most usual series were those containing degrees in which arrangements were made for completing the building of the Temple after the death of Hiram Abif. Their most important common feature was the appointment of a successor to Hiram, together with the establishment of subordinate managerial posts. These provided the superior or supervisory ranks which the French aristocracy coveted in order to secure for themselves a status higher than that of the Master Masons and their Worshipful Masters in Third Degree Lodges. This was not, in itself, enough for the aristocrats. They sought chivalric Masonic honours further to emphasise their social superiority. Additional promotion was achieved first by incorporating events from the building of the Second Temple, the 'Zerubbabel' Degrees, in which the word, lost on the death of Hiram, was recovered. This led on to one or more Degrees of a further superior sequence which culminated in Zerubbabel himself receiving a Knighthood in Babylon, Degrees known variously in Paris, Bordeaux and elsewhere by such titles as *Knight of the East*, *Knight of the Sword* or *Knight of the Eagle*[101].

It was not difficult to attach moral lessons to the supervisory, to the 'Second Temple', and to the chivalric Degrees. However, another series evolved in parallel with each of these, the so-called Vengeance or *Elu* Degrees, in which the murderers of Hiram were discovered in their various hide-outs and executed in one way or another. These events satisfactorily completed the legend of the death of the principal Architect of the Temple, not that Hiram figures as such anywhere except in Masonic traditions. It was, however, more difficult to attach moral lessons to their outcome. This may account for their adoption not at first being universal.

The Degrees from the Fourth upwards did not evolve in an orderly progression. Perhaps as early as 1750 the term 'Lodge of Perfection'[102] was being used in Bordeaux for a sequence of seven or eight Degrees beyond that of Master Mason. This system included both some half-dozen Degrees in which supervisory Offices were conferred, and also one or two of the 'Zerubbabel' Degrees in which the Word was recovered, but it did not include any of the *Elu* or Vengeance Degrees. The Bordeaux brethren also seem to have been in possession of a chivalric Degree, *Knight of the East*, by 1750. The situation was different in Paris and in other parts of France where the *Elu* or Vengeance Degrees became included in the various sequences which were being worked. Furthermore, the *Knight of the East* Degree in Paris almost certainly differed significantly from that practised in Bordeaux[103].

The Grand Lodge in Paris was little able to control events in the City itself, let alone those in Bordeaux, Metz, Lyons, Quimper and sundry others towns in France where the Brethren were generally following their own inclinations. By this time there were also French Lodges overseas which were sturdily independent, particularly in the Islands in the West Indies, the ownership of which was, in any case, inclined to change hands during the Seven Years War. Jackson himself says, "From about 1755, events are difficult to follow. There is no doubt that masonry [in France] was in a confused state."[104] Alain Bernheim puts it more delicately by stating "The 1760s and early 1770s form an intricate period in the history of French Freemasonry"[105].

Events in Paris may be briefly summarised by saying that in the 1750s the Grand Master of the *Grand Lodge of France*, the comte de Clermont, was not playing an active part in its affairs. In about 1757 he appointed a dancing-master, Jacques Lacorne, as his Deputy with limited powers[106], who presided over a self-styled *Grand Lodge* composed of Masters of Lodges. In 1760 there was a schism within Lacorne's Grand Lodge. The dissenters were led by a merchant, Pény, who set himself up as President of an assembly which he called the *Grand Lodge of Masters of the Orient of Paris*[107]. Grand Master Clermont then appointed another Deputy, Chaillon de Jonville, superior to Lacorne, and with wider powers[108]. By 1762 de Jonville was able to achieve an uneasy reunion of the two factions. In November 1762 it was agreed to appoint fourteen Commissioners to draw up new Statutes and Regulations for *The Grand Lodge of France*[109]. However, before the end of the year a master-tailor, Pirlet, had introduced a new Degree, *Emperor of the East*[110], which he conferred upon Pény. The Statutes and Regulations for the reunited Grand Lodge were approved in April 1763[111] and new appointments made to each of the Grand Offices from among the members of the two former opposing bodies. Even so, in-fighting continued. The members of the former faction led by Pény, the *'Grand Lodge of the Orient of Paris'*, were less than happy with the appointments which they had been given as Grand Officers. They found an ally in Pirlet, who had by now given the title of *'The Emperors of the East and West, Sovereign Ecossais Mother Lodge'* to the controlling body of his newly introduced Degree. Pirlet wished to dominate the uneasily reunited Grand Lodge, to secure the dismissal of de Jonville as the Grand Master's principal Deputy, and to substitute a member of his own Council in his place. He failed in his attempt, and the Grand Lodge refused "to take cognizance of present or future controversies concerning the pre-eminence and validity of the said [*Ecossais*] degrees" and a formal declaration to that effect was given to Pirlet[112]. La Chaussée, the Grand Keeper of the Seals and Archives of the *Conseil des Chevaliers d'Orient*, or *Knights of the East*[113], later made it clear that the members of this body at that time had no intent "to exert a specific influence over the administration of Grand Lodge"[114]. This was, however, a new departure[115].

Outside Paris, Bordeaux was one of the principal centres of the Higher or *Ecossais* Degrees, and several Provincial centres looked to the so-called 'Mother-Lodge' in Bordeaux for leadership, a lead which they by no means slavishly followed. The 'Lodge of Perfection' in Bordeaux itself had been considerably developed, seventeen years before these events took place in Paris, during the visit of a French expatriate, Etienne or Stephen Morin, a merchant[116] who had been born of white parents in the West Indies, probably in Martinique[117]. Several records show that Morin himself had received the Degree of *Parfait Elu Ecossais* in Antigua in 1744, the year before he visited Bordeaux for the first time. After 2 years' residence in Bordeaux, Morin returned to the West Indies and founded an *Ecossais* Lodge in Dominique. He again visited Bordeaux in 1750 for a brief stay during which he claimed the rank of 'Deputy Inspector'. Eight years later, Morin again visited France but spent much of his time in Paris, disenchanted by the action of the Bordeaux Brethren in appointing his former colleague in that city, Lamolère de Feuillas, as his Masonic superior in the West Indies. Morin joined the Parisian Lodge *La Sainte Trinité* of which Lacorne was Master. Lacorne submitted a petition requesting 'the Grand Council of the Lodges of France' to give Stephen Morin a Patent to promote Freemasonry world-wide.

The document by which this request was granted has not survived. Its supposed contents are known only from copies or copies of copies. It was issued in the name of Grand Master Clermont, although there is no evidence that he had any part in its preparation. Each surviving copy reproduces the signatures, among others[118], of de Jonville, the senior 'Deputy', as well as that of Lacorne himself. The copies are dated 27th August 1761 and in 1765, in a letter to the French Grand Lodge, Morin referred to the Patent as having been granted to him on that date. If Lacorne's signature is genuinely inserted, the Patent can hardly have been granted later than this, because Lacorne died shortly afterwards.

The object of the Patent was to regularise whatever Morin might do Masonically on his return to the Caribbean. Morin was first empowered to establish a Lodge, *La Parfaite Harmonie*, "wherever he may arrive or shall sojourn". He was then constituted "Grand Master Inspector, authorizing and empowering him to establish perfect and sublime Masonry in all parts of the world". All Brethren were exhorted to give Morin "such assistance and succour as may be in their power" and he was granted "full and entire power to create Inspectors in all places where the sublime degrees shall not already be established". The final paragraph of this copy of the Patent purports to demonstrate that the powers granted to Morin extended over the whole of the emerging system of Higher Degrees, by stating that it was signed by de Jonville as "Substitute-General of the Order, Grand Commander of the Black and White Eagle, Sovereign Sublime Prince of the Royal Secret, and Chief of the Eminent Degrees of the Royal Art"[119]. There can be little doubt that a succession of copyists embellished the wording of the Patent. The inclusion of the title "Sublime Prince of the Royal Secret" is inherently suspicious as there is no other reference to this Degree earlier than a ritual dated 1768, and there is no indication that even the name existed in Paris in 1761[120]. The original Patent may have been intended to do no more than to establish Morin as the presiding authority over the 'Craft' Degrees in the so-called New World. Indeed, Morin himself may have considered initially that this is all that the Patent conferred upon him[121].

At the end of 1761 Morin set off to return to the New World, taking with him his Patent with whatever powers it originally contained. Within a few days the ship in which he was sailing was captured by an English man-o'war, something which had also earlier happened to Morin when he was returning home in 1750. As a result, Morin spent most of 1762 in England. As a civilian, he was not treated as a Prisoner of War. He was able to move freely about the country, although there is more speculation than factual evidence about the people and places he may have visited[122]. He was, however, able to show his Patent to the Grand Master, Earl Ferrers, by whom he was kindly received, but who is unlikely to have conferred upon Morin all the distinctions which he afterwards claimed to have received from him[123].

Towards the end of the year Morin was able to continue his journey, and early in 1763 he landed in Dominique where he founded the Lodge *'La Parfaite Harmonie'* at Port-au-Prince, as his Patent entitled him to do, and he inspected the Lodges already in existence in the island. On 21st July 1763 he wrote to Chaillon de Jonville, the French Grand Master's principal Deputy, giving a Report of his activities. He received in return a copy of the new Statutes and Regulations of Grand Lodge which had been approved a few months earlier[124]. When Morin later recorded the receipt of these documents, he made no mention of receiving at the same time the so-called 'Grand Constitutions of 1762'[125].

As a result of the constant traffic of soldiers, sailors and merchants between Europe and the islands in the Caribbean, Freemasonry was well established there with English, Scottish and French Lodges in many of the Islands; there had been, for example, a French Lodge in Martinique since 1738. There were sufficient English Brethren in the so-called New World for the English Premier Grand Lodge ('the Moderns') to have appointed no fewer than six Provincial Grand Masters in the various Islands and on the mainland of America. Few of the English Brethren were interested in the 'Higher Degrees' in spite of the earlier efforts of General Matthews when Provincial Grand Master of the Leeward Islands. Those involved with Degrees 'beyond the Craft' were principally Frenchmen owing a vague allegiance to the Grand Lodge in Paris and to the 'Mother-Lodges' in the various Provincial centres. The French Brethren in Dominique, for example, had strong ties with Bordeaux.

Soon after his arrival in Dominique, Morin visited Jamaica, where he met Henry Andrew Francken, a Dutchman who had lived in the Island since 1757 and who had been naturalised a year later, then becoming a minor official of the local Admiralty Court[126]. He was already a Freemason, though there is no record of where he was Initiated. Morin may have already known Francken (although there is no evidence of their previous acquaintance) because he at once gave him high rank in the Rite which he was constructing, and appointed him 'Deputy Grand Inspector General of all the Superior Degrees of Free and Accepted Masons in the West Indies'. Thereafter, Francken worked closely with Morin until the latter's death eight years later.

After two years, Morin moved permanently to Jamaica, and, in accordance with the terms of his Patent, he transferred his Lodge, *'La Parfaite Harmonie'*, to his new home[127]. Then, with Francken's assistance, he spent his time setting up the Masonic system which is now generally referred to as 'Morin's Rite'. To gain acceptance for this, Morin required a more specific authorisation than that which was conveyed to him in his Patent of November 1761, which, in any case, had by now been revoked by the Grand Lodge of France. He had little alternative but to follow a similar course of action to that which Alan Breck proposed when he said "if I cannae beg, borrow, nor yet steal a boat, I'll make one"[128]. In spite of what earlier Masonic writers have confidently stated, it is now well established that Morin never received any 'Constitutions' from France, and that it was he, probably with Francken's assistance, or at least with Francken's connivance, who proceeded to provide what were claimed to be 'The Grand Constitutions of 1762'.

Much of the evidence for this fabrication is, admittedly, negative. The preamble to the Constitutions claims that they were

> "made in Prussia and France, Sept. 7th, 1762. Resolved by the Nine Commissioners named by the Great Council of the Sublime Princes of the Royal Secret at the Great East of France. Consequently, by the deliberations dated as above to be observed by the aforesaid Grand Councils of the Sublime Princes of France and Prussia"[129].

This cannot be so; for it is certain that no such Great Councils of Sublime Princes existed in 1762 either in France or in Prussia. The only German Rite of any significance in existence at that time was Hund's seven-degree 'Rite of Strict Observance' with which 'Morin's Rite' has nothing in common[130]. Nowhere in any records, French or German, Parisian or Provincial, is there any reference to 'Nine Commissioners' being appointed for any purpose whatsoever. The two 'High Degree' ruling bodies in Paris, Pirlet's schismatic *Emperors of the East and West* and de la Chaussée's *Knights of the East*, would hardly have assented to the production of a document which in effect subordinated each of their organisations to a new Masonic power; there is no indication that either was ever minded to do so. Nor would the French Grand Lodge have looked kindly on any such development which would have necessarily impinged on its own prerogatives in relation to the three 'Craft' degrees. Indeed, on 14th August 1766 the Grand Lodge issued a Decree "curtailing the powers of high degree colleges in respect of symbolic lodges in their area"[131]. But in the Western World there was no Ruling Body which could take exception to Constitutions which embraced the conduct of every Masonic Degree which they contained, and, in any case, the French Grand Lodge exercised no authority in Jamaica. If one invoked the principle of *cui bono?*, the answer would be that no one in Europe would receive the least benefit from the production of such a document[132].

Perhaps the most damning indictment of the preamble is the date '7th September 1762'. The Constitutions precisely follow the form and content of the Statutes and Regulations of the French Grand Lodge and these were not agreed upon until April of the following year. These Statutes and Regulations were widely promulgated and a copy was sent to Morin who acknowledged his possession of them. Not only do the 'Constitutions of 1762' reproduce their form and content, but in many of the clauses of the two documents, 'The Statutes and Regulations of the Grand Lodge' and 'The Grand Constitutions of 1762', even the wording is identical, apart from the necessary substitutions so as to refer to 'Morin's Rite' instead of to the Craft; the 'Constitutions' can only have been written by someone with a copy of the Grand Lodge Statutes and Regulations in front of him. The wide and detailed researches of Alain Bernheim and of Cosby Jackson make it almost impossible to believe that this 'someone' was other than Morin himself, in Jamaica, probably between 1765 and 1767.

It can be presumed that by 1767 'Morin's Rite' and the 'Constitutions of 1762' had been put together in all their essentials. In that year Francken took leave of absence from his Admiralty Court duties. He visited the mainland of North America, and, in December of that year, acting as Morin's Deputy Inspector, he was instrumental in setting up a Lodge of Perfection in Albany in what is now the State of New York. Francken provided a Warrant for this Lodge, and gave it a copy of the *Rules and Regulations for the Conduct of Lodges of Perfection*[133].

After Francken's return to Jamaica, Morin established the ruling body which his fabricated 'Constitutions' envisaged, *'A Grand Chapter of Princes of the Royal Secret or Ne Plus Ultra'*[134]. His efforts were not well received by all his Brethren in the Islands. He was accused of meddling in affairs without authority, his Patent having been revoked, and a successor, a Bro. Martin, appointed. He was said to have made too many innovations; this accusation may have resulted from his introducing the expanded Parisian system to Brethren in Dominique who looked to the 'Mother-Lodge' in Bordeaux. It was further rumoured that he was conferring Degrees for money. Undeterred by such criticisms he persevered with the establishment of his Rite until he died on 17th November 1771.

By the time of Morin's death Francken had evidently taken over the direction of the new Rite. He wrote a series of manuscripts setting out in each both what he claimed were the 'Constitutions of 1762' and also the Rituals of the various Degrees which composed the Rite which the 'Constitutions' governed. Three of these manuscripts survive. The earliest, which is dated 1771, was re-discovered in 1976 in the Library of the Supreme Council in England. A second copy, dated 1783, was discovered in 1855[135], also in England, but then purchased and taken to the U.S.A. where it was eventually deposited in the library of the Supreme Council of the Northern Masonic Jurisdiction. A third copy was found by Michael Spurr in Lancashire, and is now in the Museum and Library of the United Grand Lodge of England[136]. This copy is undated, but in it there is a reference to the Year 1786, so it cannot be earlier than this – nor later than 20th May 1795 when Francken died. It is believed that there was a fourth copy deposited in a Library in Lahore in India, but, if it still exists, its whereabouts are unknown[137]. With the exception of the second set of Regulations in the third copy, each of the three known copies is written in Francken's well-known and easily identifiable hand. There is no reason to doubt the authenticity of each of them.

The earliest (1771) Manuscript contains 252 pages. Originally it first set out the Rituals of the 15th to the 25th Degrees, both inclusive, but the 12 pages of what is presumably the ritual of the 25th Degree have been cut out by an unknown hand and are missing. These are followed by the Regulations for the conduct of individual Lodges of Perfection in the New World. Jackson points out

> The contents of these regulations are clearly based on the 'Statutes and Regulations for the government of particular Lodges in France and their regulations with the Grand Lodge' of 1763. Some are word for word similar to those issued by the Grand Lodge.

This is followed by a 'Masonic Tree' or list of Degrees, and then "The Great Statutes & Regulations, made in Prussia & France Sep^br 7th ; 7762". This is the earliest known copy of the so-called 'Constitutions of 1762' and consists of 32 Articles. There follow some additional instructions concerning, for example, Holy Days to be observed, and finally a copy of the "Constitution of the Ineffable Lodge of the City of Albany in the Province of New York" to which Francken had signed his name in 1767[138].

The 1783 Manuscript is more complete than that written earlier in 1771, and contains the Rituals of all the 25 Degrees of 'Morin's Rite'. Furthermore, it contains a copy of the Warrant for the Consistory of Princes of the Royal Secret which Morin erected in Jamaica in 1770 – on 30th April of that year, according to this copy. The Consistory was to supervise all Degrees from the 4th Secret Master Degree to the 25th, Princes of the Royal Secret. The Warrant appoints William Winter, the Lieutenant-Governor of the Island, as "President and Grand Commander of all Grand Chapters, Councils and Consistories". William Winter was also the Provincial Grand Master of Jamaica appointed by the 'Modern' Grand Lodge, and it is remarkable that he accepted this appointment unless he considered that Lord Ferrers' signature on Morin's Patent was a genuine endorsement of the latter's activities, even though the Patent had been revoked – of which Winter may not have been aware.

The 'Spurr' manuscript contains, written on 311 numbered pages, the Rituals of the 25 Degrees of Morin's Rite[139]. These are followed by two sets of Regulations: those "For the Government of Regular Royal Lodges of Perfection", and the "Statutes and Regulations made in Prussia and France Septemr.17th 1762" that is the so-called 'Grand Constitutions of 1762'[140].

In the early 1780s Francken continued to develop the 25-Degree Rite, appointing several Deputy Inspectors General, many of them Officers of Regiments passing through Jamaica. Among them was Major Charles Shirreff who, on his return to England, introduced several senior Freemasons to the Higher Degrees. However, Francken appears to have been less Masonically active after the violent hurricanes by which Jamaica was struck in 1784 and 1785, and which caused him serious financial loss. Francken must have been well regarded by the Jamaican colonists, because to alleviate his difficulties (he had had to sell his property in the Island) the Jamaican Assembly voted him sums of money "in recognition of his services to the public"[141]. William Winter also came to his assistance, and Francken was appointed first a Customs Inspector, then Assistant Judge of the Common Pleas in Port Royal, and finally Commissioner of the Supreme Court for the Island[142]. But before Francken's death in 1795, High Degree Masonic matters, with no firm guiding hand, had become somewhat chaotic both in the West Indian Islands and on the North American mainland. Deputy Inspectors, appointed by those who themselves had been appointed by Morin and Francken, were being less than selective in their choice of new 'Degrees' reaching the West from Europe. The stage was set for the next development.

Appendix A

The United Grand Lodge of England Library Copy of the Francken Manuscript

This Copy was found in Lancashire by Bro. Michael Spurr. When discovered it was in poor condition, and was rebound. On the first page is written

> "Received from John Caird Edinburgh
> Jas. Caird
> Liverpool
> 30th August 1815
> <u>Special</u> <u>Scholia</u> <u>up to this Day</u>
> <u>Wednesday</u> <u>the sixth</u> of <u>Sepr.</u> 1865 30th August 1830
> Hence 50 year this
> Book has been in the possession of
> Mr. N.A.Gage Half a century; it having
> been Presented to him by the above named
> Mr. John Caird of Edinburgh on the Day
> and Date above noted.
> Note also the Most Important Official
> Document at the end of this Book, it
> being no less than a copy of the Statutes
> and Regulations made in Prussia and France
> by the Nine Commissioners named by the
> Grand Council of the Sublime Princes of
> the Royal Secret at the Grand East
> of Prussia and France. It was resolved
> by the Nine Commissioners above stated that their
> deliberations dated the 7th day of Sept. 1762 shall be
> Ratified and Observed by the aforesaid Grand Council
> of the Sublime Princes of Prussia and France, by
> all the Particular and Regular Councils spread over
> the two hemispheres."

Appendix B

The Rituals of the 25 Degrees of Morin's Rite are set out on the first 311 numbered Pages of the 'Spurr' Manuscript. (These pages are preceded by an Index of the Degrees, and the comments etc. set out in **Appendix A**.) The titles of the Degrees, as set out by Francken, are as follows:

4th Degree Secret Master

5th Degree Perfect Master

6th Degree called Perfect Master by Curiosity or Intimate Secretary. Some Lodges call this degree by name of English Master.

7th Degree called Provost and Judge or Irish Master

8th Degree called Intendant of the Buildings, or English Master or Mr. in England. Many French lodges call this degree Scotch Mr. of J.J.J.

(*There is a note on the final page, p.46, of this ritual*):

> N.B. many lodges have the 27 lights by 5, 7 and 15, and seems proper to be so – and the aprons to be

lined and bordered with green, and the Ribbon of this order should have a small knot made with a green Ribbon at the end of it – all this is conformable by those who call this Degree the Scotch Master of the 3 J.J.J.

(Pages 47 and 48 are missing)

9th Degree called Chapter of Master Elected of Nine

10th Degree called Illus. Elect of 15.

11th Degree a Chapter called Sublime Knights Elected.

12th Degree Grand Mr. Architect.

13th Degree called Royal Arch

14th Degree called the Perfection the Ultimate of Symbolic Masonry.

15th Degree Masonry renew'd, or the Sword Rectified, such as is practized in the Grand Lodge of Prussia and France, the Islands of Hispaniola, Jamaica and in the Province of New York, viz. Bordeaux, Marseilles, Toulon, Cape François, Caye de Fonds, St. Mark, Port au Prince, Kingston in Jamaica and at Albany in the Province of New York established by the Most Illus. Bro. Stephen Morin & prince of the R. Secret &c &c &c grand Inspr. Genl. and Revived by H.A. Francken Prce. Of R. Sret. Depy. Inspr. General of all Superior Lodges over the 2 Hemispheres.

16th Degree Prince of Jerusalem

17th Degree Knights of East and West

18th Degree Knight of the White Eagle or Pelican, known by the name of Perfect Mason, or Kts. of the Rose Croix.

19th Degree the Subme Scotch Masonry called by the name of the Grand Pontif.

20th Degree Venbl. Gr. Mr. of all Symbolic Lodges – Sovereign prince of Masonry or Master Ad Vitam

21st Degree Prussian Knight or Noachite – otherwise called the Masonic Key.

(This is followed by) –

The second Part of the Degree of Prussian Knight called the Perfect Prussian Knight

22nd Degree Knights of the Royal Axe, or Grand Patriarchs called by the name of Princes of Libanon.

23rd Degree The Key of Masonry. Philosophical Lodge of Knights of the Eagle or Sun.

24th Degree Aparé et Lege, Dice & Tace, the Ne Plus Ultra of Masonry

(At the end is added the following) –

Note: the grd. Inspr. Stephen Morin &c in a Consistory of Princes of the Royal Secret at Kingston in Jamaica in the year of Masonry 1769, advertized the princes masons that lately a commotion had been at Paris, and that Enquiry had been made if Masons who stiled themselves Kts. of Kadoch were not in reality Knts. Templars? it was therefore Rooled in the Great East of Berlin and Paris, that said degrees in future should be stiled Kts of the White and Black Eagle, and the jewel be a black Spread Eagle &c as mentioned in this degree, and that notices should be sent to all our Inspectors abroad.

The Ne Plus Ultra or 25th Degree called the Royal Secret or Kts of St. Andrews –Faithfull Guardians of the Treasure.

(These Rituals are followed by 16 unnumbered folios containing the Regulations
* For the Government of Regular Royal Lodges of Perfection
* Statutes and Regulations made in Prussia and France
These are respectively given the improbable dates of 'the 25th of the 7th month of the year 1762' and 'Septemr. 17th, 1762', which are unacceptable for reasons set out in the foregoing text. The second set of Regulations are, of course, 'The Grand Constitutions of 1762'.)

100 There may well have been a similar, but less well-documented, creation of Degrees in Prussia also, for much the same reason as that in France – the desire of the German aristocrats to be able to set themselves apart, Masonically, from the 'common people'; there is no evidence that Frederick the Great took part in this process – in any case he would have been too preoccupied with the Thirty Years War and the Austrian Succession. See, for example, Alain Bernheim, *Did early "High" or Écossais Degrees originate in France?*, Heredom, Vol 5, p.100 (1996)

101 A.C.F. Jackson, AQC. XCVII, p.177 (1984) "Both the Paris and the Bordeaux systems made up their rituals out of events after the death of Hiram. Contemporary rituals show that the main difference was that Bordeaux relied only on Old Testament themes while Paris introduced elements characteristic of the New Testament."

102 The Bordeaux 'Lodge of Perfection' did not contain 'the Degrees from the fourth to the fourteenth, both inclusive' conferred in a 'Lodge of Perfection' in the Rite today, and should not be confused with it.

103 This account of a confused situation is considerably indebted to RC, in particular pages 37-39.

104 *Ibidem.*, p.35

105 Alain Bernheim, *The* Mémoire Justificatif *of La Chaussée and Freemasonry in Paris until 1773*, AQC, CIV, p.95 (1991)

106 *'Substitut Particulier'*

107 *Grande Loge des Maîtres de l'Orient de Paris ditte de France*

108 *'Substitut General'.* Lacorne's appointment was not revoked as has sometimes been claimed. Bernheim, *loc. cit.* p.99

109 *La Grande Loge de France*

110 *Empereur d'Orient*

111 Bernheim, *loc. cit.,*p.101

112 *Ibidem*, p.103

113 "The Council of Knights of the East, associated with the Grand Lodge of France, represented the 15° and 16°. As they named themselves as 'Chief Inspectors of the work of the Rebuilding of the First and Second Temples', it seems certain they have nothing to do with the 17°-25° [*see 'Morin's Rite', below.* C.J.M.] and were probably not concerned with the *Elu* or *Vengeance* degrees." RC p.39

114 Bernheim, *loc. cit.*, pp 102/3. (The debt owed to Alain Bernheim for the information in the foregoing paragraph is gratefully acknowledged. C.J.M.)

115 On 18th July 1761 the Grand Lodge of France had given to what was in effect the 'Provincial Grand Lodge of Lyons" Letters Patent authorising them to confer "les hauts [*sic*] grades". Mollier advances this as part of his convincing thesis that the Patent given to Morin in the following month included authority to disseminate the High Degrees as well as those of the Craft. Pierre Mollier, *Deux siècles de Rite Écossais Ancien Accepté en France*, p.37. (Éditions Dervy, Paris, 2004)

116 *'négociant'*

117 At that time, those who had such a birthplace and parentage were known as 'Creoles', a designation which did not imply any native or coloured blood.

118 The 'others' vary from copy to copy, of which there are several.

119 One version of the Patent is set out in RC, Appendix 4, p.245. "The usually accepted copy is in the archives of the Supreme Council of the Southern Jurisdiction, U.S.A. The French version from which this English translation is reputed to have been made, came from one that belonged to Jean-Baptiste de la Hogue, father-in-law of the comte de Grasse-Tilly, two men who figure later extensively in the development of the A & A Rite." *Ibidem*, p.40.

120 That 'The Emperors of the East and West' had some hand in granting his patent to Morin is a Masonic myth of long-standing – I may even in the past have been guilty of propagating it myself, and if I have misled any Brethren, I take this opportunity of apologising! C.J.M.

121 "which powers constitute me as an Inspector of all the Lodges of America under French domination, and perpetual Wor Master of Symbolic Lodge the *Parfaite Harmonie ..."* (Letter written by Morin in 1765 to the French Grand Lodge, quoted by Jackson, RC, p.41.)

122 For example, he is said to have visited Bristol and worked there one of the French Degrees.

123 On 3rd May 1764 Morin wrote "Count Ferrest, Grand Master of all the Lodges under English domination, named me Inspector of its dominion in that part of the New World and decorated me with sublime degrees giving me a certificate that I am the only one constituted for the Lodges of the Grand Elect, Knight and Scottish Prince Mason". Ferrers may well have endorsed his Patent, a common custom at that time, but this conferred no additional powers. Jackson points out that with six English P.G.M.'s in the New World, "it seems most odd that any Grand Master would give authority over them to an unknown Frenchman". RC pp56/57.

124 Morin confusingly refers to these as having been ratified on 25th November 1762, the date upon which it was agreed to appoint Commissioners to effect the reunion.

125 See, for example, RC, Chapter 5, pp.46-54

126 Francken was born in Holland in about 1720. He arrived in Jamaica in February 1757, and had become a naturalised British subject on 2nd March 1758. Yves Hivert-Messeca, *Deux Siècles de Rite Écossais Ancien Accepté en France* (Éditions Dervy, Paris, 2004). At this time he was "an Appraiser, Marshal and Serjeant at Mace in the Vice-Admiralty Court". A.R. Hewitt, *Another Francken Manuscript rediscovered*, AQC, Vol.LXXXIX, p.208 (1976)

127 Jackson speculates that Morin's move may have been brought about by the revocation of his Patent by the French Grand Lodge and his replacement by a Bro. Martin, of whom otherwise Morin appears to have taken but little notice. RC, p.58

128 R.L. Stevenson, *Kidnapped*, Chapter XXVI

129 All quotations from the 'Constitutions of 1762' are from the 1771 'Supreme Council of England' copy. (*v.i.*).

130 Gould in his *History of Freemasonry* deals at length with Hund's Rite, as does A.E.Waite in *A New Encyclopaedia of Freemasonry*. Frederick Smyth

Brethren in Chivalry pp.14/15 (Lewis Masonic, 1991) briefly summarises its salient features, making the principal points that this was essentially a 'Templar' Order, created by Karl Gotthelf, Baron von Hund (1722-76) in which "in its Entered Apprentice degree was an oath of unquestioning obedience to unknown superiors, hence the name of the rite – Strict Observance".

131 RC., p.36.

132 H.Van Buren Voorhis makes the contradictory statement "In 1762 a Sovereign Grand Council of the 25th Degree was set up, and beside a Grand Secretary, two subordinate Secretaries, one for Paris and one for Bordeaux and the Provinces, were provided. We find this in the CONSTITUTIONS of 1762, compiled by nine Commissioners in Bordeaux who issued the Morin Patent". He goes on to say that the Constitution was not prepared before Morin left France, but awaited him in Dominique where he lodged at Jacmel with the Parish Priest. *The Story of the Scottish Rite*, p.15, Henry Emerson, New York (1965). Since this is contrary to all other evidence it casts some doubt on Voorhis' account, for example that Morin's supersession by Martin (otherwise well documented) did not occur.

133 This Document still exists (RC, p.60) and is dated 25th November 1762. It is not, however, a copy of the 'Constitutions of 1762'.

134 The term '*Ne Plus Ultra*' has given rise to considerable confusion from time to time. There was never a *specific* Degree called '*Ne Plus Ultra*'. The term has been used on both sides of the Atlantic to describe the highest Degree, whichever it may have been, in various sequences of progressive Degrees – 'That Degree than which there is nothing higher'. Its use in the 30th Degree GEKHH under the Supreme Council of England etc. is something of an historic anomaly.

135 *The Freemasons' Magazine* (London), pp.506/7 (1855)

136 See **Appendix A.**

137 I am indebted to Bro.John Hamill for this information.

138 For an analysis of its provenance and contents, see A.R.Hewitt, *loc. cit.*

139 See **Appendix B.**

140 For an analysis of its provenance and contents, see J.M.Hamill, AQC, Vol. 97 p.200 (1984).

141 RC, p.61.

142 Hewitt, *loc. cit.*, p.208.

Essay 4
'1786 and All That'

By 1795 a Rite of twenty-five Degrees, universally referred to today as 'Morin's Rite', had been well established both on the mainland of America and in the Islands of the West Indies. Between Stephen Morin's last visit to France in 1762 and his death in Jamaica in 1771 he had given shape and substance to this Rite. Its Degrees were derived from those in Bordeaux, where, during his visits in the 1740s, Morin had been prominent in setting up the 'Lodge of Perfection', and from those in Paris, to which Morin, dissatisfied by the treatment he had received from his Brethren in Bordeaux, had transferred his allegiance before finally returning to his home in the New World. His Rite thereby included some of each of the various sequences of Degrees being practised in France[143]. Armed with a Patent from the Grand Lodge of France which designated him as 'G.M. Inspector' in the New World, Morin considered that his authority there was paramount. He continued to act in accordance with this belief even after his Patent was revoked, and a successor had been appointed by the Grand Lodge in Paris.

When Morin returned to the West Indies in 1763, he lived first in Dominique, but by 1765 he had left the island for Jamaica. Here he nominated a well-esteemed Public Servant, Henry Francken, as his Deputy Inspector; for eight years they worked closely together. There can now be little doubt that the so-called 'Grand Constitutions of 1762' were put together by Morin and Francken. As a pattern, they used the 'Statutes and Regulations' for the Craft Lodges in France which the French Grand Lodge ratified in 1763, and of which Morin was then sent a copy. There is not the slightest evidence that the 'Grand Constitutions of 1762' were sent to Morin from France, the more so since none of the various High Degree ruling bodies in Paris would have wished to endorse such a document which would have considerably restricted the jealously guarded powers of each. Indeed, none of their subsequent activities betrayed a knowledge of the existence of the Constitutions or of the controlling body, 'The Grand Sovereign Council', which the Constitutions envisaged. Certainly the Parisian 'Council of the Knights of the East' and 'The Emperors of the East and West' took no account of either.

Matters were very different in the New World. There was no superior body to challenge the powers which Morin assumed. After Morin's death, Francken continued to propagate the Rite. His considerable contribution was to provide manuscript Rituals of its twenty-five Degrees. Within each of his manuscripts was included a transcript both of what were claimed to be the Constitutions of the Rite promulgated in 1762 and also of the Regulations for the conduct of 'Lodges of Perfection'. These Regulations were modelled on those composed by the French Grand Lodge for its subordinate Lodges just as the 'Constitutions of 1762' had been modelled on its Statutes. Three of Francken's manuscripts are preserved and at least one other is believed to have existed[144].

During the 1780s Francken suffered serious financial losses, in spite of which he was afterwards promoted to senior office in the Jamaican Judiciary. These circumstances may have combined to diminish his enthusiasm for his Masonic labours. He cannot entirely have abandoned them because one of his manuscripts appears to have been written after 1786. Both Morin and Francken had appointed further Deputy Inspectors. They in their turn considered themselves entitled not only to appoint yet more Brethren to this rank, but also to establish bodies which conferred Higher Degrees. For example, in 1783 an American Deputy Inspector, Isaac da Costa[145], established a Lodge of Perfection in Charleston where a Council of Princes of Jerusalem was founded in the town five years later. By 1800 there were, perhaps, fifty Deputy Inspectors[146], on the American mainland. Since neither Morin nor Francken was alive, each 'Deputy' was in practice responsible to nobody but himself.

By now Masonic affairs in France were again in a state of some confusion. Soon after the duc de Chartres had been Installed as Grand Master of the Grand Lodge of France in 1772, a Grand Orient was constituted. Many of the French Lodges transferred their allegiance to the Grand Orient which attempted unsuccessfully to impose itself on the Council of the Emperors of the East and West, which formed an inner circle of the Grand Lodge. One of the objectives of the Grand Orient was to absorb all other Higher Degree systems, something which would hardly have been necessary had there been any substance to the 'Grand Sovereign Council' envisaged in the 'Constitutions of 1762' of which no one in Europe seems even to have been aware. The Grand Orient then adopted a Higher Degree system of its own after it had had a flirtation with some Lodges of a 'Rectified Scottish Rite' in Dresden[147]. In 1781, ignoring the activities of the Grand Orient, the Parisian Lodge, *Le Contrat Social,* added to its title '*Mère Loge du Rite Ecossais à l'Orient de Paris*[148]. The French proclivity for inventing new Degrees continued unabated[149], and several of these which reached the Western World were adopted by one or other of the Deputy Inspectors. Morin's carefully constructed twenty-five Degree Rite was in danger of falling by the wayside.

The fervour of the patriots in the American War of Independence was no match for the British Army which had been schooled in more formal warfare in Europe. Among those who contributed to the British defeat was the French Admiral de Grasse, the owner of extensive sugar plantations in Dominique, and the arrival of whose fleet at Chesapeke had provided the final blow to the resistance of Lord Cornwallis at Yorktown. The Admiral had a son, François Auguste[150], who inherited his father's titles, comte de Grasse Rouville, marquis de Tilly, but who is generally referred to as the comte de Grasse-Tilly. The young comte held a Commission in the French Army[151] and while serving in Paris he was initiated at the age of 19 in the *Mère Loge Ecossais du Contrat Social* on 8th January 1783[152]. De Grasse-Tilly would therefore have been aware of the Higher Degrees at an early stage of his Masonic career. Not only this, but the *Contrat Social* Lodge already had contacts with the Island of Martinique in the French West Indies.

After the death of his father, de Grasse-Tilly resigned his Commission in 1789, and went to Dominique to manage the family estates. Three years later he married the daughter of a lawyer in the Island, Jean de la Hogue[153].

An uprising of the black slave-workers in Dominique had begun in 1791, and de Grasse-Tilly, as a former Officer in the French Army, was one of those mobilised to suppress the rebellion. The colonists had little success, and many left the island, including de Grasse-Tilly and his newly wedded wife, together with his father-in-law and his family. They retreated to the American mainland[154], and took refuge in Charleston where they were hard put to it to make a living. Among other occupations, de Grasse-Tilly became a Fencing-Master, and later taught at a school opened by de la Hogue[155].

In spite of their straitened circumstances, both de la Hogue and de Grasse-Tilly resumed their interest in Freemasonry. They joined with others expelled from Dominique to form a Roman Catholic Lodge, *La Candeur*. At this time an American, Hyman Long, who had been given the rank of Deputy Inspector in Jamaica, possibly by Francken, was present in Charleston. On 12th November 1796, or so it was afterwards claimed by de la Hogue and de Grasse-Tilly, Long raised each of them, together with five others of their French refugee Brethren, to the rank of Deputy Inspector. Two months later, the seven constituted themselves into a Consistory of the 25th, or *Ne Plus Ultra*, Degree, Princes of the Royal Secret. It has never been satisfactorily explained why this should have upset the Princes of the Jamaica Consistory, but they would only recognise the Charleston body as regular after remonstrating with its members and receiving an assurance that they considered themselves subordinate to their Jamaican Brethren[156].

It is just at this time, when the Thirty-three Degree Rite was being conceived, or possibly was already newly born, that there are no trustworthy contemporary records of its nativity. There is plenty of documentation purporting to describe what occurred in the next dozen years or so – for example, in the 'Golden Books' which the members of the Thirty-third Degree of the expanded Rite were instructed to maintain – but these and other documents have so evidently been amended with later insertions and certified with later signatures[157], that they have to be treated with great caution.

Before 1800 de Grasse-Tilly and de la Hogue were apparently content with their Consistory of the Twenty-fifth Degree, and there is no reliable evidence that they were considering adding further Degrees to the twenty-five which it controlled. De Grasse-Tilly himself was also involved with more orthodox Masonic matters[158].

In 1800 the Consistory of Princes of the Royal Secret was the highest Masonic body in the Charleston area, there being otherwise only a Council of Princes of Jerusalem. The Americans were still imbued with considerable nationalistic fervour after ousting the British in the War of Independence. It would not therefore be surprising if the American Masons in the Charleston Council wanted the senior body in the district to be an all-American one, superior to a French Consistory. Be that as it may, there are several documents which record that on 25th May 1801 John Mitchell[159] presided over a meeting of a group of American Masons, some at least of whom apparently considered themselves to have attained the hitherto unknown Thirty-third Degree. At the meeting Mitchell gave Dr. Frederick Dalcho a Patent as Lieutenant Grand Commander[160] – the documents, many of which were written long after the event, diverge both as to how many were present at the Meeting, and who they were. A week later, on 31st May 1801, there was opened the first Supreme Council of the Thirty-third Degree of the Ancient and Accepted Scottish Rite with Mitchell as Sovereign Grand Commander. The Bicentenary account of this event, published in 2001 by the Supreme Council of the Southern Jurisdiction of the U.S.A., asserts that both de Grasse-Tilly and de la Hogue were Founder-Members of the Council, but their signatures on the relevant documents cannot necessarily be taken at their face value – the documents have evidently been amended, and some signatures added, at a later date. It might be thought more probable that under the circumstances the Mother Supreme Council would consist only of American members, although the Frenchmen were certainly involved in its formation. That the Supreme Council was opened on that day is, however, beyond doubt, with John Mitchell as Sovereign Grand Commander and Dalcho as Lieutenant Grand Commander.

The Founder-Members[161] of this, the first Supreme Council in the World, had done a surprising thing. They had set up a body, which, if it were accepted as regular and properly established by the other Masonic powers world-wide, was superior to any other in the 'Ecossais' or 'Scottish' Rite. As such, it had the potential to provide the unifying influence which was urgently needed to produce order out of the chaos into which the various Rites and their disparate controlling bodies had plunged the Higher Degrees. It is not surprising that it took a little time for this remarkable new enterprise to find its feet and for its members to realise of what it might be capable. It was not until 4th December 1802 that the Supreme Council at Charleston circulated a manifesto, the 'Circular throughout the two Hemispheres'[162], announcing its institution to all the more important Masonic controlling bodies, not only in North America and the West Indies, but in Europe and South America as well.

For the constitution of this Council to be accepted, an undeniable authority had to be claimed for it, and for its Rite of thirty-three Degrees. The so-called 'Constitutions of 1762' had already claimed in its first Article that

> The Sovereign Council of Sublime Princes is composed of all presidents of the Councils, particular & regular, constituted in the cities of Berlin and Paris; the Sovereigns of Sovereigns, or his substitute general, or his representative, at their head.

It had always been implicitly considered that the un-named 'Sovereign of Sovereigns' was in fact King Frederick the Second of Prussia. The Council's Manifesto was intended to sweep aside any doubts about this by specifically claiming that in 1786 Frederick the Second had personally signed new Constitutions establishing a thirty-three Degree Rite, and, moreover, that these Constitutions, or at least a true copy, were now in the possession of the Supreme Council in Charleston which had been inaugurated under their authority.

In the following year, 1803, Dr. Dalcho, the Lieutenant Grand Commander of the Charleston Council, gave a series of four Orations in which he set out the history of the Scottish Rite and the genesis of the thirty-three Degree Order. He gave no indication that he considered Frederick's authorship, and, indeed his signature, of the Constitutions of 1786, to be other than established historical fact. Among other things, Dalcho stated

> All the sublime degrees of Masonry were established before the year 1776... Only one has been established since, on 1st May 1786. By the constitutions of the Order, which were ratified on the 25th October, 1762, the King of Prussia was proclaimed as Chief of the Eminent Degrees with the rank of Sovereign Grand Inspector General and Grand Master[163] ... The Sublime Degrees are the same at this moment as they were at the time of their first formation. Not the *smallest* alteration or addition has been made to them.

This curious statement was not made to establish that what was in effect a new Order pre-dated the American Declaration of Independence, but rather that no accusation could be made that it was tainted by *Illuminism*, an anarchic doctrine set up in 1776 by Adam Weishaupt who intended to use Freemasonry to disrupt the existing political order[164]. Dalcho was determined to show that, the "Sublime Degrees" had been in existence before Weishaupt's reformist Order, apart, that is, from the thirty-third and last Degree which had been established by Frederick of Prussia who could hardly be accused of being anti-monarchical. Dalcho emphasised that, with this one exception, the Degrees of the Rite had been unchanged since "the time of their first formation", and could not therefore be contaminated by Bavarian heresies. At the uneasy period at which Dalcho wrote, with

France not yet fully emerged from the blood-bath of its Revolution, and some fears among the European establishment of how far this would spread, it was important to give this assurance if the Order were to be accepted in Britain and in other nervous European Kingdoms and Principalities.

But accepted the Constitutions were as the basis for the stabilisation of the Ecossais Masonry, now the Ancient and Accepted Scottish Rite, and for its government by national Supreme Councils in accordance with the provisions therein. Several versions of the Constitutions emerged during the first three decades of the nineteenth century, differing only in detail. In the translation from the Latin which was made by Albert Pike, the later Sovereign Grand Commander of the Supreme Council of the Southern Jurisdiction of the United States of America, Article Five, Section Three states:

> In each of the Great Nations of Europe, whether Kingdom or Empire, there shall be but a single Supreme Council of the 33rd Degree.
> In all those States and Provinces, as well of the main-land as of the islands, whereof North America is composed, there shall be two Councils, one at as great a distance as may be from the other.
> In all those States and Provinces also, whether of the main-land or the islands, whereof South America is composed, there shall be two Councils, one at as great a distance as possible from the other.
> Likewise there shall be one only in each Empire, Supreme State, or Kingdom, in Asia, in Africa, &c., &c.

Whatever the 'Act of Union' may say, the assumption has never been challenged that England, Scotland and Ireland are each 'Great Nations', and each therefore entitled to its own Supreme Council. It has also been tacitly accepted that there can be a Supreme Council in every self-governing country including those on the mainland and in the islands of North and South America, although the United States of America retains its right to have two independent Supreme Councils. There has always been rigid adherence to the converse[165], that is to say that, with the exception of the U.S.A., when a Supreme Council has been recognised by the other Councils in any 'Empire, Supreme State or Kingdom', no other Council will be recognised there.

De Grasse-Tilly went to Dominique on 21st February 1802 and established the Supreme Council of the French West Indies with himself as Sovereign Grand Commander and de la Hogue as Lieutenant Grand Commander[166]. He was then taken prisoner by the British and sent to Jamaica. Released in 1804, he was in Bordeaux on 4th July, and in September he set up the Supreme Council of France. He later established Supreme Councils in Milan in Italy[167], Madrid in Spain[168], and Brussels in Belgium[169].

That Frederick of Prussia was their sponsor became an article of faith among the Supreme Councils. For example, in 1813 J.B.P.L.Pyron, the Grand Secretary General of the French Supreme Council, published an *Abridged History of the Organisation in France of the Thirty-Three Degrees of the Ancient and Accepted Scottish Rite* in which he categorically endorsed the statement that:

> "Frederick II, presiding in person on the 1st May 1786 over the Supreme Council with whose assistance he organized and directed the Order, raised to thirty-three degrees the system of twenty-five degrees perpetuated by the Grand Constitutions of 1762 ..."

Pyron has frequently been quoted as the authority for endorsing Frederick's personal authorship of the 'Constitutions of 1786', but how far is this claim justified?

Many American authors take the same view as Pyron, foremost of them being the formidable Albert Pike. But Cosby Jackson, following Paul Naudon and R.S. Lindsay, takes the opposing view that it is almost inconceivable that Frederick himself can have had anything to do with the Constitutions. Complete versions of these comprise two distinct parts: 'The New Secret Institutes and Bases' and 'Constitutions and Statutes of the Grand Supreme Councils'. The opening paragraphs of the former have a certain philosophic libertarianism which Jackson considers not to be in accord with Frederick's opinions. He also finds anachronisms within the Constitutions, which at one point appear to refer to Frederick in the past tense. Further, fees are to be paid in "Louis d'Or of the old issue"[170] even though the gold Louis was still common currency in circulation in 1786. Since four Members at least of the Charleston Supreme Council have Jewish names[171], it is also remarkably convenient that some versions of the Constitutions state that only five members of the Supreme Council need be Christian, something which, as Jackson puts it, "in Prussia in 1786 would have been almost unthinkable"[172]. There are other provisions in the 'Constitutions' which seem to be fortunately tailored to circumstances in the

New World at the beginning of the nineteenth century. It is odd that while great Nations such as England and France might only have one Supreme Council, a string of sparsely inhabited British and French ex-Colonies on the Eastern sea-bord of North America should be permitted to have two; it was to be almost half a century before the great drive Westward took place, and the vast size of the inhabitable regions of North America was fully realised.

The original of the Constitutions with Frederick's signature and with those of the witnesses to it has never been forthcoming, although some of the unknown copyists implicitly claim to have seen at least a copy contemporary with it. For example, the English translation made by Albert Pike reproduces fragments of eight signatures[173] above Frederick's name, with the final editorial Note:

> The *asterisks* mark the places of certain signatures that have become illegible or been effaced by attrition, or by the effect of sea-water, to which the original duplicate of these documents, written on parchment, has several times been accidentally exposed[174].

Finally, there is the question of the signature of Frederick himself. Why should the King, broken in body by decades of campaigning, well-knowing that his death could not be far off but still preoccupied by serious problems of State, and who had, so far as is known, displayed no interest in Freemasonry for more than twenty years, suddenly involve himself in organising High Degree Rites which were not generally practised in Prussia? To many this provides a conclusive argument that the involvement of the King of Prussia and the date of the First of May, 1786, are alike fabrications. If this is so, the Grand Constitutions must have been composed in America, probably in Charleston itself by American members of the Charleston Council of Princes of Jerusalem, almost certainly with the assistance of the French refugees from Dominique[175]. Even so, this conclusion is not universally accepted. Several distinguished Masonic historians continue to contend that the Constitutions could have emanated from the Prussian King.

Frederick had been Initiated during the life-time of his father, Frederick William. In order to avoid his father's possible displeasure, his Initiation in Brunswick took place clandestinely during the night of 14th/15th August 1738. For several years Frederick presided over a Lodge in his Palace at Rheinsberg. Here he also formed a circle of friends to whom he gave familiar nicknames. Twelve of them formed the 'Bayard Order', a non-Masonic but serious group for discussing the Art of Warfare, albeit in archaic French.

According to a recent biographer:

> "While hunting bored him, freemasonry proved much more to Frederick's liking. He was forward-thinking and anti-clerical, and had no truck with court etiquette and outward distinctions of rank"[176]

The same author goes on to say that Bielfeld, a member of the middle-classes from Hamburg, whom Frederick had met at his Initiation, was "a good example of how freemasonry transcended the social divisions of the time"[177]. Frederick invited friends to stay with him at Rheinsberg as 'brother-freemasons'.

When Frederick succeeded to the throne of Prussia after the death of his father on 31st May 1740, he pursued his interest in Freemasonry more openly, and "Bielfeld had the job of opening the first lodge in the Prussian capital [*Berlin*]"[178]. After his accession, in whatever time Frederick could spare from campaigning, his Palace of *Sans Souci* became a centre of the arts where contemporary writers and philosophers were invited to stay. The most prominent of them was Voltaire, whom Frederick treated as more than an equal, rather as his intellectual superior[179]. Frederick was a compulsive writer – his massive correspondence was collected in thirty volumes of *Oeuvres*, of which only the final three record his military regulations and instructions. History is largely concerned with his military campaigns, but Frederick was almost a soldier in spite of himself. Jackson may have been exaggerating when he denied Frederick's liberal sentiments and wrote:

> "The freedom of speech, so often referred to in connection with Frederick's court, was in fact almost entirely restricted to Frederick himself. He never had any leanings towards 'universal equality and mutual tolerance' which Pyron attributes to him in 1813."

This does not wholly accord with the impression which is gained by the reader of Asprey's monumental biography, the subtitle of which is well-justified[180].

Lassalle has analysed in detail the arguments for denying that the 'Grand Constitutions' can be genuine.[181] He stresses the enthusiasm for 'Ecossism' in 1785. This, he considers, was not only the case in France and in the West Indies. Some Freemasons in Germany, disillusioned by "the relative failure of the Wilhemsbad Convent in 1782 where any reference to the Templars had been suppressed", also wished to see the 'Ecossais' Degrees put on a sound footing. Among these, Lassalle claims, were Stark and Wölner (sic), putative signatories of the Grand Constitutions.

Lassalle implies that prior to 1801 Mitchell possessed a 'Master Copy' of the 1786 Constitutions, and on the basis of this document he had awarded himself the Thirty-third Degree. According to de Grasse-Tilly's 'Golden Book'[182], by 27th December 1797 he and de la Hogue had Advanced Brother Joseph Jahan to the 25th Degree. De Grasse-Tilly then describes this as 'the last Degree'. It therefore must have been after this event, but before 1801, that de Grasse-Tilly became aware that there was a higher Degree, the thirty-third, to which he was Advanced by Mitchell[183]. This leaves the problem of where had Mitchell obtained his copy of the Grand Constitutions?

Lassalle is satisfied that Mitchell received it from an un-named "Prussian Brother"[184], and that all subsequent texts, including the Latin one "introduced by the Comte de St.Laurent"[185] were copied from this with varying degrees of accuracy. He then brushes aside the 'anachronisms'. He points out that the value of the Louis d'Or was reduced in 1785[186], and that there would be nothing strange if in the following year there was a reference to 'the old Louis'. So far as the sentence "The Supreme Council wields all the Sovereign masonic powers His August Majesty Frederick II King of Prussia was invested with" is concerned, Lassalle considers that far from indicating that Frederick was already dead when this was written, the phraseology is no more than the translator's misunderstanding of the French 'imperfect tense'. Lassalle's general conclusion is that the Constitutions of 1786 could at least be correctly dated.

To this one could add firstly that if the Constitutions were produced at Frederick's Court they could well have been written in French, a language in which Frederick, Voltaire's voluminous correspondent, was fluent, and in which his 'Order of Bayard' conducted its affairs. Secondly, in his last months, Frederick, though afflicted with gout and the dropsy, was no foolish incompetent, but vigorously conducted affairs of state until the day before his death[187]. It is improbable that a document of such Masonic importance, and bearing Frederick's signature, could have been concealed for more than a dozen years before being revealed to Colonel Mitchell, but it is not impossible.

Perhaps it is best simply to accept that for more than two hundred years 'The Grand Constitutions of 1786' have successfully provided 'Ordo ab Chao'[188] for the Ancient and Accepted (Scottish) Rite. They have governed the world-wide conduct of an Order from which many have derived great pleasure and considerable mental and spiritual profit, and leave it at that until time or circumstance may provide fresh evidence of their authorship.

---

143 The French sequences of Degrees included those concerned with the arrangements made after the death of Hiram, followed by the 'Second Temple' or Zerubbabel sequence, which together comprised the 'Rite of Perfection', the Elu or Vengeance Degrees, and three Knighthood Degrees culminating in the 'Rose Croix'. Above this were five Higher Degrees, the chivalric Kadosh Degree, and finally, the second of two 'Ne Plus Ultras', the 'Sublime Princes of the Royal Secret'. The anomaly among these was the Kadosh Degree, now the 30th in the Ancient and Accepted Rite. It is undoubtedly a 'Templar' Degree, its vengeance directed not against the murderers of Hiram but against the oppressors of Jacques de Molay and his Order. It is curious that it has been so tenaciously retained by the Rite. In 1766 it was vehemently condemned by the Parisian 'Council of the Knights of the East' which forbade "All Masons, Symbolic or High Degree" to "recognize, confer or accept it". Morin was aware of this disapproval, but the Degree appears in Francken's 1771 Manuscript (see below) with the diplomatic note that it "should be stiled knts. of the white and black Eagle".

144 The earliest (1771) is in the archives of the Supreme Council of England, etc., in London, a second (1783) in those of the S.C. of the American Northern Masonic

Jurisdiction, and the third (? 1787) in the Museum and Library of the United Grand Lodge of England in London.

145 Isaac da Costa had been nominated as Deputy Inspector for South Carolina by Moses Michael Hays who had himself been made a Deputy Inspector by Francken on 6th December 1768. Hays, a Dutchman, was a merchant in New York where he was President of the *Shearith Israel Congregation*. Yves Hivert-Messeca, *Deux Siècles de Rite Écossais Ancien Accepté en France,* p.60 (Éditions Dervy, Paris, 2004)

146 Harold Van Buren Voorhis in *The Story of the Scottish Rite of Freemasonry*, Appendix, Henry Emerson, New York (1965) identifies by name 45 Deputy Inspectors created after 1780. Of these, 15 were based in Charleston, 15 in Philadelphia, 3 in New York, 1 in Albany and the remainder in Dominique, Cuba and Jamaica.

147 The Dresden Lodges had constructed a 'Rectified Scottish Rite' under the influence of Willermoz, who had earlier founded 'The Rite of Strict Observance'; the Grand Orient soon withdrew its interest from this curious Rite.

148 A 'Mother-Lodge' in Marseilles had worked a 'classic' seven-degree *Ecossais* system since the 1750s. This system had been transmitted to *Le Contrat Social* Lodge via Avignon where it had acquired "grades plus ésotériques" (Pierre Mollier, *Deux siècles de Rite Écossais Ancien Accepté en France*, p.76 Éditions Dervy, Paris, 2004.) Towards the end of 1781, and throughout the following year, there was somewhat acrimonious correspondence between *Le Contrat Social* Lodge and the Grand Orient. The latter considered that *Le Contrat Social* Lodge had no right to its assumed title, and feared that, in spite of the Lodge's protestations to the contrary, it would interfere with its own ambitions. Indeed, more than one Lodge outside Paris desired a closer association with *Le Contrat Social*, for example, the Lodge *St. Charles de la Parfaite Harmonie* at Avignon, through which the Higher Degrees had come to Paris, which was threatened with suspension by the Grand Orient for so doing. See Jean-Pierre Lassalle, *Des Constitutions et Règlements de 1762 aux Grandes Constitutions de 1786*, p.29, Celebration du Bicentenaire des Grandes Constitutions de 1786, Suprême Conseil pour la France, 1986.

149 The 'Higher Degrees' were widespread in France at this time, without, in spite of the efforts of the Grand Orient, any effective central control. This is illustrated by Lassalle's comment that the Mother-Lodge, *Le Contrat Social,* "held its powers" (*tenait ses pouvoirs*) "from the Mother Lodge St.Jean d'Ecosse d'Avignon, itself proceeding from the Scottish Mother Lodge of Marseilles".

150 Lassalle, *loc. cit.* 'Alexandre François'; RC, p.282 (Index)

151 Sous-lieutenant in the 1st battalion of the Régiment du Roi.

152 Lassalle adds that de Grasse-Tilly had his servant Adnet Initiated on 15th February. On 12th March "il est passé compagnon" (Passed as Fellow-Craft? C.J.M.)

153 Jean-Baptiste Noel Marie de la Hogue, who had been

Initiated some eighteen years earlier in Port-au-Prince in the Lodge *La Parfaite* Union. In the same year he became Master of the Lodge *La Vèrité* at Cap François. 'Cape François' is one of the places noted in Francken's 1783 Manuscript where the '15th Degree Masonry renew'd, or the Sword Rectified' was 'practized'.

154 Now 'The United States of America' which had formally come into being on 21st June 1788 when New Hampshire, the last of the States to do so, ratified the Constitution.

155 Many writers have stated that de Grasse-Tilly was also employed in the new American Army in some engineering capacity, though it is hard to see what qualifications he would have had for such a position, and there is nothing to support this claim in the official Army records.

156 This was a curious transaction, because the Jamaican Consistory was not the governing body of the Rite. There was no provision in the fabricated 'Constitutions of 1762' for any Consistory to claim precedence over another – each would have been subordinate to the 'Grand Sovereign Council' if it had ever existed otherwise than on paper.

157 For example, a 33° Certificate given to Dr. Dalcho and which is dated 25th May 1801 purports to be signed by de Grasse-Tilly as Sovereign Grand Commander of the Supreme Council of the West Indies, a body which he did not found until 1803, two years later.

158 On 5th February 1787, three Lodges Warranted between December 1782 and October 1786 by the Grand Lodge of Pennsylvania (Nos.38,40 & 47) together with two Lodges Warranted by the English 'Antient' Grand Lodge (No.190, 30 Sept. 1774, and No. 236, 1786), erected 'The Grand Lodge of South Carolina of Antient York Masons'. The Officers of this Grand Lodge and of the Grand Council of Princes of Jerusalem at Charleston were often the same people. Yves Hivert-Messeca, *Deux Siècles de Rite Écossais Ancien Accepté en France*, p.29 & p.63 f/n 11. (Éditions Dervy, Paris, 2004). Jackson states that in 1801, de Grasse-Tilly was appointed Grand Marshal of the Grand Lodge of South Carolina. RC., p.68.

159 John Mitchell (1741–1816) had been born in Ireland and emigrated to Dominique in March 1764. (There is no evidence that he ever met Morin who was living in the Island at the same time.) In 1769 he left Dominique and joined his brother in Philadelphia. He fought with the American Army in the War of Independence, becoming Deputy QMG with the rank of Colonel. Ray Baker Harris, *Eleven Gentlemen of Charleston*, p.17 *et seq.* (Washington, D.C. 1959)

160 On the previous day Mitchell had conferred on Dr. Frederick Dalcho, a Londoner of Prussian extraction, the ranks of Kadosh and Prince of the Royal Secret and appointed him Deputy Inspector General, his Patents in each case being signed by, among others, Abraham Alexander, Isaac Auld, Jean-Baptiste de la Hogue, Emmanuel de la Motta, Israel De Lieben Alexander de Grasse-Tilly, James Moultrie and Sampson Simson. Yves Hivert-Messeca, *op. cit.* pp.65/6. According to Voorhis, *op. cit.* Dalcho had been an Officer in the Army of Frederick the Great.

161 Col. John Mitchell, Dr. Frederick Dalcho, Major

Thomas Bowen, Rabbi Abraham Alexander, Emanuel de la Motta, Dr. Isaac Auld, Israel de Lieben, Moses Clava Levy and Dr. James Moultrie. That there were these nine designated Founder-Members makes the claim that de Grasse-Tilly and de la Hogue were original Members of the First Supreme Council even less likely – it seems implausible that 'The Grand Constitutions of 1786' would be departed from almost before they had been adopted by having *eleven* members of the First Supreme Council.

162 Under the headings it bore each of the legends '*Deus Meumque Jus*' and 'ORDO AB CHAO'.

163 As Jackson comments with commendable brevity "He was not"! RC, p.75.

164 Adam Weishaupt, a young Bavarian social reformer, instituted the *Order of the Illuminati of Bavaria* in 1776. In the wider sense of the word, the *Illuminati* was a political organisation, through which Weishaupt sought reform by destroying established authority and superseding Christianity by 'natural religion'. One of the means by which Weishaupt hoped to do this was by incorporating Freemasonry into the Order and using it to propagate its principles.

165 With one or two obvious exceptions – Brazil, for example, as vast a country as the U.S.A.

166 Could de Grasse-Tilly have deemed this to be the second Council which the Constitutions fortuitously authorised for North America "as well of the mainland as of the Islands"?

167 5th March 1805 Voorhis, *op.cit.*, p.15

168 October 1809 *ibidem*.

169 11th May 1817 *ibidem*.

170 'Grand Constitutions of 1786' Article XVI, Section II.

171 See Footnote 18.

172 RC., p.79 There are other versions which do not even refer to Christianity, but to "the religion which most generally prevails in the particular country where it is established", and that no more than four Members of the Supreme Council are required to profess it.

173 Presumably these eight, together with Frederick himself, represented a Supreme Council of nine Members.

174 The remnants of the signatures reproduced in the 'Pike' translation are "Stark", "D'Esterno", "H.Wilhelm", "D ...", and "Wœllner" but it cannot be said whether these were genuinely appended to the original document, if it ever existed.

175 No help could be expected from Paris at that time. Organised Freemasonry had well-nigh disappeared under the revolutionary tide.

176 Giles MacDonough, *Frederick the Great, a Life in Deed and Letters*, p.113 (St. Martin's Press, New York, 1999)

177 *Ibidem*.

178 MacDonough,*op. cit.* p.133

179 Voltaire's Apron, which originally belonged to the philosopher Helvetius, was afterwards given to Benjamin Franklin. It is now in the Museum of the GODF. Pierre Mollier, An American Freemason in Paris; Benjamin Franklin W.M. of a Grand Orient Lodge in 1778-1779, p.41 and Cover Illustration, *The Chain of Union*, English Language Edition, No.2 (2004) Voltaire was Initiated into Freemasonry in Paris on 7th April 1778, and died 7 weeks later on 30th May

without leaving the City. Frederick never therefore had the opportunity of greeting him as 'Brother'.

180 Robert B. Asprey, *Frederick the Great, the Magnificent Enigma*, (Revised edition, Book-of-the-Month Club, Inc., New York, 1999).

181 Lassalle, *op. cit.* (English version) pp.64-76 (French original) pp.30-42.

182 The record of their activities which the 'Grand Constitutions' instructed all Sovereign Grand Inspectors General to maintain.

183 There is no copy of the 'Constitutions of 1786' in de Grasse-Tilly's 'Golden Book', and when in 1828 he was re-constituting the Supreme Council for the French Leeward and Windward Isles he wrote to the Supreme Council of the Northern Jurisdiction (it had been constituted in 1813) asking for a copy. Lassalle concludes that what he calls 'the family copy' was in the hands of de la Hogue. (Lassalle, *loc. cit.* (English version) p.68) But this is perplexing; without a copy how did de Grasse-Tilly set up the French Supreme Council in 1804?

184 "A letter from Moses Holbrook to J.J.J.Gourgas [*the Sovereign Grand Commander of the Supreme Council of the Northern Jurisdiction, U.S.A.*] of 30th March 1829 (some 27 or 28 years later) has these lines:

' I took the opportunity of mentioning to Br. Dalcho, to ask how Mitchell got the 33d. He replied he could not. He could not recollect; but he (Mitchell) had signed some obligation in French for it. He thinks it came from some Prussian (*a word replacing the word 'German' crossed out*) who was in Charleston, who was authorized to communicate it to him.'

Although not precise, this testimony is capital for Dalcho was still alive." Lassalle, *loc.cit.* pp35 and 68.

185 *Ibidem*, p.67.

186 "A decree of October 30th 1785 increased the number of "20 livres, Louis d'or from 30 to 32 in each mark." *Ibidem*, p.70.

187 "He was confined to a chair; but he did not cease working. He still got up between 4 and 5 a.m. and received his cabinet secretaries with the morning's business. At eight he was dressed and then worked further on state papers. For nourishment in the evening his reader fed him his favourite extracts from Cicero and Plutarch. This slightly truncated royal regime continued until 15 August. The next day he was unable to work. He died at 2.20 on the morning of the 17th in the arms of his *valet de chambre* Strützki." MacDonough, *op. cit.* p.384.

188 'Order out of Chaos'.

Essay 5
The Grand Constitutions of 1786[189]

❛ The Grand Constitutions of 1786' consists of two parts[190], each dated the First of May 1786, and each purporting to be signed in Berlin by Frederick the Second, King of Prussia. The first part, "The New Secret Institutes and Bases", sets out at some length the ostensible reasons why it was thought necessary to reorganise *The Ancient and Accepted Scottish Rite*' as an Order of Thirty-three Degrees. The second part lays down the 'Constitutions and Statutes of the Grand and Supreme Councils', its title concluding "In the name of the Most Holy and Grand Architect of the Universe, *Ordo ab Chao*". It is remarkable that while there is no certainty about when and by whom these 'Constitutions' were composed, they are still accepted throughout the world by otherwise independent Supreme Councils as the foundation of their common authority. With minor modifications to meet local conditions, and with one important exception[191], the 'Constitutions' are otherwise deemed, by tacit mutual consent, to contain the inviolable Statutes and Regulations governing the conduct of the Order, although there is no supra-national supreme body to enforce them.

The seeds of this development were sown within twenty years of the erection of the world's first Grand Lodge in London in 1717. By the mid-1730s some Brethren, both in England and overseas, considered that it was unsatisfactory to be in possession only of 'Substituted Secrets'. Their discontent resulted in the emergence of Degrees which attempted to provide answers to various questions which the hitherto stark account of the death of Hiram Abif posed to enquiring minds. These additional Degrees were not all necessarily complete fabrications. Within the embryonic Masonic system there may have been older traditions and legends which were discarded by the Premier Grand Lodge in acknowledging only the three Craft Degrees[192]. Be that as it may, while most English Brethren who were looking for something beyond the Third Degree were considerably engaged in developing that of *The Holy Royal Arch of Jerusalem*, by 1750 extended Rites had evolved on the Continent of Europe and particularly in France. These developments were beginning to produce the chaos which it was the stated intention of the 'Grand Constitutions' to reduce to order.

In the third quarter of the eighteenth century the Grand Lodge of France was barely capable of imposing its authority on events in Paris, let alone in the French Provinces where a great variety of extended Rites was being developed. Still less was it able to control matters in the Islands in the French West Indies where some of these Rites had taken sturdy root. Among others, a so-called 'Rite of Perfection', which had been developed in Bordeaux, was established in the Islands of Dominique and Martinique. This process had been considerably assisted by a West Indian Merchant, Stephen Morin, who, in the 1740s and early 1750s, made several visits to the French Western sea-port town. Returning again in 1760, Morin found himself somewhat cold-shouldered by the Bordeaux Brethren, and transferred his allegiance to those in Paris. Here he received a Patent from the French Grand Lodge which commissioned him as its representative or 'Inspector' in the so-called New World. Whatever powers the Grand Lodge had intended to confer on Morin[193], he was soon to interpret them as giving him complete freedom in his conduct of Masonic matters on the other side of the Atlantic, specifically in relation to the extended Rites with Degrees 'beyond the Craft', the *'Ecossais'* or High Degrees.

On Morin's final return to the West Indies, he soon made his home in Jamaica where he enlisted the support of a well-respected citizen of the Island, Henry Francken, whom he nominated as his Deputy Inspector. By 1767 Morin and Francken were in possession of a document entitled 'The Great Statutes and Regulations', universally now referred to as 'The Constitutions of 1762', the opening sentence stating that it was "Made in Prussia and in France, September 7th, 1762". The earliest known copy was written by Francken in the 'Constitution' which he gave in 1767 to a 'Lodge of Perfection' which he established in Albany[194]. The authenticity of these manuscripts is beyond doubt, as Francken's hand-writing and his signature are well known. What is in doubt is where these 'Statutes' originated, and who composed them.

Some Masonic historians[195] accept that these Constitutions were indeed sent to Morin from Paris although there is no record of this having taken place. The more general consensus is that between 1765 and 1767 Morin fabricated them in Jamaica, possibly with the assistance of Francken. They appear to have been modelled on the Statutes and Regulations promulgated in 1763 by the Grand Lodge of France for its Lodges of Craft Masons[196]. If this plagiarism is accepted, evidently the 'Constitutions' cannot be 'of 1762'. The Statutes which the Constitutions contain state that "They were resolved by the Nine Commissioners named by the Great Council of the Sublime Princes of the Royal Secret at the Great East of France". There is nowhere any other record of these Nine Commissioners, nor, indeed, of a "Great Council of the Sublime Princes of the Royal Secret" among the many other Parisian Masonic bodies at that time. A further telling point is that these various bodies in Paris were disputing their respective rights to preside over 'High Degrees', but none of them betrayed any knowledge of such 'Constitutions' to which they themselves would have been subject if they had indeed been promulgated, as the preamble stated, "in Prussia and France", nor took the slightest notice of any of the provisions contained therein. When in 1767 Francken was about to go to the American mainland as Morin's Deputy to propagate the 25-Degree system universally known today as 'Morin's Rite', the Constitutions conveniently filled Morin's need for the authority by which Francken could demonstrate his right to do so, which he did by giving a manuscript copy to the Council which he set up at Albany.

'The Constitutions of 1762' contain few matters of great interest[197]. The early clauses refer to administrative matters, which, with a change of titles, could be applicable to almost any Masonic Ruling Body[198]. There is no reference to the coin, a 'Louis d'Or', which appears in the later Constitutions of 1786, but the provision that "The Sovereign Grand Council of the Sublime Princes shall not grant any letters patent or constitutions unless they receive £10 sterling money for the supply of the person employed"[199], is an indication that the Constitutions were formulated somewhere where the British writ ran. It is only from Article 26 onwards, and specifically within the seven divisions of Article 29, that there is some indication of the structure of the 25-Degree Rite. The 'key figures', so to speak, in the lower Degrees of the Rite are the Sixteenth Degree Princes of Jerusalem. They have considerable privileges and specified inspectorial duties in relation to the first fifteen Degrees, the members of which are instructed to treat them with appropriate respect. Few of the Degrees superior to the Sixteenth, to the holders of which the Princes shall themselves defer, are mentioned by name in the so-called 'Constitutions'; specifically there is no mention of 'Knight of the Rose Croix'. One might wonder whether the sequence of Degrees and their rituals were fully worked out when the 'Constitutions' were first composed. However, the rituals of the Fifteenth to the Twenty-fifth Degree, Sublime Princes of the Royal Secret, were included in Francken's 1771 manuscript[200].

Morin's Rite of Twenty-five Degrees continued to be practised in the Western hemisphere after his death in 1771 and that of Francken in 1795. Each during his life-time had appointed Deputy Inspectors who considered themselves entitled to raise other Brethren to the same rank. Soon after Francken's death there were more than fifty Deputy Inspectors on the North American mainland and in the Caribbean Islands, each then owing no duty to anyone but himself. There was constant trade between the two hemispheres, and further Degrees, unheard of by Morin, which had surfaced in France, had been carried to America. Some were adopted by independent-minded Deputy Inspectors, and grafted, here and there, on to Morin's Rite. The Order which Morin had conferred on the Degrees 'beyond the Craft' was being changed once more into the Parisian Chaos of the 1760s.

Before 1800 there was in Charleston a Council of Princes of Jerusalem, the Sixteenth Degree of 'The Rite of Perfection', most of the members of which were citizens of the newly independent former British colonies. There was also a Council of Sublime Princes of the Royal Secret, the Twenty-fifth Degree of Morin's Rite, which had been set up by French refugees from the Island of Dominique where there had been a revolt of the African slaves in the sugar plantations. On 25th May 1801 several American Masons who claimed that they were Members of the Thirty-third Degree – contemporary documents differ in recording how many – attended a Meeting in Charleston. Six days later, on 31st May 1801, these Brethren opened the first Supreme Council of the Ancient and Accepted Rite of Thirty-three Degrees. This became, in due course, the Supreme Council of the Southern Jurisdiction of the United States of America, the 'Mother Council of the World', as it legitimately proclaims itself today. The Sovereign Grand Commander of the new Council was Colonel John Mitchell, himself a former resident in Dominique. In setting it up, Mitchell may have had the assistance of two Frenchmen who presided over the Charleston Council of Morin's 25-Degree Rite, the comte de Grasse-Tilly and Jean-Baptiste de la Hogue. It is impossible to be certain, because so many signatures have evidently been added to contemporary documents long after the events which they record.

Mitchell claimed to have received a copy of the Grand Constitutions of the Ancient and Accepted Scottish Rite, signed in 1786 by King Frederick of Prussia, which gave him the authority to open the Council. Unfortunately this copy, if it ever existed, has not survived, let alone the original signed by King Frederick. Further purported copies written in English, some fragmentary, appeared in the course of the next few years, one in the hand of Dr. Dalcho, the first Lieutenant Grand Commander of the new Council, but their provenance has been disputed. The first complete version, in French, did not appear until 1832 in Paris. It was followed by a Latin version, perhaps a more probable language for the original which would hardly have been written in English if it had in fact been composed in Prussia[201]. Under the authority which Mitchell claimed to have received, the Rite added eight Degrees to the twenty-five worked by Councils of Sublime Princes of the Royal Secret. Six of these were probably assimilated from French Degrees which had travelled to the Western World[202]. The Thirty-first Degree, *Grand Inspectors Commanders*, may have reached Charleston from France, or, like, apparently, the Thirty-third Degree, it may have been a new construction.

While there are several ways in which knowledge of the Degrees themselves could have reached Charleston, it is more difficult to explain the origin of the copy of the Grand Constitutions which Mitchell claimed to possess. Could the Constitutions ever have been "Settled, done, and ratified, in Grand and Supreme Council of the 33rd Degree, duly constituted, convoked and held: present and approving His August Majesty Frederic the Second, by the grace of God, King of Prussia, Margrave of Brandenburg &c., &c., &c."? The document is witnessed by eight people whose signatures are said to be largely indecipherable on the original from which it is claimed that copies were made[203]. It is finally endorsed "Approved and done at our Royal Residence in Berlin, the first day of May, in the year of Grace 1786, of our Reign the 47th", the original, it is said, being signed by 'Frederic' himself.

Many have claimed that his state of health would have prevented Frederick presiding at such a meeting in May 1786, but this claim can hardly be justified. The King contracted a fever reviewing a parade in the autumn of 1785 and he was also seriously incapacitated by gout and the dropsy. Even so, all the accounts of the final months of Frederick's life (he died early in the morning of 17th August 1786) record that he continued to discharge State business until the day before his death[204]. However, a discordant note (to which little attention has been drawn[205]) is 'Our Royal Residence in Berlin'. Frederick spent the last months of his life at his favourite Palace of Sans Souci outside Potsdam, where he died, and there is no record of his visiting Berlin in 1786. Furthermore, while Frederick himself had been Initiated in an *ad hoc* Lodge in Brandenburg in 1736, and had at first displayed a keen interest in the Craft, there is no record of his involvement with it for thirty years before his death. But, even if, in spite of these objections, Frederick had personally approved the Grand Constitutions, the stated objective of which was to produce Order out of Chaos, why did the Constitutions remain hidden for 15 years until a copy surfaced in Charleston in 1801, while the *Ecossais* Degrees in France were becoming ever more chaotic? It is an uncomfortable conclusion, but today most authorities consider that the 'Constitutions of 1786' were the work of some ingenious person in North America around the end of the eighteenth century. Not the least of the reasons for reaching this conclusion is the very prescient manner in which the Constitutions foreshadow the needs of the American brethren.

Evidently the institution of a Thirty-three Degree Rite at this time might well have accorded with the sentiments of American Brethren in Charleston. The expulsion of the British had been accompanied by an outburst of nationalistic fervour. It could have rankled with the Charleston 'Princes of Jerusalem' constantly to be aware that the senior Masonic body in their vicinity was controlled by colonial Frenchmen. If it is accepted that it is unlikely that the Grand Constitutions emanated from Frederick of Prussia, it would not be unreasonable to believe that they conveniently manifested themselves at this time to meet the aspirations of true American patriots to be masters in their own home as well of Masonry as of everything else.

The first part of the 'Grand Constitutions of 1786', after several pages of somewhat philosophical introduction, enumerates the Thirty-three Degrees of the Rite and places them in the order with which brethren are familiar today. These ascend "regularly to the Sublime Degree (the thirty-third and last), which watches over all the others, corrects their errors, and governs them: and a body or assembly whereof will be a Grand Supreme Council absolute in matters of doctrine, Defender and Conservator of the Order, which it will rule and administer, in accordance with the existing Constitutions and those presently to be enacted."

There is no doubt that the authors of the 'Grand Constitutions of 1786', whoever they may have been, were breaking fresh ground in several respects. To limit, as they did, the size of the Grand body controlling the Rite to no more than nine Members was a considerable novelty in a Masonic world in which members of Grand Lodges were apt to proliferate freely. Furthermore, by defining this body as a self-perpetuating oligarchy, they were departing from previous Masonic tradition where lip-service was at least generally paid to some form of so-called democratic election of the Rulers of the Craft. Because this conception of a Masonic ruling body was a novel one, much of the second document of the Grand Constitutions is concerned with the Supreme Council itself.

It begins by first referring to the 'Constitutions of 1762', which, it says, remain in force where they "are not contrary to these present ordinances", but "such as conflict herewith are abrogated". It is, in fact, not easy to distinguish the parts which do not conflict, and little of the 'Constitutions of 1762' remained in force, but this was an important statement – The Ancient and Accepted Scottish Rite was not to be a new Order. The Constitutions were doing no more than regularising something which, it was claimed, had long existed. It was not a novelty, tainted with the libertarian notions which had developed in Europe in the revolutionary climate at the end of the eighteenth century[206].

The Second Article formally institutes the Rank of Sovereign Grand Inspectors General of the Order. These exalted Brethren are particularly charged to preserve Charity, Union and brotherly Love, and to do the works of Peace and Mercy, as well as safeguarding the regularity, Statutes and traditions of the Order[207]. It reiterates that a body of Inspectors-General is styled a Council of the 33°[208]. The Second Article goes on to say "In places where a Supreme Council of this Degree may be properly established, authority is by these Decretals given to that Inspector who has been longest admitted to elevate another Brother to the same degree and rank". There is no specific definition here of what is meant by a place where a Supreme Council "may be properly established". However, Article IX states that no Sovereign Grand Inspector General can "exercise his individual powers" in any country where there is already a duly constituted Supreme Council which is recognised by all the other Supreme Councils. Evidently this effectively prevents any other Supreme Council invading territory where there is already a recognised Council, even to the extent of being prohibited from establishing a Chapter or Consistory therein[209].

The "Inspector who has been longest admitted", and the Brother whom he has raised to the same degree and rank are then authorised jointly to "confer the same degree on another person[210]. And thus a Supreme Council will be established.[211]". That a quorum of a Supreme Council is three (provided that the Sovereign Grand Commander and the Lieutenant Grand Commander are present) is also confirmed by Article V, § II[212].

The remaining clauses of the Second Article make it clear that a unanimous vote of the existing members is required to elect another member to the Supreme Council, and "The negative vote of one of the Inspectors, if the cause therefor shall be adjudged sufficient, shall reject the Candidate. And this shall be the rule in all similar cases". This can only be interpreted as meaning that unanimity is similarly required for election to the other Degrees with supervisory powers to which reference is made later in the Statutes.

The Third Article makes it clear that the first two Brethren who formed the nucleus of the new Supreme Council are of right respectively the Sovereign Grand Commander and the Lieutenant Grand Commander[213]. Not only this, but it goes on to say that should the Sovereign Grand Commander be removed from Office by death, resignation or other cause, the Lieutenant Grand Commander has the right to succeed to the Office. Should the Office of Lieutenant Grand Commander become vacant, the Sovereign Grand Commander has the right to appoint another member of the Council to the Office in the same way as all appointments within the Supreme Council are made by him[214].

Article IV acknowledges for the first time the different character of the highest degrees of the Rite, by providing that not only shall Sovereign Grand Inspectors General pay on their appointment *ten Frederics d'or or ten Louis d'or of the old issue*, or what, in the local currency shall be equivalent thereto" but also that any Brother who is "initiated (*sic*) into the thirtieth, thirty-first, or thirty-second degree, shall be required to pay for each such degree, the same sum of money in the same coin, or its equivalent." [215]

Article V deals with Supreme Councils themselves. In the first place, it states quite unequivocally that "Every Supreme Council shall consist of nine Grand Inspectors General of the 33rd Degree". It then adds the curious qualification that "four of whom, at least, must profess the religion that most generally prevails in the particular country where it is established". Other versions state "five of whom", thereby placing those who profess the most generally prevailing religion in a majority on the Council, but in either case it is a curious provision to insert. On the other hand it was singularly convenient for the first Supreme Council in Charleston, four of whose original members were of the Jewish Faith.

After stating the necessary quorum for a Council to be competent to transact business, to which reference was made earlier, the Article goes on to say "In each of the Great Nations of Europe, whether Kingdom or Empire, there shall be but a single Supreme Council of the 33rd Degree". It also makes the same provision about Councils "in Asia, in Africa, &c. &c." However, between these two clauses, the Article lays down "In all those States and Provinces, as well of the Main-land as of the islands, whereof North America is composed, there shall be two Councils, one at as great a distance as may be from the other"[216]. Perhaps, by permitting only a single Council in each of the populous European 'Great Nations' such as England, Prussia and France, it was intended to avoid schisms such as had occurred in Craft Masonry in England when the 'Grand Lodge of the Antients' was erected. This does not, however, explain why two Councils should be authorised for the still sparsely populated string of former colonies on the Eastern sea-board of America and in the Caribbean Islands. If this provision were in fact made in 1786, it is a further example of remarkable prescience because it made it legitimate for de Grasse-Tilly almost immediately to establish a Supreme Council for the West Indies[217].

Article VI permits a Supreme Council to delegate its authority "over the degrees below the 17th, or *Knight of the East and West*", the brethren concerned still recognising the Rank and prerogatives of Sovereign Grand Inspectors General. Article VII allows appeals to the Supreme Council, to which it is mandatory to refer "any *affair of honour*"[218]. Article VIII gave power to Consistories of Princes Mason of the 32nd Degree to elect a President, and to make "decretals", but only under strict supervision and the sanction of the Supreme Council[219]. However, the Article goes on to state, almost casually, that after the death of King Frederick, each Supreme Council "will succeed to the Supreme Masonic authority, and exercise the same throughout the whole extent of the State, Kingdom, or Empire wherefor it is constituted". This was evidently seen as being of such importance at the time when the Constitutions were drafted that it is repeated by Article XIII stating that every Supreme Council which is recognised either at that time or in the future "will, of full right, become possessed of the entirety of that Masonic authority wherewith His August Majesty is now invested". The Constitutions thereby disclaim any future intention to establish a supra-national authority. It is curious why Frederick, if it were he, was minded to divest his Masonic successor, whoever it might be, of this responsibility, but such a 'Declaration of Independence' might seem to be of evident importance to Americans who had just thrown off the Colonial yoke.

Articles IX to XI and XIII are those which are together of perhaps the greatest practical importance to English Brethren today. They refer to 'Deputy Inspectors General' which a Supreme Council is entitled to appoint. It is not easy to determine from the Constitutions precisely what powers may be delegated to them. Such Deputies need not necessarily have attained the rank of Sovereign Grand Inspector General, only that they "must regularly have received all the degrees, at least, of which a Knight Kadosh should be possessed"[220]. It is clear that supervisory powers may be delegated to members of the Thirtieth Degree, which, together with those above it, is clearly differentiated from the first twenty-nine Degrees, each of which is conferred in the appropriate Lodge, Council, Consistory or Chapter presided over by its own Master or his equivalent. In specific contrast to this, Article XI provides that "The degree of *Knight Kadosh*, and the 31st and 32nd degrees, can only be conferred on such Masons as shall have been adjudged worthy thereof, and at a meeting of, and by, at least three Sovereign Grand Inspectors General".

When some seventy years later the English Supreme Council interpreted these Articles as allowing them to delegate the supervision of Districts within its territory, a Brother to whom this responsibility was entrusted was appointed a 'Deputy Inspector General'. Generally, when appointed, such a Brother had received no more than the Thirty-first or Thirty-second degree, and on several occasions it was months, or even years before he was Advanced to the Thirty-third Degree. Today the Supreme Council customarily advances a District Inspector to the Thirty-third Degree at about the time of his appointment. This has caused some brethren within the Order to confuse 'Sovereign Grand Inspector General' which is the *name of a Degree*, just as is 'Master Mason' or 'Prince Rose Croix', with the *appointment* of 'D.I.G.', an acronym in which in the course of years 'Deputy' has become 'District', but who need not necessarily have had the *Degree* of Sovereign Grand Inspector General conferred upon him.

It is in accordance with these provisions that while today under the English Supreme Council a Brother must have been Enthroned in a Rose Croix Chapter before being Advanced to the Thirtieth Degree, Knight Kadosh is not an automatic promotion for Past Sovereigns. Constitutionally, it is potentially an Advancement to supervisory rank. Each candidate has to be recommended by a 'D.I.G.', and he is then subject to Election by the Supreme Council, and approval of the recommendation can be, and, on occasion has been, withheld.

The remaining Articles are generally concerned with the internal administration of a Supreme Council, the order of its processions[221], its days of meeting[222] (it "will be more frequently convened, if the business of the Order, to be transacted, require it" – something which its Members today know only too well!), a provision that no S.G.I.G. can individually exercise any power without authority from his own Supreme Council, which, outside its own jurisdiction, is conferred on him by a document curiously known as an 'Exequatur'[223], and that "the Illustrious Secretary and the Illustrious Treasurer of the Holy Empire" are ultimately responsible for "moneys received as revenue ... which are demandable for such degrees from the 16th to the 33rd inclusive"[224].

One other matter remains. Every Grand Inspector General, and, indeed, Deputy Inspector General, is instructed to enter into a Register "everything done by him, on pain of nullity and even of interdict", a Register which shall also contain a copy of the Grand Constitutions, Statutes and General Regulations[225]. The maintenance of these Registers, the so-called 'Golden Books', has long fallen into desuetude. Those kept by early members of the Charleston Council are valuable historical documents, but are untrustworthy because so many entries and signatures have evidently been inserted long after the event.

Whatever the provenance of these Constitutions, they still govern a flourishing and instructive Rite. In this respect it is difficult to improve on words from Jackson's conclusion to his Chapter on the Grand Constitutions:

> Surely for too long, members of the Rite have disputed whether history can prove if Frederick did take an active part in its organisation? . . In his name, our predecessors brought order out of the chaos of the Eighteenth century rites and degrees. Why should we not be grateful to them and welcome with pride the legend of our Rite?[226]

---

[189] The version of the 'Grand Constitutions of 1786' used in this Essay is that translated from the Latin by Albert Pike in 1859.

[190] There is also an Appendix to the second part describing the insignia of the Order, the regalia of the Thirty-third Degree, and the Seal of the Order. This Appendix is also signed 'Frederic'.

[191] The Constitutions provided for only two Supreme Councils in the mainland and islands of each of North and South America, but it is now accepted that while the U.S.A. alone continues to have two Supreme Councils, every nation-state in each of the Americas may have its own Council should it wish so to do, (and the majority do so wish) as is provided in the Constitutions for Europe, and " in Asia, in Africa, &c.,&c." (Article V, § III)

[192] In this context it is worth noting that as early as 1740 a Degree of "*Heredom of Kilwinning*", the descendant of which is know today as "*The Royal Order of Scotland*", was well established in London, with a Ritual containing many matters unknown to members of Lodges under the Grand Lodge.

[193] On his return to Dominique, Morin does not at first appear to have thought that he was entitled to do more than act as an Inspector of the Craft Degrees.

[194] Albany is the present-day capital of the State of New York. A further copy dated 22nd December 1768 is in the Archives of the Supreme Council for the Northern Masonic Jurisdiction of the U.S.A., another in the 'Francken Manuscript' in the custody of the English Supreme Council and a further one in the manuscript in the Museum and Library of the United Grand Lodge of England.

[195] For example, Jean-Pierre Lassalle, *Des Constitutions et Règlements de 1762 aux Grandes Constitutions de 1786*, Celebration du Bicentenaire des Grandes Constitutions de 1786, Suprême Conseil pour la France, Paris, 12th December 1986.

[196] In the majority of the Clauses of the 'Constitutions of 1762' the coincidences between their wording and that of the corresponding clauses in the French Grand Lodge Statutes of 1763 are too evident to be disregarded.

[197] Jackson uncompromisingly maintains that "They prove that the Prussian connection, later developed into the Frederick legend, was an invention made by Morin in the West Indies", but he does not expand on this assertion with which by no means every Masonic writer would agree. (RC, p.248)

[198] Article 15 displays a practical piece of worldly wisdom – "The Grand Treasurer, who ought to enjoy and be possessed of an independent fortune, shall be trusted with all the stock that shall be raised for the use of the Sovereign Grd Council and given in charity."

[199] Article 27

[200] Pages 185–196 of the manuscript, containing the ritual of the 25th Degree, have been cut out at some time by an unknown hand.

[201] King Frederick was a fluent reader and writer of Latin.

[202] Similar Degrees were known in, for example, Lyons, as well as in other French centres. To the considerable indignation of the Grand Lodge of France, the Parisian Lodge in which de Grasse-Tilly had been Initiated, the *Contrat Social*, had added *Mère Loge Ecossaise de France* to its title, and thereafter taken several 'High Degrees' from various other centres under its wing. The *Contrat Social* had also Warranted Lodges overseas. De Grasse-Tilly may have known some of the Brethren of these Lodges which had been sponsored by his Mother-Lodge, and it is possible – but unsubstantiated by any evidence – that he may have learnt from them of these Degrees which he then communicated to

Mitchell and his colleagues.

[203] It is, perhaps, curious that in the Latin version, the signatures of the witnesses on the *Constitutions and Statutes*, and on the *Appendix* to it, have received identical disfigurement, although they are separate documents.

[204] During the summer of 1786 "he was confined to a chair, but he did not cease working. He still got up between 4 and 5 a.m. and received his cabinet secretaries with the morning's business. At eight he was dressed and then worked further on state papers". Giles MacDonough, *Frederick the Great*, p.384, St.Martin's Press, New York (April, 2000). The meal he consumed on 5th August 1786, after himself approving the menu, was formidable! *Ibidem*, p.380.

[205] I know of no previous reference to this. C.J.M.

[206] For example, *Illuminism*.

[207] Article II,§ II.

[208] Article II,§ III,1.

[209] Sixty years later this provision unfortunately gave rise to unmasonically acrimonious controversy (now long since settled) between the Supreme Councils of England and Scotland as to their respective rights in the British Empire overseas.

[210] Article II,§ III,2.

[211] Article II,§ IV.

[212] The Supreme Council of England (as its Patent described it) formally came into being when Thomas Crucefix and George Oliver Advanced Henry Udall to the rank of Sovereign Grand Inspector General in late April or early May 1846.

[213] This version of the 'Grand Constitutions' is translated from a Latin text, in which the 'second-in-command' of the Council is denominated '*Vicarius-Magnus Commendator*'. Throughout his translation Albert Pike used 'Deputy' as the equivalent of '*Vicarius*'. The current title of 'Lieutenant Grand Commander' is no more than a matter of preferred translation, used throughout this commentary as being more familiar, and is not a departure from the 'Grand Constitutions'.

[214] Article III,§ IV. Thus, when in 1874 the English Supreme Council wished to appoint the Earl of Carnarvon as Sovereign Grand Commander, and similarly in 1877 to appoint Lord Skelmersdale, (later the Earl of Lathom), Nathaniel Philips who had on each occasion, as Lieutenant Grand Commander, already succeeded to the Office of Sovereign Grand Commander on the resignation of the former incumbent, immediately appointed, on the first occasion, Carnarvon as Lieutenant Grand Commander, and on the second, Skelmersdale, before resigning his own Office. On his resignation, Carnarvon and Skelmersdale respectively succeeded to the Office as Sovereign Grand Commander, and, on doing so, each at once re-appointed Philips as Lieutenant Grand Commander. This explanation may dispel the confusion into which some brethren have been cast by the succession of Sovereign Grand Commanders as set out in the 'Red Book' of the Regulations of the English Supreme Council.

[215] "Louis d'or of the old issue" has led some commentators to advance this as evidence that the 'Constitutions of 1786' must have been written after the death of Frederick and that they cannot therefore be authentic because the Louis d'Or was still current coin in 1786, and would not have been referred to as "the old issue". However, Lassalle (*loc. cit., p.36 (English Translation, pp.69/70)* has pointed out that the coin was re-valued in 1785, and to refer to "the old issue" in the following year would have been perfectly appropriate.

[216] The following paragraph makes the same provision, in precisely the same wording, for South America. For this it is difficult to suggest an explanation.

[217] Article V, §III. This is one of the few provisions of the 'Grand Constitutions' from which there has been a considerable departure. In spite of the *Act of Union* the legitimacy of separate Supreme Councils for England, Scotland and Ireland has never been challenged. The Supreme Council in the West Indies was seen as no bar to the Charleston Supreme Council delegating some of its powers to an independent Supreme Council for the Northern Jurisdiction of the American States in 1813, nor to the English Supreme Council Patenting a Council in Canada in 1874. Before the end of the Century almost every State in Central and South America had its own Supreme Council, but in what was to become the United States of America no more than two Supreme Councils have ever been recognised as legitimate, unlike the situation in the American Craft, where every State has its own Grand Lodge, and, with the recognition of *Prince Hall Masonry*, in many States two Grand Lodges are accepted as 'Regular'.

[218] In other words, the Supreme Council discountenanced duelling.

[219] This may well have been a sop to the Sublime Princes of the Royal Secret, formally the presiding body of Morin's Twenty-five Degree Rite, its *Ne Plus Ultra*, but now, as the Thirty-second Degree of the Ancient and Accepted Scottish Rite, relegated to being subordinate to the Supreme Council of the Thirty-third Degree.

[220] Article XIII,§ II.

[221] Article XIV.

[222] Article XV.

[223] Article XVII.

[224] Article XVIII.

[225] Article XVI.

[226] RC, p.83.

Essay 6
Degrees 'Beyond the Craft' in England before the Union in 1813

During the life-time of Brethren who attend Meetings today Freemasonry has been a very orderly – some might even say bureaucratic – institution. No one disputes the right of the United Grand Lodge of England in Great Queen Street and of the Supreme Grand Chapter of the Royal Arch to exercise their respective jurisdictions. In addition, many Brethren further submit themselves to the authority of the controlling bodies of other recognised Masonic Orders, not least to that of the Supreme Council of the Thirty-third Degree, all of which are careful in no way to conflict with the authority of Grand Lodge. It is not easy to visualise the somewhat less disciplined Masonic situation which existed during the hundred years before the Duke of Sussex presided over the United Grand Lodge in 1813.

Even if, in the earliest days of Speculative Freemasonry, Brethren from different Lodges might on occasion meet together, no supervisory body was recognised before the erection of the first Grand Lodge in 1717. Even then for many years this Grand Lodge had little influence on the proceedings within individual Lodges. Little is known about the earliest Speculative Meetings, but at least until the 1720s these seem to have been 'discussion groups' rather than the 'Degree factories' to which we are now accustomed. The admission of a new 'Fellow', as all early English Speculative Freemasons termed themselves, was an exceptional rather than a routine occurrence. Somehow before 1730 a system, probably with various forms of a single admission ceremony, had transformed itself into a three-Degree Rite.

This was the first Masonic revolution. While in many Lodges learned Papers on Architecture and the Liberal Arts and Sciences continued to be delivered, a series of progressive Degrees was becoming an important method of inculcating moral lessons. As early as 1726 some Brethren accepted that there were three parts to Freemasonry[227]. Harry Carr considered (but without adducing any specific evidence) that "all the essential materials of the Trigradal Rite were already in existence in the two-degree system of the Operatives"[228]. Tuckett had been the first to make an even broader speculation, putting forward the view that before 1717 "Freemasonry possessed a store of Legend, Tradition and Symbolism of wide extent. That in 1717 the Grand Lodge *selected a portion only* of this store"[229]. This conjecture might even be supported by a 1724 pamphlet if it could be taken at its face-value[230], but in its early days Grand Lodge could hardly have been strong enough to have imposed such a selection on its constituent Lodges. Prichard, however, may have made such a choice in his unofficial exposure, *Masonry Dissected*, first published in 1730, for it amalgamated two Initiatory systems, each of which was "complete in themselves and required no embellishment"[231]. While it was several years before the Third Hiramic Degree was universally accepted, its apparent ready-acceptance by so many Brethren and Lodges would have been remarkable if it had been wholly an innovation, and if there had been no tradition of a 'Raising' – one hesitates to say of 'necromancy' – already embedded in the emergent Speculative Craft[232].

It is unlikely that the precise relationship and contents of the one – or two – or three Degrees in the earliest days of Speculative Freemasonry in England will ever be known. But within five years of the publication of *Masonry Dissected* there was a further complication. In several Lodges in England the Degree of Scots or Scotch Master was being conferred on Master Masons, some of whom had already passed the Chair of their respective Lodges[233]. In spite of the assumptions made by Rylands[234], it is now generally agreed that whatever was done in these Lodges had no connection with Scottish Freemasonry. It has often been speculated, but with no conclusive evidence, that to be made a 'Scotch Master' may have been an early excursion into what afterwards became the Order of the *Holy Royal Arch of Jerusalem*.

The 1730s were a troubled period for the Premier Grand Lodge. The enthusiasm of its own early members had dwindled. Perhaps as early as 1725 a Grand Lodge had been constituted in Ireland. Then the Grand Lodge of Scotland was erected in 1736. As a result, by the end of the decade there were many Irish and Scottish Speculative Masons in London. The English Grand Lodge appears to have regarded these Brethren somewhat unfavourably, being particularly concerned about the number of spurious 'Brethren' seeking to gain admission to regular Lodges. To combat this, Grand Lodge decided to institute certain changes within the private Lodges which acknowledged its authority. Among these changes was the transposition of the 'words' of the First and Second Degrees. Many otherwise loyal Brethren considered that in doing this Grand Lodge was taking an outrageous liberty. This was not the only matter which some considered had been changed or neglected. Anderson, the author, or at least the editor, of the 'Constitutions' of 1723 and 1737, was a deist, and he had considerably influenced the de-Christianisation of the Craft. Saints' Days were neglected, and the Craft could hardly be considered any longer to be 'St. John's Masonry'. The easy-going attitude of the Premier Grand Lodge had also allowed Ceremonies to be curtailed. Many considered that candidates were no longer properly prepared, and it was asserted that the readings of the 'Ancient Charges' were neglected, as were the 'Lectures' or catechisms.[235]

In 1730 a Scotsman, Michael Ramsay, then living in France, had visited England, where he was Initiated in the Horn Lodge[236] in London. Returning to France, Ramsay became deeply involved in Masonic affairs, and in 1736 he composed a 'Traditional History' very different from that which was printed in Anderson's 'Constitutions', "TO BE READ at the Admission of a NEW BROTHER"[237]. Ramsay was to claim that he delivered the 'Oration' which contained this 'History' at the Initiation of a large number of brethren[238]. He also circulated its text widely both in England and in France. The 'Oration' gave Freemasons Christian forebears, the Knights Templar, who had sought to free the Holy Land from the Muslims. According to Ramsay, the Speculative Craft came both to England and to France by way of Scotland where the Templars took refuge after the destruction of their Order. While Ramsay stressed the chivalric background to Freemasonry, something which was very welcome to the aristocrats among the French Masons, he neither invented 'Higher Degrees', nor even suggested that they would be desirable. It is impossible to say what influence his 'Oration' had in England, but it is a curious coincidence that shortly after its circulation there were being worked in London ceremonies which had some affinity with Ramsay's speculations. These ceremonies explicitly set out "To correct the errors and reform the abuses which had crept in among the three Degrees of St. John's Masonry".

Lindsay[239] has pointed out that that this ritual working could not have been composed earlier than, say, 1725, because of its reference to the *three* Degrees of St. John's Masonry. However, by 1741 there were in the London area sufficient Chapters owing no allegiance to the Grand Lodge, but working this ritual, for a 'Provincial Grand Master' to be presiding over their activities. The Order was known as the 'Scotch Heredom or Ancient and Honourable Order of Kilwinning'[240]. From 1750 detailed documentation survives about this Order, now known as 'The Royal Order of Scotland'[241]. Lindsay[242] notes that there is no record of the 'Ancient and Honourable Order' in Scotland before 1754. The leading Scottish Masonic historians, such as Robert Lindsay himself and George Draffen of Newington, have no doubt that the Order was wholly English in origin[243].

Because the neglect of the 'Lectures' or catechisms was a major accusation brought against 'Modern' Masons in allegiance to the Grand Lodge in London, it is no surprise that the ritual of this new Order was catechetical in form. That Speculative Freemasonry had originally been Christian is firmly stressed throughout the ritual, as is that it is 'St. John's Masonry', a basic theme of the traditional history as Ramsay had revised it[244]. That it was known as the 'Order of Heredom of Kilwinning' can hardly be due to anything other than Ramsay's 'Oration'[245]. The 'Lectures', however, contain other material which does not figure either in Ramsay's 'Oration' or in what is known of earlier working of the 'Craft' Degrees, either in England or in Scotland. Neither has this material any affinity with the Rites being developed in France. While much is derived from Biblical sources, both Old and New Testaments, albeit somewhat dubiously rendered, there is a variety of other references. Many of these persisted in other Degrees and Orders which later came to the fore in England. It is tempting to accept Tuckett's view that before 1717 Freemasonry possessed a store of Legend, Tradition and Symbolism of wide extent[246]. This is not unreasonable if it is accepted that the traditional proceedings in early English Speculative Lodges were far from uniform, and that the founders of the Royal Order were seeking, among other things, to preserve these traditions[247].

It seems at least possible that the composition of *The Royal Order of Scotland* resulted from the same simmerings of discontent which led to the formation of the Committee which on 17th July 1751 declared the establishment of the *Most Ancient and Honourable Society of Free and Accepted Masons according to the Old Constitutions*, soon to be referred to as 'The Antients'[248]. By 1751 the 'Royal Arch' Degree had evolved, from whatever source it had come. It was a logical consequence of the legend in the Third Degree. If secrets were lost, one might as well set about trying to find them. At this time, the 'Moderns' totally rejected the 'Royal Arch', and this presumably contributed to the disregard in which the Premier Grand Lodge was held by many

Brethren. It is, however, remarkable that the Antients should have regarded the Degree as the touchstone of purity, if the 'Arch' had been no more than imported from Ireland or Scotland, and there had been no 'Arch' tradition somewhere in the English Masonic past. To Lawrence Dermott, the Irish Mason who was the second Grand Secretary of the Antients, it was "the heart and marrow of Freemasonry". Not only were Antient Lodges permitted, indeed encouraged, to confer the 'Royal Arch' Degree, but their members were authorised to confer any Degree of which a sufficient number of their members had the knowledge to carry out the ceremony.

It is impossible to say what were the many Degrees worked from time to time in England in one or other of the Antient Lodges, let alone from whence they came. However, the situation differed from that in France where several sequences of Degrees were also evolving. While the French systems differed in composition from one Masonic centre to another, among the welter of 'Degrees' which sprang up at this time a consistent pattern of more 'regular' rituals can be identified in spite of internecine disputes between the Rulers of the French Craft. Generally speaking, those French Rites which survived for any significant period were concerned with one or more of four broad topics – the appointment of a successor to Hiram together with arrangements for the continuation of the construction of the First Temple, vengeance on Hiram's murderers, the building of the Second Temple leading to a search for Masonic Secrets within the ruins of the First, and, finally, the conferment of Chivalric honours, even, later, of Imperial ones. With Gallic logical ingenuity, these topics were combined into Rites first of sixteen and later of twenty-five Degrees. Under American influence, the latter, 'Morin's Rite', was later further extended to become the Ancient and Accepted Scottish Rite of thirty-three Degrees.

In England Degree-sequences also developed in various Masonic centres, but they never came together as occurred in France and America to form a recognised single Rite. On the contrary, those that survived eventually gave rise to independent Orders, co-existing in varying conditions of amity under their own Rulers.

One apparent consequence of the erection of the Antient Grand Lodge was that for a hundred and twenty years the Order of Heredom of Kilwinning, the Royal Order of Scotland, disappeared from England[249]. One can only assume that the Order was no longer seen to be necessary in England in view of the revival of earlier working claimed by the Antients, together with the licence to their Lodges to work whatever Degrees they wished, a licence which presumably included much of the material in the Order of Heredom of Kilwinning[250].

Furthermore, unlike the situation both in France and in Germany, the English nobility saw no reason to separate themselves from the rest of the population in exclusive chivalric Orders. In England, 'Higher Degrees', in the modern sense of the words, were therefore generally imports rather than indigenous products. For example, during the 1750s Baron Karl Gotthelf von Hund was developing in Germany a Templar rite known as 'The Strict Observance'. Von Hund was a Freemason, whose antecedents were, to say the least, dubious. His own account of how he had come by his knowledge of the Order is inherently unlikely, if not historically impossible. Perhaps Ramsay's influence may again be seen here, because Hund claimed that the original Knights Templar had maintained a covert existence since they had taken refuge in Scotland. He claimed that for many centuries they had guarded esoteric knowledge which they were now prepared to disseminate more widely. A peculiarity of the Order's Initiatory or 'Entered Apprentice' Degree was that strict obedience had to be sworn to unknown superiors who ruled the rite – the commitment which gave its name to the Order.

Von Hund's Order achieved considerable popularity, not only in Germany but also in other Western European countries from Scandinavia to Italy. At this time English Regiments were serving on the Continent of Europe to protect the Hanoverian connection. Many of these had Masonic Lodges attached to them, several of which welcomed the introduction of von Hund's rite. Its highest Degree of Knight Templar was particularly enthusiastically adopted by the Military Lodges, which carried it back to England where it was equally well received. It was worked in Royal Arch Chapters, membership of which became the qualification for proceeding to the Degree.

In the third quarter of the seventeenth century many of these Regiments were posted to North America where their Lodges also introduced the Degree. At the same time, both in the British West Indies and also on the American mainland, Stephen Morin was establishing the Rite which he had brought with him from France and thereafter extended to twenty-five Degrees. With the authority of the Patent appointing him as 'Inspector' which had originally been given to him by the Grand Lodge of France, Morin and his colleague Francken nominated a large number of 'Deputy Inspectors'. Among these were several Officers in the British Army, for example Colonel Prevost who was appointed 'Deputy Inspector General for the Windward Isles and the British Army'[251]. Another was Charles Shirreff.

Shirreff[252] was probably aged seventeen when he was gazetted as an Ensign in the 45th Regiment of Foot on the 2nd July 1755. Later in the same year his Regiment was sent to America, and took part in the capture of Louisbourg from the French. It is probable that Shirreff was Initiated in an Antient Lodge while his Regiment was on Garrison duty in that town. The war against the French having been concluded, Shirreff was put on half-pay and went to live in the Island of Jersey[253]. Here, although himself an 'Antient' Mason, he obtained a Lodge Warrant from the 'Moderns' Provincial Grand Master[254]. Notwithstanding this, the Lodge appears to have followed the practices of the 'Antients', with two Deacons. It also probably conferred both the Royal Arch and Knight Templar Degrees.

Shirreff left Jersey in 1768, but nothing is known of his whereabouts until 1775 when the Army List shows him to have been the Fort Adjutant and Barrack Master at Fort Augustine in East Florida. Masonic government was here exercised by a Provincial Grand Master holding a Warrant from the Grand Lodge of Scotland[255]. In spite of this, Shirreff appears to have founded at least one Lodge with a Warrant from the Grand Lodge of the Antients[256]. It is presumed that Shirreff acquired his Patent as a Deputy Inspector General in Morin's 25-Degree Rite during this second tour of duty in America[257]. Certainly at about this time, Shirreff became very enthusiastic about this Rite.

While Shirreff had been in North America, a Frenchman, Pierre Lambert de Lintot[258], was prominent in Masonic circles in London. He became Master of a Lodge of previously unattached French Freemasons who had purchased its Warrant, probably formerly that of the Lodge of Integrity, No.331. This transaction was grudgingly legitimised by the Modern Grand Lodge which disapproved of such purchases. After occupying various positions under Grand Lodge, de Lintot developed his own Rite of seven Degrees. He then became Master, or *Vénérable,* of a Lodge, St. George de l'Observance, in which capacity he directed the affairs of his Rite. He obtained a Warrant for this Lodge as the Lodge of Perfect Observance No.1 from Preston's schismatic Grand Lodge South of the River Trent.

The first five Degrees of de Lintot's Rite contained many of the elements of Morin's original Rite of Perfection. The next Degree had some affinity with the Rose Croix, while the Seventh was something of a hotch-potch loosely based on the history of the Knights Templar. The First Degree, consisting of the three Craft Degrees, continued to be worked in St. George de l'Observance under the Grand Lodge, while the 'High Degrees' were worked in the Lodge Warranted by Preston.

De Lintot's Rite, which survived for little more than a dozen years, was not in itself of great importance. However, during its short life many English Freemasons were Initiated into its various Degrees, with the result that knowledge of Higher Degrees became more widely disseminated. The Templar Order was also gaining adherents[259]. De Lintot's Rite itself gave rise to one of the earliest Knights Templar Encampments, that of Observance of the Seven Degrees in London.

The American War of Independence was brought to a conclusion by the Treaty of Versailles in 1783. Shirreff, again on the half-pay list, returned to England where he settled in Whitchurch in Shropshire[260]. Here he at once wished to found a new Lodge. Although he made it clear that he intended the Lodge to follow the practices of the 'Antients', he obtained a Warrant from the Grand Lodge of the 'Moderns'. The Whitchurch Lodge being firmly established, Shirreff was instrumental in founding several other Lodges in the County[261].

In the Lodge at Whitchurch Shirreff devoted himself to presiding over the 4th to the 14th Degrees of Morin's Rite. He wrote to White, the Grand Secretary of the 'Moderns', on 1st May 1785, that he "did not propose working in the Lower Degrees of Masonry any more". Not only did Shirreff receive no reprimand for these sentiments from the 'Modern' Grand Lodge, to which one might suppose that they would have been anathema, but he entered into a considerable correspondence with its Grand Secretary. By 1788 he had sent the ritual books of several of Morin's Degrees to White, which the latter handed on to Heseltine, his predecessor who was now Grand Treasurer. By 1792 Shirreff was writing to White to say that, since he had by now given him the rituals of the whole of the first fourteen Degrees, he hoped that when he came to London he would find:

> a Brilliant Lodge, for if proper attention is given to every Degree, it will plead for itself and must Convince that every other system practic'd (*sic*) is Spurious from the 3rd and borrows in part from the true one.

For his own part, Shirreff had abandoned the more commonly practised sequence of Royal Arch followed by Knights Templar. It is uncertain for how long Morin's first fourteen Higher Degrees continued to be worked either in London or in Whitchurch – probably not after the Union in 1813. But in spite of this, the importance of Shirreff's contribution is that by the end of the eighteenth century the senior officials of the Grand Lodge of the Moderns were not only aware of Morin's Rite, but apparently were sympathetic to it.[262]

By 1791 there were sufficient Encampments of Knights Templar throughout England for Thomas Dunckerley, himself a member of the Camp of Baldwyn in Bristol, to consent to summon a Grand Conclave of which he became the first Grand Master, a position which he occupied until his death in 1795. After several changes of hands, in 1812 the Duke of Sussex accepted responsibility for the Order which he then ruled until his own death in 1843[263].

There is no evidence that Morin's Rite was widely practised in England, or that it influenced other than a few senior Masons. Other Degrees 'beyond the Craft' were however being developed in English provincial centres. It is too facile to say that poor communications provided the reason why none of these Rites spread nation-wide[264]. The more likely cause is endemic English parochialism; a dislike of uniformity which sees no shame in being different. Indeed, neither the 'Moderns' nor the 'Antients' attempted to impose uniformity on the working of the three Craft Degrees in their Lodges. In spite of the later work of the Lodge of Reconciliation, United Grand Lodge has also never attempted to curb a situation[265] in which even today a visitor to a Craft Lodge almost always sees some variation from the working to which he is accustomed.

In the North-East of England there had been for several years the obscure 'Order of Harodim'. By 1800 this was fading away, although individual members survived until the 1830s[266]. The Harodim left behind in Newcastle upon Tyne not only the 'Red Cross of Babylon' sequence including the ceremony of 'Crossing the Bridge' but it was also presumably the source of the Hagia Sophia[267] series of Degrees which are today preserved in the 'College of Holy Royal Arch Knight Templar Priests or Order of Holy Wisdom'. This Order, to which reference is sometimes made as the 'Priestly' or 'Pillars' Order, preserves a sequence of Degrees, at least by name, of which the first half dozen or so appear to be 'Temple Completion' Degrees but the remainder are Christian Degrees of little known provenance and form, differing from any in, for example, the French 'Morin's Rite'. On the other hand there are several with 'Mark' in their names, undoubtedly differing in most cases from 'the Mark' as it is known today. Both in England and Scotland a 'Mark' legend of one sort or another was evidently seen to be of more importance than it was on the Continent of Europe.

Further South, on the borders of Yorkshire, Derbyshire and Lancashire, several Degrees 'beyond the Craft' were being worked well into the second half of the nineteenth century. The unfortunately named village of Bottoms, near Stansfield, was a centre of this activity. The Degrees do not all seem to have necessarily been sequential in the sense that one led to another[268]. Among these Orders or Degrees, the position of the 'Priestly Order, or Old 33rd.' is far from clear. It does not appear to have owed allegiance to any body of the 'Holy Wisdom' Degrees practised in the North-East, nor, being a 'Pillars Degree', to have any affinity to the Thirty-third Degree which appeared in Charleston in 1801. On the other hand it seems to have considered itself to be a supervisory body of Chapters working a 'Rose Croix' Degree.[269]

Before the end of the eighteenth century another Rite or sequence of Degrees was being worked at the other end of the country, at Redruth in West Cornwall. This consisted of 25 Degrees, culminating in a twenty-sixth, 'Rosy Crusian or *Ne Plus Ultra*'[270]. Until his death in 1828, these Degrees were presided over by John Knight, who had been born in 1745, and who claimed to have received them himself in 1777. It seems probable that the rituals of the Degrees practised in Redruth, including the three Craft Degrees, had been communicated by word of mouth until Knight made manuscript copies early in the nineteenth century, with the more important parts encrypted. Knight's ritual of the '*Ne Plus Ultra*' Degree is recognisably that of the 'Rose Croix'. He evidently particularly esteemed the Order of the Knights Templar, concerning which he carried on a considerable correspondence successively with Dunckerley[271], Robert Gill and Edwards Harper.

Whatever their names might lead one to believe, the content of the Cornish rituals owes little or nothing to the work of William Finch, who, between 1801 and 1815, was an inveterate compiler of rituals, some spurious, some genuine[272]. However, in 1810 Knight added to his sequence 12 further Degrees, although initially he was dubious about their authenticity. Some of these may perhaps be identified with Finch's later emissions[273], but it is surprising that one is 'Priests Order of Seven Pillars or Priestly Order', which has strayed a long way from the home of the 'Holy Wisdom' Degrees in Northumberland.

At the same time there was in London another Order, 'The Red Cross of Palestine', which was presided over by so well a respected Freemason as Waller Rodwell Wright, who preceded the Duke of Sussex as Grand Master of the Knights Templar. Wright had been a leading figure in both the Grand Lodge of the Moderns and its Royal Arch Chapter where he had been Second Grand Principal. Very little is known about either the origin or the ceremonies in this Red Cross Order. So far as can be established, the Duke of Sussex accepted the Grand

Mastership of this Order also when Wright left England to take up an official post in the Eastern Mediterranean.

Accounts of events leading up to the Union in 1813 are properly principally concerned with the negotiations about how matters would in future be conducted within Craft Lodges – the situation of the Wardens, the role of Deacons, the necessity for an Installation Ceremony, and so on. It is easy to overlook the involvement of so many distinguished members of the two Grand Lodges – even of the Duke of Sussex himself – with Orders and Degrees outside the Craft. This involvement made the Duke's task no easier. There were many Brethren who could see no further than a crude philosophy derived from the daily task of a stone-cutter. They dogmatically rejected the contribution of the learned Speculatives of the sixteenth and seventeenth centuries to the rich vein of allegory and symbols in which the Craft was veiled and by which it was illustrated. On the other hand, many influential Brethren, both 'Antients' and 'Moderns', were not prepared to forgo their involvement with the accretions which the Royal Art had acquired. To obtain agreement to a statement, however ambiguous and however short-lived, that, while the Craft consisted of three Degrees and three Degrees only, three Degrees which somehow included that of the 'Royal Arch', the Degrees of Chivalry could still legitimately be practised, was a diplomatic feat which today we may sometimes under-estimate.

227 For example, Drake's speech at York on 27th December, 1726 – "that three Parts in four of the whole Earth might then be divided into **E – P – F – C – M – M**." Douglas Knoop, G.P. Jones and Douglas Hamer, *Early Masonic Pamphlets*, p.203, Manchester University Press (1945)

228 Harry Carr, *The Conjoint Theory*, AQC, LXVI, p.44 (1953).

229 J.E.S. Tuckett, AQC XXXII, p.4. (1919).

230 "... long before the Knights of St. *John* of *Jerusalem* or the Knights of *Malta*, to which two *Lodges* I must nevertheless allow the Honour of having adorned the Antient *Jewish* and *Pagan* Masonry with many Religious and Christian Rules." *A Letter from the Grand Mistress* (1724), Douglas Knoop, G.P. Jones and Douglas Hamer, *The Early Masonic Catechisms*, p.235 Manchester University Press (2nd. Ed., edited by Harry Carr, 1963).

231 George Draffen of Newington, comment on Eric Ward, *Early Masters' Lodges and their relation to Degrees*, Part 1, AQC,LXXV, p.136 (1962). 'Initiation', as it is known today, is self-evidently an example of a widespread rite in which 'Enlightenment' is thus gained, so widespread that a Yoruba Chief could not be made a Freemason because he refused to be hood-winked, on the grounds that he had already been restored to light in this way when made a Chief and was not prepared to undergo it again. (R.W.Bro. Sir Lionel Brett, Private communication to present author.) 'Raising' from a spiritual death is an equally common 'Initiation', a more dramatic analogue of being hoodwinked, as in the Eleusinian Mysteries and in Mithraism.

232 The Graham Manuscript of 1726 refers to the raising of Noah in language almost identical to that referring to the Raising of Hiram in *Masonry Dissected*. Knoop,

Jones and Hamer, *op. cit.* p.93

233 For example, at the Lodges held at the 'Bear' at Bath (now Royal Cumberland No.41) 28 Oct 1735, 8 Jan 1747, 24 Nov 1754, 17 Feb 1756, 14 Apr 1758 and at the 'Rummer' at Bristol 7 Nov 1740, also at a Lodge Constituted in Salisbury in 1732, 19 Feb 1746. Eric Ward, *Early Masters' Lodges and their relation to Degrees*, Part 2, AQC, LXXV, p.156, (1962). Also a Minute in *The Records of the Lodge Original No.1, now Lodge of Antiquity No.2*, Ed. W.Harry Rylands, Vol. 1. p.105 (2nd. Edition, Revised) (Privately printed by Harrison and Sons for the Lodge of Antiquity, 1928) states that on 17 June 1740, nine members of the Lodge, including the Master, Senior Warden and Secretary, "were this evening made Scotch Masters" by a visiting Brother.

234 *Op. cit.*

235 For a more detailed summary of the matters leading to discontent, see, for example, Bernard E. Jones, *A Freemason's Guide and Compendium*, pp.200 *et seq.*, Harrap & Co.(1950). So far as the 'Lectures' were concerned, it must be appreciated that many of our Brethren at this time considered them to be the most important work of the Lodge, to which the admission of Candidates was almost an interruption.

236 The Lodge of which Dr. Desaguliers was a member.

237 "The Constitutions of the Free-Masons" (1723), page 1.

238 On 2nd August 1737 Ramsay wrote, in English, to Carte, an English Jacobite, saying that he had delivered his 'Oration' at various times at the Initiation ('Acception') of eight Dukes and peers, and of two hundred Officers of the first rank and highest nobility. Bodleian Library MS No.226, folio 398, quoted by Paul Tunbridge, *The Climate of European Freemasonry, 1750–1750*, AQC, LXXXI. p.96 (1968).

239 Robert Stratheam Lindsay (Ed A.J.B.Milburn), *The Royal Order of Scotland*, Wm. Culross & Son, Coupar Angus (1971)

240 "Scotch Heredom or Ancient and Honourable Order of Kilwinning". An advertisement for a meeting of this Order "at the sign of The Swan in Great Portland Street" appeared in a London broadsheet on 26th November 1743.

241 By 1750 there were five Chapters of the Order in London, as well as one at the Hague, and one in Norfolk, Virginia.

242 Lindsay, *op. cit.* p.39 *et seq.*

243 Lindsay points out (*op. cit.*) that various Scottish references, for example to 'Icolmkill' and to 'Scots Money', do not appear in the earliest rituals of the Order. which were amended to include them only after the headquarters of the Order became established in Edinburgh in the mid-1750s.

244 According to Ramsay the first Patron of the Order, 'St. John of Jerusalem', was neither the Baptist nor the Evangelist, but 'John the Almsgiver'.

245 "James, Lord Steward of Scotland, was Grand Master of a Lodge established at Kilwinning in the West of Scotland in 1286, shortly after the death of Alexander III, King of Scotland, and one year before John Baliol mounted the throne. This Lord received Freemasons into his Lodge, the Earls of Gloucester and Ulster, the one English, the other Irish." (Ramsay's 'Oration'.)

246 *op. cit.*

247 It may be no more than a curious coincidence that those practising 'Degrees beyond the Craft' were known as Scotch Masters in England and Maitres Ecossais in France, that the 'reforming Order' in England was known as 'Heredom of Kilwinning', and that Ramsay's 'Oration' claimed a Scottish parentage for both English and French Speculative Freemasonry. Jackson was of the opinion that Ramsay's 'Oration' was not the seminal document but that there was a common source possibly connected with the Order of Harodim which flourished in the North-East of England and of which too little is known with any certainty. (A.C.F. Jackson, AQC XCI, p.143 (1978), comments on N. Barker Cryer *op. cit.* P.117 *A New Look at the Harodim*).

248 Many, almost certainly the majority, of the members of the six Lodges which came together to erect the Grand Lodge of the Antients were originally Scottish or Irish masons. For this reason its establishment is perhaps more properly described as that of a rival to the Premier Grand Lodge, 'the Moderns', rather than as a 'schism'. Bernard E. Jones, *A Freemason's Guide and Compendium*, p.196, George G. Harrap & Co. (1950).

249 In 1756 the headquarters of the Order were re-established in The Hague where there was already a Lodge of the Order. A few years later it was transferred to Edinburgh, where the Scots adopted it as their own, embellishing it with several items of local colour.

250 A further reason may perhaps have been that after the 'Forty-Five', when Bonnie Prince Charlie's advance as far as Derby had led to near panic in London, it was no recommendation for an English organisation to have a Scottish background.

251 Jackson, *op. cit.*

252 Much of the following material relating to Major Charles Shirreff (including that this was the spelling which he himself used when signing his name) is taken from A.C.F.Jackson, AQC, LXXXVI, pp.178-188 (1973).

253 Shirreff was possibly employed in the Island in some minor military capacity, as he was restored to full-pay in December 1765.

254 Lord Carysfoot (Grand Master of the 'Moderns', 1752/3) had appointed Thomas Dobrée, a Guernsey Merchant, Provincial Grand Master for 'Guernsey, Jersey, Alderney, Sark and Arme in ye British Channell'. (A.C.F.J. is at a loss to construe 'Arme'; could this not be 'Herm'?)

255 On 15th March 1768 James Grant, Governor of East Florida, had been commissioned by the Grand Lodge in Edinburgh as 'Provincial Grand Master over the Lodges in the Southern District of North America'.

256 All the Records of the Scottish Provincial Grand Lodge were lost when the Spanish occupied East Florida in 1783.

257 There is little doubt that Shirreff possessed such a Patent even though the principal evidence is his own correspondence. After his return to England he claimed to have shown it to, among others, the Chevalier Bartholomew Ruspini and to Sandland, who is said to have been an intermediary between Shirreff and W.H.White, the Grand Secretary of the 'Moderns'.

258 De Lintot was an engraver by profession. He engraved a Plate for his rite of Seven Degrees. It included the inscription "Ordre Royal D'Ecosse Tenu en Francois en Faveur des Estrangers" This design was later adopted by Thomas Dunckerley for the Certificates of Knights Templar, after blocking out this inscription, and also the words Heredom and Kilwinning. RC, p.97

259 For example, on 21st October 1778, the Royal Arch Chapter of Friendship in Portsmouth recorded in its Minutes that Thomas Dunckerley had written to say that they 'might make Knights Templars' if they wanted to and so resolved. Frederick Smyth, *Brethren in Chivalry*, p.17, Lewis Masonic, 1991). Jackson, however, refers this record to the Phoenix Lodge No.257 at Portsmouth. R.C. p.92.

260 There is no evidence that Shirreff had any previous Shropshire connections.

261 Shirreff founded sufficient Lodges to constitute a Province, of which, on account of his ill-health, he would accept only the Deputy Provincial Grand Mastership.

262 During the Seven Years and Napoleonic Wars there were in England several thousand French Prisoners of War, many of whom were allowed to live in so-called 'Parole Towns' under conditions of restricted liberty. In several of these towns the French prisoners founded Lodges, in many of which the 'Higher Degrees' were worked. Many Englishman joined these French Lodges. Whitchurch was a 'parole town' as early as 1757. In the "Catalogue des Ouvrages **** composent la Bibliothèque Maç.·. du G.·. O.·. de France, 1882" there is reported to have been an entry – "A94. Règlements MS – Tableau des membres et déclaration des prisonniers de guerre français sur

parole composant la Loge la *Triple Union* sous les auspices du Grand Orient de France France à l'O.˙. de Whitchurch, Comté de Shropshire, Angleterre, 5813, avec signatures". John T. Thorp, *French Prisoners' Lodges*, p.289 (2nd Edition, augmented) The Lodge of Research No.2429, Freemason's Hall Leicester (1935). Anyone who tries to relate Shirreff's choice of Whitchurch to French Prisoners *en parole* is almost certainly clutching at straws!

263 The Duke of Kent, one of the Royal Brothers of the Duke of Sussex, was Royal Grand Patron of the Order. Dunckerley had been succeeded by Lord Rancliffe, who himself died four years later. The Duke of Kent did not then summon Grand Conclave to meet for four years, after which for two years he presided himself as Grand Master. He then appointed Waller Rodwell Wright in his place, who resigned in 1812 in favour of the Duke of Sussex.

264 There is evidence from the file containing original correspondence, principally between John Knight and the Masonic authorities in London, that in 1810 a letter posted in London on a Friday would regularly be delivered in Redruth in Cornwall on the following Monday. (Files etc. in John Coombe Masonic Library, Hayle, Cornwall, and John Knight File in the Museum and Library of United Grand Lodge of England in London.)

265 Apart, that is, from certain specific matters, such as removing the 'Traditional Penalties'.

266 According to Dr. Henry Leeson, Sovereign Grand Commander of The Supreme Council in 1867, in the Cross of Christ Encampment of Knights Templars, of which he was a member, the 'Rosae Crucis' Degree (which Leeson had taken in 1837) was not 'conferred under powers derived from the Encampment Warrant' but 'under the direction of individual members of the Ancient Order of Harodim who belonged to that Chapter'. A & A. p.52, quoting from The Supreme Council Minute Book.

267 Αγια Σοφια; 'Holy Wisdom'.

268 In addition to the three Craft Degrees with their associated Lectures, "Bottoms also conferred the degrees of Mark, Ark, and Link, Veils with Royal Arch, Rosy Croix, Old Mark, St. Lawrence, Mediterranean Pass, Knights of Malta, Eleven Ineffable Degrees, Priestly Order, or Old 33rd., Red Cross of Babylon, White Cross Knight, Knight of Constantinople. Ark Mariners." John E. Craven, *An Historical Sketch of Freemasonry at Bottoms, Eastwood, Near Todmorden, Yorkshire*, p.8 (John Heywood, Manchester, 1886).

269 Even so late as July 1871, twenty-five years after the Supreme Council in London had received its Patent, the controlling body at Bottoms purported to Warrant a Rose Croix Chapter in Rochdale (Warrant in The Supreme Council's archives). The Rose Croix Chapter at Bottoms continued to work independently until it petitioned for a Warrant from The Supreme Council which it was granted on 12th July 1892 as High Greenwood Chapter No.124 "free of charge in consideration of an old Chapter, unconnected with this Supreme Council, having existed in that place from Time Immemorial".

270 In Redruth, after 'Entered Apprentice' and 'Fellow Craft', 'Mark Man' was interposed before 'Master Mason'. This was followed first by 'Mark Master', then by 'Master of Arts and Sciences or Passed the Chair', before half a dozen Degrees, each with a faint resemblance, if only in name, to the earlier Degrees in the 'Rite of Perfection' in 'Morin's Rite'. The 'Royal Arch' was divided into five 'Points', each considered to be a separate Degree, as if to enable the total to be brought to 25. This is followed by 'Ark Mariners', 'Knights Templar' (of which John Knight had been appointed 'Provincial Grand Commander' by Dunckerley), 'Mediterranean Pass', and 'Knights of Malta'. After this, before the '*Ne Plus Ultra*' are the four Degrees of the Eastern, Western, Northern and Southern Knights, the ceremonies of which in each case seeming to consist of little more than the communication of the Sign, Token and Word. John Knight, manuscript notebook, *F__E M_____Y FROM THE E_____D AP_____E TO THE N.P.U.,* Shelf Mark 7, John Coombe Masonic Library, Hayle, Cornwall. 1810. (This is one of several similar manuscripts written by John Knight 1800-1821.)

271 Dunckerley appointed John Knight the 'Provincial Commander' (today, Provincial Prior) of the Knights Templar in Cornwall.

272 F. M. Rickard, *William Finch*, AQC LV (part 2), p.163 (1944).

273 At least one circular directed by Finch to a lodge in Cornwall is in existence. 'William Finch' file in United Grand Lodge of England Museum and Library.

Essay 7
French Attempts to Establish Higher Degrees in England

The Union in 1813 of the two competing English Grand Lodges – 'Antients' and 'Moderns' – was a considerable achievement. The three Craft Degrees of Pure, Ancient Masonry have ever been the bedrock upon which the Masonic edifice rests. There is good Biblical precedent for saying that a House divided against itself cannot stand, and one can only wonder what the future of English Freemasonry would have been had there been no reconciliation of the opposing Brethren. But the first Grand Master of the United Grand Lodge of England, the Duke of Sussex[274], had to steer a careful course. With the co-operation of his Royal Brother, the Duke of Kent, he had brought all English Freemasons together into one body, but the fragility of the Union can be seen by anyone who reads the original[275] Minutes of the proceedings of the Lodge of Reconciliation. Hemmings, who presided, was a 'Modern' Mason who was evidently determined to go so far, but no further, and Goldsworthy, who hankered after greater concessions being made to 'Antient' practices, had to be somewhat ignominiously expelled. The Act of Union had conceded that the Orders of Chivalry could still be practised, but too much emphasis on this could well have led to the withdrawal from the Union of the more hide-bound former adherents of the former Grand Lodge of the 'Moderns' which was, after all, the Premier Grand Lodge in the world.

Since 1812 the Duke of Sussex had been Grand Master of the Military, Religious and Masonic Order of Knights Templar. In addition, he seems also to have succeeded to the Grand Mastership of the Order of the Red Cross of Palestine when Waller Rodwell Wright had to relinquish that Office also, but little or nothing more is heard of this. The Knights Templar were fortunate in having in their senior ranks two able and dedicated masons, John Christian Burckhardt, whom the Duke appointed Deputy Grand Master *ad vitam* in 1812, and Robert Gill, the Grand Vice-Chancellor and Registrar. After the Union, with the Order in such capable hands, the Duke of Sussex was able to show no overt concern for its governance. It is generally assumed that for twenty years he privately kept a watchful eye on its conduct. Possibly prior to 1820 one or two new Conclaves were given Dispensations, under which they could meet without Warrants, but in that year Gill's house in Soho burnt down, and many early records of the Knights Templar were destroyed in the conflagration. There is a record of a Grand Conclave having been held on 31st January 1820, and between 1824 and 1830 three new Encampments were certainly Founded[276]. But it was not until 1834 that the Duke of Sussex evidently considered that it was appropriate for him publicly to assert again his Grand Mastership of the Order by signing a Warrant for the Royal Sussex Encampment at Torquay[277].

However, fifteen years before this, the Duke of Sussex had had to employ all his diplomatic skills when another proposition had been made to him[278]. By 1819 the Ancient and Accepted Rite of Thirty-Three Degrees had gained a considerable foothold in many countries in Europe. The comte de Grasse-Tilly, having played some part in erecting the 'Mother Supreme Council of the World' in Charleston, South Carolina, in 1801, returned to Europe in 1804 after forming a Supreme Council of the Thirty-third Degree for the French West Indies. By the end of that year he had also established a Supreme Council in Paris with himself as Sovereign Grand Commander. At this time there was a multiplicity of Higher Degrees in France, the members of which owed allegiance to no single governing body. The new Supreme Council was welcomed by the majority of those who had hitherto acknowledged one or other of the various independent French Higher Degree bodies and who now placed themselves under its direction.

The establishment of de Grasse-Tilly's Supreme Council did not, however, wholly resolve the problems which still existed in Freemasonry in France. The symbolic Lodges which practised the Higher Degrees or '*Ecossais*' Masonry formed themselves into a *Grande Loge Générale Ecossaise* which although in amity with the Supreme Council over which de Grasse-Tilly was presiding, did not become part of it. There was in addition a further long-established Masonic governing body, the Grand Orient, some of whose members, after receiving the Thirty-third Degree, created their own College of Rites[279].

The Emperor Napoleon, himself a Freemason[280], made a series of interventions in order to regularise matters. The Grand Chancellor of the Empire, Prince Jean Jacques Régis Cambacérès, already Assistant Grand Master of the Grand Orient, was appointed Grand Master of the *Grande Loge Générale Écossaise*. De Grasse Tilly, who had held a commission in the French Army before he went to the West Indies fifteen years earlier, had resumed his Military duties. Before he went on active service in 1806 he was apparently forcibly 'persuaded' to resign as Sovereign Grand Commander of his Supreme Council so that Cambacérès could take his place. With one man in charge of all Higher Degree Masonry in France it seemed possible that the previous conflicts between rival bodies would be brought to an end. The Supreme Council under Cambacérès' direction at first made its Grand East in the Galerie de Pompéi, and then in 1812 moved to a more permanent home in the Rue Saint-Honoré. But matters again became further complicated when six members of the Supreme Council which de Grasse-Tilly had formed in the French West Indies, left the Islands and came to Paris, taking over the vacated premises in the Galerie de Pompéi, in consequence of which they were commonly referred to as the 'Council of Pompéi'. The newcomers included the Lieutenant Grand Commander of the West Indian Supreme Council, Jean-Baptiste de la Hogue, the father-in-law of de Grasse-Tilly, and its Grand Secretary General H.E., Tessier de Marguerittes. All of them at once claimed Honorary Membership both of what was now Cambacérès' Supreme Council, which appears to have conceded this to them, and also of the Council of Rites of the Grand Orient, which did not.

The defeat of Napoleon by the Allied Powers in 1814 changed the face of French Freemasonry once more. Cambacérès left the scene, together with those of the members of his Supreme Council who had been prominent supporters of the Emperor. When de Grasse-Tilly[281], who had suffered the misfortune of being made a Prisoner of War[282], returned to Paris, he claimed that his enforced resignation eight years earlier had been illegal. In the meantime, the Grand Orient, the members of which had been less prominent supporters of Napoleon, remained in being, and they, together with some Members of the original Supreme Council who still remained in Paris, formed a new body under the title of 'Grand Orient, Supreme Council for France and the French possessions'[283]. The remaining Members of the original Council considered this action to be illegal, and in 1815 they declared that the Supreme Council legitimately set up in 1804 was still in existence, but temporarily in abeyance.

De Grasse-Tilly then established yet another new body, a purported Supreme Council with its Grand East in the Restaurant de Prado[284]; inevitably it became known as 'the Supreme Council of the Prado'. Several distinguished Masons became Members of this Council: comte de Fernig as its Lieutenant Grand Commander, Vice-Admiral comte Allemand, and comte Decazes.

In 1818, shortly after the Supreme Council of the Prado had been set up, de Grasse-Tilly had to leave Paris – the circumstances of his departure are uncertain, and he may have been under a cloud. Be that as it may, the Council of the Prado deposed him from his position as its Sovereign Grand Commander. This deposition might have been justifiable if de Grasse-Tilly had been formally convicted of moral turpitude, but his replacement by three 'Conservators'[285], in defiance of the 'Grand Constitutions of 1786', was indefensible, and removed any claim to regularity which the Council might have had. On his return to Paris, de Grasse-Tilly briefly joined the 'Council of Pompéi', but then unsuccessfully attempted to set up yet another Supreme Council. The organisation of the French Higher Degrees was becoming chaotic. Fortunately matters were taken in hand by comte Decazes, a member of the 'Prado', and a considerable figure in French politics at that time, being a personal friend of the restored King Louis XVIII, whose Prime Minister he became in 1821. Decazes brought together from the Councils of Pompéi and of the Prado sufficient Members who could realistically claim to have derived their authority from the Supreme Council regularly set up in 1804 by de Grasse-Tilly for Decazes to be able to claim in 1821 that this Supreme Council, placed in temporary abeyance in 1815, had now been legitimately revived.

However, in 1819, this rationalisation had not yet been accomplished and there were four French Masonic bodies each claiming to be a Supreme Council:

- The 'Supreme Council, or Council of Rites of the Grand Orient'.
- The Supreme Council regularly set up by de Grasse-Tilly in 1804, but in abeyance since 1815.
- 'The Supreme Council of Pompéi', in reality the Supreme Council of the West Indies 'in exile'.
- 'The Supreme Council of the Prado', whose regularity had always been doubtful, but which it had in any case forfeited by deposing de Grasse-Tilly.

In spite of this, it was from the last of these that an embarrassing offer to set up a Supreme Council of the Thirty-third Degree in England was presented to the Duke of Sussex.

This offer was made by one of those curiously flamboyant characters who from time to time emerge from the ranks of Masonic brethren and achieve some temporary acceptance, and frequently notoriety. Joseph Glock was the son of a peasant farmer, Nicholas Glock, and of Barbe Orthlieb whom Nicholas subsequently married[286]. As a young man Joseph had been to the Antilles, possibly as a conscript in the Napoleonic Army. There is no factual evidence of his career before 1818 when he appeared in Masonic circles in Paris, claiming that he had visited Haiti, Mexico and 'New Spain', acquiring various high Masonic ranks, including the Thirty-third Degree, during his visits[287]. Not only this, but the peasant farmer's son was soon claiming both nobility and membership of the landed gentry by assuming the aristocratic 'particle', and the name of his birthplace – he was now known as Joseph de Glock D'Obernay, and under this name he became a member of the bodyguard of King Louis XVIII in which de Grasse-Tilly was also serving.

D'Obernay's Masonic credentials were accepted by the governing body of the 'Council of the Prado', and probably by others as well. D'Obernay persuaded the 'Prado' to mandate him to establish the Ancient and Accepted Rite of Thirty-three Degrees in countries where there was as yet no Supreme Council, although it is questionable how far D'Obernay's intentions arose solely from a desire to spread enlightenment. His subsequent conduct indicated that his principal concern was his personal financial gain. However, the 'Conservators' of the 'Council of the Prado' seem to have considered that for it to be seen as a 'Mother Council' would enhance its reputation and status in France. D'Obernay's eventual destination was to be the Americas, where he boasted of high-ranking Masonic contacts, but he decided first to discover what he could achieve in the British Isles.

D'Obernay therefore went to Ireland with a letter of introduction from an Irish Brother in Paris, F.W. Jones. The letter was addressed to John Fowler, the Grand Commander of the Council of Rites which controlled the Knights Templar and Rose Croix Degrees in Ireland. Fowler, the Deputy to the Grand Master of Ireland, the Duke of Leinster, had apparently already tried to obtain information from Jones about Degrees higher than the Rose Croix. In spite of Jones' commendation, D'Obernay failed to persuade anyone in Ireland to pay the excessive fees which he proposed to charge for Patents for the Higher Degrees. He then went to London, where he had a meeting with the Duke of Leinster himself on 18th August 1819. The Duke was cautious in his dealings with D'Obernay, and expressed his disquiet in a letter to his Deputy. Fowler was, however, anxious for the Higher Degrees to be communicated in Ireland if the cost were not unreasonable. Ireland had early adopted Higher Degrees 'beyond the Craft', and there were no 'Moderns' to be conciliated, as the Duke of Sussex had to be careful to do in England. D'Obernay evidently told the Duke of Leinster that he was willing to confer these Higher Degrees upon him personally. On behalf of his College of Rites, Fowler therefore sent Leinster a Certificate[288] authorising the Duke to accept these Degrees so that he himself could later communicate them in Ireland, presumably at a more moderate cost.

So far this was no more than a matter of Irish domestic interest. However, before he received the Certificate from Fowler, the Duke of Leinster had written a letter of introduction for D'Obernay to the Duke of Sussex. As Grand Master of the recently United Grand Lodge, the Duke can hardly have welcomed D'Obernay's intervention. It interposed a potential minefield under the delicate path along which the Duke was walking in his efforts to preserve the Union. He was in a cleft stick. If he refused to receive D'Obernay, there was nothing to prevent the latter himself establishing a legitimate Supreme Council of the Thirty-third Degree in England, legitimate, that is, if D'Obernay's position as a Sovereign Grand Inspector General was as regular as he claimed it to be. (The Duke could hardly have been aware of the confusion caused by the multiplicity of French Supreme Councils.) It would be inevitable that the Duke's refusal to take part in its formation would become public knowledge, and this would upset the members of the Higher Degrees whose interests the Duke was covertly seeking to protect. On the other hand, to receive the Higher Degrees himself and to establish an active Supreme Council under his own direction could equally undo all that he had achieved, even resulting in the more die-hard former 'Moderns' withdrawing from the Union. However, there was the benefit that if such a Council were to be regularly Patented, England would no longer be 'Open Territory'. No one else could legitimately claim to establish another Supreme Council in the 'Kingdom', and the problem could not arise again.

The Duke therefore conceived a 'damage limitation' exercise, but one which contained within itself further potential perils. He first met D'Obernay on 6th September 1819. Subsequently a preliminary agreement was made to set up a Supreme Council not just for England, but, according to the later Patent which established it, for "the Kingdom of Great Britain, Ireland and its possessions in America and the Indies". For the Grand Master of the Grand Lodge of England thus to intrude on two neighbouring independent Masonic jurisdictions, Ireland and Scotland, would indeed have been playing with fire had the Duke intended that the proposed body should have any reality. However, this device enabled the Duke of Leinster to become the second Member of the proposed Council without the involvement of any senior English Freemason. By this time Leinster had received the Certificate from the Irish College of Rites. In October he signed an endorsement on the reverse of this document: "I hereby empower our Illustrious Brother His Royal Highness the Duke of Sussex to receive for me such communications in the higher degrees of Masonry as he thinks proper from Brother J.D.D'Obernay". It is probable that, having done this, Leinster took no further part in the machinations which the establishment of the new Council involved.

The Grand Constitutions of 1786 provide that three Members form a quorum of a Supreme Council, and for the new body to come into existence a third member was therefore required. To fill this vacancy the Duke of Sussex selected his confidential Masonic Secretary, Hippolyte da Costa[289]. The Patent for the Council would come from the 'Council of Prado' and a draft was prepared for D'Obernay to take back to Paris for its approval. While awaiting passage at Gravesend, D'Obernay wrote to the Duke soliciting a hundred guineas for the expenses of his journey. Within a month D'Obernay had returned with the necessary documents including a Concordat setting out the terms of the recognition of the 'British' Supreme Council by the 'Council of the Prado', describing itself as 'The Supreme Council . . . . . [of the] G[ran]D∴.OR[ient]∴.ECOSSAIS for France and her possessions in America and the Indies', a very questionable description. The original of the Concordat no longer exists. There is a reputed copy in the archives of the *Grande Loge de France*, a copy which, if it is an accurate reproduction of the original, is so full of clerical errors that it is possible that it was D'Obernay's own production, and that the Conservators of the 'Prado', if, indeed, their signatures were genuine, did no more than sign it.

On 13th October 1819 D'Obernay conferred their Patents of the Thirty-third Degree upon both the Duke of Sussex and da Costa – the Duke of Leinster was not present, and Sussex acted as his proxy. The Supreme Council of 'Britain' was duly and covertly constituted with its three members, and there was then, as was the custom of the day, a positive orgy of conferring Honorary Memberships. The Concordat provided that the Dukes of Sussex and Leinster, together with Hippolyte da Costa, should become Honorary Members of the sponsoring Supreme Council, the 'Prado'. Seven members of the latter, of course including D'Obernay, were made Honorary Members of the 'British' Council[290]. By the 21st October D'Obernay was again at Gravesend, on this occasion awaiting his passage to Jamaica. Two days later, following his usual mendicant custom, he wrote to da Costa asking him to request the Duke of Sussex to settle his bill at the Inn at which he was staying. On 14th November 1819, after D'Obernay had departed for the New World, the 'Council of the Prado' conferred Honorary Membership of their Council on four further Members of the 'British' Council, their names to be selected by the Duke of Sussex. The Duke acknowledged this courtesy on 29th November, but said that he could make no nominations for the present because "it is not proposed to fill the number of the Supreme Council for England, Great Britain, Ireland and the possessions in America and the Indies until everything has been organised and the location chosen, which has not yet been done". It never was, although Sussex accepted a box of 16 official seals sent to him by the 'Prado'[291].

The formation of the "Supreme Council for Great Britain" had attracted no publicity, and few people other than Sussex himself, Leinster and Hippolyte da Costa were aware of it. With D'Obernay safely in the West Indies, the Duke of Sussex would have been entitled to heave a sigh of relief. However, D'Obernay exaggerated the powers which he claimed that Sussex had conferred upon him[292]. In Jamaica D'Obernay met the Provincial Grand Master under the United Grand Lodge of England, Surgeon-General Dr. Michael Clare, and proceeded to interfere with his rule of the Craft in his Province. Next, D'Obernay went to Cuba, where, claiming to be an emissary of the Duke of Sussex, he formed a 'Lodge of Adoption', that is a Lodge for both men and women, and also proposed to form a Royal Arch Chapter. After then visiting Haiti he went to New York, where he again claimed to be the Duke's Representative for all the Degrees practised in England, including the Higher Degrees of the Ancient and Accepted Rite. Indeed, he described himself as such in a series of letters which he sent to England. By this time Dr. Clare had also written to the United Grand Lodge of England enquiring about D'Obernay and complaining of his conduct. The Officials of the United Grand Lodge of England were faithful supporters of the Duke of Sussex. This correspondence may even have been the first that the joint Grand Secretaries, William White and Edwards[293] Harper, had heard of 'The Supreme Council of Britain'. Realising the damage which public knowledge of this might cause, they sent the letters to da Costa without even entering them in the Grand Lodge records. Da Costa wrote severely to D'Obernay, reprimanding him, pointing out the 'confusion' which he had caused in Grand Lodge, and making it clear to him that while Sussex may have conferred Grand Chapter rank upon him, this did not entitle him to interfere with the work of a Provincial Grand Master.

All these matters were successfully 'hushed up', D'Obernay retired to the island of Haiti where he died in 1839, and during the life-time of the Duke of Sussex the Ancient and Accepted Rite did not further disturb the tranquillity of the United Grand Lodge of England.

There can be little doubt that the Ancient and Accepted Rite was the oldest of the extended Higher Degree systems. More recently there had emerged two further Rites, each with a multiplicity of imposing-sounding Degrees, those of Memphis and of Misraim. It was claimed that the Rite of Memphis was a Christian development of the ancient Egyptian mysteries, and that it had been communicated to the Templars. *Inter alia*, it included the Degree of Rose Croix as its 46th Degree. Nothing but its own traditional history supports the claim that the Rite emerged in Egypt at the end of the eighteenth century under the auspices of a certain Samuel Honis who is reputed then to have brought to France a cumbersome Rite of 97 Degrees.

The Order of Misraim was only mildly more conservative, claiming a mere 90 Degrees, of which, as in the Ancient and Accepted Rite, that of 'Rose Croix' was the 18th. It appears to have been 'invented' in Milan in 1805 by a brother Lechangeur who died in 1812. After his death, Michel Bédaride, together with his brothers Marc and Joseph, brought the Rite to Paris to add to the High Degree confusion there. A few Lodges were founded, in spite of opposition from the Grand Orient. By 1816 de Grasse-Tilly appears to have joined the Order and to have held senior rank in it[294]. As occurred when 'The Supreme Council for Britain' was established, Honorary Memberships were widely distributed, though it is uncertain whether the recipients, who included the Duke of Sussex, were in all cases aware of the 'honour' conferred upon them[295].

According to the Rite's own records, Jacques-Etienne Marconis de Nègre joined a Misraim Lodge in Paris on 21st April 1833[296]. He was expelled two months later, for, it was claimed, abusing the confidence of several individuals, whatever that may have meant. However, he was given a Warrant for a Misraim Lodge in Lyons[297] in October 1835, and was admitted to the 66th Degree[298]. Marconis may have considered that this was an insufficiently rapid promotion, and one which did not give him sufficient opportunity for financial reward. Two years later he resigned from the Lodge in Lyons, and went to Brussels where on 21st March 1838 he consecrated a Lodge similarly named *La Bienveillance,* but a Lodge of the Rite of Memphis, for which he was promptly expelled from that of Misraim.

Three months later, Marconis consecrated a further 'Memphis' Lodge, *Osiris,* at the Prado in Paris, the home of the former irregular Supreme Council. The socially respectable élite members of *Osiris* included two noblemen. Also among them was a Scotsman, "The thrice Illustrious Bro. Morison de Greenfield, Physician to H.R.H. the Duke of Sussex[299], Grand Inspector General 93°, Sublime Pamphylach"[300]. Marconis consecrated three further Lodges, to which he appears to have had no difficulty in obtaining recruits, and he was elected Hierophant Supreme Chief.

Marconis' activities do not seem to have disturbed the civil authorities, but they exasperated the brothers Bédaride, whose Rite of Misraim was suffering loss of members, and their income was thereby reduced. They laid information, without, so far as is known, any factual basis, that the members of the Rite of Memphis engaged in disruptive political activity. On being told this, the Prefect of Police ordered their Lodges to close. Accordingly, on 15th June 1841, Marconis, the Grand Hierophant, suspended the Order's activities.

For Freemasonry in England the timing of what proved to be a temporary dissolution might be considered fortuitous. More than one Englishman had been attracted by these grandiloquent degrees. When the Duke of Sussex died in 1843, renewed development of the 'Orders of Chivalry' could take place. The Grand Conclave of the Knights Templar could be re-constituted. The supervision of the Degrees of 'Rosae Crucis' and 'Kadosh', hitherto worked in its Encampments, could be transferred to a legitimately Patented Supreme Council of the Ancient and Accepted Rite[301] without, however, the distraction of 'Misraim' and of 'Memphis', at least until their amalgamation in England under John Yarker many years later.

It was to be many years before the few local assemblies working Higher Degrees in, for example, Newcastle upon Tyne, Stansfield, Redruth, Bath and Bristol, gave their allegiance to the Grand Conclave on the one hand, or to the newly constituted Supreme Council on the other. When the members of the Baldwyn Rite in Bristol did so, they were conceded considerable freedom to retain their traditional rituals. This was not conceded to the Knights Templar Camp of Antiquity at Bath, which in its early days had included the Degree of Royal Ark Mariner among the Higher Degrees which it worked – its Minute Book Records that in 1790, William Boyce, who was later Commander of the Encampment for ten years, took "all the degrees of ye Red Cross also Royal Ark Mariners"[302]. Indeed, there is further evidence of the involvement of the Ark Mariners in the Higher

Degrees in a Warrant dated 1793 naming the Duke of Clarence as the Commander of the Grand and Royal Ark Lodge, which refers to "this and other Degrees belonging to Ark Mariners which are Mark man, Mark Master, Excellent and Super-excellent which are to be conferred for a fee of 5/3 and those of Knights of the Red Cross, Knights Templar, Meditterranian [sic] Pass etc. etc. etc. for a fee of 10/6"[303]. John Dorrington endorsed this Warrant as having received it as Grand Master of the Order in 1816. That no more is heard of this Order for some years may perhaps be explained by an obituary note in *The Freemason* in May 1871 stating, *inter alia*, that Dorrington had been "one of the guardians of the Emperor Napoleon at St. Helena"[304].

274 The Duke of Sussex had been born in 1773, the sixth son and ninth child of King George III and Queen Charlotte.

275 The actual manuscript Minutes of the Lodge of Reconciliation are preserved in the Museum and Library of the United Grand Lodge of England and may be viewed by those who can persuade the Librarian that they are genuine students of Masonic history. Otherwise only a typewritten transcript is made available; regrettably this contains several errors and omissions.

276 Hugh de Payens (Canada) 1824, Cornubian (Falmouth/Truro) 1826, and Loyal Brunswick (Plymouth) 1830. None of the three is now on the English Register.

277 Now No.25 on the Register of the United Orders.

278 I make no apologies for the heavy reliance of this and the immediately following paragraphs on Chapter 14 of A.C.F.Jackson's *Rose Croix* (Revised Edition, Lewis Masonic, 1987). I know of no other comparably lucid account of affairs in France at this time.

279 According to the records of the 'Grand Collège des Rites', several Englismen, who have not otherwise been identified, received the 33rd Degree from the College. They include (spellings *sic*) Colonel Sir John Scott Lillie, Bart, 'Jean-Marie-Etienne Godefroi-Forvil, Chevalier de la Tour d'Auvergne, capitaine de haut bord de S.M. Britannique', Major Joseph Kelly 'de cavalerie anglaise', Major Sir Josias Coghill-Coghill, Bart 'de cavalerie', Joseph Ritchie 'au service diplomatique anglaise', Major Christopher Satter 'de cavaleries anglaise', George-Hamilton-Chichester 'comte de Belfast, pair d'Angleterre', Williams-Henry-Hugh-Cholmondeley,'pair d'Angleterre', Sir Joshua-Colles-Meredyth Bart 'd'Irlande, chevalier de Malte', Samuel-Zaliffe Tuffenel, ministre de l'église anglicane', and 'William (Thomas), docteur en médecine,a l'île de Wight'. M. Pierre Mollier, Private Communication to Author, 19 September 2001.

280 Napoleon's reputed Masonic apron is preserved at the Grand East of The Supreme Council of England, etc., at No.10 Duke Street, London.

281 De Grasse-Tilly had served first in Italy and then held the rank of 'Captain of Horse' in Spain where he had been made a Prisoner of War. He had earlier established the Supreme Council of Spain on 4th July

1811. John T. Thorp, (Ed. Lionel Vibert), *French Prisoners' Lodges*, (2nd Edition, augmented), p.47, The Lodge of Research, Freemasons' Hall, Leicester, (1935).

282 De Grasse-Tilly had enjoyed restricted liberty in the 'Parole Town' of Abergavenny where he had presided over a Higher Degree Lodge *Enfants de Mars et de Neptune* under the French Grand Orient, signing several Certificates (still extant) for Englishmen who joined the Lodge. *Ibidem*, pp.46-69 *passim*.

283 This body survives today as 'The Grand College of Rites'.

284 The Restaurant de Prado was a dance-hall in the Quai aux Fleurs, on the Ile de la Cité near the Cathedral of Notre Dame.

285 Two of the 'Conservators' were Admiral comte Allemand and baron de Marguerittes.

286 The Glock family lived at Obernay to the South of Strasbourg.

287 A.C.F. Jackson points out that R.F. Gould (*History of Freemasonry*, vol 3, p.355,1882-1887) must almost certainly be in error when he claims that Joseph Glock was involved in a revival of High Degree Masonry in Paris in 1810. Glock was then no more than 19 years of age, and could hardly at that time have had the opportunity to acquire the distinctions which Gould attributes to him. A.C.F. Jackson, AQC Vol XCIV, p.43 (1981).

288 The Certificate was dated 30th August 1819, and signed by Fowler and his two Wardens.

289 Hippolyte da Costa was a Portuguese, but had lived in America before coming to England and being engaged as his Secretary by the Duke of Sussex. The Duke had appointed him Grand Scribe for Foreign Correspondence in the Royal Arch Chapter. He had also given him the little more than nominal position in the Craft of 'Provincial Grand Master for Rutland'.

290 D'Obernay, the duc d'Aumont, Admiral comte Allemand, the marquis de Massiac, baron de Marguerittes, comte Decazes, and the duc de Tarante.

291 On 9th July 1889 The Supreme Council acknowledged the receipt from Shadwell Clerke, then the Grand Secretary of the United Grand Lodge of England, but previously Grand Captain General of The Supreme Council, of a "Box containing 16 seals

of the A and A Rite, formerly the property of H.R.H. the Duke of Sussex, and believed to have been presented to him by the Grand Orient of France". These seals are now preserved at 10 Duke Street.

292 The Duke appears to have done no more than to make him a Past Third Principal in the recently Constituted Supreme Grand Chapter, although its Minutes do not contain a record even of this appointment.

293 Harper's father, Thomas, had married Anne Edwards, which accounts for the son's unusual first name.

294 A.C.F. Jackson AQC XCIV, p.47 (1981).

295 Comte Decazes might or might not have been surprised to have been given the rank of 90° in 1818, but, if they were aware of it, the Dukes of Sussex, Atholl and Leinster can hardly have failed to be startled at being awarded the same grade in 1821/2. *Ibidem.*

296 Ellic Howe AQC XCII, p.2 (1979). These paragraphs are considerably indebted to Bro. Howe's *Inaugural Address* of 9th November, 1978. Marconis had been born at Montauban on 3rd January 1795. His father, Gabriel-Mathieu Marconis, may have been associated with Samuel Honis in founding the *Grande Loge des Philadelphes* at Montauban in 1813. *Ibidem* & f/n 3.

297 *La Bienveillance.*

298 'Grand Inquisitor Commander'

299 In 1846 Doctor Charles Morison obtained a Patent for a Supreme Council of the Ancient and Accepted Rite for Scotland from that of Spain. Subsequently he had this endorsed by each of the French Supreme Council, that of the Grand Orient, and also by the Council which claimed somewhat shaky continuity from that established by de Grasse-Tilly in 1804. It was the latter actions which offended the Supreme Council of the Northern Masonic Jurisdiction of the U.S.A.

300 Howe, *op. cit.*, p.3

301 Some authorities state that there was a 'Compact' by which the Grand Conclave agreed that Encampments under allegiance to it would no longer work the 'Rosae Crucis' and 'Kadosh' Degrees. There may well have been such a Compact, formal or informal, but the present author has been unable to find any trace of it.

302 This Minute seems to dispose of the supposition that the Ark Mariners did not become 'Royal' until after the Royal Brethren joined the Order in 1796.

303 '10/6' is half a guinea, and '5/3' half of that.

304 "The Lodge was in mourning owing to the decease of one of its members, Bro. J. Dorrington, Past Great Commander, 33°, P.Z., P.M., Past Grand Mark Master, &c. who had been a very active member of most of the ancient orders in masonry, and indeed had attained the highest honours in them. Bro. Dorrington was one of the guardians of the Emperor Napoleon at St. Helena, and had enjoyed for many years a pension from the government for long, faithful and meritorious service." Report of a Meeting of 'The Royal Clarence Lodge of Royal Ark Mariners. No.1' on 23rd March 1871. *The Freemason*, Vol IV, p.231 (15th April, 1871).

Essay 8

The events leading to the Patenting of 'The Supreme Council for England'

His Royal Highness Augustus Frederick, Duke of Sussex, died on 21st April 1843 at the age of seventy, in his thirtieth year as the first Grand Master of the United Grand Lodge of England. For all this time he had steered a careful course. The two former competing Grand Lodges, the 'Antients' and the 'Moderns', were united after sixty years of disagreement, and the Duke had been determined that the Union, achieved with such difficulty, should not be dissolved. The brethren who adhered to the 'Modern' Grand Lodge, the Premier Grand Lodge in the world, had been unwilling to acknowledge that pure, Ancient Masonry extended beyond the three Craft Degrees including the Supreme Degree of the Holy Royal Arch, and even the latter Order had only been somewhat grudgingly accepted by some of the more die-hard 'Modern' Brethren[305]. Furthermore, 'Modern' Brethren had accepted with even less enthusiasm the rider to the Articles of Union which stated that it was "not intended to prevent any Lodge or Chapter from holding a meeting in any of the degrees of the Orders of Chivalry, according to the constitutions of the said orders". Indeed, this clause was deleted by the United Grand Lodge in 1817.

It has been said that the Duke of Sussex "was a devout, if unorthodox, Trinitarian, but he held liberal views"[306]. He was certainly strong-minded, and did not welcome opposition. In his opinions he displayed a curious dichotomy. On the one hand he considered that Freemasonry should be 'generalist' and that the Christian references within the Craft should be eliminated so that they offered no hindrance to those of other Faiths[307]. However, in 1810 he had accepted Office as the Grand Master of the Military, Religious and Masonic Order of the Knights Templar, an undoubtedly Christian Order, and he was not prepared to renounce it. This Order was fortunate in having two able and dedicated Knights among its senior Officers – John Christian Burckhardt[308], the Deputy Grand Master *ad vitam*, and the Grand Vice-Chancellor and Registrar, Robert Gill. The Duke could safely leave the conduct of the affairs of the Order in their capable hands, maintaining a distant oversight of its proceedings, without offending the former 'Modern' Brethren by publicly demonstrating his own connection with the Order. In the years immediately following the Union, perhaps half a dozen Knights Templar Encampments were founded, meeting under Dispensations[309]. It was not until 1834 that the Duke considered that bygones had sufficiently become bygones for him to put his own signature to a Warrant for a new Encampment[310]. However, even then he did not display any enthusiasm for the expansion of the Order. In his life-time no further Meeting of its controlling body, the Grand Conclave, was summoned. His own retention of the rule of the Order may have been considerably dictated by a wish to prevent its direction falling into other and more vigorous hands which might have provided a focus of opposition to his 'Generalist' views. On the other hand, he made no attempt to suppress it.

However, only six years after the Union, the Duke of Sussex had been placed in a difficult position by Joseph de Glock D'Obernay, the emissary of a Supreme Council of the Thirty-third Degree of the Ancient and Accepted Rite in Paris, a Council which had little claim to regularity. D'Obernay proposed that the Duke should become the Sovereign Grand Commander of a Supreme Council of the Rite, not just for England, but for "the Kingdom of Great Britain, Ireland, and its possessions in America and the Indies". Even setting aside the implication that this would infringe upon two neighbouring jurisdictions, Scotland and Ireland, it would have been highly inexpedient at this time for the Duke to be seen to be associated with such a High Degree body, something which in any case would have been contrary to his own 'Generalist' convictions. On the other hand, if he refused D'Obernay's offer, there was nothing to stop the Frenchman independently setting up in England a Supreme Council which might even claim the right to confer the three Symbolic Degrees of Craft Masonry. The carefully crafted Union might well then be seriously disrupted.

The Duke of Sussex surmounted this potential hazard to the untroubled existence of the United Grand Lodge by agreeing to accept a Patent of the Thirty-third Degree on his own behalf, and on that of the Duke of Leinster (who took no further part in the proceedings, but mandated Sussex to act as his proxy). A third Patent was therefore given to Hippolyte da Costa, the Duke's confidential Masonic Secretary. The Duke of Sussex nominated no further Members of the Council, and intended that nothing more should be heard of it – few became aware even of its existence.

The Degree of Knights Templar, and, in some cases, that of the Knights of Malta together with the Mediterranean Pass, had not been the only Degrees being worked in English Templar Encampments in the early nineteenth century. Many (if not all) of them worked a 'Rosae Crucis' Degree, together with, at least in some cases, a 'Kadosh' Degree, as a progressive sequence following that of the Templar Degree itself.

There were several local variants of this sequence. The Royal Kent Chapter in Newcastle upon Tyne was considerably influenced by the old *Order of Harodim*[311], until in April 1812 it received a Warrant from the Grand Conclave under the title of "Knights Companions of the Royal Exalted Religious Order of the Temple and Sepulchre of St. John of Jerusalem, HRDM KDSH". At Redruth, in Cornwall, John Knight[312] presided until his death in 1828 over a system of 26 Degrees, of which the last, or *Ne Plus Ultra*[313] was a '*Rosycrusian*' (*sic*) or 'Rose Croix Degree'. The best-authenticated of these sequential workings is that still practised in Bristol, and which, after *circa* 1810, became known as the 'Rite of Baldwyn'. Before the Union of the Grand Lodges in 1813 this was a fully progressive system of seven Degrees, of which the first three were those of the Craft. At the Union, in order to maintain their regularity under the United Grand Lodge of England, the 'Symbolic Degrees' were divided from the 'Higher Degrees'[314]. Under the terms of a Concordat with the Supreme Council signed many years later[315], the 'Rose Croix' Ritual derived from the progressive system is still used in the Camp of Baldwyn[316]. A somewhat similar sequence was employed in Bath in the Camp of Antiquity. There may have been other less well documented local variations, for example at Stansfield on the borders of Derbyshire, Lancashire and Yorkshire, but the Knights Templar Encampments in London are not known to have worked additional Degrees other than 'Rosae Crucis' and 'Kadosh'[317]. There was thus a great variety of ceremonies being worked, nominally at least, under the Grand Conclave, at least two of which, 'Rosae Crucis' and 'Kadosh', were essentially Degrees of the Ancient and Accepted Rite, now well established in many countries outside the British Isles, but without any supervisory control of their performance being exercised in England.

The 'Rosae Crucis' or *Rosycrusian* Degree conferred in these Chapters and Encampments was one of several versions of what is generally known as the 'Rose Croix'. The Masonic Legend, accepted by many past writers, is that the 'Rose Croix' Degree originated at a Chapter held in the French town of Arras in 1745, and even that it was given a Charter by the 'Young Pretender', Charles Edward Stuart. This myth has long been exposed as a pleasant fabrication[318]. The Degree may have had a basis in the Rosicrucian ceremonies practised in Germany around the middle of the eighteenth century. The first definitive evidence of its existence comes from documents preserved in the French town of Lyons. Here, some time shortly after 1761, Jean-Baptiste Willermoz assembled a Rite of twenty-five Degrees of which the highest was *Knight of the Eagle, of the Pelican, Knight of St. Andrew or Mason of Heredom*. Willermoz completed this essentially 'Rose Croix' Ritual in 1765[319]. By 1768 there was a Sovereign Chapter Rose Croix in Paris. From this time on the Degree grew in popularity, perhaps because it re-introduced the teachings of Christianity into a system which had become deistic and even secular.

There were many sources from which the 'Rosae Crucis' and 'Kadosh' Degrees may have arrived in England. In the 1780s de Lintot brought together several of the Degrees then being worked in France into his Rite of Seven Degrees, but the 'Rose Croix' does not appear to have figured prominently in this. There seems little doubt that a Degree of 'Rose Croix', more 'orthodox' than that in de Lintot's Seven Degree Rite, was introduced to Irish Knights Templar Encampments in the 1780s by a Swiss, Emmanuel Zimmerman, together with a Frenchman, Pierre Laurent. In 1782 Laurent was in London, and received a 'Kadosh' Degree from de Lintot's Rite, and Zimmerman may have similarly progressed, perhaps in 1785. There was continual traffic between Dublin and the West Coast English ports, and the Degrees worked under what later became the Irish 'Council of Rites' would certainly have become known in the West Country.

But it may have been the Lodges formed by French Prisoners of War which provided the most fertile ground in which Higher Degrees, and specifically the 'Rose Croix', were propagated in England. During the Napoleonic Wars there were at times several tens of thousands of these prisoners in England[320]. Officers were frequently allowed to live on parole in certain designated towns[321], and many formed their own Masonic Lodges[322]. Indeed, those in Ashby de la Zouch, Chesterfield, Leek and Northampton[323] obtained Warrants from the Grand Lodge of the Moderns, having received a sympathetic hearing from the Deputy Grand Master, the Earl of Moira, who had himself been a Prisoner of War in France. Towards the end of the first decade of the nineteenth century French prisoners had opened Higher Degree Chapters in several English towns[324]. Not only did many Englishmen join these French Lodges and Chapters, but numbers of Frenchmen joined English Lodges. De Grasse-Tilly, sometime Sovereign Grand Commander of the Supreme Council of the West Indies, and later of the Supreme Council of France, was himself taken prisoner, and lived on parole in Abergavenny. Here he proceeded to confer Higher Degrees, and sign appropriate Certificates[325]. Doubtless the fees charged for such promotions were an important consideration for the generally poverty-stricken French prisoners, but, be that as it may, the Higher Degrees became widely disseminated among English Brethren. From whatever source individual Encampments had acquired the Degrees of 'Rosea Crucis' and 'Kadosh', at the latest by the 1830s they were being widely worked as progressive Degrees for those who were already Knights Templar.

Among those who progressed in this way was Dr. Robert Thomas Crucefix. After qualifying at St. Bartholomew's Hospital, and spending a short time in India, Crucefix had returned to England where in 1829 he was Initiated in the Burlington Lodge[326]. In 1831 Crucefix had practised in Edinburgh for a short time, and it was there that he was Installed as a Knight Templar in the Scottish Grand Conclave. Returning to England in the same year he joined the Cross of Christ Encampment[327] where, in accordance with the English custom, he received both the 'Rosae Crucis' and the 'Kadosh Degrees'.

Crucefix found himself in serious disagreement with the autocratic Duke of Sussex. In 1834 he had proposed the foundation of an 'Asylum for Aged and Decayed Freemasons'. The Duke doubted if Freemasonry could support more than its two existing Charities. Crucefix expressed his contrary views freely in *The Freemasons' Quarterly Review* of which he was the founder and editor[328]. Furthermore, not surprisingly Crucefix received no support from the Duke for his claim that the 'Rosae Crucis' and 'Kadosh' Degrees were properly part of the Ancient and Accepted Rite. In his *Quarterly Review* Crucefix more than once expressed his concern that a body, that is, a Supreme Council, should be set up to control the uniform conferment of, in particular, the 'Rosae Crucis' or 'Rose Croix' Degree. However, in the life-time of the Duke, it was impossible for any such body to function - after all, the Duke himself was nominally Sovereign Grand Commander of a non-existent Supreme Council. He had no intention of further propagating Christian Masonry or of bringing Masonry 'beyond the Craft' forcibly to the attention of those former 'Modern' Masons who still felt strongly about the limits of 'Pure Ancient Masonry'. The Duke of Sussex viewed both Crucefix and his *Quarterly Review* with considerable disfavour because of his advocacy of each of these causes.

Doctor George Oliver[329] became a frequent contributor to *The Freemasons' Quarterly Review*, and struck up a warm friendship with Crucefix. He was a much respected writer on Masonic topics, who had gained a particularly high reputation in the United States of America. His opinions were so authoritative that in 1829 he had been entrusted with the task of preparing a further revised edition of Preston's *'Illustrations of Masonry'*, then the standard work on the Craft.

Oliver had been born in 1782, and had been initiated in St. Peter's Lodge in Peterborough shortly before his twenty-first birthday[330]. In December 1826 the Duke of Sussex had appointed Charles Tennyson D'Eyncourt Provincial Grand Master of Lincolnshire. D'Eyncourt was a Barrister and a liberal-minded Member of Parliament, whose views evidently appealed to Sussex who appointed him his Equerry. He was not Installed as Provincial Grand Master until 1832, and on 11th October in the following year he appointed George Oliver as his Deputy. Oliver, the accepted authority on Masonic matters, disapproved of the reluctance of his Provincial Grand Master to hold Meetings of the Provincial Grand Lodge, pointing out that the 'Book of Constitutions' laid down that these should be held once a year. He believed, *inter alia*, that these Meetings gave Brethren from different Lodges the opportunity to meet each other and that this led to the wider dissemination of Masonic knowledge. Such more 'open' dissemination of Masonic matters was something which Crucefix propagated in the columns of *The Freemasons' Quarterly Review*, but it was another matter of which the Duke of Sussex strongly disapproved.

In 1837, after considerable argument, and in spite of the Grand Master's opposition, Grand Lodge accepted a proposition that the foundation of an Asylum for Aged Freemasons was 'expedient'. Oliver persuaded his Provincial Grand Lodge to support the Asylum project, and solicited contributions from the Lodges in the Province. In November 1839 Crucefix presided at a Committee to further the foundation of an Asylum, but some of the proceedings were so outspoken that the Board of General Purposes suspended Crucefix and two of his colleagues. Crucefix then had an angry confrontation with the Duke of Sussex, wrote him an insubordinate letter and published it in his *Review*. He only saved himself by making a formal apology in Grand Lodge which thereupon rejected the Motion for his expulsion on a divided Vote, D'Eyncourt having urged his expulsion and voted for it.

By January 1840 the Asylum project had received considerable contributions from both home and abroad. In November 1841 there was a Meeting at which the proceeds were to be presented to Crucefix, and of which Oliver was persuaded to take the Chair. He opened the proceedings with an Oration, praising both the *Review* and Crucefix to whom he gave the credit for "the recent growth of the Craft, both at home and abroad". Publication in the *Review* further angered the Duke. D'Eyncourt asked for Oliver's resignation as his Deputy, and, failing to receive it, dismissed him on 3rd May 1842. Many Brethren, in England and elsewhere, were outraged by this, and Crucefix fanned the flames in his publication.

Among others who strongly supported George Oliver was Henry Udall. Udall was a Barrister who was at that time Secretary of Westminster and Keystone Lodge No.10, in which he had been Initiated six years earlier. He was also a member of the recently re-constituted Encampment of Faith and Fidelity of which he had been the Eminent Commander. His attack on D'Eyncourt published in the *Quarterly Review* was vicious. "I much regret that there is no effectual method of teaching that brother that his elevated provincial Rank is conferr'd upon him for other purposes than that of attempting a stigma on one who is held in the highest esteem by all those whose good opinion in Masonry is worth obtaining". Many were of a similar opinion, though expressing it less forcibly. On the other hand, the Duke received strong support from those who considered that he had acted properly. That it was the Duke who had persuaded D'Eyncourt to act as he did is generally accepted. The Duke's animus against Crucefix and Oliver is more difficult to explain. His attitude towards Christian Masonry has been the subject of so many contradictory opinions expressed by eminent Masonic researchers that a consensus can hardly be reached[331].

The death of the Duke of Sussex on 21st April 1843 changed everything. There were, however, other theoretical obstacles to forming a Supreme Council of the Ancient and Accepted Rite for England. First, If the Council over which the Duke of Sussex had nominally presided could claim regularity, the 'Grand Constitutions' would not allow the formation of another in the same Kingdom. The Irish Masons had already ignored this by obtaining a Patent from the Supreme Council of the Southern Jurisdiction of the U.S.A. in 1826. But if the 'Kingdom of Great Britain and Ireland' was one 'Great Nation' within the terms of the 'Constitutions', the existence of the Irish Council would itself prohibit the formation of one in another part of that Kingdom.

No weight seems to have been given to either of these objections by Henry Beaumont Leeson[332], who had been born in 1803, six years after Crucefix. He was a Graduate of Cambridge University who had then qualified at St. Thomas's Hospital where he later became a Lecturer in Forensic Medicine, also being appointed Coroner for Greenwich. Having been Initiated in St. Mary's Lodge[333], he was Installed as a Knight Templar in the Cross of Christ Encampment on 16th December 1836, the same evening as that on which Crucefix was elected as its Eminent Commander. Leeson received the 'Rosae Crucis' and 'Kadosh' or *Ne Plus Ultra* Degrees from Crucefix in the following May. For some unexplained reason Leeson resigned from the Cross of Christ Encampment in the following December and shortly afterwards joined that of Faith and Fidelity where Henry Udall was also a member.

There is strong presumptive evidence that shortly after the death of the Duke of Sussex, Henry Leeson made his first visit to the Grand Orient of France in Paris, and opened negotiations with its Supreme Council; indeed, he may have been in touch with its Members somewhat earlier. This was not the self-styled legal successor of the Supreme Council founded in 1804 by de Grasse-Tilly which by now itself had somewhat dubious antecedents. The Council attached to the Grand Orient was not recognised as regular by either of the two American Supreme Councils. Even so Leeson appears to have had no scruples in maintaining his contacts; it has been said that he may even have reached the point at which he was prepared clandestinely to confer the 33rd Degree himself.

As its Director of Ceremonies, Crucefix was playing a leading part in the resurrection of the Grand Conclave of Knights Templar, but this did not distract him from his desire to see the Degrees of the Ancient and Accepted Rite brought under the supervision of a Supreme Council. He was more scrupulous than Leeson about the regularity of either of the French Supreme Councils. He therefore wrote to the Supreme Council 33° of the Northern Masonic District and Jurisdiction of the U.S.A. on 26th October 1845, requesting their authority for him to establish a Supreme Council of the Ancient and Accepted Rite in England. He indicated that there was some urgency about this in order to frustrate any attempt to establish a Council under the auspices of an irregular French body. It can only be presumed that, in saying this, Crucefix had Leeson's activities in mind. Furthermore, the 'Rosae Crucis' degree, the conferment of which Crucefix wanted to regularise, was as Christian as the Trinitarian Knights Templar Encampments in which it was being conferred.

It may be presumed that it was for this reason that Crucefix addressed his request to the still Christian Supreme Council of the Northern Masonic Jurisdiction of the U.S.A. and not to that of the implicitly 'Generalist' Southern Jurisdiction, 'the Mother Council of the World', which was, furthermore, in some disarray at this time.

On 10th November 1845 Crucefix again wrote to the Northern Jurisdiction emphasising the urgent need to frustrate any attempt from some other source to establish a Supreme Council in England. Both this and his earlier letter were brought before the American Council at its next Meeting on 23rd/24th December 1845. The Council did not act hastily. Both "the pressing state of matters in England" and the proposal made by Crucefix to ameliorate them were "fully investigated" before the Council resolved "That the interest of our Ill[ustriou]s. Order and its stability would no doubt be much forwarded and advanced in that Country by compliance to the wishes of our Petitioning Ill[ustriou]s. Brother". The Grand Secretary General, Charles Moore, was ordered to write officially to Crucefix to convey the decision of the Council, and to set out the grounds on which it had made it.

Moore's letter to Crucefix was dated 29th December 1845. He expressed the anxiety of his Sovereign Grand Commander, J.J.J.Gourgas, that there should be "a perfect harmony in the working and proceedings between the Supreme Grand Councils of the United States, of Scotland and of Ireland" and his belief that this would "be promoted, and the sooner secured, by the co-operation of our distinguished Sublime Brethren in England operating through a regularly and lawfully constituted Supreme Council". Moore then went on to say, "He is the more anxious on this point, in view of the irregular and unmasonic course which has been adopted and pursued by the Grand Orient of France; against any alliance with which, so far as Sublime Freemasonry is concerned, he particularly desires me to caution you."

Moore further emphasised the point by setting out "the conditions and sanctions under which the Patent you desire will be forwarded to you". He made it clear that the decision of his Supreme Council to grant a Patent had been considered "justifiable only by the emergency of the case". The Council had considered that it was only the opposition of the Duke of Sussex which had restrained "the high Masonic powers at Paris" from attempting to extend their jurisdiction to England, and "that restriction no longer existing they will soon, if they have not already [done so], direct their efforts to the attainment of this cherished object. To thwart them in this, should be the desire of every friend of our own pure and unadulterated rite." All this having been set out at considerable length, Moore only then went on to state the manner in which the English Supreme Council should be constituted. After this diatribe, Crucefix could hardly have been unaware of the views of the North American Council. However, when, in accordance with the instructions which he had been given, he appointed first Dr. Oliver as his Lieutenant Grand Commander, and then selected his "Grand Treasurer of H.E.", to which Office he appointed Henry Udall, each of whom had been his allies in his recent contretemps with the Duke of Sussex, he does not seem to have communicated, at least to the latter, the strictures against the French Grand Orient which Moore had set out in his covering letter. As instructed, each of the three counter-signed the Obligations of the two others, and Crucefix returned all three documents to Moore with a covering letter on 6th February 1846.

The American Council held meetings on the 20th and 27th March 1846, when it deemed the letter from Crucefix "A most satisfactory Communication". It then proceeded to nominate Crucefix "as an Honorary Member of our Supreme Council with full power and authority to form organize and establish agreeably to our Degree and its Grand Constitutions dated Berlin first May 1786 'The Grand and Supreme Council of the M[ost] P[uissant] Sovereigns Grand Inspectors General of the 33d degree for England to hold their Grand East in the City of London' whereof and of Right we appoint constitute and acknowledge him the said M.Ill. Robert Thomas Crucefix to be the founder and its first Most Puissant Sovereign Grand Commander *ad vitam* &c. &c. &c. *Ordered* that a *Patent* to that effect be furnished him dated 26 October 1845."[334] The Patent was to be sent to Crucefix by the steam-packet leaving on the first of April, together with full copies of the Rituals of the 30th, 31st, 32nd, and 33rd Degrees, a copy of the Grand Constitutions of May 1786, a copy of "Gd. Inspr. Stephen Morin's Patent of 27 August 1761", and a copy of the Oath of Allegiance. However, the package was ordered only to include the "S.W. g. t. & ob. of R + of h.r.d.m[335]." with no mention of the full Ritual of the 18th Degree.

The choice of Oliver as the first Lieutenant Grand Commander was inevitably well received by the Supreme Council of the Northern Masonic Jurisdiction. He had long been associated with Crucefix, and his writings were well known in the U.S.A. where they had made him perhaps the most highly esteemed English Freemason of his day. Henry Udall had also been closely associated with Crucefix for some years, but he was, perhaps, hardly an ideal choice because, although he had Chambers[336] in London, he was frequently absent from the Metropolis, being a member of the Northern Circuit.

However, with the addition of Henry Udall the 'English' Supreme Council was formally established in accordance with Article V, § II of the 'Grand Constitutions'[337]. Any attempt by Henry Leeson to obtain the sponsorship of the French Grand Orient had been thwarted by the promptitude with which the Supreme Council of the Northern Jurisdiction had acted. Apart from any niggling doubt about whether England, Ireland and Scotland were each 'Great Nations', and therefore each entitled to have its own Supreme Council, there was now a Supreme Council for England (Wales was nowhere mentioned in the Patent), the regularity of which was beyond question. There was, however, a formidable task to be faced – the new body had to be accepted as being responsible for the Degrees of 'Rosae Crucis' and 'Kadosh', and must persuade the Encampments throughout the country to allow these Degrees to be assimilated within the thirty-three Degrees of the Ancient and Accepted Rite.

305 "There was to be no Fourth degree as the Duke had anticipated, nor was any provision made for the government of the Royal Arch in the new *Book of Constitutions*." P.R. James, The Prestonian Lecture for *1962, The Grand-Mastership of HRH the Duke of Sussex,* The collected Prestonian Lectures (Vol. 2) p.22, Lewis Masonic (1983)

306 P.R. James, *Grand Lodge*, p.146 (O.U.P., 1967).

307 "The process of de-Christianising the Craft ritual and ceremonies, gradual since 1717, was now completed." P.R. James, The Prestonian Lecture for 1962, *loc. Cit.,* p.15.

308 Burckhardt had been appointed Deputy Grand Master *ad vitam* by the Duke of Sussex in 1812.

309 Hugh de Payens (Canada) 1824, Cornubian (Falmouth/Truro) 1826, and Loyal Brunswick (Plymouth) 1830, none of which is now on the English Register, are known to have been so founded, and there were probably one or two others prior to 1820 when Robert Gill's house in Soho was burnt down, and most of the early records of the Knights Templar Order were lost.

310 The Royal Sussex Encampment at Torquay, now No.25 on the Register of the United Orders.

311 For a time there may have been both a Rose Croix Chapter and also a Chapter of the Harodim Order meeting in the city. W.Waples, *An Introduction to the Harodim*, AQC, LX, p118, 1947.

312 In June 1795 Thomas Dunckerley had appointed Knight "Provincial Grand Master of Knights Templar for the County of Cornwall". 'Mitchell File', John Coombe Library, Hayle Masonic Centre, Cornwall.

313 *'Ne Plus Ultra'* is a phrase in the interpretation of which great caution has to be used. On some occasions it may have been used to denote a 'Rosae Crucis' or 'Rose Croix Degree', on others a 'Kadosh' Degree, and on rare occasions something quite different.

314 At about the same time, "About the year 1813 the

members of Baldwyn applied to the Emperor Napoleon of the French Grand Orient, for the correct working of the Orders of Chivalry (outside that of the Knights Templar and Hospitaler [*sic*]). The request was granted." Cecil Powell, 'Keeper of the Provl. Archives, Bristol', Preamble to a transcription of an old 'Baldwyn' Ritual ("which is very similar to that which we now follow" C.P.), signed and dated November 18th 1908. Numbered '1' in the Ritual Archives of The Supreme Council of England etc., 10 Duke Street, London.

315 The 'Articles of Agreement' were signed on 10th May 1881.

316 The Degrees in the 'Baldwyn' working are – *Elect of Nine, Scots Knight of Kilwinning, Knight of the East, Sword and Eagle, Knight Templar* and *Knight of the Rose Croix.*

317 Apart, that is, from the Mediterranean Pass and Knight of Malta.

318 See, for example, RC, p.24 *et seq.*

319 Willermoz corresponded with the Master of one of the Lodges in Metz, Meunier de Précourt, from whom he may have obtained information about German Rosicrucian Rites.

320 "it is computed that between the year 1803 and the signing of the Treaty of Paris of May, 1814, upwards of 122,000 enemy soldiers and sailors arrived in England, many of whom had been taken prisoners during the Peninsular War, in the West Indies, and in numerous naval engagements." John T. Thorp (Ed. Lionel Vibert), *French Prisoners' Lodges*, p.14 (2nd, Edition, augmented) The Lodge of Research No.2429, Freemasons' Hall, Leicester (1935)

321 Between 1803 and 1813 there were eventually 50 of these so-called 'Parole Towns', including 15 in Scotland and 5 in Wales. Thorp, *op. cit.*, p.22.

322 Lodges have been traced in 32 of the Parole Towns. *Ibidem*, p.30.

323 *Ibidem*, p.29.

324 It was the French custom, at least under the Grand Orient, that a Lodge could be regularly formed by 7 Masons in a town where there was no Lodge, or by 21 if there were already a Lodge there. The Rite generally practised was the *Rite Française en Moderne*, a 7-Degree Rite which had been adopted by the Grand Orient of France in 1786. It culminated in the 6th Degree, Knight of the East, and the 7th Rose Croix. Thorp, *op. cit., passim.*

325 The French Lodge in Abergavenny was the *Enfants de Mars et de Neptune.* 6 Certificates (Craft and Rose Croix) with de Grasse-Tilly's signature exist from 1813/4. For example, there is one in the name of Benjamin Plummer, the Grand Superintendent of the Baldwyn Knight Templar Encampment dated 20th July 1813. There was no Lodge under the United Grand Lodge of England in Abergavenny, and many local Brethren joined *Les Enfants*. When the prisoners returned home in 1814, 11 of these local Brethren, having first formed a Lodge of Instruction, received a Warrant for Philanthropic Lodge No. 658 (now No.818, in whose Lodge-room the Certificates are preserved). Plummer and Husenbeth were deputed to consecrate the Lodge, of which the first WM was the Vicar of Abergavenny, the Revd. William Powell. Thorp,*op.cit.,* pp46-69.

326 Now No.96. Crucefix subsequently joined Peace and Harmony Lodge (now No.60) which he represented as a Grand Steward in 1832, after which he was appointed to the Board of General Purposes of United Grand Lodge on which he served for five years, being promoted to Junior Grand Deacon in 1836.

327 Now the Preceptory of St. George No.6.

328 The first number of the *Freemasons' Quarterly Review* was published in April, 1834.

329 Oliver's Doctorate was a 'Canterbury' and not a Medical distinction.

330 The original St. Peter's Lodge was erased from the Grand Lodge Register in 1830 for non-payment of dues. After an abortive attempt to revive it, in 1836 Oliver was delegated by the Grand Master to constitute its present successor, St. Peter's Lodge, No.442.

331 For a more detailed account of these contumacious affairs see
•   P.R. James, *The Grand-Mastership of the Duke of Sussex* (The Prestonian Lecture for 1962). The Collected Prestonian Lectures 1961-1964, p.11, Lewis Masonic (1983);
•   P.R. James, *The Crucefix Oliver Affair,* AQC LXXIV, p.53 (1961);
•   R.S.E. Sandbach, *Priest and Freemason*, pp. 68-121, *passim*, Revd. Edition, Lewis Masonic (1993).

332 Leeson did not receive his MD until 1841, having been elected FRCP in the previous year, and becoming FRS eight years later. (J.W. Daniel – Private Communication, 2 Oct 2001.)

333 Now No.63.

334 There is no direct evidence as to why the Patent was back-dated to the date of the despatch of the original letter from Dr.Crucefix, rather than the date on which the decision to issue a Patent was taken, or even the date upon which the letter was received. It can only be speculated that this was to pre-empt the priority of any possible Patent from France, or, perhaps, so that it would pre-date the French Patent for a Supreme Council for Scotland.

335 'Sign, Word, grip, token and Obligation of the Rose Croix of Heredom'.

336 Essex Court, in The Temple.

337 "When the Most Potent Sovereign Grand Commander and the Deputy Grand Commander of THE ORDER are present, three members will constitute a Council, competent to transact the business of THE ORDER."

Essay 9
The early years of the 'Supreme Council for England'.

The Duke of Sussex had died in April 1843. There was no immediate rush to develop the Christian Higher Degrees about which, for various reasons, the Duke had been less than enthusiastic[338]. However, in 1819 he had found it expedient to become Sovereign Grand Commander of a Supreme Council of the Thirty-third Degree for 'Britain'. He appointed no more than the two additional Members necessary to give the Council a legal existence, and then successfully smothered it, with few being aware that it had ever existed. In 1826 the Duke of Leinster, the Lieutenant Grand Commander of the Duke's Supreme Council, had established a Supreme Council for Ireland, which presumably was considered to have made the Duke's 'British' Council a dead letter.

Many English Brethren were anxious to see the establishment of a Supreme Council for England. There were two principal reasons for this. Evidently the first was to work the thirty-three Degrees of the Ancient and Accepted Rite under proper authority, as was already being done in the territories of most of the principal Masonic powers on both sides of the Atlantic. Several English Brethren, among them senior members of the Craft, had already acquired, in one way or another, at least some of these Degrees. Secondly the 'Rosae Crucis' Degree, broadly equivalent to the 'Rose Croix' Degree of the Ancient and Accepted Rite, was being worked in the majority of Knights Templar Encampments as a progressive Degree from that of Knight Templar itself, without there being any superior body controlling its ritual and procedures.

In the 1830s and '40s there were two Supreme Councils in France. One could claim a somewhat shaky descent from the Supreme Council regularly established in Paris by de Grasse-Tilly in 1804. The other, the Supreme Council of the Grand Orient, had little claim to regularity, but was probably the more active of the two bodies. It has become evident that Doctor Henry Beaumont Leeson, possibly even before the death of the Duke of Sussex, had been in contact with the Supreme Council of the Grand Orient with a view to its sponsorship of a Supreme Council in England.

Leeson had been born in 1803, and was a graduate of Cambridge University. He qualified at St. Thomas's Hospital where he subsequently became a Lecturer in Forensic Medicine, also being appointed Her Majesty's Coroner for Greenwich[339]. He had been initiated in St. Mary's Lodge[340], and he was later Installed as a Knight Templar on 16th December 1836 in the Cross of Christ Encampment[341], receiving the Degrees of 'Rosae Crucis' and 'Kadosh' in the following May. Leeson resigned from the Cross of Christ Encampment in December, and later joined the newly Warranted Encampment of Faith and Fidelity[342].

On the same night as that on which Leeson had been Installed in the Cross of Christ Encampment, Doctor Robert Thomas Crucefix was elected as its Eminent Commander. Crucefix was six years older than Henry Leeson. He had qualified at St. Bartholomew's Hospital, after which he had spent a short time in India. On his return to England he was Initiated in the Burlington Lodge. In 1831 he practised for a short time in Edinburgh, where he was Installed as a Knight Templar in the Scottish Grand Conclave. On his return to London, Crucefix joined the Cross of Christ Encampment, receiving there the Degrees of 'Rosae Crucis' and 'Kadosh'. He joined Peace and Harmony Lodge[343] which he represented as a Grand Steward in 1832, and then for five years he served on the Board of General Purposes of United Grand Lodge, being promoted to Junior Grand Deacon in 1836.

His progress in Grand Lodge did not prevent Crucefix having a serious disagreement with the somewhat autocratic Grand Master, the Duke of Sussex. The original *casus belli* (that is not too strong a term) was the desire of Crucefix to found an 'Asylum for Aged and Decayed Freemasons'[344], a project of which the Duke disapproved because, so he said, he the Craft could not support another Charity. That Grand Lodge endorsed the foundation of the Asylum in spite of the Duke's opposition did nothing to endear Crucefix to his Grand Master. Crucefix compounded his offence first by promoting the concept of a Supreme Council in his journal, *The Freemasons' Quarterly Review,* of which he was the founder and Editor, and then by his vigorous support of the Reverend George Oliver, a Doctor of Divinity[345], whom Crucefix, in common with many others, considered had been unjustly deposed as Deputy Provincial Grand Master for Lincolnshire. Oliver, now more than fifty years of age, was recognised on both sides of the Atlantic as the leading authority on Masonic symbolism.

Crucefix had written in some haste to the Supreme Council of the Northern Jurisdiction of the United States of America on 26th October 1845 seeking a Patent for a Supreme Council in England, expressing his fear that if it were not forthcoming a Patent might be issued by the irregular Supreme Council of the French Grand Orient[346]. At its Meeting on the 23rd and 24th December 1845, the Council agreed to give a Patent to Doctor Crucefix. The Americans had the same fear of irregular French activity, and in their letter confirming their intention to provide a Patent, Crucefix was warned in the strongest terms to have nothing to do with the Grand Orient.

While these negotiations were in progress, preparations were being made in the Encampment of Faith and Fidelity to separate the Degrees of 'Rosae Crucis' and 'Kadosh' from that of Knights Templar. The 'Council' (in reality, the 'Standing Committee') of the Encampment had been asked to consider the matter, and its President, Henry Udall, reported their conclusions to the meeting of the Encampment on 31st January 1846. The recommendations were read out by Davyd Nash, the Knight Marshal, and, on Udall's proposition, it was thereupon agreed that the Encampment should be divided into three quasi-autonomous components. Henry Udall would be Grand Superintendent of the Encampment and continue to be the President of its Council. Within the Encampment itself only the Degrees of "Knights Templars, Knights of Malta and of the MP[347]" would be worked. There would then be "an Illustrious College of Knights KH and NPU" with Richard Lea Wilson as its President. Finally, Henry Beaumont Leeson was to be "MWS of the Sovereign Chapter of Princes Rose Croix".[348]

A Supreme Council may be established in 'unoccupied Territory' by a Sovereign Grand Inspector General being specifically delegated to do so. The ensuing Council has a legal existence when three of its members have been obligated. The American Supreme Council therefore first sent Crucefix three copies of the Obligation for the Thirty-third Degree. He selected Doctor Oliver as Lieutenant Grand Commander[349] and Henry Udall as Grand Treasurer General of the new Council, each of whom signed his own Obligation, and counter-signed those of the other two. Oliver's reputation in America as a Masonic writer ensured his acceptability by the Northern Supreme Council. Henry Udall, the Grand Superintendent of the Faith and Fidelity Encampment, was an obvious choice as "Grand Treasurer of H∴E∴". Moreover, he had supported Crucefix in his opposition to Oliver's dismissal from his Office in the Province of Lincolnshire. He was a well-respected Barrister with Chambers in the Temple, but his frequent absences from London as a Member of the Northern Circuit were to make his future position difficult.

When the Supreme Council of the Northern Jurisdiction received the signed Obligations, Crucefix was elected an Honorary Member of the Council, and as such he was empowered to establish the English Council in accordance with the 'Grand Constitutions of 1786'. He was also sent the Patent which established the Supreme Council for England (it contained no reference to Wales).[350] The Patent was dated 26th October 1845, the date of Crucefix's original letter to the Northern Council, presumably to frustrate any French attempt to establish priority for another Council. With the Patent, Charles Moore, the Grand Secretary General of the American Council, also conveyed to Crucefix a further strongly worded injunction from his Sovereign Grand Commander, J.J.J.Gourgas, to have no Masonic communication with the Supreme Council of the French Grand Orient. Henry Udall was afterwards to maintain that Crucefix did not tell his two colleagues about this prohibition at the time.

Since the 'Grand Constitutions' state that three members of a Council are competent "to transact 'the business of the Order'" there was therefore no immediate need for hurry in filling the remaining vacancies on the Council of nine members. What was more important was that although there was now a regularly established Supreme Council to govern the Order, there was as yet no Order for it to govern. However, a nucleus was provided by the steps which had already been taken in the Encampment of Faith and Fidelity to separate the 'Sovereign Chapter of Princes Rose Croix' from the working of its other Degrees. Moreover the Report which the Encampment had adopted charged Udall, Wilson and Leeson "to take such measures, as they may deem necessary, for the consolidating and establishing of those Degrees respectively"[351]. Evidently the three Brethren interpreted this as including permission to seek recognition from the new Supreme Council for the 'Sovereign Chapter'.

The 'Supreme Council for England' appears to have held its first formal Meeting on 24th June 1846. Evidently the Council maintained a record of its proceedings because it later recorded its frustration when Davyd Nash, the first Grand Secretary General H∴E∴, took its first Minute Book with him to Bristol when he gave up his Office in 1854. It was never seen again[352].

At its Meeting on 24th June 1846 the Council approved a Warrant (or 'Patent' as reference was then made to these authorisations) for its first subordinate Council. Six days later, on 30th June, there was a regular Meeting of the 'Sovereign Chapter of Princes Rose Croix' of the Encampment of Faith and Fidelity at which it transferred its allegiance to the new Supreme Council, accepting a Patent as the 'Metropolitan Chapter' (later to be called the 'Grand' Metropolitan Chapter)[353]. Leeson, the MWS of the Encampment's 'Sovereign Chapter' took the Chair, with Henry Udall acting as 'Pontiff' (Prelate). The only surviving report of this Meeting is that which appeared in *The Freemasons' Quarterly Review*. It records, *inter alia*, "... The Chapter was opened before four o'clock, and on its opening the M.W.Sovereign announced to the members that they had the honour of having for a visitor the illustrious Brother, Thomas Wright, S.G.I.G. 33rd, and Grand Secretary to the Grand Council in Ireland, who had come from Dublin to honour the first Chapter held under a warrant from the English Supreme Council ... It was then announced by the Most Wise Sovereign that, having accepted the duties of the Chair, his first duty was to inform the Chapter that their proceedings were entirely in accordance with the constitution of the Order, as he was acting under the express sanction of the Supreme Council for England and Wales... There were several eminent Brothers admitted to the distinguished rank of Princes Rose X, the entire proceedings being conducted with great solemnity ... At the end of the service, the Illustrious Brother, Thomas Wright, spoke in terms highly eulogistic of the whole proceedings, and characterised it as quite pure; he also, delivered a message from His Grace the Duke of Leinster, who (*sic*) he had this morning seen, stating his satisfaction felt by his Grace that the illustrious Brother was able to attend on the occasion ..." Two points of interest emerge from this. Evidently Leeson had not yet been Obligated as a member of the Supreme Council – had he been, he could hardly have forborne to mention it. Secondly, the new Supreme Council was evidently anxious to obtain the approval of the Supreme Council of Ireland, whose Sovereign Grand Commander, the Duke of Leinster, had been one of the three Members of the abortive Supreme Council which the Duke of Sussex had unwillingly formed in 1819. Indeed, the English Council maintained a close contact with that in Ireland for many years.

At the Meeting of the Supreme Council of the Northern Masonic Jurisdiction held on 23rd July 1846, it took note of an official communication from Dr. Crucefix stating that he had duly established the Supreme Council, for the first time described as "for England and Wales" although there was no mention of Wales in the Patent, that it would meet at Freemasons' Hall, London, and that this had been publicised in *The Freemasons' Quarterly Review*. The American Council then ordered further manuscript documents to be sent to Crucefix "by the Steamer of the first of August". These included "Statutes & Regulations for the 14th degree dated 25 October 1762, in 37 Articles for Lodges of Perfection (that is, 'The Grand Constitutions of 1762'), together with a variety of other documents.[354] The Council also took note that Henry Leeson, Richard Lea Wilson[355], Davyd Nash[356] and Thomas Pryer[357] had now been obligated as Members of the Council. (This brought the number of Members to seven, leaving two vacancies.) It was ordered that a Notice proclaiming the regular Constitution of the Supreme Council for England and Wales should be published in *The Freemasons' Monthly Magazine* at Boston. More contentiously (to what trouble this was to lead later!) the Supreme Council of the Northern Masonic Jurisdiction dismissed the legitimacy of the Supreme Council of the "33° Rite ancien et accepté for Scotland"[358], and proclaimed the Council of which Crucefix was now Sovereign Grand Commander as "the *only* Grand and Supreme Council of the 33d degree in *Great Britain* which they do or can recognise or acknowledge as constitutional and legal".

Although the American sponsor of his Supreme Council had cautioned Crucefix against having anything do with the Supreme Council of the French Grand Orient, on 3rd August 1846 Davyd Nash, as Grand Secretary General, addressed two letters to it. The first is headed by the regular seal of his Supreme Council, bearing the legend 'SUPREME COUNCIL XXXIII SOV GD INSP GEN'. It announces the formation of a Supreme Council in London, and seeks to establish "des relations intimes et fraternelles" by exchanging representatives. But the second letter, also received by the Grand Orient at the same time[359], differs significantly. While the note-paper bears the seal of the Supreme Council, as does the first letter, below it there is a second seal, apparently produced by a rubber-stamp, with the inscription 'GRAND COUNCIL OF RITES FOR ENGLAND AND WALES' and the letter is headed "A l'Orient du Grand Conseil des Rites pour Angleterre et Galles assemblé à Londres". It announces to the Council of Rites of the Grand Orient of France that the Grand Council of Rites for England and Wales had been "regulièrement formé organisé et assemblé" and, as does the first letter, seeks an exchange of Representatives. Whatever was going on? A Council of Rites had been established in Ireland for several years, ostensibly to absorb the irregular Orders of Misraim and Memphis, with, it subsequently stated, no intention of doing anything except to suppress them, but there were no grounds for the statement in Nash's letter. There is no doubt that the English Supreme Council had close relations with that of Ireland, and one can only suppose that Nash, at least, considered it appropriate to follow the Irish example. A rubber-stamp would hardly have been commissioned and impressed if Nash, at least, had not been serious about 'The Council of Rites', but no other reference to it has been found.

The Grand Orient considered both these two letters at its meeting on 17th August 1846, and apparently decided to ignore the second one referring to a 'Council of Rites', as there is no record of a reply to it. However, it treated with amicable caution the request, set out in the first letter, for recognition of the new Supreme Council. On 29th August it replied, seeking further information, which the Council in London provided in a voluminous response dated 21st September 1846. This included a manuscript facsimile transcription of the Patent which had been received from the Supreme Council of the Northern Masonic Jurisdiction. This was subscribed by a statement, signed both by Udall as Grand Treasurer H.˙.E.˙. and by Leeson as Grand Chancellor[360], "We hereby certify and declare that the above is a faithful and correct copy and was examined and compared by us with the original Warrant as Witness our hands and seals this twenty First day of September 1846" – except that it wasn't! The copy states that the new Supreme Council was for 'England Wales &c', while the original specifies 'England' only. In spite of this significant emendation, the Council in London carefully headed both its covering letter and its list of Members only as 'pour l'Angleterre'[361].

The covering letter contains one other matter of interest. It not only expresses the pleasure of the English Supreme Council at the friendly tone of the letter which had been received from the Grand Orient, but also offers its thanks for the kindness shown by the Grand Orient to Dr. Leeson[362], "récemment à Paris". This is the only specific contemporary reference extant to Leeson visiting the Grand Orient[363].

Before the end of 1846 William Tucker[364] had been Obligated as a member of the Supreme Council and appointed Grand Almoner, leaving one vacancy to be filled.

On 24th February 1847, Crucefix presided over a meeting of the Supreme Council at which International relations were discussed. The appointment of Bro. Edward A. Raymond was confirmed as the representative of the English Supreme Council near that of the Supreme Council of the Northern American Jurisdiction, which had already accepted Henry Udall as its representative near the English Council. But, in view of the admonition conveyed in Moore's earlier letters, it is extraordinary that Leeson was accepted by the other Members of the English Supreme Council as the representative in England of the Supreme Council of the Grand Orient of France, and Bro. A. Bugnot as the representative of the English Council near that of the Grand Orient, the more so since Crucefix had apparently been aware of the doubtful antecedents of the latter even before he had received the views of the American Supreme Council. It is hard to believe that the appointments would have been approved had the Members of the Council been fully told of the contents of Moore's letter of 29th December 1845 in which he had made it clear that the grant of the Patent was consequent upon no such relationship being established.

The appointment of these Representatives was published in *The Freemasons' Quarterly Review*. When this was brought to the attention of the Supreme Council of the Northern Masonic Jurisdiction, they reacted swiftly. Dr. Crucefix received a sealed package with a covering letter dated 3rd September 1847 saying that the seals were only to be broken at the next formal meeting of the Council. When this took place on 23rd September, and the sealed package was opened, its Members were confronted with "a denunciation of our proceedings in the Paris affair and a declaration that all intercourse must cease with them until we had returned to the principles contained in the Grand Constitutions of the Order and had attended to the instructions sent to us in the letter of their Secretary Genl. Br. Moore"[365]. According to Henry Udall, it was then for the first time that the Members learnt of the contents of Moore's letter which had preceded the issue of the Patent and "we found we had done what was quite unjustifiable and could only excuse ourselves on the ground of ignorance". It is possible that the relationship with the Grand Orient was not the only matter in which the Supreme Council of the Northern Masonic Jurisdiction considered that the English Council had departed from "the principles contained in the Grand Constitutions of the Order". In the fairly full reports in *The Freemasons' Quarterly Review* there is no mention of the conferment of any of the 'Intermediate Degrees' by the English Supreme Council before December 1847. Knights Templar who now wished to become Princes Rose Croix may well have considered themselves already qualified to do so without going through the rigmarole of the 'Intermediate Degrees'.

Perhaps the English Council was unduly influenced by Leeson or considered it injudicious to antagonise him; the Council was as yet hardly well established and a French Patent for a rival Council would have been disastrous had Leeson withdrawn with the intention of setting up such a body. At all events, its Members seem to have ignored the strictures which had been placed upon them, and there is no record of any reply being made to the North American Council at this time.

Indeed, Leeson was evidently continuing to foster his close friendship with the Supreme Council of the French Grand Orient. On 15th September 1847 he was sent, as a token of his appointment as their Representative, a sash or "Cordon du G[rand].˙.O[rient].˙.". Subsequent events were to prove that common courtesy was not always Leeson's predominant characteristic and his acknowledgement of this was not received by the Grand Orient until 13th March in the following year. Leeson excused himself for this delay by saying that on several occasions he had had to be away from London. His letter of thanks is written in sufficiently idiomatic French to make a literal translation almost impossible, unlike Nash's more pedestrian writings. The intimate relationship which Leeson maintained with his French Brethren is illustrated by his addressing his reply personally to Pillote, "Secretaire du G.˙.O.˙.de France", while Nash's letters were formally addressed to the French Council.

At the meeting of the Council on 9th December 1847, it first received "a highly satisfactory account of the financial affairs of the Supreme Council" from Henry Udall. Nash then repeated the announcement not only of the appointment of the representatives to and from the Northern Masonic Jurisdiction Supreme Council, but also those of Leeson and Bugnot to and from the Supreme Council of the French Grand Orient, this last presumably occasioned by Leeson's receipt of the Grand Orient sash. Curiously, in spite of the severance of all communications by the Supreme Council of the NMJ, at the meeting of the English Council on 12th June 1848 it was informed that it had been among the recipients of a manifesto from the American Council denouncing the spurious Councils of Joseph Cerneau[366] and of Elias Hicks. At a meeting later in the year (at which representatives of the Supreme Council of the 'Brazils' were also present), the healths were drunk of J.J.J. Gourgas, the Sovereign Grand Commander of the Supreme Council of the NMJ, and of his fellow S.G.I.G.'s, as if nothing had happened.

In September 1846 the four-year reign of John Harris as Eminent Commander of the Mount Calvary Encampment of Knights Templar had come to an end and Thomas Pryer succeeded him, being Installed on St. John's Day, 27th December. At that Meeting, there was set up a Committee to consider the future conduct of the 'Superior Degrees' in the Encampment, as 'Faith and Fidelity' had done in the previous year. On 28th February 1848 Pryer reported the result of the Committee's deliberations and it was resolved to seek a Patent for the Encampment's Rose Croix Chapter from the Supreme Council. The Patent, dated 6th June 1848, is signed by the 7 Members of the Supreme Council whose names had appeared in the American Council's announcement with the addition of that of Tucker, strong presumptive evidence that at this time there was still one unfilled vacancy. The Rose Croix Chapter was consecrated on 12th June, but there was no further meeting until 17th December 1849, and though Pryer continued as its MWS until his death in 1851, the Chapter did not meet again in his life-time. Indeed, for several years the Encampment appears to have regarded its involvement with the Supreme Council as more or less a formality and the Chapter's Patent as one of Confirmation rather than of Constitution[367].

On the other hand in the years after its Constitution, Metropolitan Chapter met on several occasions to Perfect Brethren. From time to time the Supreme Council also constituted itself into a Rose Croix Chapter for the same purpose. Since for some years, many of the Officers of Metropolitan Chapter were Members of the Supreme Council, this has led to some confusion, even to statements that Metropolitan Chapter was simply"'the Chapter of the Supreme Council'. The Supreme Council also performed other Advancements, and not only to the 30th, 31st, and 32nd Degrees. It seems possible that some attempt was made to work the 'Intermediate Degrees' in extenso. Otherwise it is difficult to know what to make of the Press report that on 17th December 1847 there was held "a Grand Council of Princes of Jerusalem of the 16th degree", at which it was resolved "That the petition of the Grand Scotch Knights and Knights of the Sword and the East, this day presented and read to this Grand Council, being in form and approved, the degree of Grand Princes of Jerusalem shall be conferred on the petitioners at the next meeting of the Grand Council on the 9th of February next". Incidentally, the Report of this meeting is the first occasion on which The Supreme Council is described as "for England and Wales and the dependencies of the British Crown".

Again, on 12th June 1848 two Brethren were admitted to the Thirty-second Degree, two to the Thirty-first, and then "several Knights of St. Andrew, 29th, of the Sun, 28th, and others" were Advanced to the Thirtieth Degree. One of the Brethren Advanced to the Thirty-second Degree was John A. D. Cox, which negates the claim which has frequently been made that Cox was a member of the Supreme Council as early as 1847[368].

Finally, it is uncertain for how long Pryer retained his seat on The Supreme Council after the acceptance of a Patent by the Mount Calvary Chapter. There is only one further mention of him in the Press reports, and it seems probable that at some time before 1850 he resigned, thereby creating a second vacancy on the Council, the number of nine members then being completed by the election of Henry Emly and Frederick Winsor.

Appendix

Verbatim extract from Henry Udall's explanatory letter to
Sir John de la Pole dated 3rd July 1856

"Not very long after the English Council had been formed Dr. Leeson the then Grand Chancellor of the Order went to Paris and was after his arrival there accredited to the Supreme Council in the Grand Orient which is regarded as a Spurious Council and had, without my knowledge or the knowledge of Dr. Leeson, been so declared in the most solemn manner by our Parent Council; the only body ever acknowledged by it in France being "The Supreme Council of France" established AD 1805 by the Supreme Council of the Southern Jurisdiction of America, holding its Grand East at Carolina. When the fact that we had fraternised with the Grand Orient came to the knowledge of our Parent Council no time was lost by its members in communicating their views of our conduct. At the next meeting of our Council our late Sov Commr Dr. Crucefix produced a package from America unopened, addressed to the Supreme Council and he was further instructed by letter that the seals were not to be broken until after the Supreme Council had been solemnly opened under the most formal obligations of the Order. In opening the package, we found a denunciation of our proceedings in the Paris affair and a declaration that all intercourse must cease with them until we had returned to the principles contained in the Grand Constitutions of the Order and had attended to the instructions sent to us in the letter of their Secretary Genl Br Moore. On their letter being referred to, we found we had done what was quite unjustifiable, and could only excuse ourselves on the grounds of ignorance. This transaction necessarily impressed itself strongly on my mind and I came to a determination to make myself fully acquainted with the laws of the Order and the letters containing the terms on which the American Council granted us our Warrant (*sic*). Our Parent Council remained highly displeased with us for some years, when being myself the Representative in our Council of the American Council I wrote a letter in 1851 to our Representative on the American Supreme Council, extracts of which you will find enclosed with this statement. Matters from that moment began to amend and before the end of the year, I had a letter from the Ills Br Yates Lt Gd Commr stating that my letter had given great satisfaction to their Council and in a letter dated the 5th of May AD. 1852 the Ills Br Gourgas wrote to me thus 'Last Summer during my stay in the vicinity of Boston our brethren handed me over your communication to Br R. I then directed them to answer it forthwith *reestablishing* at once on the most friendly footing our former fraternal relations which I always regretted had been interrupted through an early ill advised mismanagement'. In June 1852 at one of the most important meetings ever held of the Order, in the presence of the Earl of Donoughmore, General Chatterton and other distinguished brethren, I, on giving out the Patents of several Rose Croix Chapters, took occasion to explain the organization of the Order and the obligation we were under to see that that organization was not departed from. To prevent any error of my own in a matter of this importance I read from the letters sent by the American Council their instructions as to that organization. The substance of what took place was published in the June number of the Masonic Quarterly (to which I would thank you to refer) and from that time the greatest good feeling has existed between the respective Councils. In a letter dated Oct 4th 1852 Ills Br Gourgas writing to me said 'I felt much gratified to perceive by the published account in the June number of the Quarterly Magazine that your Supreme Council was so far favourably progressing in the *regular constitutional organization* of the "Ancient and Accepted Rite" and that you had taken special pains not only to explain but also to invigorate the good work by sound precepts for the *strict performance* of those duties to which we are all equally so sacredly bound.' The American Council has from that time spoken of us in the published reports in terms of the highest praise and especially on the ground of our pursuing *a course of strict legality*."

338 John Burckhardt did not summon the Grand Conclave of Knights Templar, of which he was the Deputy Grand Master *ad vitam*, for nearly three years after the Duke's death, although he gave Warrants to two new Encampments over his own signature while attempting to maintain contact with all the Encampments that had survived.

339 Leeson did not receive his MD until 1841, having been elected FRCP in the previous year. Eight years later he was elected a Fellow of the Royal Society. (J.W. Daniel, private communication, 2 Oct 2001.)

340 Now No.63.

341 Now Preceptory of St. George, No.6, Warranted 26th October 1795.

342 Now No.26, Warranted 12th September 1838.

343 Now No.60.

344 Now the Royal Masonic Benevolent Institution.

345 Oliver had been awarded a 'Canterbury' and not a University Doctorate.

346 There is no certain evidence as to the reason why Crucefix applied to the Council of the Northern Masonic Jurisdiction, and not to that of the Southern, 'The Mother Council of the World'. While the Southern Council had always been, to all intents and purposes, 'Generalist', the Council of the Northern Jurisdiction was still Christian. Crucefix wanted the 'Rosae Crucis' and 'Kadosh' Degrees to be worked under his new Supreme Council, and since the Order of Knights Templar which currently worked the Degrees was explicitly Trinitarian Christian, it can only be presumed that he preferred to have Christian sponsors.

347 (Mediterranean Pass.)

348 Matthew Christmas, *A Short Account of the Origins and Early History of the Grand Metropolitan Chapter*, p.4 (July 1996).

349 Among the stipulations in Moore's letter of 29th December 1845 for the issuing of the Patent was "you will, if possible, appoint Dr.Oliver, your Lieut∴ Grand Commander".

350 Crucefix was also sent a wealth of documentation together with the Rituals of the Degrees up to and including the Thirty-second, with the exception that in respect of the Eighteenth there is only a record of his being sent the Sign, Token, Word and Obligation of the Degree.

351 Matthew Christmas, *op. cit.*

352 Because of the absence of a Minute Book and other contemporary Council records, its history prior to July 1854 (when its first extant Minute Book commences) has to be pieced together from the Minutes of old Chapters, surviving contemporary correspondence, and reports in the Masonic Press, the latter treated with particular caution because of the endemic fallibility of journalistic reporting. A notable source is a bundle of letters written by Henry Udall, and other relevant correspondence found in the archives of the Supreme Council in 10 Duke Street. Another more exotic source is the files containing letters written from the English Council to the French Grand Orient in defiance of the American prohibition. These files were seized by the Germans in Paris and formed part of an anti-Masonic exhibition in Berlin in 1942. They were subsequently discovered by the Russians and taken to Moscow. Since the year 2000 the Russian authorities have returned these documents piecemeal to the Grand Orient, and photocopies of those relevant to the English Supreme Council have been made available through the courtesy of M. Pierre Mollier, Directeur de Service, Bibliothèque-Archives-Musée, Grand Orient de France, to whom the present Author's grateful thanks are due.

353 Subsequently given the Number '1'; Chapters did not receive 'permanent' numbers until 1880, the first Chapter to be given a number on its Warrant being 'Albert Edward' on 7th December of that year.

354 These documents included "Statutes and Regulations for the 15th Knights of the East, 16 art., Duties and Privileges Princes of Jerusalem 16th Degree, 13 art., ordinances Sov. Pces. R **+** of h.r.d.m.18th Degree". (The last is the only one of these documents which has so far been provisionally identified in the Archives in 10 Duke Street.) Also "Signs, Words and Tokens from the 4th to 18th, 19-29" noting that those for the 30th, 31st and 32nd had already been sent.

355 Wilson had been born in 1807, and Initiated in 1830. He was Installed a Knight Templar in the Cross of Christ Encampment, thereafter taking the 'Rosea Crucis' and 'Kadosh' Degrees in April 1835. He also became a member of 'Faith and Fidelity', and was nominated as 'President of the College of Knights KH and NPU' therein (*vide supra*).

356 Davyd Nash was a Bristol mason who had been initiated in 1832 in the Royal Sussex Lodge of Hospitality on that City. He was a member of the Encampment of Faith and Fidelity of which he was Knight Marshal.

357 Thomas Pryer was a Solicitor who had been initiated in1841 at the age of 26. Two years later he was Installed as a Knight Templar in the Cross of Christ Encampment. He received the remaining Degrees conferred in the Encampment on Trinity Sunday,1845, becoming its Eminent Commander in 1847. It may be presumed that such a relatively inexperienced Brother was elected to the Council with a view to obtaining the adherence of the Rose Croix Chapter of the third of the influential London Encampments.

358 The Supreme Council for Scotland had accepted a Patent from the Supreme Council in France which was abhorred by the Council of the Northern Jurisdiction.

359 The file reference numbers of the G.O. are consecutive – 3/418 and 3/419 – and both letters were considered by the G.O. on 17th August.

360 Leeson also added ' H∴E∴' to his title.

361 'du Saint Empire' is appended to the appointment of *each* of the five Members (Udall, Leeson, Wilson, Nash, Pryor) other than Crucefix and Oliver.

362 'son ambassadeur prés de vous' (*sic*).

363 There is also a reference to Leeson's visit in Henry Udall's long letter of explanation which he addressed to the Supreme Council on 3rd July 1856.

364 William Tucker was a West Country Mason who had been Initiated in 1842. Not only had he been appointed Provincial Grand Master for Dorset in the Craft in 1846, but he was also Provincial Grand Master of Knights Templar in the County, as well as Eminent Commander of the Coryton Encampment of which Colonel Charles Kemeys Kemeys Tynte, shortly

to be elected Grand Master of the Grand Conclave of Knights Templar, was also a Member.

365 Udall letter file.

366 Whether de la Motta's Supreme Council of the Northern Jurisdiction erected in 1813 or 1815 had any more claim to legitimacy than that purported to have been established by Cerneau is still a matter for dispute, although the passage of time has in practice made the argument irrelevant. See, for example Michael Poll, *The philalethes*, p.84 *et seq.* (June 2001).

367 See:
Ewen McEwen, *The Mount Calvary Encampment* pp.21-24 undated (? 1990).
H.V. Wiles, *Mount Calvary Chapter Rose Croix, No.3*, 1848–1948, pp.36/37 (1948).

368 It is noteworthy that so many of those brethren who were anxious to see The Supreme Council established as the Governing Body of, *inter alia*, the 'Rosae Crucis' and 'Kadosh' Degrees conferred in Knights Templar Encampments, were Officers of Grand Conclave. At the Meeting of Grand Conclave in April 1848, Dr. Leeson succeeded Henry Udall as 'Grand Second Captain', John A.D. Cox was appointed Grand Registrar, Matthew Dawes was re-appointed Grand Chamberlain, Henry Emly was in the second year of a four-year appointment as Grand Almoner, and Captain Vernon was appointed First Great Aide de Camp. In addition, William Tucker was Provincial Grand Commander of Knights Templar in Dorset, and Thomas Crucefix himself was Provincial Grand Commander for Kent. Furthermore, in 1848 and 1849 influential members of the A & A Rite were in the majority on the Grand Conclave Committee – Crucefix, Udall, Leeson, Wilson and Cox.

Essay 10
1850-1854 – Henry Udall guides the affairs of the Supreme Council.

The loss of its first Minute Book adds to the difficulty of discovering what took place within the Supreme Council prior to July 1854. Before Thomas Crucefix died after a long illness on 25th February 1850, the Supreme Council probably had its full complement of nine Members[369]. On the death of Crucefix, Oliver, the Lieutenant Grand Commander, automatically took his place as Sovereign Grand Commander in accordance with the Second Section of Article Three of the 'Grand Constitutions'. These do not, however, provide a statutory right for any particular Brother to be promoted to Lieutenant Grand Commander when a vacancy occurs in that Office. It is not easy to see why the Grand Chancellor, Dr. Henry Leeson, was appointed. Henry Udall, the Grand Treasurer General, as the third of the Founders of the Council, might have been expected to have succeeded Oliver, but he apparently waived whatever claim which he might have had. There is no doubt that Leeson had a forceful personality, and it may have been considered inadvisable to oppose his wishes. Possibly there was a more practical consideration. Henry Udall was frequently absent, undertaking his professional legal duties in the North of England, and Oliver himself rarely visited London. It may have been thought undesirable, if not impractical, for both of the two most senior Members of the Council frequently to be unavailable[370].

The vacancy in the Council numbers left by the death of Crucefix was not filled until the election of John Astell Deacon Cox in the following year[371]. He may well have been considered a valuable acquisition. As Grand Registrar of the Grand Conclave of Knights Templar from 1848 to 1860 he was in a position of some influence from which to encourage 'Rosae Crucis' Knights Templar to affiliate to the Supreme Council.

In the spring of 1851 Dr. Oliver resigned his Office at the Head of the Council, and reverted to that of Lieutenant Grand Commander. The reasons for his decision to step down as Sovereign Grand Commander are as obscure as are those for Leeson's earlier promotion. Five years later Oliver's letter of resignation as Lieutenant Grand Commander casts only a little light on them. Oliver wrote "I have long felt the incongruity of retaining the Incumbency of an Office whose duties I do not feel myself physically competent to discharge. Brother Udall and others are acquainted with the reasons which originated the policy of this measure, but these no longer exist and therefore in April 1851 I not only resigned the dignity of Most Puissant Sovereign Grand Commander which devolved on me at the death of our late Illustrious Brother Crucefix in favour of Dr. Leeson but requested leave to retire from the Lieutenancy. It was not at that period considered expedient, and I was pressed to retain it for a few years longer.[372]"

There may have been a pressing reason why the Council did not accept the resignation of George Oliver in 1851, persuading him to remain a Member by reverting to the position of Lieutenant Grand Commander. When the Supreme Council of the Northern Masonic Jurisdiction had granted the Patent for the English Supreme Council, it had categorically stated that this was conditional upon the English Council having no relations with the Supreme Council of the Grand Orient of France. Even if Henry Leeson had been aware of this prohibition, he had ignored it. As a result, in 1848 the Northern Masonic Jurisdiction had broken off relations with the English Council. Now, three years later, Henry Udall, who in some way seemed to consider himself to be the conscience of the English Council, was anxious to engineer a *rapprochement* with its sponsors. This might well have been impossible if Leeson, whose French connections made him mistrusted by the Northern Jurisdiction, became Sovereign Grand Commander of the English Council, while Oliver, whom the Americans esteemed and trusted, was then no longer seen to be playing a part in its affairs, if only in name. Udall, anxious not to offend the Northern Jurisdiction further, would have been well aware of this, and Oliver's statement may indicate that his unwilling re-acceptance of the Office of Lieutenant Grand Commander was in some measure due to Udall's urging.

The first Meeting of the Supreme Council with Henry Leeson at its head appears to have taken place on 8th May 1851. Henry Emly and Frederick Winsor had 'retired'[373] from the Council, and their places had been taken by Sir John Robinson, Bart. of "Rokeby Hall, Dunlear"[374], and by Captain Arthur Quinn Hopper.

Leeson evidently considered that the Supreme Council was sufficiently well established to broaden its activities. On 16th May 1851, after a meeting at which the Thirtieth Degree was conferred on several Brethren, the first Meeting of "The High Grades Masonic Union" took place. This body was to "banquet together four times annually; no Brother being eligible for election who has not attained the rank of 30th Degree of the Order"[375]. Furthermore, at the same time Colonel Vernon was appointed as the Chairman of a Board of Stewards to arrange a Summer Festival of the Order at which would be entertained visitors from other Jurisdictions visiting the Great Exhibition at the Crystal Palace[376].

A few weeks later Nash, the Grand Secretary General, circulated a Summons dated 6th June 1851, in which he stated that the Supreme Council would hold a 'Solemn Convocation' on the following 3rd July. The document went on to say that:

> all S.P. of the R.S. of the 32nd degree, all members of the 31st degree, and all G.E. Kts. K.H. of the 30th degree are required to attend.
>
> A Grand Council of G.E. Kts. K.H. will be holden as above for the reception of Candidates; after which a Sov. Chapter of Princes R. + of H.R.D.M. of the 18th degree will be opened, at which all Princes R. + of H.R.D.M. will be admitted.
>
> Brethren wishing to be exalted to these degrees should write to me, directed "Freemasons' Hall, London".[377]

It may be possible to read too much into this wording. However, it perhaps indicates that Leeson was prepared to depart in some measure from the 'Grand Constitutions', not only by omitting the conferment of the Intermediate Degrees before Princes Rose Croix (and subsequently Knights Kadosh) were 'exalted', but even by ignoring the necessity for Brethren to be elected to the Higher Degrees by the Supreme Council *per se*.

However, a month earlier, in May 1851, Udall, wishing to restore the regularity of the English Council in the eyes of its North American sponsor, had written, as its former Representative in England, to his opposite number in Boston, Edward Raymond. He first said that since "the melancholy death of our late Commander I have had the opportunity of carefully looking over parts of the American correspondence that took place between your Council and our late lamented Commander", presumably, that is to say, Moore's letters of 29th December 1845 and 20th March 1846, each of which pronounced an anathema on the Supreme Council of the French Grand Orient. Udall then goes on to say that "if those letters had been before me I should have considered that we on receiving your Warrant morally contracted with you that we should govern our Council by those leading principles so ably stated in the letters", and goes on to accept that the Council's dealings with the Grand Orient in Paris were contrary to this. He does not, he continues, seek "to exculpate myself. Considering the responsible position I occupied in the Council I ought to have asked to have the whole correspondence before me." Had he done so, he then says, he would not have consented to the error being made, and, he adds, that was also the view of other members of the Council. Udall pleads that it was an accident – after denying that it was a proposition made by Crucefix, he explains that Leeson was in Paris, waiting for instructions, and "had refused an introduction to meet 'the Duc de Cayes'[378] (*sic*) the head of the Supreme Council and he wished to be instructed how he was to act, it having become known that a Member of our Supreme Council was in Paris. We were all very insufficiently acquainted with the history of the Order and at the moment thought that we ought to fraternise with the G.O and this seems to have been done by acclamation. I recall well what had influenced me at the time in consenting to that act was the scandal maliciously disseminated in this Country against your honoured Commander and the character of your Supreme Council by one whom we believed to represent the Sentiments of the Supreme Council of France. It has luckily happened that nothing had been done to revive our official correspondence since Bro. Leeson was in Paris, the all absorbing event of the Revolution having made all other subjects except Politics too tame for National intercommunication. No doubt in this year of universal fraternity many of the most distinguished members both of the G.O. and the Supreme Council will be guests at our Banquet. Our hospitality will compel us to give them a hearty welcome but until we are very much better acquainted than we are with all the proceedings and *a better understanding exists* in both Hemispheres I believe no attempt will be made *certainly not with my consent* to revive any such official connection on the Continent"[379].

It seems probable that it was indeed the events of 1848 – 'The Year of Revolutions' – that had prevented further intercourse between the Supreme Council and the Grand Orient, rather than any deliberate decision on the Council's part. The "year of universal fraternity" referred, of course, to the "Great Exhibition of 1851" during which the 'Summer Festival' of the Supreme Council was to be held. Each of these occurrences was in a sense fortuitous – the one had ended correspondence with the Grand Orient, and the other provided a reason for being unable to avoid a renewed contact.

Udall's letter, and his explanation of the Council's actions, might be thought to be a shade unconvincing, but before the end of the year he received a reply from Giles Yates, the Lieutenant Grand Commander of the Supreme Council of the Northern Jurisdiction, in which he said that Udall's letter had given the Council "great satisfaction". This was followed by a letter to Udall, dated 5th May 1852, from J.J.J. Gourgas, the Sovereign Grand Commander of the Supreme Council of the Northern Jurisdiction, in which he said that "Last Summer during my stay in the vicinity of Boston our brethren handed me over your communication to Bro.R[aymond]. I then directed them to answer it forthwith *reestablishing* at once on the most friendly footing our former fraternal relations which I always much regretted had been interrupted through an early ill advised mismanagement."[380]

The second Summer Festival of the Supreme Council took place on 9th June 1852. It was said to be held "under the sanction of the Supreme Council of Sovereign Grand Inspectors for England and Wales and the Dependencies of the British Crown", the first time this unauthorised designation had been used. Udall took the opportunity to clarify the manner in which its North American sponsor expected the Degrees of the Rite to be conferred. Before he did so, Cox opened Metropolitan Chapter, of which he was now MWS, "and exalted several Brethren to the rank of Sov. Prince Rose Croix". Neither Leeson, the Sovereign Grand Commander, nor Oliver were present at the Festival, and Udall took over the meeting. He first said that the Supreme Council had acceded to four Petitions for 'Patents' for Rose Croix Chapters. Three of these, he said, he was able to hand over to the respective Most Wise Sovereigns, that for Coryton to William Tucker, for Vernon to Colonel Vernon and that for Palatine to Matthew Dawes. (The three recipients were respectively the Provincial Grand Commanders of Knights Templar for each of the Provinces in which the new Chapters were situated.) William Hancock, the first MWS of Weymouth Chapter, the second Chapter in Tucker's Templar Province of Dorset, was not present to receive his 'Patent' in person.

Then, as Udall afterwards wrote, "in the presence of the Earl of Donoughmore, General Chatterton and other distinguished brethren, I, . . took occasion to explain the organization of the Order and the obligation we were under to see that that organization was not departed from. To prevent any error of my own in a matter of this importance I read from the letters sent by the American Council their instructions as to that organization."

The letters were presumably the documents referring to the 'Intermediate Degrees' which had been sent to Crucefix by the steamer of 1st August 1846. According to the report in the *Masonic Quarterly Review*, Udall started by saying that "as the laws of the Order were given to them with great precision, and as the Grand Lodges of Perfection, Princes of Jerusalem and Sov. Chapters would have to abide by them, he would state to the Convocation the organisation that they, as Sov. Grand Inspectors, must see enforced". After stressing that the A. & A. Rite did not interfere with "Craft or symbolic Masonry", and that the Rite "begins *from* that of Master Mason", and that only Master Masons from Regular Lodges could be received into it, he described the bodies which should be established under a Supreme Council. Udall was evidently envisaging the 'Intermediate Degrees' each being conferred in full in a distinct Lodge or other appropriate convocation, each with its own Officers, as is the case both in the U.S.A. and under the Supreme Council of France today. There should, he said, then be a Grand Lodge of Perfection having Jurisdiction over the Degrees 4th-14th inclusive. "This," the report of his statement continues, "should, as far as possible, be a Representative Council, and be composed of those who are in authority, as being head of the Degrees over which it had control." He went on to say that there should be a second body "A Grand Council of Princes of Jerusalem, which exercised jurisdiction over the Fifteenth and Sixteenth Degrees, and all Grand Lodges of Perfection. The body," he continued, "should be so composed as to represent fairly the Lodges and Chapters over which it had control". A Sovereign Chapter Rose Croix exercised authority over the Seventeenth and Eighteenth Degrees. Finally, Udall said, "A Sov(ereign) Grand Consistory of S.P.R.S. ... confers from the Nineteenth to the Twenty-ninth Degree inclusive of its own right," adding that of course each body was subject to the Supreme Council which alone conferred the Thirtieth and Higher Degrees[381].

Whether, and if so, to what extent, this complex organisation was put into effect (and there may have been some attempts to do so), the report in the Masonic Press of Udall's considerable oration was well received in the U.S.A. On 4th October 1852 Gourgas wrote to Udall that he "felt much gratified to perceive by the published account in the June number of the *Quarterly Magazine* that your Supreme Council was so far favorably progressing in the *regular constitutional organization* of the 'Ancient and Accepted Rite' and that you had taken special pains not only to explain but also to invigorate the good work by sound precepts for the *strict performance* of those duties to which we are all equally most sacredly bound". The published reports from the Northern Jurisdiction thereafter stress the Council's satisfaction with the manner in which the English Council was carrying out its duties.

Whatever procedure was in reality initially adopted by the English Council in respect of the 'Intermediate Degrees', there is little doubt that its primary concern was with the Eighteenth 'Rose Croix' Degree. One of the explicit reasons for seeking to establish a Supreme Council in England was the lack of a supervisory body to ensure that the 'Rosae Crucis' Degree was conferred in Knights Templar Encampments in a regular and uniform manner. In the early days of Metropolitan Chapter, many of its Officers were themselves members of the Supreme Council, who could thereby satisfy themselves of the propriety of the Chapter's proceedings. But when in March 1852 'Patents' were given to Chapters in places far distant from London – Dorset, Somerset, Warwickshire and Lancashire – such personal supervision could no longer be exercised at every Meeting. Furthermore, there was no certainty about the details of the Ritual which should be used. The Supreme Council of the Northern Masonic Jurisdiction had sent Thomas Crucefix many documents relating to the Ancient and Accepted Rite, including the full Rituals of the Degrees from the Thirtieth to the Thirty-third, but for the Eighteenth 'Rose Croix' Degree there is no record that he was sent other than the Sign, Word, Grip, Token and Obligation. With these, recognition was assured, but it was important that they were communicated in a uniform manner. It was desirable to eliminate the French influence which is apparent in one early post-1845 manuscript 'Rose Croix' Ritual in the archives of the English Supreme Council. Furthermore the Ritual adopted would preferably be compatible with that used in the generality of 'Rosae Crucis' Chapters working within Knights Templar Encampments, so that possessors of the 'Rosae Crucis' Degree could be affiliated to 'Rose Croix' Chapters 'Patented' by the Supreme Council without their acceptance as members of the Rite appearing anomalous.

It is apparent that in 1852 Henry Udall made a definitive recension of the Ritual of the 18th 'Rose Croix' degree for use in the newly 'Patented' Chapters. The original copy of this has not been found, but that it existed is indicated, *inter alia,* by a note in each of two early manuscript Rituals of the provenance of which there is no doubt. The first of these is that prepared for William Tucker, the first MWS of Coryton Chapter. At the end of the manuscript text there is a note in Tucker's handwriting, "Copy made for me from Udall's M∴S∴S∴ by Bro. W∴B∴Hancock of Weymouth this 4th day of April 1853. William Tucker 33∴.". The identical Ritual used by Charles Vigne, the first MWS of St. Peter and St. Paul Chapter in Bath, is prefaced by 'Directions' for conferring the Degree, and is subscribed "Signd Bro. Udall 26th October 1852". This is not in Udall's handwriting, but it is difficult not to conclude that the Ritual given to Vigne had been copied from an original which had been signed by Udall himself.

This evidence seems to leave little doubt that within three months of the statement which Henry Udall had made to the General Meeting of the Order in July 1852, he had also provided a Ritual of the 18th Degree to be used by all the new Chapters. The 'Directions' for conferring the Degree refer primarily to the Intermediate Degrees, the Fourth to the Seventeenth, both inclusive. Perhaps it would be unjust to accuse Udall of having been devious. His statement about the organisation of the Order had served its purpose in 'gratifying' the Supreme Council of the Northern Masonic Jurisdiction. But the 'Directions' over the copy of his signature in the 'Vigne' Ritual, and those in the 'Tucker' Ritual, state:

> In conferring the degree of Rose Croix, you will first give the degrees by name from the 4th to the 14th, in a Grand Lodge of Perfection.
>
> You will then declare a Grand Lodge of Princes of Jerusalem opened, and confer the 15th and 16th degrees by name.
>
> You will give the Knights of the East and West or 17th degree by name, and then, the Rose Croix in extenso.
>
> The great length of time necessary is sufficient excuse for not giving the others in that manner.

In spite of this instruction (of which they may not have been aware) the Supreme Council of the Northern Jurisdiction continued to be 'gratified', and at the Higher Degrees Meeting on 4th November 1852 Udall drew attention to the commendatory letter which he had earlier received from Gourgas.

It therefore appears almost certain that, within three months of the statement which Henry Udall made to the Summer Festival of the Order in July 1852, he had provided a Ritual of the Eighteenth Degree to be used in all the new Chapters. The procedure seems to have been that the first MWS acquired a copy of the full ritual of the Degree, and he then made further copies containing no more than their own 'parts' for each of the Officers of the Chapter[382]. While the Ritual is recognisably that in use in Chapters under the Supreme Council for England, etc., today, the Opening is, however, more verbose. It was evidently soon amended because at the end of the 'Vigne' Ritual there is added "Opening, Dr. Leeson. June 1855", the wording of which is almost identical to that in current use[383].

Both Leeson and Oliver were absent from the Summer Festival of the Order in July 1853, as they had been from that held in the previous year. Udall again presided. The Thirtieth Degree was first conferred upon Lord Leigh, the Provincial Grand Master for Warwickshire. John Deacon Cox opened Metropolitan Chapter and Perfected several Brethren. According to his usual custom Udall then gave a long address, first expressing his pleasure at the "true Masonic, as well as civil qualifications of every candidate" who had been admitted into the new Chapters to which he had referred in the previous year. He went on to say:

> Application had been made to the Supreme Council, for a patent for a Rose Croix Chapter, at Bath, to be called after the patron saints of that ancient city, St. Peter and St. Paul. This Patent he had hoped to have been able at this convocation to have delivered into the custody of its MWS, the Illustrious Brother Chas. John Vigne who would be assisted in it by the Chaplain of the High Grades Union, the Rev. George Bythesea. The patent of constitution was, however, not quite ready.

Vigne[384], who lived in Bath[385], had been Perfected by William Tucker at Coryton. He had been among those Advanced to the Thirtieth Degree at the Higher Degrees Meeting in the previous November. He was evidently well suited to preside over the new Chapter. Otherwise, Udall's statement has some curious features. In the first place, the Patent for St. Peter and St. Paul Chapter bears the same date, 21st March 1852, as that of the other four Chapters which had received their Patents in the previous year, in spite of which that for St. Peter and St. Paul was "not quite ready". Secondly, other early Chapters Patented by the Supreme Council were each associated, one way or another, with Encampments of Knights Templar. There was in Bath the Encampment of Antiquity, but it appears to have been dormant from 1822 to 1855[386]. It is not known to have conferred the 'Rosae Crucis' Degree before St. Peter and St. Paul Chapter Rose Croix was Patented. However, Bladud[387] Encampment was Warranted in 1852, and it may have been the potential source of candidates which this provided that fired the imagination of Charles Vigne[388].

Udall went on to inform those present at the Festival that at the Convocation of the Northern American Supreme Council which had been held in the previous March, Gourgas had said, referring to the English Council, "Its interests are in able and discreet hands, and the present indications are, that it is destined at no very remote period, to take its stand at the head of all the Supreme Councils of Europe, for character, ability, and efficiency."

It was perhaps Dr. Leeson's professional duties which accounted for his absence from several Meetings of the Supreme Council and of the 'Convocations of the Higher Degrees' both during 1853, and in the early part of 1854. Leeson certainly spent some time at his home in the Isle of Wight, and in addition to his Masonic commitments he was both the Coroner for Greenwich and a Lecturer at the Medical School of St. Thomas's Hospital. On the occasions when Leeson was not present, it was generally Henry Udall who presided in his place, and the reports in the Masonic Press demonstrate that he never neglected the opportunity to set forth his views on the Order at some length to the assembled gatherings. Dr. Oliver was by this time almost a recluse, and although the frequently absent Leeson was the Sovereign Grand Commander, it is probably no exaggeration to say that at the beginning of 1854 Udall was the most prominent and respected figure in the Order. Indeed, in spite of the inaccuracy about the immediate successor to Crucefix, there is no reason to doubt the validity of the comment made by Davyd Nash in a letter which he wrote to *The Freemason* in April 1858, "On the death of Dr. Crucefix, Dr. Leeson was elected Sovereign Grand Commander; but for some years the real management of the Order was in the hands of Bro. Henry Udall."

369 Crucefix, Oliver, Udall, Leeson, Wilson, Nash, Tucker, Emly and Winsor.

370 Although Leeson's home was 'Pulpit Rock', Bonchurch, Isle of Wight, he had a London *pied-à-terre* at Grove House, Greenwich.

371 According to *The Freemasons' Quarterly Review*, among those present at the Banquet after a Meeting on 18th March 1851 was "Ill. Bro. J.A.D.Cox, S.P.R.S. 32nd" The list appended to a Report of a Meeting of the Supreme Council held on 8th May 1851 includes as one of the nine Members John Astell D. Cox. Evidently Cox was Elected to The Supreme Council in April/May 1851, possibly at the Meeting on 8th May. (In the following year Cox was Enthroned as MWS of Metropolitan Chapter – Matthew Christmas, *A Short Account of the Origins and History of the Grand Metropolitan Chapter*, p.6 [1996]).

372 A & A, p.36.

373 The announcement of their retirement is followed by a note – "but are appointed, by Patent, specially to assist the Supreme Council in superintending Provincial Districts", but there is no further reference to what would have been an early appointment of 'District Inspectors General'. At the Meeting of Grand Conclave in the previous month, Emly had been promoted from Grand Almoner to Grand Chancellor, an Office which he was to occupy for the next 3 years, and, like Cox, he was therefore also in a position to encourage the affiliation of 'Rosae Crucis' Knights.

374 There is a footnote to the Report of the speeches at the Banquet after the Summer Festival on 9th June 1852 to the effect that Sir John Robinson "took his 30th degree in the Supreme Council of England. He was advanced to the 31st degree by the Supreme Council of Scotland with the assent of the Supreme Council of England. On a vacancy taking place in the Supreme Council, he was made a Sov. Grand Inspector General. He is also on the Registry of Ireland."

375 A Report in February 1853 notes that it was "a bye-Law of the 'High Grades Union' that none but Brethren who have dined at one of the banquets of the Union are eligible for election into that body. A Brother, therefore, who has attained the rank of the 30th Degree is admitted to dine once before joining that the Brethren may be the better acquainted with him before he goes through the ordeal of the ballot."

376 *The Freemasons' Quarterly Review* reported that the Summer Festival, which was held on 3rd July 1851, was "as important a Masonic meeting as ever took place in the annals of Freemasonry". Those present included Alderman Hoyte, the Grand Chancellor, and other Members of the Irish Supreme Council, and the Hon. A.F.Jocelyn, the Past Sovereign Grand Commander of Scotland.

377 I am grateful to Bro.John Hamill for drawing my attention to this document.

378 Udall's reference is presumably intended to be to Count Decazes, a personal friend of King Louis XVIII of France, whose Prime Minister he had become in 1821. At about that time Decazes brought together as a Supreme Council various Brethren who could claim to have been sometime members of the Supreme Council legitimately established in Paris by de Grasse Tilly in 1804. Decazes presided over this as the Supreme Council of France, in opposition to that of the Grand Orient, but both its continuity and the legitimacy of its membership were dubious, and the Americans regarded it with equal disfavour. However, Decazes' Council had granted the Patent for the Supreme Council for Scotland shortly after Crucefix had obtained that for England.

379 *Sic* – but the punctuation has been amended. Udall letter file.

380 See **Appendix** to 'Essay 9' for Udall's subsequent fuller account of these transactions. (p.80)

381 The Brethren in those days must have had considerable stamina! At the Banquet after this long meeting "the cloth being cleared and the National Anthem sung", there were no fewer than 14 more or less lengthy speeches.

382 That apparently made by Vigne for the 'High Pontiff' (Prelate) of St. Peter and St. Paul Chapter is still preserved in the Archives in 10 Duke Street.

383 There have been a few major changes in the Ritual procedure (Swords were abandoned at about the time of the First World War, Scriptural passages during the Candidate's ascent of the ladder were introduced in 1917, 'proving' the Princes was discontinued in 1951, the 'Sign of Admiration' was changed to 'Adoration' early in the twentieth century, and is no longer given as part of the Opening, the recitation of 'The Agonies of Christ' was omitted in the 1860s, and various musical items are no longer mandatory – or today even permissive) but apart from these, with minor verbal amendments made from time to time, the Ritual currently issued by the Supreme Council is to all intents and purposes the 'Udall Recension'.

384 Charles Vigne had been Initiated in the Lodge of Honour (now No.379) in Bath in 1849, becoming its WM two years later. He was one of the earliest candidates for Perfection in Coryton Chapter. Gerald Bryant, *A History of the First 150 Years of St. Peter and St. Paul Chapter No.6*, p.16 (2003)

385 Westfield House, Weston, Bath. *Ibidem*.

386 "There was a gap in the Minutes from 30th April 1822 until 15th June 1855." *Ibidem*, p.21.

387 Now No.40 on the Register of Great Priory.

388 Vigne was an enthusiastic member of the Ancient and Accepted Rite, who, on his election to the Supreme Council in 1855 held for a time the Offices both of Grand Treasurer General and Grand Secretary General. He afterwards held the Office of Sovereign Grand Commander from 1869 to 1874 when he gave place to the Earl of Carnarvon.

Essay 11
The Supreme Council encounters rough water —
August 1853 to July 1856

Since 1846 William Tucker had been Grand Almoner in the Supreme Council which now styled itself "of England and Wales and the Dependencies of the British Crown". In addition, Tucker was Provincial Grand Master for Dorsetshire in the Craft, and also Grand Commander of Knights Templar in that Province. That he acted in a somewhat eccentric manner on 18th August 1853 seems to have been ignored, or at least condoned, by Dr. Leeson and the other members of the Supreme Council. At the Meeting of his Provincial Grand Lodge on that day Tucker, according to his own statement, had worn the "robes of an S.G.I.G. 33°" (whatever these may have been) "in addition to my full clothing as a Prov[incial] G[rand] M[aster]". When he addressed his Provincial Grand Lodge, Tucker had made clear his high opinion of the Ancient and Accepted Rite, deplored the failure since the Union for it to be recognised by the United Grand Lodge as an integral part of the Masonic system, and recommended all young Masons to take "an advancing course". The Grand Master of United Grand Lodge, the Earl of Zetland, refused to accept Tucker's explanation, and in November 1853 he deprived him of his Provincial Office[389]. This had no effect on Tucker's position on the Supreme Council[390].

At a poorly attended meeting on 5th July 1854[391], Leeson announced that the Grand Secretary General, Davyd Nash, had retired from the Council. Nash had returned to Bristol, taking with him the Council's Minute Book, together with whatever other Council documents he may have possessed, none of which were ever recovered[392]. In spite of Lord Zetland's displeasure which Tucker had incurred little more than six months earlier, Leeson had no scruples in appointing him as Grand Secretary General in Nash's place. The vacancy on the Council resulting from Nash's 'retirement' was filled by Sir John de la Pole on 1st November 1854[393].

In 1854 there were seven Chapters Rose Croix owing allegiance to the Supreme Council. Five of these had been granted Patents dated 21st March 1852[394] after each had regularly submitted a Petition requesting its constitution. The two others were derived from Knights Templar Encampments in which the 'Rosae Crucis' Degree had customarily been conferred. Each of these two latter, the Encampment of Faith and Fidelity first, and later that of Mount Calvary, had resolved to work the 'Rosae Crucis' Degree separately from the Installation of Knights Templar. Each then requested the newly formed Supreme Council to grant a Warrant under which the Degree of 'Rose Croix' might be conferred under the Council's auspices[395]. The Supreme Council agreed to this in each case, but while the Chapter formed from Mount Calvary retained the Encampment's name, that from Faith and Fidelity was Patented as Metropolitan (later Grand Metropolitan) Chapter[396]. Metropolitan Chapter flourished, with frequent meetings to Perfect Brethren. Many of its Officers were Members of the Supreme Council. Although the Chapter was a quite separate body, its Members later, but without justification, regarded it as having been in its early days the 'private Chapter' of Supreme Council. The confusion was understandable; on several occasions the Supreme Council itself Perfected Brethren, having formed itself for the purpose into a Rose Croix Chapter, many of the Officers of which were also Officers of Metropolitan Chapter[397].

Those Brethren who were the original Members both of Metropolitan and of Faith and Fidelity Chapters, together with the majority of the Founders of the five other Chapters which received the early Patents, had taken the 'Rosae Crucis' Degree in their Encampments, but had not been Perfected as Sovereign Princes Rose Croix. To regularise their position, they were excused going through the Ceremony of Perfection provided that they took an Oath of Allegiance to the Council. This procedure, which was termed 'Affiliation', continued to be extended for many years to Knights Templar who had taken the 'Rosae Crucis' Degree, but who wished to join Chapters under the banner of the Supreme Council. The Ceremony of Affiliation could only be carried out by a Member of the Supreme Council, using a form of words which continued to be employed almost to the end of the century[398].

The Thirtieth Degree was another matter. The Supreme Council never permitted affiliation directly as a Grand Elected Knight Kadosh. The status of those Knights Templar who were Affiliated, but who had previously progressed to the 'Kadosh' Degree in their Encampments, evidently presented the Supreme Council with a problem. To confer the Thirtieth Degree of the Ancient and Accepted Rite on all those who might consider themselves entitled to it was proving time-consuming. In the Minutes of the Meeting of the Supreme Council on 14th February 1855, after noting that the Council "proceeded to consider the best mode of practically extending a knowledge of the Ancient and Accepted Rite of 33° which was adjourned at the last meeting"[399], it is briefly recorded that the establishment of a Grand Metropolitan Chapter KH 30° was discussed and approved. Leeson was authorised to invite 'The High Grades Union' to submit a Petition for the establishment of such a Chapter[400].

In the following month, Tucker, the Grand Secretary General, died at the early age of 39[401]. Charles Vigne was Elected a Member of the Council in his place, and Obligated, but he was not formally 'Admitted' as a Member until the following November when Leeson at once appointed him Grand Secretary General[402]. Only then was Vigne authorised to purchase a Minute Book. The book which he purchased contains the records of Meetings of the Council for the previous eighteen months to which reference has already been made. However, Vigne can only have entered these from notes taken earlier by others before he himself was a Member of the Council. Their accuracy and completeness is therefore open to question. In particular, the earlier Minutes record no further details of any discussions about the formation of the 'Grand Metropolitan Chapter KH'.

There is little doubt that it was Leeson who was most anxious for the Degree of GEKKH to be conferred in a 'Grand Metropolitan Chapter KH' rather than at a Meeting of the Supreme Council itself. When Leeson first proposed this, Udall, according to the statement he later made, had expressed his doubts whether the Supreme Council of the Northern Masonic Jurisdication would accept its regularity. He also believed that there would be further discussion within the Council before a Warrant was granted.

There is no record in the Minute Book of a Meeting of the Council in April 1855, and there is no reference to the GEKKH Chapter at the Meeting in June 1855 at which Udall was present. However, after the recorded Minute of this June Meeting, there is interposed on the same folio a note dated 16th February 1855 recording the presentation of the Petition for the Chapter KH on that date. There is no indication as to why this note was interposed, but if it is a true record, it is surprising that the fact was not reported at the June 1855 Meeting. Furthermore, Leeson must have acted with remarkable haste to convey the invitation to the Union, and the Union then to have prepared the Petition with extraordinary speed, in order for it to be presented it within 48 hours. But, as noted earlier, the reliability of the Council's Minutes prior to Vigne's Election in November 1855 is questionable.

The Petition for 'The Grand Metropolitan Chapter KH' was signed by 14 Members of the Higher Degrees, headed by Henry Emly. According to the Minutes, the final decision to grant the Warrant was taken at the Council Meeting on 1st November 1855, a Meeting at which Henry Udall was present, but the Minutes do not record any discussion, or dissent on Udall's part.

Udall had given notice that his professional duties would prevent him attending the Council Meeting which was to be held on 14th February 1856. Henry Emly was ill, and at the Meeting it was agreed to transfer the 'Patent' for the 'Grand Metropolitan Chapter GEKKH' from him to John A. D. Cox who had been elected to the Supreme Council in 1851. Then, in spite of Udall's absence, and apparently without previous reference to him, a Resolution was passed that he, as Grand Treasurer General, should produce, at each Meeting of the Council, a statement of the funds which he held on its behalf. This was relatively innocuous – no criticism of Udall's conduct appears to have been implied, and his audited Accounts had been accepted at the corresponding Meeting in the previous year. However, the Minutes of the Meeting record the Council's approval of some more contentious matters. These included that each appointment of an S.G.I.G. as a Member of the Council should be for a three-year period, that (without previous notice having been given) the 'retired' Council member, Frederick Winsor, should be reinstated and appointed 'Master of Ceremonies', and that the Grand Secretary General should be authorised to employ a 'Copying clerk' at the Council's expense.

The Consecration, or at least the first meeting, of the 'Grand Metropolitan Chapter KH' may have occurred even before its Warrant (or 'Patent') had been signed – the Minutes are not wholly clear on this point. Blank copies of 'Patents' were then held by the Grand Treasurer General who was responsible for obtaining the fees for their issue. It appears that Vigne, as Grand Secretary General, wrote to Udall for such a form. On 16th March 1856 Udall replied to him from the Northern Circuit, "I have written to London to a relative to go to my Chambers with my keys and see if the patent you want can be got – if so it will be sent to you." He goes on to say, in the most cordial manner, "I am sorry to learn that you have been suffering from Rheumatism – I am rather better but this bleak weather is very trying in our courts. In haste, Yours truly, Henry Udall"⁴⁰³. Udall appends below his signature:

"Although I have stated that I should do nothing to oppose the formation of the K.H. as proposed, on account of my deference to Dr. Leeson, yet I am by no means satisfied that the thing is right *or that under the present great changes that any good will come of it* and I thought you and I and Dr. Leeson agreed in this when we talked it over – I have always thought that the K.H.'s made would owe their rank not to the Patent itself but to the Supreme Council authorizing them to be made in the presence of three of their own body⁴⁰⁴. There are a great many other things I wished to discuss but cannot do so by letter."

However, while Udall was evidently concerned about the actions proposed by the Supreme Council, there is no indication, either in the Minutes or in Udall's later letters, that at this time there was any serious rift between him and the Council in general or Dr. Leeson in particular.

The next Meeting of the Council had been arranged for 8th April 1856. Shortly before it took place, Udall, then on the Northern Circuit in Liverpool, wrote to Leeson⁴⁰⁵ that "at great inconvenience" he had made arrangements to attend the Meeting, but that he now found "that it would be impossible for me to do so on account of some fresh business". He went on to point out that "According to the days now fixed for the Meetings the only one which I can with certainty attend is that in July as I am always away from London on the other days." Evidently Udall was concerned that his absence from the February Meeting had prevented him from presenting his financial statement to the Council. He reminded Leeson that "As I mentioned to you on the day before the last Meeting, all the accounts ordered to be paid were done so (*sic*) and nothing is due for the year except the account due to the Tavern and as the time for disputing the assignment is now passed that may now be safely paid." Udall then went on to say: "The Years receipts fully equalled the payments, but that and other matters must be examined at the July Meeting. Be good enough to ask Bro. Vigne to receive what money is to be paid to the Trea[surer]. Gen[era]l." Udall concluded in the most friendly manner by saying that he had now to go to the other end of the County before returning to London, from which, he said, he had now been absent for seven weeks, "and sick enough I am of moving about although this is the best Circuit I have had".

Before the Council met on 8th April 1856, its former member, Henry Emly, who had earlier been too ill to assume the Mastership of 'The Grand Metropolitan Chapter KH', had died. He had certainly been one of the leading lights in the 'High Grades Union', the body to which those who had been Advanced to the 30th Degree were eligible for Election, and he had apparently been its Treasurer. At the Council Meeting it was agreed, *inter alia*, that Vigne should write to the absent Udall "expressing the regret of the Council that his Accounts were not furnished to the present Meeting; requesting him to pay forthwith the sum of £261.16.9 being the balance in his hands on 14th February 1855 to the Account of the Supreme Council of England and Wales with the London and Westminster Banking Company, Holborn Branch, and that he be particularly requested to have his Accounts ready for audit at the next meeting as promised in the letter to the Most Puissant Sovereign Grand Commander". That Udall should present his accounts for audit some fifteen months after the last occasion on which this had been done was not an unreasonable request. That the Supreme Council apparently considered that Udall would still hold the same balance as he had held in February 1855 was extraordinary in view of the fact that five months earlier the Council had authorised him to pay from it bills totalling some seventy pounds.

His letters indicate that Charles Vigne held Henry Udall in considerable respect as one of the original Members of the Council, and, indeed, as a personal friend. In his letters to Udall, Vigne frequently expresses his regret that, in his Office as Grand Secretary General, he has to carry out the instructions of the Council by transmitting somewhat peremptory Resolutions to its Grand Treasurer General. On this occasion he forwarded extracts of the Minutes to Udall, under cover of what was evidently intended to be a conciliatory letter, starting by writing in the most cordial way, "though I must rejoice that the increase of business was the cause that prevented our having the pleasure of your company at the Council". He goes on to say that had Udall been present he would "have been witness of the feelings which induced us all to pass such resolutions". He then makes it clear that it was not primarily any default on Udall's part which gave rise to these feelings, but that they "were engendered by the very unpleasant position a body or Order is placed in when having to deal with the Executors of a Treasurer, the fatal delay in procuring the Accounts and money, is only too unfortunately apparent in poor Emly's case and was so strongly felt by all as to induce us to frame the enclosed minutes in which we felt convinced you would have participated had you been present, and have most thoroughly concurred". In other words, the Council wished to avoid a repetition of what had had to be dealt with after Emly's death, should any mischance befall Udall.

By 1st May 1856, Vigne had received no reply to his letter, and again wrote to Udall, saying "I have received enquiries if the Balance has been paid into the London & Westminster Bank; as I do not like to ask the question of any body but yourself, please give me an early reply that I may answer the query." Vigne added a postscript – "Will you kindly call at the L. & W. Bank (Holborn Branch) and add your name to those of the Supreme Gd. Council on a paper authorizing them to pay cheques subject to the conditions in the minutes."

Udall replied on 5th May, saying that he had just received Vigne's letter which had been "forwarded to me in the country", and that it was only when Vigne had sent him the full Minutes that he had learnt of what he described as "the extraordinary proceedings of the late meeting of the Supreme Council". Either Udall had read the Minutes without having had the benefit of first reading the conciliatory letter which Vigne had sent with the extracts – the Minutes as recorded in the Council's Minute Book make no reference to the problem with the deceased Emly's Accounts – or he had ignored Vigne's tactful indication that it was this which lay behind the Resolutions, and had taken these as being criticisms of his own conduct. He pointed out that the £261.16.9 mentioned in the Council's Minute was, he presumed, "taken from our late friend, Tucker's minutes of the Audit – the whole of my papers and accounts of the same having been left by me at the meeting of that Council as mentioned by me at the time (the day being that on which Dr. Leeson you and myself dined together) and have not been seen by me since".

He next turned to the Resolution about the opening of a Bank Account. "I would have no objection in placing the money, which I, as the Treasurer General of the Order, only, have legally the right to hold, in the London & Westminster Bank but I certainly never will allow the control of it go out of my hands by allowing other persons to draw checks for it. Quite independent of this – the illegal resolution passed to open an account in the name of Supreme Grand Council would make the account itself one of endless anxiety – for should notice be given to the Bank, by anyone alleging himself interested in the fund as a member of the order, all checks would assuredly be refused by the Bank[406]."

Udall then returned to the Accounts themselves, and the question of an Audit. "As to that part of the resolution in which I am requested to have the accounts ready for Audit in July, thereby with the context intimating that the reason the audit did not take place was because the accounts were not ready, I must characterize as most unjustifiable. When I saw Dr. Leeson and yourself the day before the meeting of the Council in February and when as I understood we all agreed that no matter of importance would be brought forward at the Council, I was as I stated ready to go into the audit that afternoon but could not be present next day. Why then should such a resolution have been passed and published in the Circular and how can the Council be kept together if such things are done? There are several other things done quite illegally – that especially of limiting the election of S.G.I.G.33rds to the Council for three years. Again how can the appointment of Ills. Br. Winsor to the office of M.C. be supported, he not being a member of the Council?

"As I do not intend to give my sanction to any of the matters alluded to, all done be it remembered without previous notice having been given that they would be discussed, I shall have to consider before the meeting in July what is proper for me in my position to do and to assist me in coming to a right conclusion I have intimated to a friend of mine in the North, in whose judgment I can rely, who will be in London before the middle of next month that I wish his advice in a matter of some importance and on his determination in the matter I shall act. Immediately this is done I shall communicate fully to the whole of the members of the Council so that the subjects of this hasty letter may be fully before them at the meeting in July. I have never quarrelled with any body of men I have yet acted with and that this may be averted in the present case I propose not to enter into these matters further except in the way I have stated. I should not have done so now had it not been necessary in replying to the question you put to me in your letter."

Udall concludes his letter, for the first time somewhat testily, "I have not been acquainted, which surely I ought to have been, with what was done during the various meetings you had. I hear from your letters there was a meeting of K.H. on the Friday, how was that? I expected that when you did not pull up your Cab on our meeting in the Strand on the Saturday that I should have seen you here" (Udall had headed his letter 'The Temple' where he now had Chambers at 9 Kings Bench Walk) "in the course of that day."

Vigne acknowledged this letter two days later. Thanking Udall for his explanation, Vigne was evidently anxious to prevent this official disagreement disrupting their personal relationship, for he went on to say, "I quite agree that we had better not mention this matter any more until you have consulted your friend or at our next Meeting, for, whatever *we* may say *to each other* can avail nothing and may cause some unpleasant feeling which between us I am most anxious to avoid, so, if we meet in town let this be a forbidden subject between us recollecting that in the execution of my duties as Secretary, I am obliged to write as so directed." Somewhat optimistically, Vigne goes on to say: "I have no doubt that time and a quick discussion will enable us to arrange all these subjects harmoniously." A comparative newcomer to the Supreme Council, Vigne apparently did not see that Udall was standing firm on his own interpretation, as a professional lawyer, of the provisions of the 'Grand Constitutions'. Vigne may well have been unaware that these even existed – it was not until July 1859 that the Council requested Leeson to make the members aware of the provisions contained therein – and Leeson, unwilling to be frustrated in his plans, perhaps did not care. But Vigne was punctilious in refuting any implications of discourtesy. "I wish to explain the reason why I did not pull up when I passed you in the Strand. Henry Leeson and I were going to the London Bridge Station and when we started from Bacon's [Hotel] we had only 25 minutes out of which I had to call at a shop in the Strand. We only just hit it off." He ignored the suggestion that he might have called later upon Henry Udall!

On 5th June, Udall received a further letter from Vigne saying that Leeson had written to him, asking him to enquire from Udall "if we may depend on your presence at the next Council meeting (8th July) of which he has given me instructions to issue notices with the following Agenda:

"To take into consideration the Subject of Finance
To consider any communication from the Ill.Gr.Treasurer Genl. in reference thereto and also to Audit his Accounts and to take such steps as may be considered necessary in case of non compliance with the Orders of the Supreme Grand Council."

This was at once both fair warning of Leeson's feelings, and also an opportunity for Udall at least to resolve his difference with the Council about its finances, but the manner of its transmission only served further to irritate the Grand Treasurer General. On the following day Udall replied tersely from Westminster Hall, to which his clerk had brought Vigne's note, "as you wish for an early answer be good enough to say that I shall have great pleasure in answering any enquiry Dr. Leeson may make to me himself, but I object to answer questions put in this triangular mode". Vigne does not seem to have received this brusque answer[407] (perhaps Udall's clerk diplomatically overlooked the despatch of this ungracious reply!), but had apparently met Udall, because he wrote on the following day: "I have not received the letter of the 6th June from Westminster Hall in which you object to the Triangle." Udall wrote again saying that he could not understand how this happened, because "after copying it on the fly leaf of yours of the previous day I put it among the letters for Post in our Robing Rooms". He went on to say that "I was not able to leave London for Newcastle on Sunday night, but hope to sleep at Doncaster tomorrow night; my address for the next seven weeks will be Northern Circuit".

Udall then composed a lengthy statement – 12 closely written foolscap pages headed 'July 3rd 1856' – containing his views on the manner in which the Supreme Council was discharging its duties. This homily – for that is what it amounted to – is of some interest as indicating the interpretation which could be placed on 'The Grand Constitutions of 1786' by a lawyer such as Henry Udall. Not all of his views would be accepted today, although they are not unworthy of consideration, but they were certainly at variance with the autocratic approach of Henry Leeson; above all, Leeson wanted to retain the Council's contact with the Supreme Council of the French Grand Orient, and he would have had no wish for those ignorant of the matter to be made aware of the displeasure of the Supreme Council of the Northern Masonic Jurisdiction regarding this, and of Udall's part in averting it.

In thus bringing matters to a head in the Summer of 1856, Udall undoubtedly considered that he was acting in the best interests of the Ancient and Accepted Rite. Together with Crucefix and Oliver he had been instrumental in setting up the Supreme Council, and as the only survivor of the trio he considered that he had a special responsibility. His over-riding concern was to maintain the Supreme Council's regularity in the eyes of the Northern Jurisdiction – he appears to have regarded the Supreme Council almost as his client and he was not prepared to see its case go by default.

Appendix
Procedure for Affiliation

S.G.I.G. 33°. You will take the volume of the Holy Law in your hand and assure me that on the penalty of all your former obligations; on your word as a Master Mason; and on your word as a gentleman you are duly qualified to be affiliated to our Order *as a Sovereign Prince Rose Croix* under the Supreme Grand Council of England & Wales.

Prayer

Oh Almighty & Sovereign Architect of the Universe who penetratest into the most secret recesses of the hearts of men, purify ours with the sacred fire of Thy Divine Love. Banish from this Holy Sanctuary the impious and the profane, & grant that we, being solely occupied with the great work of our redemption, may be enabled to distinguish the precious metal from the dross, and may not be deceived in the choice of him we are now about to affiliate. And may the bond of our union be ever cemented by Peace Benevolence and good will. Now unto the King Eternal, Immortal, Invisible, the only true and Wise God be the kingdom, the honour and the Glory, now and for ever. Amen

I must now call upon you to take a solemn obligation.

! - - - - - - - - being a Free & Accepted Master Mason regularly initiated, passed and raised in a warranted lodge most solemnly promise and swear faithful Allegiance, Fealty and submission to the Decrees of the Most Puissant Sovereigns Grand Inspectors Generals of the 33°, duly, lawfully and constitutionally established on the 26th October 1845, sitting in Grand & Supreme Council at their Grand East in London for England & Wales & the Dependencies of the British Crown. I do further promise to hold no Masonic fellowship intercourse, or communion whatever in any of the Ineffable and Sublime degrees of Ancient, Free & Accepted Masonry with any Mason or body of Masons which at any time have or hereafter may be established in Great Britain or its Dependencies by any Authorities whatever except with such as are, or may be duly recognised and acknowledged as lawful by the aforesaid Supreme Council. And I do further declare that I will (after my affiliation) as soon as a convenient opportunity shall occur, sign my name in the Roll of the Golden Book of the Order.

Salute the Sacred Volume

By virtue of the Power vested in me as S.∴G.∴I.∴G.∴ 33° I hereby affiliate you to our order as an Illustrious & Sovereign Prince Rose Croix under the Supreme Gd. Council of the 33° for England & Wales & the Dependencies of the British Crown.

N.B. Only a Member of the S.G.C. 33° can affiliate.

(Transcribed from the manuscript Ritual given to Invicta Chapter No.10 in 1864. C.J.M.)

389 Accounts of this extraordinary affair can be found in the papers by F.J.Cooper, AQC, LXXXIII, 125, 1970 and by J.W.Daniel, AQC, CVI, 75/76, 1993.

390 Tucker did not, however, attend its Meeting on 31st October 1853 when Lord Methuen, the Provincial Grand Master in the Craft of his neighbouring Province of Wiltshire, was Advanced to the 30°. He may have been too involved in presenting his case to the Craft authorities! He was present at the Council Meeting on 9th December when the 31° was conferred upon three Brethren who were later to be elected Members of the Supreme Council — Sir John de la Pole, Charles Vigne, and George Beauchamp Cole. Each of the three was further Advanced to the 32° on 5th July 1854.

391 Leeson himself presided. Henry Emly and Arthur Hopper attended, although they were 'Retired members', but of the actual Members only Henry Udall and William Tucker were present.

392 Davyd Nash was a Bristol Mason. The Encampment of Baldwyn in Bristol showed no inclination to submit either to the Grand Conclave or to the Supreme Council. It is impossible to say what pressure was brought to bear on Nash, but he effectively severed his connection with the Supreme Council and upheld the autonomy of the 'Camp of Baldwyn'.

393 At this time the procedure for the admission of a new Member to the Supreme Council appears to have been that his name was proposed by the Sovereign Grand Commander at a Meeting of the Council, and, if unanimously approved, he was then Obligated at that Meeting. He then attended the next Meeting, and during the course of it, frequently not before the second day of the Meeting, the Member-designate was "admitted in Ancient and Solemn Form a Sovereign Grand Inspector General of the 33rd. Degree". (Minutes of Meetings of 5th July and 31st October 1953 [de la Pole] and of 29th June and 1st November 1855 [Vigne].)

394 Coryton, Weymouth, Vernon, St. Peter and St. Paul and Palatine. (Chapters under the Supreme Council were not given formal numbers until 1870.)

395 See: Matthew Christmas, *A Short Account of the Origins and Early History (1846–c.1874) of the Grand Metropolitan Chapter*, p.4 (1996); Ewen McEwen, *The Mount Calvary Encampment*, p.23, (?1990); H.V. Wiles, *Mount Calvary Chapter Rose Croix, No.3 1848–1948*, pp.36/37 (1948).

396 For several years Mount Calvary Chapter played little part in the development of the Ancient and Accepted Rite in England. Between 1852 and 1860 the Chapter did not meet, and it narrowly escaped having its 'Patent' withdrawn on the grounds that it was in abeyance. McEwen, *op. cit.*, pp.24/25; Wiles *op. cit.*, p.38.

397 The Supreme Council has always exercised the right to act, without a Warrant, as a Chapter Rose Croix. For example, today at the Consecration of a new Chapter, the Presiding Officer first opens a Rose Croix Chapter, the Officers of which are either Members of the Council, or S.G.I.G.'s appointed temporarily to fill some of the Offices.

398 See Appendix.

399 There is no record of any earlier discussion.

400 On 31st January 1846 the Encampment of Faith and Fidelity separated the Degrees of 'Rosae Crucis' and 'Kadosh' from that of Knights Templar. It was the consequent 'Sovereign Chapter of Rose Croix' which then accepted a Patent as 'Metropolitan Chapter'. There is, however, no indication that 'The Grand Metropolitan Chapter KH' was in any way related to 'The Illustrious College of KH and NPU' also separately formed by the Encampment of Faith and Fidelity – or of what subsequently became of the 'College'.

401 Tucker died on 11th March 1855. The cause of his death entered on his Death Certificate was Pulmonary Phthisis. It has been suggested that his erratic conduct for which he was deposed as Provincial Grand Master was due to 'Spes Phthysica', a mental condition which sometimes occurs in sufferers from this ailment. S.Vatcher, AQC, LXXXIII, p.138 (1970).

402 Charles Vigne also succeeded Tucker as Provincial Grand Commander of Knights Templar for Dorsetshire, where he was a member of the Coryton Encampment of which the Grand Master of the Knights Templar, Colonel Kemeys Tynte, was also a member. In addition to this appointment, the Supreme Council continued its influential representation in the Grand Conclave of Knights Templar – Henry Emly was in his fifth year as Grand Chancellor, John Cox in his sixth as Grand Registrar, and Henry Udall was a member of the Executive Committee of the Conclave from its 'revival' in 1847 until 1856. In addition Captain Arthur Hopper had been Second Grand Captain in 1853.

403 The Patent which Vigne had requested can only have been that for the 'KH Chapter', for no other application for a Patent was received by the Supreme Council between that dated 21st March 1852, and issued in July 1853 (St. Peter and St. Paul), and that on 12th January 1858 (Royal Kent).

404 It is impossible to disagree with this statement, because it is precisely what is specified in the *Grand Constitutions of 1786*.

405 As can be seen from later correspondence, Udall evidently felt that in his position it was more appropriate for him to deal directly with the Sovereign Grand Commander rather than through the intermediary of the Grand Secretary General.

406 Presumably the point which Udall was making was that the Supreme Council was not yet Incorporated (this was to be done some years later) and not being a Body Corporate there might be some confusion about who could give instructions concerning the Account at the Bank.

407 Vigne later annotated a copy of this "N.B. this note never came into my hands. Chas.Jno.Vigne".

Essay 12
The Henry Udall Affair

In the summer of 1856 there was a division of opinion among the members of the Supreme Council for 'England'[408]. Dr. Henry Beaumont Leeson had succeeded Dr. Oliver as Sovereign Grand Commander. Of the original three members of the English Council, only Henry Udall, the Grand Treasurer General, was among its present Members[409]. He had contrived to restore amicable relations with the Supreme Council of the Northern Masonic Jurisdiction of the U.S.A. which had severed them because of Leeson's determination to maintain his relationship with the irregular Supreme Council of the French Grand Orient, something of which Udall deeply disapproved. Udall was probably the only Member of the Council, apart from Leeson himself, who had studied the 'Grand Constitutions of 1786'[410], and he took a lawyer's view of the need to observe them to the letter. He considered that several things which Leeson intended to do contravened either the 'Grand Constitutions' or the usages of civilised society. Specifically, among the former was the establishment of a 'Grand Chapter KH' in which to confer the Thirtieth Degree, and also Leeson's wish to deprive the Grand Treasurer General of the custody of the Council's funds, and among the latter, coming to decisions at Council Meetings, in particular about Elections to the Council, without giving formal notice. On the other hand Leeson considered that Udall was being negligent about accounting for the funds for which he was responsible.

At the meeting of the Supreme Council on 8th April 1856 a letter was received from George Oliver. His earnest wish was granted that his resignation as Lieutenant Grand Commander should be accepted[411]. The Council also received the resignation of Richard Lea Wilson[412], the only current member of the Council, other than Leeson himself and the absent Henry Udall, who had been elected before 1851. Oliver and Wilson being no longer Members of the Council, and apologies for his unavoidable absence having been received from Henry Udall, at the April Meeting, Henry Leeson, the Sovereign Grand Commander, had been a Member of the Council for five years longer than anyone else. He encountered no opposition when he began to exhibit the latent autocracy which was to bring about his own resignation as Sovereign Grand Commander twelve years later. He first said that for the time being he proposed to defer the appointment of a Lieutenant Grand Commander in Oliver's place. Next, Wilson, having been the 'Master of Ceremonies' of the Council, Leeson, without giving the customary notice, said that he proposed to re-instate the 'retired' Member of the Council, Frederick Winsor[413], and appoint him Master of Ceremonies in Wilson's place. Similarly without notice, and also apparently without seeking the concurrence of his fellow-Members, Leeson then announced that he "nominated to the Council the Sublime Prince of the Royal Secret Matthew Dawes to complete the number of the Council"[414].

Because of the reservations which Udall had already expressed, Leeson would have been unlikely to welcome him to succeed Oliver as Lieutenant Grand Commander, an Office to which Udall might be thought to have some claim if he had desired the Office. It may be that Leeson's determination to defer the Appointment was not unconnected with his next proposition. The Council resolved that Charles Vigne, the Grand Secretary General, should write to Udall "expressing the regret of the Council that his Accounts were not furnished to the present Meeting; requesting him to pay forthwith the sum of £261.16.9 being the balance in his hands 14th February 1855 to the Account of the Supreme Council of England and Wales with the London and Westminster Banking Company, Holborn Branch". That Udall should present his Accounts for Audit some fifteen months after the last occasion upon which this had been done was not an unreasonable request. That the Supreme Council apparently considered that Udall would hold the same balance as he had held in February 1855 was extraordinary in view of the fact that five months earlier the Council had authorised him to disburse from this Balance some ninety pounds.

During the early summer of 1856 Udall and Vigne exchanged several letters. Vigne evidently liked and respected Udall, and expressed his regret at having to convey to the latter the ever more peremptory demands of the Council – and since the Supreme Council did not meet between April and July, this can only have been under instruction from Leeson. Udall was indignant that a Bank Account should have been opened without consulting him as Grand Treasurer General[415]. In early June Vigne notified him that, for the next meeting of the Supreme Council on 6th July, Leeson had given him:

"instructions to issue notices with the following Agenda
To take into consideration the Subject of Finance
To consider any communication from the Ill. Gr.Treasurer Genl. in reference thereto and also to Audit his Accounts and to take such steps as may be considered necessary in case of non-compliance with the Orders of the Supreme Grand Council[416]'.

Confronted with this, Udall composed a lengthy statement – 12 closely written foolscap pages[417] headed 3rd July 1856. Unfortunately his commitments to the Northern Circuit would again prevent him attending the forthcoming meeting. Udall's statement covered the whole range of the activities of the Supreme Council and not only the question of Finance. It must be read in the context that Udall had carefully studied 'The Grand Constitutions'.

Curiously, Udall's statement was addressed neither to Leeson nor to Vigne but to Sir John de la Pole. De la Pole had been Obligated as a Member of the Supreme Council on 5th July 1854[418] and may well have been unaware of the Council's rupture with its American sponsors six years earlier. At the same time Udall wrote to Vigne, telling him what he had done, and said that he had asked de la Pole "when he has read it to send it to you. It is of course of such a nature that I am obliged to make all copies myself"[419].

In his letter, Udall first details the correspondence which he has had with Vigne since the Council Meeting in February. To put this in context, he then sets out at length the circumstances of the rift with the Supreme Council of the Northern Masonic Jurisdiction, making clear that the prime cause of this was Leeson's liaison with the French Grand Orient. He next recounts the actions which he himself had taken to restore harmony, concluding with the American Council's approbation of the "course of strict legality" which it considered that the English Council was now pursuing. It was evidently this "course of strict legality" – or at least his interpretation of it – which Udall intended should continue, and of which he wished de la Pole to be aware.

He went on to say: "I mention this matter" (that is, the necessity for a 'course of strict legality') "in our past history for two reasons. First, a most strange doctrine has got abroad that a Supreme Council has the power within its own jurisdiction of organizing the order in what way it pleases. Secondly, to shew the reason why I have never sanctioned and in fact without making an unseemly opposition having steadily attempted to thwart the formation by members of a body distinct from the Supreme Council for giving the ceremonies of the 30th degree of the Order – such being a division not sanctioned by the American Council although it is by the Grand Orient of Paris".

Udall then sets out at some length those circumstances in which he himself had been involved which led to the Warranting of the 'Grand Metropolitan Chapter KH', emphasising his strong view that "the brethren who took the 30th degree under an Officer appointed by its authority would receive no valid rank by virtue of it, but would owe such rank to the authority of the three Sov. Gd. Insp. Gen. deputed by the Supreme Council to be present at the ceremony", going on to say: "I have always doubted the legality of our Supreme Council granting such a Warrant, and on full and further consideration of the subject am convinced that those doubts are well founded. I hold that the rank of Kt. K.H. of the 30th degree can only be *regularly* conferred by the Supreme Council itself, or by special delegation in each particular instance to the Grand Consistory of Princes of the Royal Secret, and then, of course, in the presence of three Sovereign Gd. Insp. Gen. – the same being as I understand the practice, at the present day, in the American Council."[420] Udall concluded, "Surely we ought after one rupture with our Parent Council to have been especially careful not to run the risk of a second."[421]

Udall then went on to express his disquiet with some more domestic matters, in which Dr. Leeson was exhibiting that autocracy which characterised his term of office as Sovereign Grand Commander. "I proceed next to call your attention to the appointment of Ills. Br. Winsor to fill the vacancy of Master of the Ceremonies in the Council caused by the resignation of the Ills. Br. R[ichar]d. Lea Wilson. The Ills. Br. Winsor formally and in writing resigned his seat in the Council in the year 1851. What then can be more illegal than appointing him to an office in the Council without a fresh election, after the usual notice given? I can conceive nothing more calculated to make the acts of a body null and void[422].

"I next proceed to the resolution that all future elections to the Council shall be limited to three years and with the power of re-election (which in my opinion makes the matter worse)." Udall based this objection on the more questionable interpretation of the 'Grand Constitutions' that Election as a Member of a Supreme Council was "for life that he may exercise the functions of his office independently of the dictation of others, and that he may not be trammelled by the mere authority of those around him.[423] He takes no obligation of fealty to his own Council but binds himself religiously to observe the Statutes and Ordinances of the Order and without any favour, partiality or affection to discharge his duties as a S.G.I.Gen[era]l.; wedded as such anew to the order, his country and his God." He repeats his contention that a Supreme Council is not a legislative body, a view which he supports by quoting a letter which he had received from Gourgas, the Sovereign Grand Commander of the Supreme Council of the Northern Jurisdiction.

Udall concludes his long diatribe by assuring the Council that all its funds are safely in his hands, in spite of what he claims is an attempt to abolish the Office of Grand Treasurer General. He then complains of the lack of courtesy because Meetings had been arranged at times when he had given forewarning that he would not be able to be present, and concludes with a Postscript to the effect that "he would be happy to work with the other members of the Council" if its recent acts were annulled, and his own position restored[424].

Does this final paragraph and Postscript amount to a statement of at least conditional resignation – "I can only resume my Office if the Council's recent actions are rescinded"? If this was Udall's intention, it would at least explain his acceptance without recorded comment of the decisions taken at the following Meeting of the Council, something which it is otherwise hard to explain. But whatever were the rights and wrongs of the Council's actions of which Udall complained, he himself had not produced the Grand Treasurer General's accounts. By failing to do so, he had left himself open to the accusations which were now to be made against him, and, being absent on the Northern Circuit until the beginning of August, he was in no position to rebut them.

The Quarterly Meeting of the Supreme Council was held on 8th July 1856. George Oliver's resignation having been confirmed, Leeson now appointed George Vernon as Lieutenant Grand Commander. That Udall had in fact met Charles Vigne before the Meeting, and complied with at least some part of the Council's demands is indicated by Vigne's ability to inform the Council that there was £140 in the Bank and cash in hand of £10.3.4d[425]. After the disbursements which the Council had earlier authorised Udall to make, these Balances might have been considered realistic. Had there not been Leeson's apparent animus against Udall, this information might have been accepted as adequate until such time as the Accounts were presented for audit. The figures hardly gave grounds for any implication that funds had been misappropriated. Indeed, evidently the Balance had been paid into the Bank as Udall had been requested to do.

At the Meeting no reference was made to Udall's long letter of 3rd July, nor to the charges of irregularity which he had made therein, although by this time de la Pole, Vigne, and, indeed, Leeson himself[426], would all have read it. Leeson evidently wanted no more interference with his command of the Council, and in particular with his flirtation with the French Grand Orient. That Udall had informed de la Pole and Vigne in detail of the disapproval of the Supreme Council of the American Northern Jurisdiction[427] could have been awkward for Leeson if Udall's statements had been taken at their face value and the matter debated.

It is therefore difficult to escape the conclusion that, while Udall's failure to provide financial information, and his refusal to give the Bank a specimen signature, were made the *casus belli* within the Supreme Council, it was his opposition to other measures favoured by the Sovereign Grand Commander which led to his downfall. The seven most recently elected Members of the Supreme Council were almost certainly unaware of 'The Grand Constitutions', and may have discounted Udall's concern about departures from them. There may have been a fundamental misunderstanding of the place of the *Ancient and Accepted Rite* in International Freemasonry. Indeed, two of Udall's statements about the limited powers of the Supreme Council might well have been incomprehensible to them, and for this reason, to have been ignored. They may have seen Udall's effusion as no more than an attempt to divert attention from his apparent wish to retain his personal control over their finances, and to have dismissed as a smoke-screen his historical account of matters disposed of several years earlier. They were continuing to have friendly relations with what they considered to be their neighbouring French 'opposite numbers', and, perhaps, saw no reason why they should be told to abandon these by far distant Brethren in their former American Colonies. All this can be no more than speculation, but it is difficult otherwise to see why the Council acted in the way in which it was about to do.

In his long letter, Udall had made the specific statement that on the day before the February Meeting of the Council, he had met both Leeson and Vigne, and told them that his Accounts were then already prepared for Audit – this statement was not contradicted; it was not even mentioned. But Leeson was determined to continue his relationship with the French Supreme Council. He can hardly have wanted Udall to continue to use his position as a Member of the Council to criticise both this and his departures from the 'Grand Constitutions'. If Udall remained a Member, and persisted in his views, Leeson's own position might be in jeopardy.

Henry Udall was, however, held in great respect by many Members of the Order, and in particular by those Members of the Higher Degrees who had attended his various orations. If what was to amount to his expulsion from the Council was to be accepted by the Order in general, and by its senior Members in particular, it was necessary that doubt should be cast upon the validity of his high reputation. To the Victorians, financial probity was the ultimate test of respectability. That the Supreme Council had grounds for considering that Udall had seriously mismanaged its finances would condemn him in the eyes of all respectable members of the Establishment who were unaware of how flimsy was the evidence for this. Udall was given no chance to defend himself. In his unavoidable absence, and disregarding his explanatory letter, the Council agreed a preliminary Statement. It then passed three Resolutions. While the Statement was true in substance, if not in detail, the third Resolution imperfectly concealed an implication for which the Statement gave no grounds:

"that the repeated neglect of the Illustrious Grand Treasurer General Henry Udall in regard to the presentation of his Accounts, the imperfect manner in which those accounts have been kept[428], his frequent absence[429] without forwarding such Accounts although requested to do so and notwithstanding ample notice have been matters of the most painful regret and inconvenience to the Supreme Grand Council.

"Resolved: That the absolute refusal of the Illustrious Grand Treasurer, either to furnish any statement of Accounts[430], or to comply with the Orders of the Supreme Grand Council render it imperative on them to put an end to such contempt of their authority and they therefore have no alternative but to dismiss him from the Office of Illustrious Grand Treasurer General and from all Station, Office, Power, and Dignity in the Supreme Council of the 33rd Degree.

"Resolved: That Brother Henry Udall be dismissed accordingly from the Office of Illustrious Grand Treasurer General and from all Office, Station, Power and Dignity in the Supreme Grand Council for the 33rd Degree for England & Wales and the Dependencies of the British Crown, and that this resolution be communicated to Brother Henry Udall by the Illustrious Grand Secretary General.

"Resolved: that the Most Puissant Sovereign Grand Commander be empowered to take such steps as he may legally be advised in respect to the recovery of the Monies in the late Treasurer General's hands, and be requested to report thereon to the Council."

Vigne, as Grand Secretary General, did not at once notify Udall of the Resolutions which had been passed at the Council Meeting, and on 10th July he replied to Udall's last brief letter:

"I have received your note announcing that you have found the Golden Book and I laid this communication before the S.G.C. As your friend, I only wish this notice had been accompanied by the Book itself and the Accounts and however much you may feel disposed to doubt it, I assure you, one and all deeply deplored the resolution you have taken in this matter."

Two days later, Vigne wrote from his seat at Hilton Park formally to inform Udall of his dismissal:

"I cannot find words to express the very deep regret I feel that in virtue of my office I am obliged to forward to you the accompanying extract from the Minutes and can only repeat my assurance that one and all of the Council most truly lament the very painful necessity that existed for passing the same."

Undoubtedly Udall had been both careless and discourteous, but in spite of the implication in the third Resolution, no evidence was adduced that the respectable barrister had either misappropriated or misapplied the Council's funds, or that there would be any difficulty about the 'recovery' of the Balance. It might be considered that natural justice should have allowed him to defend himself before the Council took the drastic and damning action which had this implication. But for any response which Udall might subsequently make to be ineffective, it was necessary that the dubious verdict of the Council should be accepted before Udall could defend himself. No time was therefore lost in sending out letters to each S.P.R.S. 32° setting out the Council's three Resolutions over the signature of the newly appointed Lieutenant Grand Commander.

That this was, from Leeson's point of view, a wise move, is evident from the reply of the Staffordshire S.P.R.S., Thomas Ward, who wrote to Vernon:

> "Thank you for the Inform. contained in your letter recd. this morning which has perfectly *astounded* me. From his position in Society, & his apparent love of Masonry, & Zeal for our Order the Grd. Tr. is the last person I should have expected of the disreputable conduct you describe!"

In a postscript, Ward added: "I was not aware that there had existed any unpleasant feeling between the Council and the Ex. G.T. so that your information took me quite by surprise".[431] Similarly, Lt. Colonel Edward Dering[432], S.P.R.S., just returned with his Regiment from Malta, wrote on 19th July: "I much regret the intelligence conveyed by your letter, I had always thought our Bro. U. so devoted to the interests of our Order that I am quite at a loss to understand how he could have refused to comply with the wishes of the Council."

It is only fair to note that other members of the 32nd Degree were less surprised. The prominent Oxford Mason, R.J. Spiers, wrote on 17th July: "I am truly sorry to hear of it, though I am not surprised at your taking this step. I resigned my membership of the Faith & Fidelity Encampment, of which Bro. U. is Registrar, principally because of the irregularity & uncertainty attending everything connected with it." On the following day George Cole[433] wrote: "I am not surprised at the Council having arrived at the determination you mention I have long seen that some such result was inevitable, & although it must be a matter of regret to all concerned the individual has only himself to blame." In the absence of any evidence of financial malpractice, one is left with the impression that the busy Barrister had simply 'taken too much on'.

From Udall himself there seems to have been no reaction. When at the end of July Vigne wrote to Udall requesting the return of the blank Warrant forms and the Council's Seals, Udall replied from the Northern Circuit: "I can do as you wish as before leaving London I had everything Masonic packed and sent from my Chambers," adding in the most friendly manner: "I hope you will have good sport when the season commences"[434]. Again, one can only speculate, but Udall seems to have anticipated the reaction his letter would provoke, and had decided to wash his hands of the whole affair.

Henry Bowyer[435] was Elected to the Supreme Council in Udall's place at the next Meeting on 14th October. Under Leeson's guidance the Council then took two inconsistent decisions. First, it was agreed that copies of the Resolutions regarding Udall should be sent to the North American Supreme Council, with the hope that it "will still be pleased to continue their friendly relations with this Council". Then Leeson announced his intention of renewing the relationship with the French Grand Orient, the very relationship which eight years earlier had led to the rift with the Council's North American sponsors, and of which, of course, he now took no steps to make them aware.

Vigne wrote to Charles Moore, the Grand Secretary General of the American Council on 16th October, enclosing extracts from the Minutes of the two previous Meetings. In his covering letter, Vigne made no reference to their contents, but only hoped that the American Council would approve of the new official form which had been adopted for such communications. The Americans could do no other than accept the findings of the English Council at their face-value. On 22nd November Moore replied:

> "While thanking you for your kindness in promptly communicating with this S.C. we cannot forbear to express our extreme regret at the unauthorised and unlooked for defection of Bro. Udall. Yet we are assured by the course you have pursued in reference to him that you will not tolerate unmasonic conduct in the Members of your Council, but will keep and preserve it in a sound healthy condition.[436]"

There is no record of any reaction from Henry Udall while this correspondence was taking place. On 9th November Vigne wrote to him saying that he had been directed by the Council:

> "to request that you will send me at once all books, papers, letters, Certificates, Seals, I.O.U.'s, and anything else you may have belonging to, or relating to the affairs of the G.C. together with a schedule which I will sign and return. I am also authorised to ask you for a statement of Accounts with the balance in your hands for which I will send a receipt in proper form."

This is curious, because in reply to Vigne's earlier request, Udall had stated on 7th August that "before leaving London I had anything Masonic packed and sent from my Chambers". It is odd that Vigne had not already received it. But even more extraordinary is the request for the Statement of Accounts. Leeson had requested Vigne to act for the time being as both Grand Secretary General and Grand Treasurer General. He had produced the Accounts at the Meeting on 14th October, and they had been Audited and Accepted; the Credit Balance was £143.14.5d. If any money was unaccounted for, the deficit can only have been trivial.

On 12th November Udall's only reply to Vigne's latest request was to ask him to "be good enough to forward to me the names of those whom you designate S.G.C. of the 33rd (sic) who have desired to make the request contained therein". Vigne patiently replied on 14th November[437].

Nothing more is recorded in the Minute Book about either property or funds, apart from regular Annual Statements of Accounts and one curious entry six months later[438].

On the other hand, the matter of intercourse with the French Supreme Council was far from closed. At the Meeting of the Supreme Council on 13th January 1857, it was informed by Dr. Leeson that Frederick Winsor, who was going to France, had agreed to renew this, but that this contact had had to be postponed because Winsor had cancelled his visit. The ties of friendship were, however, maintained when Brother Bugnot, the English Council's Representative near the French Grand Orient was sent a Collar and Jewel of Office. In January 1859 the English Council received "Ill. Bro. Hyde Clarke 32° under the Grand Orient of France", and greeted him as such after he had produced the Certificates of his several Degrees[439]. The Supreme Council of England continued to recognise the Supreme Council of the Grand Orient and Brethren holding Degrees under it for a further twenty years[440].

There is no doubt that Henry Udall had been remiss – perhaps 'casual' would be a better word – in conducting the financial affairs of the Supreme Council, and possibly of other bodies as well. It is hard to believe that Dr. Leeson did not use this as an excuse to allay Udall's criticisms of his own conduct by removing him from Office. However, at least his advice about the 'Grand Metropolitan Chapter KH 30° bore fruit. Like the 'High Grades Union', it soon disappeared without trace.

408 It now also styled itself 'of Wales and the Dependencies of the British Crown'.

409 Henry Udall was a barrister, a member of the Northern Circuit. For the past half-dozen years he had played a leading role in the affairs of the Council, but at this time his legal commitments caused him frequently to be absent from its Meetings.

410 It was not until the Meeting of the Supreme Council on 12th July 1859 that it was resolved "that the Members of the Supreme Council, feeling that they are not sufficiently acquainted with the Obligations and Prerogatives of their position, have to request that the M.P. Sov. Grand Commander will sanction and authorise the Regulations, Ordinances and Grand Secret Constitutions to be communicated to them". A & A, p.42.

411 At the following Meeting in June, the Supreme Council received a letter from George Oliver, thanking the Members for accepting his resignation, and pointing out that he had not wanted the Office in 1851, and that he considered that now the reasons which at the time made it expedient for him to accept the position no longer existed. It can only be presumed that in saying this he was referring to the restoration of fraternal relations with the Council's American sponsors.

412 Richard Lea Wilson had been a Member of the Supreme Council since 1846. Wilson had been the President of the "Illustrious College of Knight KH and NPU" which the Encampment of Faith and Fidelity had established when they separated the Knights Templar Degrees (KM, KT and MP) from those of the Ancient and Accepted Rite.

413 His name is inconsistently spelled in the Minutes and in the Masonic Press as 'Windsor', 'Winsor' and 'Winser'.

414 Since 1849 Matthew Dawes had been the Provincial Grand Commander of Knights Templar in Lancashire, having been Grand Chamberlain for the first three years after the 'revival' of Grand Conclave. He was evidently a very suitable choice to assist in the expansion of the Order. After his 'nomination', the nine Members of the Council were Henry Beaumont Leeson, Henry Udall, John A.D. Cox, Frederick Winsor, Sir John Robinson, George Vernon, Sir John de la Pole, Charles Vigne and Matthew Dawes.

415 Udall was particularly indignant that every member of the Council should become an authorised cheque signatory, his own signature only one among nine.

416 The ostensible reason for this sudden preoccupation with Finance was that when Henry Emly died, he had been Treasurer of the Higher Degree 'Dining Club',

the 'High Grades Union'. Apparently some confusion of his affairs had led to difficulties in acquiring the balance due to the Union from Emly's Executors, and Leeson did not want to be put in a similar position should anything happen to Udall.

417 For those only conversant with modern usage, 'foolscap' was a paper size similar to A4.

418 De la Pole was Elected in place of Davyd Nash.

419 As the only surviving one of the three 'original' Members of the English Supreme Council, Udall appears to have considered that he had a responsibility towards the more recently elected Members. He started his letter to de la Pole by writing "I request your attention to the following statement that you may the better be able to perform the duties that devolve on you arising from your exalted masonic dignity as Sov. Gd, Insp, Genl. in the Supreme Council of this country, and for the purpose of your more fully appreciating my motives in the course I am pursuing as a Member of that Council and Grand Tr. Genl. of the Holy Empire."

420 To this Udall added: "I direct your attention more especially to this matter because I find in the June number of the Masonic Magazine that Ills. Br. Davyd Nash is reported to have said at a meeting of the Bristol Kt. Templars that he believed that the Supreme Council intended to establish what he termed Consistories of the 30th Degree of Kt. K.H. in several places in England – one pressing reason I had for attempting to thwart the printing of such a Warrant was the conviction I felt that the American Council would consider it an innovation in the organization pointed out for our guidance."

421 Here Udall's interpretation can hardly be gainsaid. Article XI clearly states "The degree of *Knight Kadosh*, and the 31st and 32nd degrees, can only be conferred on such Masons as shall have been adjudged worthy thereof, and at a meeting of, and by, at least three Sovereign Grand Inspectors General".

422 Udall added: "I must say also for myself I should have strongly remonstrated against his re-introduction and should have given these reasons:
1st. That from the time of his being an S.G.I.G. he has shown no activity to do anything to benefit the order nor has he so far as my recollection serves me attended any meeting of the order in any of its Degrees.
2ndly. I have a reason against it as Tr:Genl. – for although he put the order to some expense which I need not particularize he never paid the ordinary fee of an S.G.I.G. Surely when we have so many eminent and distinguished brethren in the ranks we ought not to pass them over and let a vacancy be filled by a Br. who notwithstanding he is of the highest dignity in the order has witheld from us his assistance."

423 The 'Grand Constitutions' are not easy to construe in this respect. Article II, §I, clearly states "The 33rd Degree invests those Masons who are legitimately in possession thereof, with the character, title, privileges, and authority of Sovereign Grand Inspectors General of the Order". Article V, § I, states that "EVERY SUPREME COUNCIL shall consist of Nine Grand Inspectors General of the 33rd Degree". However, it says nothing about their terms of Office. Other articles

certainly appear to envisage there being S.G.I.G.s who are not members of a Supreme Council.

424 According to the copy which Vigne later made of this letter, Udall enclosed with this screed an extract from the letter which he had written in May 1851 to the SC,NMJ.

425 That Udall and Vigne had indeed had met prior to the Meeting of the Council is confirmed by a hurried note which the latter received from Udall on the following day – "I forgot to tell you in the excitement of our meeting that the turn-out of my Chambers in moving, the roll of the Golden Book was found".

426 Vigne annotated a letter which he received from Udall before the Meeting "Bro. Udall requesting me to shew my copy to Dr. Leeson, 5 July 1856". Vigne's correspondence indicates the respect in which he held Henry Udall, and, being punctiliously conscientious, he is unlikely to have failed to comply with Udall's request.

427 Neither de la Pole nor Vigne might be aware of this because it took place several years before either had been Elected to the Council: de la Pole, in November 1854, and Vigne in June 1855.

428 Only eighteen months earlier, in February 1855, Udall's Accounts had been Audited, accepted and adopted. According to his own statement, 12 months later he had announced that another year's Accounts were ready for Audit, but, admittedly, had not yet been produced. It is hard to say on what evidence the statement could be made "the imperfect manner in which those Accounts have been kept".

429 Of each of which Udall had given formal Notice on account of his legal duties.

430 At the Meeting Vigne had been able to make a statement of the Cash at Bank and in Hand.

431 If one takes Udall's letter of 6th July at its face-value, six months earlier there seems to have been none.

432 Colonel Dering was Elected to the Supreme Council on 9th July 1862.

433 George Beauchamp Cole was Elected to the Supreme Council on 21st April 1857.

434 Udall's reply is dated the seventh of August, five days before the start of the Grouse-shooting Season, the 'Glorious Twelfth'.

435 Captain (later Colonel) Henry Bowyer, the Deputy PGM of Oxfordshire, was the fourth 'Provincial Grand Commander' of Knights Templar to have a seat on the Supreme Council. (The others were Matthew Dawes [Lancashire], soon to be succeeded by Albert Hudson Royds (Supreme Council, May 1868), George Vernon [Staffordshire], and Charles Vigne [Dorset].) Henry Vernon [Worcestershire] was to take his seat on the Council in 1860. The Supreme Council was then well placed to influence Knights Templar to affiliate under its Banner, with another prominent member of the Ancient and Accepted Rite, Dr. Henry James Hinxman, having succeeded Thomas Crucefix as Provincial Grand Commander for Kent.

436 Moore also requested the nomination in Udall's place, of a Representative of his Council near that of what he was careful to refer to as 'England and Wales'. ('The new official form' stated 'of England & Wales and the Dependencies of the British Crown'.) Vigne was then placed in a position of some difficulty.

Having written to Moore to say that he would place his request for a Representative before his Council, he had to write again on 20th January 1857 to say that "Our M.P.S.G.C. has himself selected one of our Council to act as your representative whose name he purposes himself forwarding to your M.P.S.G.C. Bro. E.A.Raymond being desirous by so doing of paying him and your Council the greatest compliment and attention in his power". In spite of this somewhat obsequious approach, the American Supreme Council accepted the name of John Astell Deacon Cox when Leeson eventually forwarded it.

437 "I send the names of the S.G.C. as you require. Dr. Leeson, Sir J. Robinson. Sir J. de la Pole, F.A.Winsor, J.A.D.Cox, M.Dawes. Col. Vernon. C.J.Vigne and Capt. Bowyer Elected."

438 The Minutes of the Meeting on 14th July 1857 record that Messrs. Elkington, of the Freemasons' Tavern, had sent the Supreme Council an Account for a sum which they claimed was due to them from the 'High Grades Union'. The Secretary (*sic*) was instructed to reply, somewhat tartly "that the Council had nothing to do with the meetings of the High Grades Union, and the order having been given by Mr. Udall, he having money in his hands is accountable to them for it". There is no record that Udall took over the funds of the 'High Grades Union' after the death of Henry Emly. Indeed, Vigne's earlier letter seemed to indicate that the Council had, with difficulty, dealt with the matter itself, and certainly did not ask Udall to intervene.

439 However, when in April of the following year Hyde Clarke sent the Supreme Council a letter about the wish of some Brethren in Smyrna to hold a Chapter under the English Supreme Council, suitable caution was displayed and the matter seems to have been ignored.

440 On 13th September 1877 the Grand Orient of France declared it to be unnecessary to require of Candidates for admission into Freemasonry a declaration of belief in the G.A.O.T.U, and the V.S.L. was no longer mandatorily displayed in its Lodges and Chapters. The United Grand Lodge of England withdrew recognition from the Grand Orient, and, following its example, all English Masonic bodies, including the Supreme Council, severed all connection with it.

PART TWO

THE EIGHTEENTH OR 'ROSE CROIX' DEGREE

Essay 13
The Earlier Rituals of the 'Rose Croix' Degree

It would be no exaggeration to say that if we knew the full story of how and why the Degree which we now know as the 'Rose Croix' was absorbed into Speculative Freemasonry, we would understand better how the Craft itself came into being. It would be naïve to insist that 'Rose Croix' is wholly unconnected with the 'Rosicrucians', the imaginary Brotherhood conceived by Johann Andreae at the beginning of the seventeenth century. There is no evidence that this Brotherhood was other than a figment of his imagination – Andreae himself admitted that his so-called *'Manifestos'*[441] were no more than a *ludibrium*, a fable or academic joke[442]. They have something in common with the myth in *The New Atlantis* which Francis Bacon published at about the same time as the *'Manifestos'* were appearing. Although the Rosicrucian Brotherhood conceived by Andreae had no physical existence, the ideas put forward in the *'Manifestos'* had a considerable influence on philosophical thought in the seventeenth century, at the very time when the Speculative Craft was taking shape. Anyone to whom this is of more detailed interest is well advised to study the works of the late Dame Frances Yates[443].

'Rose Croix' did not emerge as a Masonic Degree until the middle of the eighteenth century. Earlier Masonic writers[444] claimed that it originated in a Chapter in the French town of Arras in or about the year 1745, and was conferred by the 'Young Pretender', Charles Edward Stuart, upon some of his Jacobite adherents by means of the so-called 'Charter of Arras'. This pleasant story is now dismissed as a complete fabrication[445]. The first definitive evidence of the existence of the Degree comes from documents preserved in the French town of Lyons. In the 1760s Jean-Baptiste Willermoz assembled here a Rite of Twenty-five Degrees of which the highest was *Knight of the Eagle, of the Pelican, Knight of St. Andrew or Mason of Heredom*. Willermoz had corresponded with the Master of one of the Lodges in Metz, Meunier de Précourt, from whom he may have obtained information about German Rosicrucianism. In 1765 he completed what was essentially a Ritual of the 'Rose Croix' Degree[446]. By 1768 there was a *Sovereign Chapter Rose Croix* in Paris. From this time the Degree grew in popularity, possibly because it reintroduced the teachings of Christianity into a system which had become deistic and even secular.

Perhaps the most remarkable thing about the 'Rose Croix' Degree is that so little of its format, and even of its wording (in literal translation), has changed in the course of almost two hundred and fifty years. Naudon considers that the two earliest surviving manuscript rituals of the Degree were written in about 1765, one of which he reproduces in a book published in 1978[447], the other being in the Bibliothèque Historique de la Ville de Paris[448]. Jackson pointed out the "surprising similarity" of all subsequent texts to the 1765 original[449]. Indeed, much of the wording of a printed French ritual of the Degree dated 1770 is identical to that in each of the 1765 manuscripts[450]. This printed ritual, *The Royal Art of the Knight of Rosecroix*, purports to have been published as an anti-Masonic 'Satyr', but most Masonic scholars regard both the Ritual and its dating as being genuine, though not its claim to have been printed in England[451]. It contains everything necessary for the conduct of a Rose Croix Chapter, not only the ritual wording and rubrics, but, for example, a specimen Knight's Certificate, the detailed description of the layout of the rooms required for the Ceremony, and instructions as to how, when and where Chapters should meet[452].

So that there can be no mistake in regard to the ambiance of the Degree, this Ritual explicitly states in respect of the rooms in which the Ceremony takes place that "The first represents Mount Calvary and the second the tomb of J.C. The two together are intended to represent allegorically the events of his death and resurrection." Lest there should be any mistaken confusion with a Sacrament, under "The meal of the Knights", the Ritual states "This is the only table-Ceremony practised in a Rosecroix Chapter, but it is essential, being in memory of the meal attended by J.C. at Emaus (*sic*) when he again met with his disciples after his resurrection"[453]. This is, of course, chronologically appropriate, since 'the Third Point', as it is known today, follows the Ceremony in the 'second room', which, as this Ritual has already made clear, is "Representing the moment of the resurrection of J.C.".

The Opening is simple, similar to that with which English Brethren are familiar today, except that there is no Prelate. It is the 'first Warden' who answers the question as to the time, relating the customary catalogue of disasters, and interposing the phrase "when the tools of Masonry were broken"[454] after "when the Light was obscured". The Master then opens the Chapter after the words "since masonry has suffered such a calamity (*une tribulation*) let us devote our cares to a new labour, to recover the lost word ...".

The Candidate enters 'the first room' after the Master of Ceremonies has repeated to him the series of calamities to recover from which the Chapter has been opened. In this room, the Master sits beside the Altar, in front of which there is a drawn curtain, and the grieving Brethren "are sitting on the floor in a state of confusion, each with his right hand under his chin, his left in front of his face, and his elbow on his knee." Thereafter the Ceremony proceeds in the familiar way. The Master again describes the disastrous situation with which the Brethren are confronted, the curtains being drawn apart at "the veil of the Temple is rent in twain". The aid of the Candidate to assist in recovering the 'Lost Word' is solicited, and he is instructed to travel for 33 years, which, he is informed, will be symbolised by 7 circuits of the room[455]. The Candidate finds the initials of the three Virtues at the three Pillars, after which he takes an Obligation[456]. The Candidate is then told that "all is accomplished" (*consommé*)[457].

Thereupon all the brethren are instructed to travel[458] in order to attempt to recover the 'Lost Word' with the assistance of the three Virtues. Seven circuits of the room are then made, at the third, fourth, fifth and sixth of which, the Master, Wardens, Officers and Brethren respectively pass through into the second room. At the Candidate's seventh circuit the Master of Ceremonies prevents his departure, tells him that he must now humbly pass through the most serious trials, and removes all the Candidate's regalia. He then covers him with "a black cloth smelling of ashes", and leads him three times round "the room where Hell is represented"[459]. He is then instructed how to answer the 'four questions' ("Whence come you?", "Where have you passed" and so on.) before the Candidate, still veiled, is introduced to the brethren in the 'Red Room'. There is no reference to a ladder in the Ritual, but the Candidate replies to the four questions, and is instructed "to take up the initial letter of each word" – Judea, Nazareth, Raphael, Juda[460]. The Master congratulates him on thereby finding the 'Word', and proceeds to instruct him in the Signs and Tokens, which are almost identical to those given in a Chapter today, save that the first sign is known as that of 'Admiration'. The Candidate is then invested, with a Sash (not an Apron or Collar), and the senior Warden says (all the Bn. placing their hands on the Candidate) "by the power which I have received from the sovereign Chapter of heredon (*sic*) your mother L. and home I create and constitute you Prince, Knight of the Eagle, perfect mason, free of heredon, under the title of Rosecroix".

As in many Rituals of the period, this is followed by a question and answer 'Lecture' in which the Ceremony is recounted. When this is concluded, the Master asks "What is the hour?" and receives the familiar answer informing him that everything is now restored, including "our Working Tools have resumed their proper form". After this response, alms are collected, and the Master asks "if any Knight has anything to propose for the good of the order or of the Chapter". As to the actual closing, the Ritual says no more than that "the Chapter is closed with the Ceremonies and ritual used in similar cases with the difference that the Master leaves his seat and embraces each of the Knights saying to each of them deep peace (*paix profonde*)"[461].

The Master then says "let us go and take the refreshment which our labours deserve and depart in peace". The Brethren take off their boots, put on slippers, and are given a white wand by the Master. The two most lately joined Brethren "go into the middle chamber" and lay a white cloth on a table upon which they place a loaf of white bread on a plate surrounded by three candles. All the Brethren then follow the Master into the room and stand round the table "in no particular order". The Master takes up the bread, breaks off a piece for himself, and then passes the loaf round to the other Brethren. "The last-joined" then places on the table a goblet of wine, from which the Master himself drinks before passing it also to the other Brethren. Any wine remaining is poured on the fire, after which each Brother is again "embraced by the Master saying Peace be with you to which each replies And also with you". The Brethren leave the room, replace their boots and disperse. The final instruction is "note that the last-joined clears the table & that during the whole Ceremony of the Banquet the most profound silence is observed & no one acts as servant to the Brn., all being equal[462]".

The identity in the wording extends even to the heading of the specimen Certificate set out both in the 1765 manuscript and in the 1770 printed versions – "De l'Orient de l'Univers et du lieu très secret de la Métropole Loge d'Ecosse par les nombres 77", although the Certificate in the printed version is considerably expanded. Many of the questions and answers in the 'Lecture' which follows the ceremony are identical in both the printed and manuscript versions, though each has some questions which the others do not include, and omits others. It is difficult not to believe that each was derived from a common source, possibly the original Ritual of Willermoz. These Rituals, together with other early versions, do, however, exhibit one curious inconsistency. In some, the 'Third Point' is conducted before the Chapter is closed, and in others, after the Closing.

In the West Indies during the 1760s Stephen Morin had developed a 25-Degree Rite which included the 'Rose Croix' Degree as its Eighteenth. After Morin's death in 1771, Henry Francken took over the direction of Morin's Rite. He wrote a series of manuscripts setting out in each what he claimed were copies of 'The Grand Constitutions of 1762', and the Rituals of the Degrees of the Rite which these 'Constitutions' were considered to govern. The earliest of these manuscripts is dated 1771[463], a second is dated 1783[464], and a third, undated, was written between 1786 and Francken's death in 1795[465].

The text of the Francken manuscripts is, for the most part, a literal translation of the wording in the French Rituals to which reference has already been made, even to the inclusion of the three-times spoken 'huzza' which is characteristic of French masonry at this time. The Penalty in the Obligation bears the same reference to Christ's suffering upon the Cross. In each of these Rituals, the regalia includes a cordon or sash. It is curious that while in the French Rituals this is worn over the left shoulder 'à droit', in the Francken rituals it is worn from the right shoulder to the left. In spite of this minor detail, it is almost impossible to believe that Francken did not have access to a copy of a 'Rose Croix' Ritual derived from the same source as were the French Rituals. In Francken's manuscripts there is, however, one extraordinary omission – there is no reference to the 'Third Point'. This seems to imply that not only did the Third Point form no part of Morin's Twenty-five Degree Rite, but also that it may have been absent from the initial formulation of the Ancient and Accepted Scottish Rite of Thirty-three Degrees under the first Supreme Council in Charleston in 1801.

In the last quarter of the eighteenth century Christian Chivalric Degrees were being practised in Engand in Encampments of Knights Templar. There is no certainty about the source from which these were derived. The Templar Degree featured in von Hund's 'Rite of Strict Observance' from which English Military Lodges adopted it and, presumably, introduced it to England on their return from service in Europe. At the same time various European sequences of 'Higher Degrees' were becoming known in England. For example, in the 1780s, de Lintot, a member of one or more of the French Lodges in London, also developed a 'Rite of Seven Degrees' which incorporated, in a garbled form and with much extraneous matter, some of the material in the first thirty Degrees of today's Ancient and Accepted Rite, together with a mish-mash of historical Knights Templar Degrees[466]. By 1791 there were several Knights Templar Encampments in England, each deriving its authority from a Chapter of the Holy Royal Arch, and many of them having adopted Degrees other than those of Knights Templar, Knights of Malta and the Mediterranean Pass. In that year Thomas Dunckerley[467] secured the independence of the Encampments from 'The Grand and Supreme Royal Arch Chapter' by establishing a new Ruling Body, the all-embracing nature of which can be seen from its comprehensive title 'The Grand Conclave of the Royal, Exalted, Religious and Military Order of H.R.D.M. Grand Elected Masonic Knights Templars, K.D.S.H. of St. John of Jerusalem, Palestine, Rhodes, etc'[468]. In the course of the next few years, most English Encampments successively gave their allegiance to the newly formed Grand Conclave of which the Duke of Sussex became Grand Master in 1812.

In the majority of these Encampments, previous Exaltation in a Royal Arch Chapter continued generally to be the only qualification required of a Candidate before Installation as a Knight Templar, although, as Smyth points out[469], there is little logic in this tradition. There were exceptions: possibly in Newcastle upon Tyne, probably in Cornwall, and certainly in Bristol[470]. Elsewhere in England, most, if not all, Encampments, while retaining the Royal Arch as the only essential prerequisite for Installation, extended the Rite by subsequently conferring the Degrees of 'Rosae Crucis' and 'Kadosh' to each of which reference was confusingly made from time to time as the *Ne Plus Ultra*, 'than which there is nothing more'[471]. There is no authoritative record of whence the Encampments derived their authority to confer these Degrees, or of how they came to be aware of them[472].

Few 'Rosae Crucis' rituals have survived. In 1908 Cecil Powell, the Keeper of the Archives in Bristol, presented the Librarian of the Supreme Council[473] with a copy which he had made of a manuscript endorsed 'Richard Smith 6 May 1821'[474]. In his introductory notes, Powell suggested that this was translated from the French before the receipt of the Grand Orient rituals on which the present 'Bristol Working' is based[475]. However, nowhere in this manuscript is there any reference to the Degree of 'Rose Croix', *per se*. The Candidate is announced as seeking to be admitted a Knight 'Rosae Crucis', and thereafter there are several references in the manuscript to the Degree as such, including two in the Obligation. It is therefore possible that this manuscript is an example of the 'Rosae Crucis' ritual generally used in Knights Templar Encampments. This likelihoood is increased by the Conclave being referred to as "of Mt. Calvary" and not "of H.R.D.M.", and by the list of Officers being the same as that found in contemporary Knights Templar Encampments, including '2 Generals' and a 'Prelate'. The presiding Officer is the 'Grand Master', the customary title of the Presiding Officer in a Knights Templar Encampment at the turn of the eighteenth century, and is addressed as "Most Wise Prince"[476]

The Ceremony is markedly different from that set out in the 1770 French *'Rosecroix'* ritual, and from that subsequently adopted in English 'Rose Croix Chapters', although some of the wording would be familiar to 'Rose Croix' Brethren today. However, in the Opening, the Brethren are summoned to stand in two lines or columns ("all the Sr. Knights draw their Swords and put on their hats") and they and the Outer and Inner Guards communicate the Sign, Token and Word to one or other of the Generals[477]. But when the Master of Ceremonies confirms that "the gates of the Castle are secure", (an evident reminiscence of the Knights Templar ceremony) and the Most Wise has been thus assured, he opens the Conclave with the familiar recital of calamities (including the breakage of the tools and columns of Masonry). He then asks the Prelate "What remains for us to do?", and receives the reply, as in the ritual today ("To respect the Decrees of Providence" and so on), and the Knights are told that that shall be their aim.

That this Degree follows on from that of a Knight Templar is then repeatedly stressed. The Candidate is received "in the Habit and Decorations of a Kt. Templar", and has to prove himself as such. Having done so, he enters the first room (where all the Companions 'lay down on the floor in a mournful posture'), and is questioned by the 'Most Wise'[478]. The Candidate then visits the Pillars to find the Initials, F, H and C[479], but there is no reference to seven circuits. In the Obligation, before pledging himself to secrecy, the Candidate has to declare that he has been regularly Installed as a Knight Templar. After the Candidate "Kisses the Book", he withdraws to be veiled, and, on his return, takes part in the seven circuits during which all except the Prelate, the Master of Ceremonies, the Inner Guard and the Candidate himself "depart quietly to the joyful apartment".

From this point, the Ceremony, while preserving its general familiar form, differs considerably from any subsequent 'Rose Croix' Ritual. It is in the first, or 'dark' room that the Prelate asks the 'Questions', the answers to which reveal the 'Word', and this is then shown to the Candidate inscribed on the Cross on the Altar. The Candidate then ascends a ladder, apparently a real one, repeating successively on its seven steps *first* the 'Word Letters', and *afterwards* the initials of the 'Virtues'. The ladder is then moved so that the Prelate can physically use it to ascend in order to remove the 'Word' from the Cross, after which a procession is formed to carry the 'Word' into the "joyful room". Here it is presented to the Most Wise, who pronounces it aloud, "to which the Prelate answers 'Miserere nobis'", and the 'Word' is fixed "in its usual place, which must be done with pins only, so as to be easier removed when required. As soon as it is fixed, all the Companions fall on their Knees & point their Swords at it as a Mark of Respect". The Candidate is then Installed, and afterwards invested with regalia which differs substantially from that of the present-day 'Rose Croix' Degree. However, the Signs, Token and Words which are communicated are, for the most part, the familiar ones. The 'Feast', (which is nowhere referred to as the 'Third Point') then takes place. The exhortation of the M.W. to take part in this is similar to that in later 'Rose Croix' Rituals, and afterwards the 'Word' is consumed by fire, but the wording of the necessity to do so is somewhat different. The Conclave is then closed in the 'lower apartment', the Prelate stating that it is "The 9th or last hour, the hour of a perfect Mason", his explanation of which being given in the familiar words, as are the closing words of the Most Wise.

Although this is distinctly a 'Rosae Crucis' Ritual, it has been described above in some detail, as it may well have been similar to that used in the earliest Chapters held under the Supreme Council of England. There is no record of an 18th Degree 'Rose Croix' Ritual being included in all the documents sent to England by the Supreme Council of the Northern Jurisdiction of the U.S.A. in the course of Patenting the English Supreme Council, in spite of the assertion to the contrary by Baynard.[480] Indeed, further study of the contemporary correspondence, including that which has only recently come to light, strongly indicates that no Eighteenth Degree Ritual was received in England from America, whatever Leeson may have obtained from France. It is therefore impossible to be certain what Ritual was used at the first meeting of a Chapter under the jurisdiction of 'The Supreme Council for England'. This took place at the Freemasons' Hall on Tuesday the 30th of June 1846 with Dr. Leeson in the Chair, and Henry Udall, one of the three earliest Members of the Council[481], as 'High Pontiff' or Prelate[482]. Leeson and Udall were both members of the Faith and Fidelity Encampment under the auspices of which this first Chapter meeting was initially held, its Rose Croix Chapter then receiving a 'Patent' from the Supreme Council as 'Metropolitan Chapter'[483].

To establish the independent identity of the new Supreme Council, there would have been an evident need to distinguish the Degrees conferred under its jurisdiction from the 'Rosae Crucis' and 'Kadosh' Degrees of the Knights Templar Encampments, even though, for the time being, the Supreme Council deemed these as equivalent to its own Degrees. It is conceivable, though no direct evidence of this can be adduced, that the first steps taken to achieve this can be found in a manuscript ritual[484] in the Archives of the Supreme Council, and which shows signs of considerable use. It is written on both sides of sheets of plain paper, stitched together. It appears to be in the handwriting of Henry Udall who, for the next few years, was preoccupied with ensuring the regularity of the proceedings of the Council. This ritual, while similar in some respects to the transcription of the pre-1815 Baldwyn Ritual to which reference has already been made, is more probably an independent translation from a French original[485]. It commences by the Brethren being asked to assist in opening a Chapter specifically of *Rose Croix* of Mount Calvary, and, unlike the pre-1815 transcription, the words *Rosae Crucis* appear nowhere in the text. The exhortation after the Obligation refers to the 'altar' and not to 'this sacred tribunal', and the description of the elaborate regalia of a Knight 'Rosae Crucis' is omitted. There is, however, no doubt, that the Candidate is considered to be qualified to receive the 'Rose Croix' Degree by having been previously installed as a Knight Templar; at this early stage in the existence of the Supreme Council for England it might not have occurred to any of those present that this should not be the case. In the absence of other evidence, it is at least possible that this was the first 'Rose Croix' Ritual used under the new Supreme Council. Thomas Wright, the Grand Secretary General of the Irish Supreme Council, attended the first meeting on 30th June 1846, apparently as the personal emissary of its Sovereign Grand Commander, the Earl of Leinster. The report of the meeting states that "Wright spoke in terms highly eulogistic of the whole proceedings, and characterized it as quite pure". Knights Templar references would not have seemed to him to be irregular, because the Irish Council required this qualification. The Northern Masonic Jurisdiction was given no information about the Ritual being employed by its daughter Council, but greeted the first conferment of the Degree in England with enthusiasm[486].

It might well have seemed 'irregular' to the American Brethren if those 'Advanced' to the 'Rose Croix' Degree in this first ceremony had necessarily been Knights Templar, because under neither American Supreme Council was there any connection between the two Orders[487]. On the other hand, in many English Encampments there had been for several years a custom or tradition of semi-automatic progression to the 'Rosae Crucis' Degree within a short time after Installation as a Knight Templar. There had apparently been an agreement that English Knights Templar who had already progressed to the Degree of 'Rosae Crucis' would be deemed Sovereign Princes Rose Croix if they so wished. This could be effected by affiliation, which involved taking an Obligation of Allegiance to the Supreme Council. Those Knights Templar who had not yet so progressed were an evident source of Candidates to be Perfected within the Ancient and Accepted Rite. But, accustomed hitherto to look forward to more or less immediate progression, such Brethren would be understandably unwilling to suffer the delay of passing through fourteen Intermediate Degrees. There might well be pressure to maintain the system to which they were accustomed. A formula was therefore necessary by which lip-service was paid to the conduct of the Rite as desired by the Americans while dealing with practical problems in England. No one was better equipped to do this than the experienced lawyer, Henry Udall, and it appears that it was he who devised the compromise which has endured to the present day.

The ritual authorised by the Supreme Council of England and Wales etc. for use in its Rose Croix Chapters today differs little in its essentials from that attributed to Henry Udall, which was circulated in 1852[488]. Minor changes in the wording and one major addition[489], are recorded from time to time in its Minutes as having been authorised by the Supreme Council. We can, however, be well assured that when a Candidate is perfected today we are following closely in the footsteps of our predecessors in the 1850s, and, indeed, are straying little from those imprinted nearly a century earlier.

441 The 'Confessio', the 'Fama' and the 'Alchemical Wedding'.

442 Frances A. Yates, The Rosicrucian Enlightenment, pp.80/1 (Paladin Edition, 1975).

443 In particular, The Rosicrucian Enlightenment, Chapters 15&16, pp.249-278 (Paladin Edition, 1975) and The Occult Philosophy in the Elizabethan Age, Part 3, pp.167-191(Routledge & Kegan Paul, London, 1979)

444 For example, A.E.Mackey in his Encyclopaedia of Freemasonry.

445 Among the reasons for dismissing this story are the facts that there is no evidence that Prince Charles ever visited the town, that there was no Chapter in Arras until 1765, that there is no reference to the Charter itself until the 1760s, that it is highly unlikely that the Prince would have referred to himself in a document as 'Pretender to the English Crown', and even less likely that in his father's life-time as ''We, Charles Edward, King of England, France, Scotland and Ireland'.

446 Alice Joly, Un Mystique Lyonnais et les Secrets de la Franc-Maçonnerie, 1730-1824 (1938) Reference is made to this in RC, p.25, but the present author regrets that he has been unable to locate a copy of this work.

447 Reproduced in Paul Naudon, Histoire, Rituels et Tuilleur des Hauts [sic] Grades Maçonniques, Annexe 1, p.375, 3d. Edition, refondue et augmentée, Dervy-Livres, Paris (1978). This ritual came to light during the disposal sale of the Library of the Château de Brigon in Amsterdam on 25th January 1856.

448 Reproduced in Renaissance Traditionelle, Nos.5-7 (1971).

449 RC, p.28.

450 Wolfstieg No.35.724.

451 "Masonry was illegal in France [at various times] during the periods 1730-1800 though the ban was only used against people who could not protest against the police. The fact [is] that there were many of the aristocracy and clergy in the Masonic lodges, so the easiest victims on which the crime of being a mason could be pinned were the authors and printers of masonic rituals etc. though such documents were required by the lodges. This is the reason why:
(a) The correct place of printing was never shown. I have seen Jerusalem, Berlin shown as printers, while London, where Masonry was not a crime, figures often. All of course were written and printed in France.
(b) Masonic writings i.e. rituals etc. were given an anti-masonic basis as a justification. Hence the 'Satyr' in this case."
A.C.F. Jackson, private communication.

452 A photocopy of this text, together with a translation (E. & O.E.!) by the present author, is available at the Grand East of the Supreme Council for England & Wales at 10 Duke Street, London.

453 St. Luke, Chapter 24, verse 13 et seq.

454 Reference to the breakage of the Masonic Working Tools is made in nearly all of the early rituals, although it is omitted in Rituals under the Supreme Council of England & Wales today. Jackson has pointed out (see 'Essay 15') that today "there is less emphasis on the destruction to humanity resulting from the loss of the Word, that is, the Crucifixion, and more upon the rewards for finding it, that is, the Resurrection and man's salvation."

455 The Candidate is instructed to genuflect each time he passes the Altar.

456 The Obligation includes among the Penalties an account of Christ's sufferings during His Passion and Crucifixion. Significantly it ends with "In addition I promise and give my word of honour that I will never reveal the place nor those who have received me".

457 Evidently this is the appropriate place for the Words from the Cross 'Consummatum Est' to be recited. How they ever became transposed elsewhere is a mystery.

458 As in various other respects, there seems to be a reminiscence here of the Royal Order of Scotland.

459 That is, our 'Chamber of Death' where today the Candidate meditates.

460 In no ritual from any source prior to 1995 is the fourth word anything other than 'Juda' or 'Judah'.

461 This is still the practice under the Supreme Council of France where each departing Brother is saluted on the forehead by the MWS.

462 It may be of interest to note that in the 18th Degree Ceremony worked by the Supreme Council of France which is in amity with the G.L.N.F, the customary address to the Brethren by the presiding Officer is "My Brothers and Equals".

463 This copy is in the custody of the Supreme Council of Engand and Wales.

464 This copy was discovered in England in 1855, and subsequently purchased and deposited in the Library of the Supreme Council of the Northern Masonic Jurisdiction of the U.S.A.

465 This copy is deposited in the Museum and Library of the United Grand Lodge of England.

466 See William Wonnacott, AQC 39, The Rite of Seven Degrees in London, p.63 (1926)

467 This is the spelling with which Dunckerley signed his name to his letters, many of which are extant.

468 Frederick Smyth, Brethren in Chivalry, page 23 (Lewis Masonic, 1991).

469 Ibidem, p.44.

470 See Ritual numbered '1' in the archives of the Supreme Council of England, etc.

471 In North Cornwall, in the first half of the nineteenth century, John Knight, appointed by Thomas Dunckerley as 'Provincial Grand Commander of Knights Templar in Cornwall' and his successors propagated a 25 plus 1 ('Ne Plus Ultra') Degree system, to which Knight, possibly influenced by William Finch, eventually added a further 12 Degrees.

472 There are various sources from which it has been postulated that these Degrees might have come to England. For example, several Englishmen received the Degrees in France. Then the Supreme Council for Ireland was established in 1826 and there was constant traffic between Dublin and the English West Coast ports. Possibly the most prolific sources were the Lodges established in 'Parole Towns' by some of the tens of thousands of Frenchmen taken prisoner in the Napoleonic Wars, in which Lodges, for example that in Abergavenny, there is conclusive evidence that English (and Welsh) men received 'Higher Degrees'.

473 Edward Armitage, a native of Tasmania, who was

advanced to the 33º in 1902 and appointed Librarian to the Supreme Council. In 1905 he was appointed to a Committee to review the Ritual, and his visit to Bristol in 1906 may well have been in connection with this task. [Armitage was elected to the Supreme Council in 1912, serving as Lieutenant Grand Commander from 1924 until his death in 1929.]

474 'Ritual No.1', v.s.

475 Powell pointed out that these Rituals comprise "the system of Clermont", the "Hauts *[sic]* Grades du 1er.˙.2me.˙.3me.˙. et 4me.˙. Ordre, savoir Les Elus, les Ecossais, le Chev. D'Orient et le sublime grade de Rose Croix". The 'Richard Smith' Ritual differs considerably from the present Bristol working of the 'Rose Croix' Degree, which is set out in a manuscript Ritual also in the Archives of the English Supreme Council, and which formerly belonged to Col. S.E.Taylor. It includes, for example, the elaborate addition of the 'Opening of the Seals'.

476 That this is a translation from the French is further indicated by the Officers other than the Grand Master, Generals and Prelate being addressed as 'Most Respectable' ('très respectable')

477 This was also the procedure during the opening of Knight Templar Encampments, a procedure somewhat more positive than the response today to the instruction "See that none are present but true Brethren of the Temple.

478 It is, perhaps, again of interest that the 'Most Wise' refers to 'our Royal Order'.

479 'The Pillar of Strength F' is in the West and the 'P. of Wisdom in the North C' and not vice versa as in a Rose Croix Chapter today.

480 S.H. Baynard, Jr., *History of the Scottish Rite of Freemasonry*, (1938).

481 The other two were Dr. Robert Crucefix and Dr. George Oliver. Dr. Leeson only became a Member after the formal establishment of the Council by Crucefix, Oliver and Udall.

482 So far as is known, all the Brethren who became members of the Supreme Council in its earliest years had received both the 'Rosae Crucis' and 'Kadosh' Degrees in Encampments of Knights Templar; for example, Crucefix, Leeson and Wilson in 'Cross of Christ' (now St. George No.6); Udall in 'Faith and Fidelity', now No.26; Pryer in 'Mount Calvary, now No. 'D'; Tucker (probably) in Coryton, and Davyd Nash presumably in 'Baldwyn'.

483 'Metropolitan Chapter' the 'Patent' of which is dated 24th June 1846, later became 'Grand Metropolitan Chapter', and received the number '1' when Chapters were formally numbered in 1880.

484 Numbered '10' in the Supreme Council archives.

485 For example, the senior Brethren present are addressed as *'Respectable'*, as was (and is) the French custom. The newly perfected Candidate is addressed as "a Prince of the Rose of the Cross" as if a French title had been literally translated. The words given with the Sign of the Good Shepherd are 'E' and 'P.V.', something which nowhere appears in the pre-1815 Baldwyn transcription. In the 'Lecture' appears the answer "In the most respectful situation, my heart penetrated with the solemnity of the obligation", typical French verbiage, literally translated with an

infelicity of expression which appears nowhere in 'Baldwyn'. A point which the present author has seen nowhere else is of some interest. When the Candidate is asked who gave him 'the true Word', he replies "It is not permitted to any one to give it, but to find it by our own perseverance assisted by the Author of Life". When then pressed to give it to his interrogator, the reply is "I dare not, but if you will ask me the particulars of my journey &c. you will force it from me."

486 *The Freemasons' Quarterly Review*, 13, p.367 (1846).

487 Although in Albert Pike's Ritual the 30th Knight Kadosh Degree was to be even more specifically a 'follow-on' from the actual history of the Knights Templar than is the GEKK under the Supreme Council for England and Wales etc. today.

488 The Reverend George Bythesea of St. Peter and St. Paul Chapter, a High Churchman who was influential in the affairs of the Ancient and Accepted Rite in the early days of the Supreme Council for 'England', may have been responsible for several scriptural references which appear in no later Ritual, and which are now omitted, although a few others have been added.

489 In 1917 the Scriptural extracts to be read after the last four steps of the ladder were added, the Minute indicating that this was a revival, but there is no reference to these readings in any earlier Ritual, English or foreign.

Essay 14
The Third Point

[This Essay is based on the first part of a Paper written by the late V.˙.Ill.˙.Bro A.C.F.Jackson 33°, but never published, dated January 1994, and entitled "A Study on the History and Symbolism of the *Third Point* of *The 18th or Rose Croix Degree* of the Ancient and Accepted Scottish Rite". The text is as Brother Jackson wrote it, only omitting the 'Schedule of Rituals used' and a few other minor interpositions, and with the paragraph headings absorbed into the text, together with some similar editing in order to make the paper more suitable for delivery[490]. Few would argue with the facts as stated by V.Ill.Bro.Jackson, although some of the opinions expressed in this Paper (to which the editor has drawn attention) may be debatable. C.J.M.]

The title 'Rose-Croix' has always been a popular one for religious and fraternal organisations because of the many Biblical allusions to the rose. Perhaps the most famous of these philosophical systems, known as 'Rosicrucianism', started early in the seventeenth century but it had no direct connections with Freemasonry. Some of its material did however come into various masonic Degrees and by the eighteenth century there were several with titles similar to 'Rose Croix'. Such Degrees, on the Continent of Europe, were usually called 'Scottish' or *'Ecossais'* though there was no proven connection with Scotland. These degrees have died out, except for the one with which we are concerned and which has, in England, and in many other countries, become the 18th degree of the Ancient and Accepted Scottish Rite. The word 'Scottish' was dropped from its title by the Supreme Council for England and Wales in the nineteenth century though most other Supreme Councils retain it.

It is believed that this 'Rose Croix' Degree originated with a Frenchman, Jean-Baptiste Willermoz, an enthusiast behind a group of Freemasons in the French town of Lyons, who in 1761 were forming a new Rite. Their Degree had several names including Knight of the Eagle, of the Pelican, of St. Andrew, and of Rose Croix of Heredom. It was little more than a framework until Willermoz, using his contacts with members of the Rite of Strict Observance, a German order, produced a Degree that contained some elements of both Templarism, the Strict Observance and Rosicrucianism, but which was based on a central Christian theme. The Degree has not changed its basic idea from its start, but it is now less dramatic, and there is less emphasis on the destruction to humanity resulting from the loss of the Word, that is, the Crucifixion, and more upon the rewards for finding it, that is the Resurrection and man's salvation. The culminating part of the Degree – the Third Point – has only changed in presentation: its principles remaining unaltered.

The history of the Third Point itself is possibly less uncertain than that of the 'Rose Croix' degree of which it forms the final part. It is a reasonable conjecture that the Third Point stemmed from the table Lodges which formed an integral part of all early French Masonic meetings. These French Lodges were held around a table at which, at the end of the Masonic Ceremonies, food and drink were served with elaborate formality. Each degree seems to have had its own Ceremony. Descriptions of such Ceremonies appear in several French exposures from about 1740 and it seems logical that the Rose Croix Third Point grew out of them. Reference will later be made to two 1765 manuscript rituals of the Degree which confirm this theory to some extent – no other theory seeming possible[491]. As the 'Rose Croix' was Christian from its start, their table procedure naturally had a Christian element.

It is curious that one of the 1765 rituals seems to have been given a theoretical background of an even earlier date as it includes elements of the Biblical feast of the Passover[492]. Obviously the many early French 'Rose Croix' Lodges had varying procedures but these have gradually grown into the Third Point. The stages as to how the various procedures grew into our present day Third Point Ritual will be described after referring to the general symbolism now practised.

The basic concepts of the Third Point conducted under the Supreme Council for England and Wales are almost certainly practised by the majority, if not all, of the other Supreme Councils throughout the world. The sharing of the essentials of nourishment has always been a sign of friendliness and fellowship, principles which are of course among the bases of Freemasonry. In the Third Point of the 'Rose Croix' degree these principles are exemplified by a secular feast, based on a combination of eastern and western Ceremonies implying both loyalty to the Order and fraternal affection. Such Ceremonies have come down to us from time immemorial. Some examples are worth quoting. One of the earliest references to the use of food to show friendliness is that of the Patriarch Abraham entertaining three angels with 'a morsel of bread'[493]. There are many similar examples in early literature, but a particularly appropriate one is that of the meals eaten by the early Christians after their prayer meetings. In the early days of Christianity such meetings were regularly held. They were called 'agapé'[494], a Greek word meaning approximately 'charity'. There was often danger, and in Rome the catacombs sometimes had to be used, but the agapé were nevertheless occasions of fellowship and friendliness.

It is not difficult to recall many similar feasts throughout history where friendship was often combined with charity, and this is the theme exemplified by the Supreme Councils of many countries. A quotation from the English version of the ritual of the Netherlands Supreme Council shows this clearly:

> "My brethren, the first Christians broke bread together and partook thereof with gladness and singleness of heart; let us also, as children of the same Father and brethren of the same family, with gratitude towards Him to whom we owe this great privilege, partake of this humble meal for the promotion of Unity and Brotherly Love."

The Supreme Council for Scotland, with the same principles, takes a more Eastern view:

> "... among the wandering Arabs of the desert those who have been admitted to their tents, and who have partaken of their bread and salt, are henceforth bound to them in the closest bonds of love and friendship[495]."

The Supreme Council for Ireland entitles the 'Third Point' ceremony as that of the 'Loving Cup':

> "... before we separate let us renew our vows of Friendship and Fraternity by partaking together of Bread and Salt, the inviolable pledge of Friendship with the Eastern Nations, and let us drink together of the Loving Cup which symbolises the Cup of mingled joy and sorrow which Providence has prepared for every man that lives."

Under the Supreme Council for England and Wales the Third Point is held in the same setting as that of the Second Point. Though some Chapters dim the lights, the Ceremony is usually held in a room brightly illuminated and decorated with roses and red hangings. This may be for convenience but it adds to the portrayal of happiness which a darkened room does not[496].

The constituents of the 'Feast' (as reference is made to it in early Rituals), or, to use a technical term derived from the liturgy, its 'elements', are naturally simple and from the earliest days of the Degree, they have always included bread and wine.

Bread has been characterised as man's staple diet since the Garden of Eden and the sin of Adam – "In the sweat of thy face shalt thou eat bread till thou return unto the ground"[497]. There are many occasions upon which reference to bread is made in the Bible. Perhaps the best-known examples are the feeding of the multitude by Jesus[498] and by His referring to Himself as "the Bread of Life"[499]. One of the most apt Biblical quotations for the Third Point comes, however, from St Paul:

> "Therefore let us keep the feast not with the old leaven, neither with the leaven of malice and wickedness; but with the unleavened bread of sincerity and trust."

For Christian Freemasons of all periods, however, the symbolism of bread used at a feast would be summed up in the words: "Give us this day our daily bread". For many years the Supreme Council for England and Wales has authorised the use of plain biscuits as an alternative to bread, presumably for convenience of handling. Though this may have diminished the symbolic position, the change emphasised the fact that any connection between the Third Point and the bread used in religious services is quite untenable.[500]

In the Bible, there is no prohibition on the use of wine but only on its misuse. In fact, on many occasions its use is encouraged as something that "maketh glad the hearts of men"[501]. The miracle by which Jesus turned water into wine to ensure the success of the wedding feast at Cana[502] is well known, but a less familiar quotation from Isaiah is particularly appropriate for those taking part in the Christian *agapé* and therefore applicable to the Third Point: 'everyone that thirsteth, come ye to the waters, and he that hath no money; come ye and eat; yes, come, buy wine and milk without money and without price'[503]. Even St. Paul, who was very strict in his views about personal abstinence, urges Timothy: "Drink no longer water; but use wine for thy Stomach's sake and thine own infirmities"[504].

Examples of the use of wine as a token of friendship can be found so often throughout history that it is not necessary to quote them, but the Loving Cup Ceremony practised now at many masonic gatherings is a reminder of what has always taken place in the outside world. One of the lasting examples of this is the 'stirrup cup' still used at meetings of Hunts. This Ceremony of friendship and fellowship of men about to take part in a common enterprise is not restricted only to England but it is a normal procedure in many countries[505].

Salt has always had a special significance, primarily as a symbol of permanence and honesty, and as such it has been commonly used to seal a covenant. "And every offering thou shalt season with salt, with all thy offerings thou shalt offer salt"[506] is a familiar quotation to Brethren who have attended the Consecration of a Lodge. Less familiar may be "It is a covenant of salt for ever before the Lord unto thee and thy seed with thee"[507]. It would not be becoming to Freemasons to apply to themselves Our Lord's words to His disciples: "you are the salt of the earth"[508], but it is perhaps a salutary reminder that before they are Perfected, all Rose Croix Brethren have passed through many tests of merit, and have undertaken to live up to high standards. Sharing our salt with our Brethren should remind us that if we fail to honour our obligations, we will have lost our savour, and wherewith shall we then be salted?

Reference has already been made to the significance of salt in Eastern countries. European writers have recorded similar sentiments. The sixteenth century Spanish author Miguel Cervantes' wrote: "It is a true saying that a man must eat a peck of salt with his friend before he knows him", a sentiment echoed by his English contemporary, George Herbert, when he wrote: "Before you make a friend, eat a bushel of salt with him". Rudyard Kipling was a Freemason who seems to have had a knowledge of Degrees of which he may not himself have been a Member, but one of his early verses is peculiarly apposite for the Third Point:

> "I have eaten your bread and salt,
> I have drunk your water and wine
> The deaths you died I have watched beside,
>   And the lives ye led were mine."

The 'Living Circle' is an important part of the Ceremony of the Third Point. As already noted, Masonically a circle of this type probably has its origin in the days when Members of a Lodge met around a table. However, the only early written references to this custom come from French sources. *Le Secret des Francs-Maçons,* an exposure written in 1742, describes what is referred to as *La Chaine d'Union* – "Everybody rises & they form the chain, that is to say, that each grasps the other's hand, but in a rather singular manner; they cross & interlace their arms, so that he who is on the right holds the left hand of his neighbour, & similarly he who is on the left, holds his neighbour's right, thus forming a Chain all round the Table'[509]. Similarly in *La Franc-Maçonne* of 1744 there is "these happy Brethren ... take each other by the hand ... while they sing with vivacity:

> Let us join hand in hand
> Binding us firmly together
> Let us tighten the knot divine
> Whose charm unites us."[510]

Over the years, there have been many minor modifications to the Third Point procedure. There are examples of the Brethren standing opposite each other in two parallel lines, facing each other, and this is still done by some Supreme Councils. This may be a relic of some older procedure, but it seems to miss the personal contact achieved by welcoming a Brother into the circle of his friends.

For Brethren who belong to Craft Lodges where the Initiate's Chain Ceremony is used, the 'Living Circle' of the Third Point will not be a novelty. Even to Brethren to whom this is familiar, the admission of the new

Member of the Rose Croix into "the living circle of our hearts" as practised in the Third Point in Ceremonies under the Supreme Council for England and Wales must be an emotional moment, and leave a lasting impression on any Candidate.[511] The Living Circle is a symbol of unity, involuntary perhaps, but inevitable, a unity which should eliminate all personal preferences. By the Circle, the individual loses his personal importance and becomes part of a society – in this case a Member of the Rite that he has just joined.

The two earliest Rituals of the 'Rose Croix' Degree which describe the Third Point are each dated 1765, the year in which Willermoz is believed to have put the finishing touches to the Degree. The description of the Third Point in the first of these[512] is as follows:

> "The brethren go into a room in the middle of which is a table covered by a white cloth. On this table is placed a loaf of white bread in a basin in the middle, with three yellow candles round it. The Most Wise and the other brethren take off the buckles of their shoes ... [and] the last admitted gives each a wand at least six feet in length.
> "They stand round the table with their wands in their right hands. The Most Wise says "Sovereign Creator of all things, who foresees the needs of all, bless the nourishment that we are about to take so that it may serve to Thy glory and our satisfaction; so mote it be". The Most Wise takes the bread, breaks a piece, and gives it to him who is on his right and so on ... Then taking the wand in the left hand and eating ... then the last admitted collects the cup and gives it to the Most Wise who drinks and passes it to his right ... When the cup has been round, the Most Wise throws the remnants into the fire as a sort of burnt offering.
> "The Most Wise says 'To Order' ... all the brethren make the sign of the Good Shepherd ... and make the heavenly sign[513]. The Most Wise embraces all, saying 'Peace be with you': the brethren reply 'So mote it be'. All the brethren return to the 1st Chamber[514] and disperse, and during the ceremony observe the most complete silence. As the ceremony is in memory of Easter it should be observed on Shrove Thursday[515] and is the Chapter feast day.

The second Ritual of the same date[516] describes a very similar procedure[517]. Confusingly the presiding Officer is referred to indiscriminately as 'Grand Master', 'Most Wise', or simply as 'Master'. The sign which today is known by a different name is here referred to as that of 'Admiration' as it is in the rituals of the Supreme Council of England and Wales until early in the twentieth century. The occasion which the 'Table Ceremony' commemorates is made clear in the preliminary to the description of the Third Point – "the appearance of J.C. to his disciples at Emmaus." The 'newest members' are sent out to prepare the room for the Third Point, and when it is ready, the Brethren remove the buckles of their shoes which they then wear 'slipshod'. They are given a wand of rose wood, and enter in procession behind the Master who alone among them is not bare-headed. "No servants can be present to serve. All the brethren are equal, having the same rank". (It is here noted that there are some Chapters where one can eat a roasted lamb having the head and four feet cut off before it is eaten and thrown on to the fire as a victim and sacrifice.)

> "Note that there can be only one large goblet on the table and one large knife, but never a bottle as it is the rule that all use the same goblet. The bread must never be cut, it is broken, and then all the Knights are round the table and the Master makes the following Prayer:
> "'Sovereign Creator of all things who provides for the needs of all, bless the human food which we are about to take and that it be to thy greater glory and the satisfaction of all the Brother-Knights of the Rose-Croix.'"

After this, the Ceremony proceeds exactly as in the ritual already described.

The Editor of *Renaissance Traditionelle* (the journal in which this latter ritual is reproduced) mentions a number of similar Rituals, apparently each slightly later than these two. They are certainly all from the eighteenth century, and he suggests that they come from a common ancestor. Perhaps this is the original Lyons degree of Willermoz.

A book published in 1767[518] deals with a special Rite which had a short popularity in eighteenth century France. It claims to give the ritual of *Le vrai Rose-Croix*. This is actually a ritual similar to the legends of the Fifteenth and Sixteenth Degrees of the *Ecossais* Rite which later was promulgated in various chapters in France, and then, in about 1770, by Stephen Morin in Jamaica. There is therefore no Third Point.

In 1772 H.A. Francken, a Dutchman living in Jamaica and who was the assistant to Stephen Morin, wrote in manuscript a book which contained many of the Degrees of the *Ecossais* Rite that Morin had compiled[519]. In 1782 Francken wrote a similar book which contained all the Degrees of Morin's rite from the Fourth to the Twenty-fifth. This latter book was copied by an American in 1794 and the copy is in the Library of the United States Northern Masonic Jurisdiction[520]. In none of Francken's manuscripts is a Third Point included in the 'Rose Croix' Degree. Some or all of these books must have been used, or have been known to, those Freemasons in the United States who formed the first Supreme Council of the Ancient and Accepted Scottish Rite in Charleston in 1801. Thus it may be, that in the early days, the Rite in America did not use the Third Point, although it was certainly normal in Rose Croix Chapters in Europe at this period.

In 1787 a printed book, *Le Recueil Précieux de la Maçonnerie Adonhiramite*, appeared in two volumes. The Adonhiramite Rite was one of High Degrees and had a limited popularity before dying out towards the end of the eighteenth century. The Seventh Degree of this Rite was known as *Le Vrai Rose Croix* and was presumably of the type used in Rose Croix Chapters at this period. It included a Third Point but more developed than those given in 1765. The following extracts from this Ritual describe a Ceremony which includes additional features with which we are familiar today. It takes place in the main Lodge room in which is added a small table in the centre.

> "This is covered by a cloth and there is a loaf and a cup full of wine on it. ... A small piece of paper on which is written the sacred word of the Rose-Croix is also placed on the table. Everything thus prepared, everyone takes a wand in his hand. All the brethren place themselves in two lines, that is to say to the North and South. The Wardens are at the head, and the Most Wise between them . . . . Then the travels begin as follows. The Most Wise, followed by all the Brethren, goes round the Chapter seven times, starting by the South. Then he stops opposite the East, makes the sign, takes the loaf from which he breaks off a small piece before giving it to the First Warden who is on his right. The latter also breaks off a small piece and passes the loaf to the Brother who is on his right; and this is continued so that the remains of the loaf arrives at the Second Warden who eats it. The Wine is circulated in the same way. The First Warden turns towards the Most Wise who gives him the grip saying E . . . . and the Warden answers P. . V. . . . . The cup passes and the ceremony continues as far as the Second Warden who returns the cup and gives the grip. The latter shows the Brethren that the cup is empty. Then advancing to the table, he takes the paper, lights it, and puts it in the cup. When the paper is completely burnt the Most Wise makes the sign and says 'Consummatum Est'. All the Brethren then make the Sign. The Most Wise then closes the Chapter."

It should be noted that the stationing of the Brethren in two lines facing each other, not in a circle, is similar to the procedure now used by the Supreme Council for the Netherlands. The present-day Netherlands Ceremony is naturally more elaborate and there is no burning of the word – their Ceremony seemingly being no more than a Masonic fraternal feast[521].

In 1845 Richard Carlile published the exposure *Manual of Freemasonry*[522]. It is known that Carlile took much of his material from another exposure writer, William Finch, who wrote about the turn of the century. There is no reason why Carlile's book should not accurately represent the procedures used in some Chapters at that period[523]. His last Ritual is the "Rosicrucian or Ne Plus Ultra Degree". It is similar to, though shorter than, a previous 'Rose Croix' example, but it includes a Third Point which the previous one omits. Carlile suggests that the Third Point was not an essential part of the Degree, but we know from other early Knights Templar rituals that the '*Ne Plus Ultra*' as the 'Rose Croix' was often called in England did use the Third Point.

Carlile's Third Point Ritual is as follows[524]:

> The third point is never held, except after the second, and then when it is held, the preceding point is not held for it[525]. A sideboard is prepared. This is covered with a table cloth, and on it are placed as many pieces of bread as there are Knights, and a goblet of wine. The paper with the sacred initials upon it is deposited on the altar. Every Knight has a white wand in his hand. The M.W. strikes his upon the earth twice, and declares that the Chapter is resumed. Then he leads seven times round the apartment, and is followed by all present, each stopping in front of the transparency, to make his sign. At the last round, each Knight partakes of the bread; and, still preserving the form of a circle, the M.W. takes the goblet,

drinks out of it, and passes it around. When it comes to him again, he places it upon the altar, and the Knights give each other the grip. The paper, with the sacred word upon it, is put into the empty goblet and burnt. The Knights make the sign, and the Most Wise says:

CONSUMMATUM EST.

It is not known what Ritual was used by the Supreme Council for England and Wales in 1846 after it had received its Patent in the previous year. The sponsoring Supreme Council, that of the Northern Masonic Jurisdiction of the U.S.A., originally sent over documents connected with the Thirtieth to the Thirty-third Degrees, but only the Obligation of the Eighteenth. Soon afterwards what was said to be the complete Ritual of the Eighteenth Degree was sent over, but there is no evidence as to what this was or whether it was adopted. As can be seen from the examples already given, there were many 'Rose Croix' rituals already in existence. Some may have come from France and have been adopted by the Knights Templar Encampments already working the 'Rosae Crucis' Degree, or they may have been imported by soldiers returning from the West Indies or from the U.S.A. after the War of Independence.

[*V. Ill. Bro.Jackson then discusses at length some of the post-1852 rituals in the archives of the Supreme Council, but without having had access to the whole collection, his analysis is inevitably incomplete. This 'Essay' could well be concluded by the following words which are not those of Brother Jackson:*]

It was not until 1852 that a Ritual, in which the Third Point differed little in its essentials from that in use in its Chapters today, was promulgated on behalf of the Supreme Council for England and Wales by Henry Udall, the Grand Treasurer General H.E.

---

490 In his covering letter to the Grand Secretary General dated 1.9.1993 with which he enclosed this Paper, Brother Jackson wrote "My present writing is not suitable, of course, for any form of publication, but, when completed, might form the basis of a lecture". I can only hope that in publishing this edited version, Brother Jackson would consider that I am adequately carrying out his wishes. C.J.M.

491 A.C.F.J.'s conclusion – these are his *ipsissima verba*.

492 [It should be noted that this would be an anachronism – all the rituals agree that the Third Point follows the symbolic Resurrection, while the Last Supper, an enactment of the Passover, precedes it. C.J.M.]

493 Genesis XVIII, vv.3-8.

494 αγαπε

495 [Some Speculative Brethren may see in this wording a reminiscence of the Inner Working in another Order which claimed to be associated with the Degree of HRDM at the end of the eighteenth century, and into which it otherwise seems a curious intrusion. C.J.M.]

496 In his letter to the Grand Secretary General of the Supreme Council dated '1.9.1993' noted above, Brother Jackson wrote, *inter alia*, "On a general point, my personal view is that we are inclined to treat the 3rd. Point too solemnly. I am not suggesting that it should not be worked with reverence, but I look on it

as a feast of joy and rejoicing, the sequel to the prayer meetings of the early Christians when they ate together, rich and poor alike".

497 Genesis III, v.9.

498 St.John, VI, v.11.

499 *Ibid*. v.35

500 [I can only hope that Brother Jackson is right. In fact, all the Rituals, manuscript and printed, in the possession of the Supreme Council for England and Wales, and which apparently have been used in its Chapters, specify 'biscuits', from the earliest manuscript tentatively dated circa 1850 to the printed Rituals in use today. Unfortunately Jackson admits that the Supreme Council of England etc. Ritual of 1870 was the earliest he had seen. Had he known that biscuits appear to have been specified in England from at least 1850, it would be interesting to know what he would have made of this. It is to be hoped that (particularly in view of the Pauline quotation) biscuits were not seen by our early 'Rose Croix' Brethren as more nearly resembling unleavened matzos. The matter was raised in 1922, when John Tower replied "To break bread and to break biscuit are really synonymous as biscuit is a form of bread." A & A, p.879. C.J.M.]

501 Psalm CIV, v.14.

502 John II, vv.1-9.

503 Isaiah LV, v.1.

504 I Timothy, V, v.23.

505 [It may be noted that when this Ceremony is carried out in many of the London Livery Companies, the man on the right of the drinker turns round so as to guard the back of the man drinking. No such action is required in Masonic meetings, the mutual trust among Brethren evidently being higher than that among Liverymen! C.J.M.]

506 Leviticus II, v.13.

507 Numbers XVIII, v.15.

508 Matthew V, v.13.

509 Harry Carr (Editor) *The Early French Exposures,* p. 65, Quatuor Coronati Lodge No.2076 (1971).

510 Ibidem, p.148.

511 [In every manuscript Ritual provided by the Supreme Council for England and Wales from 1852, while the Brethren were properly instructed to form a 'living circle', the newly Perfected Brother was then welcomed into 'the *loving* circle of our hearts'. 'Loving' appeared here in the first printed Ritual authorised by the Supreme Council of England and Wales in 1899, but in the second edition in 1901 it had become *'living* circle of our hearts' without any authority for the change in the Supreme Council Minutes, and it has remained so ever since. C.J.M.]

512 Paul Naudon, *Histoire, Rituels et Tuilleur des Hauts* [sic] *Grades Maçonniques,* p.375 *et seq.,* 3d. Edition, refondue et augmentée, Dervy-Livres, Paris (1978). [This Ritual was found at the public sale of the library of the Château de Brigon in Amsterdam on 25th January 1956.]

513 A.C.F.J. notes that this may have been what is now the first part of our second sign.

514 A.C.F.J. notes 'which is the dark room'.

515 A.C.F.J. notes 'Our Maundy Thursday'.

516 *Renaissance Traditionelle,* No. 7, p.241 *et seq.,* (1971). [This ritual is in the Bibliothèque Historique de la Ville de Paris. C.J.M.]

517 [To avoid unnecessary repetition (A.C.F.J. gives the wording in full) this has been re-written, and only the salient points of difference are noted here. C.J.M.]

518 *Les Plus Secrets Mystères des Hauts* [sic] *Grades de la Maçonnerie.*

519 This book is in the custody of the Supreme Council for England and Wales in London.

520 [A third Francken manuscript was discovered by Bro. Spurr in Lancashire when he was conducting his researches into 'The Grand Lodge of Wigan', and is now in the Museum and Library of the United Grand Lodge of England in Freemasons' Hall in London. I am informed by Bro. John Hamill that there was another copy in Calcutta, but all trace of this has now been lost. C.J.M.]

521 [It should also be noted that in none of these rituals is there any mention of salt, and also that both the bread and the wine are passed to the right, that is, anti-clockwise, the opposite of what is the custom in Chapters today under the Supreme Council for England and Wales. This is also the procedure today under the Supreme Council of France. Perhaps I may add on a personal note, that attending a Third Point in France, and finding myself standing on the left of the Most Wise, I observed the bread being passed to the right. However, when the Most Wise was presented with the cup, from force of habit I turned to my right ready to respond to his invocation, which sufficiently confused him that he passed the cup to me, and it circulated to the left, causing some minor consternation in the West, when the Wine, travelling in the opposite direction, met the Bread. C.J.M.]

522 [Carlile concludes the Introduction to this work with the words "I am sure that secrecy is a vice; and I therefore expose and explain Freemasonry". (p.xv.) C.J.M.]

523 [These are A.C.F.J.'s own words. What Chapters, where? There were none in England before 1846. However, the second of two approximately 'Rose Croix' Rituals quoted by Carlile may represent the 'Rosae Crucis' degree worked in Knights Templar Encampments. C.J.M.]

524 Richard Carlile, *Manual of Freemasonry,* pp.310/311, Reeves and Turner, London (?1845).

525 [Whatever this means. C.J.M.]

Essay 15
The Intermediate Degrees, 4th to 17th, both inclusive

Before the 'Supreme Council for England' received its Patent from the Supreme Council of the Northern Masonic Jurisdiction of the U.S.A., two 'additional Degrees' were being worked in many English Knights Templar Encampments. These Degrees were known as the 'Rosae Crucis' and the 'Kadosh' or *'Ne Plus Ultra'*[526]. Between the time of the Union of the two rival English Grand Lodges in 1813 and the death of the Duke of Sussex in 1843, the Grand Conclave of Knights Templar was effectively in abeyance. The Duke had no wish to arouse the opposition of the more die-hard former Members of the Grand Lodge of the 'Moderns' by promoting Christian chivalric Degrees. For thirty years there was therefore no active superior body ensuring uniform working even of the Degrees of Knights Templar and of Knights of Malta, let alone of the two additional Degrees which had a considerable affinity with Degrees of the Ancient and Accepted Rite. When Grand Conclave was resuscitated in 1845 with Colonel Charles Kemeys Tynte as Grand Master, one of its early tasks was to propagate an 'official' Ritual of the Degree of Knights Templar.

However, by the summer of 1846 the English Supreme Council was regularly established. All its early Members had themselves taken the Degrees of *Rosae Crucis* and *Kadosh* in Encampments of Knights Templar. The Grand Conclave agreed that these Degrees should no longer be worked in Knights Templar Encampments, but that they should respectively be considered as equivalent to the Eighteenth 'Rose Croix' Degree and to the Thirtieth Degree of Grand Elected Knights Kadosh under the jurisdiction of the newly constituted Supreme Council of the Ancient and Accepted Rite. Whether this was done in true English fashion by the usual processes of consultation or if there were any formal concordat it is impossible to say; no formal resolution to this effect has come to light. But two influential Knights Templar Encampments in London, *'Fidelity'* and *'Cross of Christ'*, both of which worked the 'Rosae Crucis' and 'Kadosh' Degrees, and to one or other of which most of the early Members of the Supreme Council belonged, formed Rose Croix Chapters out of their existing membership. They then accepted 'Patents' or Warrants for these Chapters from the Supreme Council[527].

The Degrees from the Fourth to the Fourteenth, the 'Rite of Perfection' which formed part of what was then known as 'Morin's Rite', had been worked in England by Charles Shirreff in about 1785, both in his Lodge in Whitchurch, and in the 'Brilliant Lodge' in London[528]. It has been alleged that some Knights Templar Encampments had also adopted these Degrees[529]. Otherwise the 'Rite of Perfection' was little known in England. Certainly in most Encampments the Knights Templar Degree led directly to that of the 'Rosae Crucis' with no intermediate gradations. The newly formed Supreme Council was therefore faced with an awkward problem. It had little choice but to acquire a following by deeming that the 'Rosae Crucis' Degree was equivalent to the Eighteenth Degree of the Ancient and Accepted Rite and affiliating as many as possible of those who already possessed it. But before the establishment of the Supreme Council those Knights Templar who had not already progressed to the Degree of 'Rosae Crucis' would have expected shortly to do so. These Knights would hardly be encouraged to place themselves under the jurisdiction of the Supreme Council if they had first to suffer the delay of acquiring *in extenso* each of the fourteen Intermediate Degrees before being eligible for that of 'Rose Croix'. On the other hand, the Rite of which the Supreme Council had accepted a Patent to establish was one of thirty-three Degrees. The first three Symbolic Degrees could be deemed to be equivalent to those which had necessarily already been conferred on each Brother in a Regular Craft Lodge, but the fourteen succeeding Degrees were an integral part of the Rite. Evidently some compromise had to be reached about these Degrees.

An explanatory pamphlet setting out the contents of the Intermediate Degrees is today presented to every brother who is Perfected in a Rose Croix Chapter under the Supreme Council for England and Wales. Suffice it to say here, therefore, in the words of the current Ritual of the Eighteenth Degree, in a Lodge of Perfection are conferred "the first nine of these degrees, from the fourth to the twelfth, [in which] the legend of Hiram Abif is continued in a series of allegories. Collectively they portray the confusion caused by the death of Hiram and the steps taken by King Solomon to complete the building of the Temple"[530]. Then "the thirteenth and fourteenth degrees refer to the legend of the secret vault and its contents".

"The Council of the Princes of Jerusalem" follows "The Lodge of Perfection". In the Council are conferred "the fifteenth degree, Knight of the Sword, or of the East, and the sixteenth degree, Prince of Jerusalem. These two degrees are known as the 'Historical Degrees' or 'Orders of Chivalry'. They give an account of the assistance received from Cyrus and Darius in the task of rebuilding the Temple after the Babylonian captivity."

The final preliminary to the 'Rose Croix' Degree is the seventeenth, "Knight of the East and West" which is described in the ritual as "the first of the 'Philosophical Degrees' and forms a fitting preface to the principles of Christianity represented in the eighteenth degree". It is necessary for a Candidate for Perfection to know at least the words of the seventeenth Degree, although in the present working these are given for him by the Marshal, as are also his credentials[531]. In some early Rituals the latter were also communicated to the Candidate in addition to the Signs and Tokens of the seventeenth Degree, before he was admitted to the First Point, and he had to answer for himself.

No Supreme Council Minutes have survived for the period from 1845 to 1854, and for the most part the complete series of Minutes after the latter date contain few references to Ritual matters. It is therefore very difficult to discover how in its early years the Supreme Council dealt with this matter of the Intermediate Degrees. The search is made more complicated by much of the evidence appearing to be contradictory.

The first recorded meeting at which the Degree of 'Rose Croix' was conferred under the Supreme Council for 'England' took place on 30th June 1846[532]. It was reported in *The Freemasons' Quarterly Review*[533], of which the first Sovereign Grand Commander, Thomas Crucefix was the founder and editor. The Press Report says no more than "There were several eminent Brothers admitted to the distinguished rank of Princes Rose Croix, the entire proceedings being conducted with great solemnity". It is not even certain whether these "eminent Brothers" were Knights Templars, who were Perfected, or whether they were holders of the 'Rosae Crucis' Degree who were affiliated; the word 'admitted' is somewhat ambiguous. The only further comment in the Report is that the Grand Secretary General of the Supreme Council of Ireland, Thomas Wright, who attended as the representative of the Irish Sovereign Grand Commander, the Duke of Leinster, "spoke in terms highly eulogistic of the whole proceedings, and characterized it as quite pure".

There is next a Report[534] of a meeting on 17th December 1847 at which a Grand Council of Princes of Jerusalem of the 16th Degree was held at which it was resolved "That the petition of the Grand Scotch Knights and Knights of the Sword and the East, this day presented and read to this Grand Council, being in due form and approved, the degree of Grand Princes of Jerusalem shall be conferred on the petitioners at the next meeting of Grand Council on the 9th of February next". ("Scotch Knight of Perfection" – "Grand Scotch Knights" – are alternative names for the fourteenth Degree, Grand Elect Perfect and Sublime Master.) This brief report seems to imply that the Intermediate Degrees, or at least the fourteenth and above, were at this time being worked in full. There is, however, no report of the meeting on 9th February 1848. Next, a Report in the *Quarterly Review*[535] of a meeting of the Supreme Council on 12th June 1848 is followed by undated Reports, "Metropolitan Chapter. Several candidates were installed as S.P.R.C. of the 18th degree, and became members of this distinguished chapter", and "Mount Calvary Chapter ... several distinguished brethren were advanced to the rank and privileges of S.P.R.C.", in each case without any mention of a Council of Princes of Jerusalem or other preliminary. Similarly in December 1850, after reporting the death of Dr. Oliver, the *Quarterly Review*[536] gives notice of a meeting to be held "during the month of January, probably Thursday the 23rd." when "the Metropolitan Chapter, which will also meet will confer the degree of Rose Croix". There is no report in the *Review* of this meeting, but a Report[537] of a Meeting held on 18th March 1851, at which John Cox opened a Chapter Rose Croix, also states "Several candidates were exalted in this most interesting degree", again without reference to any preliminaries.

Three years before this the Supreme Council of the American Northern Jurisdiction, which had issued the Patent to the English Supreme Council, withdrew recognition from its daughter-Council because of Dr. Leeson's refusal to sever his connection with the irregular Supreme Council of the French Grand Orient. In the early 1850s the 'English' Supreme Council was accustomed to hold a 'Summer Festival of the Ancient and Accepted Rite'[538]. In 1852 this took place on Wednesday the ninth of June. Henry Udall, the Grand Treasurer General, who had been one of the three original members of the English Supreme Council, took advantage of this gathering to further the process in which he was engaged of restoring amicable relations with the North American Council. According to the Report in the *Quarterly Review*[539], John Cox first opened the Metropolitan Chapter Rose Croix and "several Brethren, who had obtained the degree of Knights of the East and West [*that is, the seventeenth Degree, with no mention of those preceding it*] were examined by the High Pontiff[540], were afterwards introduced, and exalted to the rank of Sov. Prince Rose Croix. The anthems and sacred music of the degree were given by a full choir conducted by Brother Jolly. After the exaltation had been concluded, the Ill. Grand Treasurer of the Order addressed the Convocation, and said that, in the absence of the Sov. Grand Commander, he had now to announce that the Supreme Council had, since the last Convocation, had several petitions presented to them from various parts of England for the establishment of Grand Lodges of Perfection, Grand Lodges of Princes of Jerusalem, and Sov. Chapters of Rose Croix. The Supreme Council had acceded to the request in several instances, and such Grand Lodges would for the future be holden at Birmingham, at Bolton, at Manchester, at Liverpool, at Axminster[541], and at Weymouth."

According to his own later statement, Udall, an experienced barrister, had by now studied with meticulous care the 'Grand Constitutions of 1786', a document of the existence of which no other member of the Supreme Council, with the probable exception of Dr.Leeson, seems at this time even to have been aware. In his evident desire to ensure that the North American Council could not find any fault with the manner in which the English Supreme Council was presiding over the Rite, Udall emphasised to the gathering the importance of strictly adhering to the letter of the 'Constitutions'. As he afterwards wrote "in the presence of the Earl of Donoughmore, General Chatterton and other distinguished brethren, I ... took occasion to explain the organization of the Order and the obligation we were under to see that that organization was not departed from. To prevent any error of my own in a matter of this importance I read from the letters sent by the American Council their instructions as to that organization"[542]. According to the Report in the *Quarterly Review,* Udall then said that "as the laws of the Order were given to them with great precision, and as the Grand Lodges of Perfection, Princes of Jerusalem and Sov. Chapters would have to abide by them, he would state to the Convocation the organisations which they, as Sov. Grand Inspectors, must see enforced". He went on to say that the Illustrious Founder (here presumably referring to Frederick the Great) had intended "to secure to every Council the exclusive jurisdiction over sublime Freemasonry in the country in which it should be established and to protect it against foreign interference". He stressed that there was no encroachment upon or interference with "Craft or Symbolic Masonry". The Rite, he said, "begins *from* that of the Master Mason because no person under that degree can be received in any of its subordinate bodies. It is the duty of those bodies to see that no persons irregularly admitted as Masons should be received by them."

Udall then went on to describe the 'bodies' which should be established under the Supreme Council, and which had this responsibility, starting with the Grand Lodge of Perfection. "This should, as far as possible, be a Representative Council, and be composed of those who are in authority, as being the head of the degrees over which it has control." He outlined the history of the Grand Lodges of Perfection, pointing out that these were subject to the earlier 'Statutes of 1762', some of which he read out. He then described a second body, "A Grand Council of Princes of Jerusalem which exercised jurisdiction over the fifteenth and sixteenth degrees, and all Grand Lodges of Perfection. The body should be so arranged as to represent fairly the Lodges and Chapters over which it had control." Thirdly a Sovereign Chapter of Rose Croix of H.R.D.M. exercised authority over the 17th and 18th degrees.

The Report in *The Freemasons' Quarterly Review* of this lengthy oration was duly brought to the attention of the Supreme Council of the Northern American Jurisdiction in Boston. Its Sovereign Grand Commander, J.J.J.Gourgas, himself wrote to Udall on 4th October 1852 saying that he "felt much gratified to perceive by the published account in the June Number of the *Quarterly Magazine* that your Supreme Council was so far favorably progressing in the *regular constitutional organization* of the 'Ancient and Accepted Rite' that you had taken special pains not only to explain but also to invigorate the good work by sound precepts for the *strict performance* of those duties to which we are all equally most sacredly bound".

Henry Udall had left the Council eighteen months before its Bye-Laws were first printed in 1858, and he could therefore have had no hand in their preparation. But, fully in accord with Udall's earlier exposition, these 'Bye-Laws' (unfortunately they are not numbered) state:

- "A Warrant for a Sovereign Chapter Rose Croix will include authority to hold a Grand Lodge of Perfection and a Council of Princes of Jerusalem. The Grand Lodge of Perfection will govern the degrees from the 4th to the 14th inclusive; the Council of Princes of Jerusalem the 15th and 16th Degrees; and the 17th and 18th Degrees will be placed under the immediate administration of the Rose Croix Chapter."
- The specimen 'form of Petition' in the Bye-Laws includes "And we do further recommend our Brother ... to be nominated the first Most Wise Sovereign of the same [our Brother ... to be the most Equitable Sovereign Prince Master of the Council of Princes of Jerusalem; and our Brother ... to be the Thrice Potent

Master of the Lodge of Perfection]."
- Under the heading 'CONSECRATION' the Bye-Laws state:
Whenever a warrant is granted by the Supreme Grand Council 33∞ to hold any Lodge of Perfection, Council of Princes of Jerusalem, or Sovereign Chapter Rose Croix ... Copies of such Bye-laws as may be agreed on by any Lodge of Perfection, Council of Princes of Jerusalem, or Sovereign Chapter Rose Croix, shall be sent to the..... etc."
- "Every Lodge of Perfection, Council of Princes of Jerusalem, or Sovereign Chapter Rose Croix shall once in each year ... fill up the printed form which will be sent ... with the names, offices and descriptions of Subscribing and Honorary Members....."
- "A Prince of Jerusalem who visits an inferior Council or Lodge, should present himself clothed with the dress and ornaments of a Prince; and when his approach is announced ... he shall be received under the Arch of Steel ... and seated on the right hand of the Presiding Officer."
- "Princes have the right of being covered in all subordinate Lodges, Chapters or Councils, and of addressing the Chair without first asking permission."

and so on, and so on. The titles of the Officers both of a Council of Princes of Jerusalem and of a Lodge of Perfection are set out at length in the body of the Bye-Laws[543].

It seems unlikely that the Supreme Council would have gone to the trouble of publishing Bye-Laws particularising in such detail if these arrangements were not intended to be practised in at least some of the Chapters which it had Warranted. Indeed, there is further evidence that this was so.

- In 1857 the Supreme Council gave a dispensation to the MWS of Grand Metropolitan Chapter to confer the Degrees 4th–17th *per saltum* on four Candidates, with the evident implication that otherwise they would have to have been conferred *in extenso*.
- Also in 1857, when Dr. Kent took 'Letters of Credence' from the Supreme Council to Australia, these initially only authorised him to Warrant bodies for conferring the 4th–17th degrees (as did those given to Hugh Sandeman for Bengal), although they were then amended. Even so, Kent gave only a provisional Warrant to the (Melbourne) Metropolitan Rose Croix Chapter, to which the Supreme Council sent an 18th Degree Warrant in April 1859 after Kent had reported back to it.
- In October 1860 the Supreme Council refused a request to open 'a Grand Lodge of Perfection & Council of Princes of Jerusalem at Oxford – nothing is said about a Sovereign Chapter Rose Croix, and it was to be 12 years before a Chapter was consecrated in Oxford.
- As late as April 1866 the Grand Secretary General replied to a letter "relative to the working *in extenso* of the degrees from the 4th to the 17th inclusive ... saying that the 14th degree ... should be first carefully and perfectly worked" and that he was requested by the Council to give instruction to the MWS of each Chapter on the signs and words of each Degree 4th–16th inclusive[544].
- The Minutes of the meeting of William de Irwin Chapter (now No.28) on 12th January 1871 record that "The MWS appointed the presiding officers under The Grand Lodge of Perfection, Council of Princes of Jerusalem and Knights of the East and West as follows", and the Minute enumerates them, name by name and Degree by Degree[545].

From a consideration of this evidence it is hard to arrive at any conclusion other than that perhaps as early as 1847 and certainly as late as 1871, at least some Chapters were working *in extenso* some or all of the Intermediate Degrees, and that by its Bye-Laws the Supreme Council was encouraging them to do so. There is the problem that no copies of the Ritual used in the conferment of these Degrees have so far been found in the archives of the Supreme Council itself, or in those of several old Chapters whose Recorders have been very helpful in searching for them. A detailed perusal of the early Minute Books (where these still exist) and of archival material in the possession of other Chapters Warranted before, say, 1885, both at home and overseas (including those Warranted by the English Supreme Council, but which have now transferred their allegiance to another jurisdiction) might throw further light on this question[546].

Persuasive as this evidence appears to be, it cannot be considered to be conclusive. At the Summer Festival which took place on 9th June 1852, Patents or Warrants were presented for Rose Croix Chapters to be held in several places including Coryton[547], the seat of the Grand Secretary General, William Tucker, and Weymouth[548]. The Ritual used by William Tucker is preserved in the archives of the Supreme Council[549]. The title-page is inscribed "Old working of Reception 18°". That this Ritual is what it claims to be is authenticated by the manuscript inscription at the end "Copy made for me from Udall's M∴S∴S∴ by Bro. M∴B∴Hancock of Weymouth this 4th day of April 1853 [*signed*] William Tucker 33°". The Candidate is received as being a Knight of the East and West[550], with the implication that at least the last of the Intermediate Degrees had already been conferred elsewhere.

Complications, however, set in with the Consecration of St. Peter and St. Paul Chapter in Bath. Although its Warrant bears the same date as that of the Chapters at Weymouth and Coryton, St. Peter and St. Paul was not Consecrated until 25th October 1853 with Charles Vigne[551] as its first MWS. Vigne's copy of the Ritual is also preserved in the archives of the Supreme Council [552]. The text is similar to that of Tucker's Coryton Ritual, with one important exception. On the verso of the second folio is written 'Directions', and under this:

"In conferring any degree of Rose Croix you will first give the degrees by Name from the 4th to the 14th in a Grand Lodge of Perfection.
You will then declare a Grand Lodge of Princes of Jerusalem opened, and confer the 15th and 16th degrees by Name.
You will give the Knights of the East and West or 17th degree by Name, and then, the Rose Croix in extenso. The great length of time necessary is sufficient excuse for not giving the others in that manner.

Signd. Bro Udall 26th Oct 1852."

This signature and date are not in Udall's handwriting and, together with the 'Directions', are presumably copied from Bro.Udall's manuscript as was the transcription made for Tucker by William Hancock. The 'Directions' are followed by a list of the Intermediate Degrees[553]. There is then the instruction that each of the three 'Grand Lodges' shall be opened "By the power in me vested", and this is followed by the signs, tokens, knocks and words of the Seventeenth Degree set out at length, the 'Words' written only with the concealment of being back-to-front.

In the 'St. Peter and St. Paul' Ritual, the 'Directions' for conferring the Intermediate Degrees are little more than an outline of the procedure to be adopted. In the Ritual being used in Weymouth Chapter in 1855 or 1856[554] they have been expanded to provide a procedure differing little from that set out in the Ritual today, including an Obligation which has, however, been later inserted in the original text.

Another manuscript Ritual, this one copied in 1864 by Matthew Cooke of Invicta Chapter also gives the detailed procedure for conferring the Intermediate Degrees, Fourth to Sixtenth by name, together with the 'Secrets' of the Seventeenth. A further copy of the Ritual[555], prepared in 1871, probably one of the first to be copied by Hyde Pullen, the Assistant Secretary to the Supreme Council, has the same 'Directions'. The authenticity of this Ritual can hardly be in doubt, for it is authenticated not only by no less than three of the Council's Seals, but also by the full signature of Nathaniel Philips, the Lieutenant Grand Commander.

The riddle posed by the Intermediate Degrees cannot be solved without more information, which, it is hoped, may come to light among some as yet unexamined Masonic records. But it is hard to see what lay behind the Bye-Laws published by the Supreme Council in 1858, when at the same time apparently 'Official' Rituals contained Directions for the Intermediate Degrees to be conferred by name only. That this publication was no accident can be seen by the Council eight years later requesting the Grand Secretary General to give instruction to the MWS of each Chapter on the signs and words of the Degrees fourth to sixteenth inclusive. Both the Tucker 'Coryton' and the Vigne 'St. Peter and St.Paul' Rituals refer to a manuscript written by Henry Udall, and the latter gives its date as 26th October 1852. Is it possible that Udall had given those present at the Summer Festival the exhortation to confer the Intermediate Degrees *in extenso* for no other purpose than to please the American brethren? But the 'Directions', which are to all intents and purposes the same as those contained in the Supreme Council's Ritual today for the conferment of the Intermediate Degrees, have the name of Henry Udall appended to them in two manuscripts. To make such a volte-face only four months after his dogmatic statements at the Summer Festival is seemingly inexplicable.

All that can be added is that in the current Edition of the 'Rules of the Supreme Council' it clearly states:

"**6.** The The Supreme Council administers all the degrees of the Rite. It authorises its Chapters to confer on qualified candidates the 18th Degree in extenso, and the 4th to the 17th Degree by name only but no Chapter or member of the Order other than a member of the Supreme Council may otherwise confer or attempt to confer or demonstrate any degree of the Rite unless permitted to do so by dispensation."

For at least the last hundred years, no Chapter in England, other than King Edward the Seventh Chapter of Improvement, has received such a dispensation which even in this case has to be annually renewed.

Appendix A

Extract from the November 1858 Bye-Laws of the 'Supreme Grand Council' of the Ancient and Accepted Rite for England and Wales, and Dependencies of the British Crown'.

"Officers of bodies subordinate to a Sovereign Chapter Rose Croix of H.R.D.M.

COUNCIL OF PRINCES OF JERUSALEM

1. Most Equitable Sovereign Prince Master
2. High Priest
3. Most Enlightened Senior Warden
4. Most Enlightened Junior Warden
5. Valorous Keeper of the Seals and Archives
6. Valorous Treasurer
7. Valorous Master of the Ceremonies
8. Valorous Master of the Entrances
9. Valorous Tyler.

LODGES OF PERFECTION

1. Thrice Potent Master
2. Hiram King of Tyre (his Deputy)
3. Senior Warden
4. Junior Warden
5. Keeper of the Seals
6. Treasurer
7. Secretary
8. Orator
9. Master of Ceremonies
10. Captain of the Guards

The Thrice Potent, on each election night, shall appoint one or two Tylers, also an Almoner"

(I may be clutching at straws, but it could be relevant that Coryton Chapter, Warranted June 1852, had *two* Tylers ('S.B.' – Serving Brothers), when working both at Coryton and also at Axminster, but only one after its move to Exeter, and its union with Rougemont in 1870. C.J.M.)

Appendix B

WILLIAM de IRWIN CHAPTER No.28

Extract from minutes of meeting of the Chapter held on 12th January 1871.

"The MWS appointed the presiding officers under The Grand Lodge of Perfection, Council of Princes of Jerusalem, and Knights of the East and West as follows:

Ex & PP;s : Cox	The Most Powerful Master of the 4° or Lodge of Secret Master
" " : Jones	Rt. Worshipful Master of the 5° or Lodge of Perfect Masters
" " : Butter	Most Ill. Master of the 6° or Lodge of Intimate Secretary
" " : Mathias	Thrice Ill. Master of the 7° or Lodge of Provost and Judge
" " : Wiltshire	Thrice Potent Master of the 8° or Lodge of Intendant of Buildings
" " : Taylor	Commander of the 9° or Lodge of Elect of Nine
" " : Vizard,W.J. Ill.	Commander of the 10° or Lodge of Elect of Fifteen
" " : Pigot Thrice Ill.	Commander of the 11° or Chapter of Sublime Knights Elected
" " : Davies	Most Potent Commander of the 12° or Chapter of Grand Master Architect
" " : Inskip	Grand Master of the 13° or Chapter of the Royal Circle of Enoch
" " : Vizard, F.	Thrice Potent Grand Master of the 14° or Chapter of Grand Lodge of Perfection
" " : Townsend	Sovereign Master of the 15° or Council of Knights of the East and West or Knights of the Red Cross of Babylon
" " : Clarke	Most Equitable Sov. Master of the 16° or Council of Knights of Princes of Jerusalem
" " : Mumbee	Most Puissant Ven. Master of the 17° or Council of Knights of the East and West"

(After a transcript supplied by Ill.˙.Bro. N.G.Wilkins 32°, District Recorder, District of Somerset, personal communication to C.J.M., 24 Jan 2000)

---

526 The phrase 'Ne Plus Ultra' ("Than which there is nothing further") can be found attached to many Degrees, indicating no more than the highest Degree in a sequence in a particular Rite. It is not the name of any specific Degree, though used to describe several – towards the end of the eighteenth century the term was frequently attached to the eighteenth 'Rose Croix' Degree (RC p.30). Its use to describe the Thirtieth Grand Elected Knight Kadosh Degree of the Ancient and Accepted Rite is an historic anomaly, but it has become intrinsic to that Degree although within the Rite there are three higher Degrees.

527 Matthew Christmas, *A Short Account of the Origins and Early History of the Grand Metropolitan Chapter*, p.4 (July 1996)
  Ewen McEwen, *The Mount Calvary Encampment*, pp.21-24 (Undated - ? 1990).
  H.V. Wiles, *Mount Calvary Chapter Rose Croix, No.3, 1848-1948*, pp.36/37 (1948).

528 A.C.F. Jackson, AQC, pp.173-188 (1973).

529 RC pp.93-95 and Appendix VIII, p.272.

530 It should be noted that, of these, the ninth, tenth and eleventh Degrees describe the vengeance taken on Hiram's assailants, and from which it is not easy to derive any moral lessons which are acceptable in today's politically correct climate.

531 In earlier Rituals of the Supreme Council, the Candidate did not have to exchange the words with the MWS but had to prove himself by signs.

532 This was in effect a meeting of the Rose Croix Chapter of the Encampment of *Faith and Fidelity* which had accepted a 'Patent' (Warrant) from the Supreme Council six days before the meeting as 'Metropolitan Chapter' (later Grand Metropolitan Chapter No.1). *Vide* Matthew Christmas, *Op. cit., supra.*

533 A & A, p.13.

534 A & A, p.14.

535 A & A, p.15.

536 A & A, p.16.

537 *Ibidem*

538 The first had been held in 1851 to welcome the many Masons from other Jurisdictions who visited London to attend the Great Exhibition which took place in that year.

539 A & A, pp.19 *et seq.*

540 The 'Prelate' of a Rose Croix Chapter was then known as the 'High Pontiff'.

541 (Coryton).

542 Udall letter file In the archives of the Supreme Council.

543 Appendix A.

544 Supreme Council Minutes.

545 Appendix B.

546 The Grand Secretary General would be extremely grateful to any Brother who located such material and informed him about it.

547 "Axminster".

548 In fact, that for Weymouth could not be presented "but as the Most Wise Sovereign was not present, the patent must be presented at another time" which was evidently done.

549 A black hardback note-book of 48 sheets (the last four blank) numbered '6' in the Supreme Council archives.

550 "The Candidate should have on the Jewel and Insignia of his Masonic rank as a Knight of the East and West and other Jewels, but not any Jewels or Insignia of his rank as a Knight Templar, if he be a Knight Templar."

551 Charles John Vigne was to become both Grand Secretary General and also Grand Treasurer General of the Supreme Council, and afterwards Sovereign Grand Commander from 1869 to 1874.

552 This manuscript Ritual is written in a well-formed hand, but not copper-plate, in a hardback, leatherette-bound note-book with clasp fastening and red silk bookmark. It is numbered '7' in the archives of the Supreme Council and consists of 92 sheets (of which the last 19 are blank) with the text for the most part, but not exclusively, written on the *recto*. There is little doubt that it is Vigne's original personal copy, and has the names of the first Officers of St. Peter and St. Paul Chapter written in pencil in what appears to be Vigne's hand.

553 The Fourteenth is entitled "Grand Elect Perfect and Sublime Master".

554 This manuscript Ritual is written in copper-plate in a red leatherette-bound note-book numbered '3' in the Supreme Council archives. It contains 40 sheets, the majority of which are written on both *recto* and *verso*.

The fly-leaf contains a clear impression of the Seal of the The Supreme Council, with below it an indecipherable symbol alongside the initials 'C.J.V.' Charles John Vigne was Grand Secretary General from November 1855 until J.A.D. Cox was appointed to that Office in 1857. The Ritual was evidently not originally prepared for a specific Chapter; a space is left for the name of the Chapter in the request by the M.W.S. 'be pleased to assist me to open ... Chapter" with "this Weymouth" inserted in pencil.

It is tempting to assume that this was one of the earliest, if not the first, of the 'Official' manuscript Rituals issued to Chapters, which were authenticated by the impression of the Seal and the initials of the Grand Secretary General.

555 This Ritual, numbered '11' in the archives of the Supreme Council is written in copper-plate in a red leather covered note-book which became the standard format for official Rituals issued by the Council. It may well have been prepared for Sandeman Chapter, then meeting in Calcutta, but which transferred to Bournemouth, England, in 1972.

Essay 16

The evolution of today's English 'Rose Croix' Ritual
Part One. Manuscript Rituals prior to 1899

In 1845 the Supreme Council of the Northern Masonic Jurisdiction of the United States of America granted a Patent to Robert Thomas Crucefix to establish a regular Supreme Council for England[556]. Together with the Patent, several documents were then sent to Dr. Crucefix, and others followed in the next year. These specifically included the Sign, Grip, Token and Word of the Eighteenth 'Rose Croix' Degree, but it is uncertain whether a full Ritual of the Degree was ever received from America[557]. The first meeting at which the 'Rose Croix' Degree was conferred under the auspices of the Supreme Council for England was held on 24th June 1846, but there is no record of the Ritual which was used either on that occasion, or on similar occasions in the course of the next five years.

Even had the English Supreme Council received an American Eighteenth Degree Ritual, it might well have been thought appropriate to make some modifications to it. For many years the progressive Degree of 'Rosae Crucis' had been conferred in Encampments of English Knights Templar. It was agreed that this should no longer take place, and that Brethren who had already proceeded to this Degree should be deemed to possess the Eighteenth 'Rose Croix' Degree provided that they would affiliate to the Ancient and Accepted Rite[558]. Evidently the Degree to which they were deemed to proceed should not be so different from that of 'Rosae Crucis' that affiliation appeared to be an anomaly. But so as to underline the independence of the Ancient and Accepted Rite, it was, of course, essential that Candidates for the 'Rose Croix' Degree should not wear the regalia and jewels of a Knight Templar nor be called upon for the pass-words of that Order as happened in the 'Rosae Crucis' Degree. Neither could there be included major elements of the 'Rosae Crucis' Degree Ritual which appeared in none of the early Rituals of that of the 'Rose Croix'[559]. On the other hand, it might have seemed appropriate to retain minor items of wording and procedure which could give newly affiliated 'Rosae Crucis' Knights a sense of familiarity with their new surroundings in a Chapter. Whether it were done by accident or by design, several Knights Templar references were retained in the early Rituals of the 'Rose Croix' Degree worked under the Supreme Council; indeed, some can still be identified in the Ritual used today[560].

Until the summer of 1852, all admissions of brethren to the Eighteenth Rose Croix Degree under the authority of the newly-formed Supreme Council for England took place in London. These Ceremonies were conducted either in the Supreme Council itself or in either Metropolitan Chapter which had been formed from the Knights Templar Encampment of *Faith and Fidelity*, or *Mount Calvary* Chapter, which had similarly been formed from the Encampment the name of which it retained[561]. On each of these occasions the principal Offices were generally held by Members of the Supreme Council which was therefore in a position to control the Ritual used.

It was not until 9th June 1852 that Henry Udall, the Grand Treasurer General, one of the three original Members of the Supreme Council, announced that the Council intended to give 'Patents' or Warrants to Chapters to be held outside London[562]. No longer, therefore, would Members of the Supreme Council be able to supervise every Ceremony conducted, and it would evidently be desirable for there to be a standard Ritual for all Chapters. The earliest Supreme Council Minute Book contains entries only from 1854, and there is no contemporary record of such a Ritual being authorised or prepared. However, in the archives of the Supreme Council there are manuscript Rituals of three of the earliest Chapters Warranted outside London, those of Coryton at Axminster, and of Weymouth, each Consecrated in 1852, and that of St. Peter and St. Paul at Bath, Consecrated in the following year. There is no doubt of the authenticity of each of these three Rituals. The title-page of the Coryton Ritual[563], is inscribed "Copy made for me from Udall's M∴S∴S∴ by Bro M∴B∴ Hancock of Weymouth this 4th day of April 1853" and is signed by its first MWS, "William Tucker 33°"[564]. Similarly, that used by Charles Vigne, the first MWS of St. Peter and St. Paul Chapter, not only has annotations in his handwriting, but on its third page are set out 'Directions', below which is written "Signd. Bro Udall 26th Oct 1852", evidently copied from an earlier document, as the signature is not Udall's. That used in Weymouth Chapter is undated, but it was originally almost identical to each of the other two, although many amendments had subsequently been made. This is, however, the first Ritual which can claim to be 'Official'. The fly-leaf contains a clear impression of the Seal of the Supreme Council, alongside the initials 'C.J.V.', that is Charles John Vigne, who was Grand Secretary General from November 1855 until the Summer of 1857. It can therefore be considered to validate 'Udall's MSS'.

It therefore seems probable that Henry Udall, who in 1852 was playing a leading role in the affairs of the Supreme Council, prepared the rescension of the Eighteenth Degree Ritual from which all later Rituals of the Eighteenth Degree under the Supreme Council of England etc. have been derived, with only a few major, but many minor, changes. There is, however, the curious anomaly that permission to confer the Intermediate Degrees by name only is specifically attributed in the St. Peter and St. Paul Ritual to Henry Udall, who in June 1852 had instructed those present at a general Meeting of the Ancient and Accepted Rite that, in order to conform to the 'Grand Constitutions', these Degrees must be given *in extenso*.

The earliest French Rituals of the 'Rose Croix' Degree date from 1765-1770. Jackson, writing originally in 1980, pointed out that "there seems to be far less alteration in this degree than in any other of the Rite in the two centuries since it was first produced"[565]. The French Rituals and the putative Udall recension are each recognisably the Degree which we work today[566]. Indeed, much of both today's working and also that in the earliest English manuscript Rituals (some of which contain additional Templar references, in particular in the Ritual used at Coryton[567]) are no more than a literal translation of major parts of the early French Rituals.

The 'Openings' in the earliest English Rituals are very 'Templar'. At Coryton "the outposts are properly secured", and "The Trumpeter sounds the ordinary Military Summons" to proclaim the assembling of the Chapter. The Generals then prove the Princes by receiving from each the Sign, Token and Word. Indeed, this latter procedure persisted in English Chapters for many years. It is, however, specifically stated that the Candidate must not wear "any Jewels or Insignia of his rank as a Knight Templar". On the other hand the Candidate has to present a lengthy written petition seeking admittance, as was the case in contemporary Knights Templar Encampments. The suitability of the Candidate was then tested by the 'High Pontiff', as the Prelate was then known, before the former entered the Black Room, but, after these preliminaries, the First and Second Points proceed using words almost identical to those in today's Ritual. As was also the custom for many years, the curtains before the Altar were drawn apart at the words "the veil of the Temple is rent in twain". The detailed references to Our Lord's Sufferings, which are omitted in later versions, are included in the Coryton Ritual, both in the wording of the Obligation, and also in the recital by the 'High Pontiff' of Christ's 'Seven Agonies' before the Candidate ascends the symbolic ladder. On the other hand, again the case for many years, there is no formal explanation of the regalia. So far as the Signs and Words are concerned, the Sign which we know as that of 'Adoration' is described as that of 'Admiration', the name which had consistently been handed down for it from the earliest Rituals of the Degree. There is an additional word, to which reference can be made as 'O'[568], which also has an early origin. While the Third Point is conducted somewhat differently, the essential features which are practised today are there, with the exception that the Word is burnt with the words "Consummatum Est" immediately before the final Closing of the Chapter[569].

It is probable that William Hancock, the first MWS of Weymouth Chapter, also made the copy of the Ritual which Charles Vigne used in St. Peter and St. Paul Chapter in Bath[570]. It contains much material additional to that in the 'Coryton' Ritual, including a long "Explanation of the Jewel worn by Sir Knights of the Rose Croix by Sir Knight Brother W.B.Hancock MWS, Weymouth". This is a very worthy exposition of what might be termed 'Masonic Theology', but that it did not become incorporated in the regular Ritual should not be a cause of any great regret! There is also a "Notice relative to the 3d. Point", which is a masterpiece of unreliable history, the demise of which should also not cause concern![571] However, in addition, the manuscript contains more precise instructions for conferring the Intermediate Degrees, including the full signs of the Seventeenth Degree, precisely as they appear in the Ritual today, together with the Words, which are imperfectly concealed by being written backwards. The original 'Opening' still displays undue 'Templar' influences, but that this was not appropriate was evidently soon recognised. Appended to the text there is a procedure headed 'Opening. Dr. Leeson June 1855'. This 'Leeson' version retains the practice of the Generals receiving the Word and the Sign from each of the Princes who stand in two columns in the North and South, and the Castle gates are also duly guarded, but when the MWS has been assured of this, all further 'Templar' matter is omitted, and the wording is precisely the same as that used today[572], the only addition being that before "Save we beseech thee ..." the Princes give the Sign of Admiration "and repeat Seven times Hoschea or Hoshazannah".

The original manuscript sets out the 'proving' by the 'High Pontiff', but this has been scored out by pencil strokes, as has the reading of the somewhat Uriah Heep-like Petition. The Candidates now had to do no more than "write their names, abode, profession and Masonic titles (Knights of the East and West) on a Petition", to which the Marshal added the age "33". The ballot was then taken, and the Candidate admitted for the customary examination commencing "Who and what are you?". The explanation of the situation in which the Chapter found itself was given in words almost identical to those in use today.

There is still no Scripture reading from Isaiah while the Candidate perambulates to the Pillars, but there is the instruction "The music plays 'By the Waters of Babylon' ". The reference in the Obligation to the Sufferings of Our Lord on the Cross has been heavily scored out in black ink. The Pauline commendation of Charity is recited, though slightly truncated[573]. In the Second Point the recital by the 'High Pontiff' of the Seven Agonies of Our Lord has been crossed through in pencil, but, after that elision, the only significant difference from today's wording is that, to the question "What supported you?", the Candidate replies, "The example of our Saviour's sufferings and Crucifixion". The Candidate is invested, without explanation, with the Collar and Jewel – no reference is made to an apron with which the Candidate was invested in the First Point - the Signs and words are communicated as today, with the exception of the first Sign again being 'Admiration', but when the newly Perfected Prince takes his seat, "Trumpet sounds. All applaud . . . . . . O saying Hosannah, Hosannah, Hosannah, On earth Peace and Goodwill towards Men". The Third Point and the closing are as in the 'Coryton' Ritual.[574]

The 'Weymouth' Ritual was almost certainly written after this in 1856[575]. It was evidently used in the Chapter for many years, the manuscript bearing several successive amendments[576]. It is the first English manuscript Ritual which contains a diagram of the Altar in the First Point, together with a drawing of each of the two Tracing Boards, inserted as the first three pages after the fly-leaf. The Ritual is of particular interest as the many amendments illustrate the developments which took place in the course of the next dozen years or so. Unfortunately none of them is dated.

As in the St.Peter and St.Paul Ritual, the Intermediate Degrees are first conferred by name in almost the same words as those in which they are conferred today, save that there are no explanations of the groups of Degrees as in the latest Rituals. The differentiation of the fourteen Degrees of the 'Rite of Perfection' is, however, indicated by the Candidate being Obligated never to reveal "the several Degrees of the A & A Rite from the 4th to the 14th both inclusive and from the fifteenth to the seventeenth both inclusive" instead of "from the first to the seventeenth". There is also one interesting emendation. The knocks at the Opening were originally written !!!!!! - !.. This has been crossed through and "o o – o o – o o – o", substituted with the Note "The report of the 17° which must be used when there are candidates until they are perfected"[577].

The 'Weymouth' Ritual is the first of the English Rituals in which there is a detailed description of the rooms in which the Ceremony of Perfection is conferred[578]. This differs in some respects from that to which Princes Rose Croix are accustomed today. In particular, it refers to the disposition of the Tracing Boards, which were specified as part of the normal Chapter furnishings until the end of the nineteenth century[579]. This manuscript, authenticated by the Supreme Council, is the earliest record of the physical arrangements which the Council wished to see uniformly adopted for conferring the Degree. The only specific point to which attention may be directed here is that "Beside the Altar there should be a couch for the M.W.S. to recline on", a feature of all the earliest 'Rose Croix' Rituals.

The Opening retains the procedure of the Brethren standing in two lines, with drawn swords, to communicate the Sign, Token and Word to the Generals, the 'Outer Guard' temporarily entering the Chapter to communicate them to the Marshal. The 'time' originally is still "The Sixth or first hour of the day", but this has been eventually amended to "It is the ninth hour of the day"[580]. The opening then proceeds in the same words as are used today, with a few trivial exceptions[581]. In spite of the amendment in the 'Intermediate Degrees' that the Knocks should be !!.!!.!!. 0 "when there are Candidates until they are Perfected", this is now amended to 0 0 0 0 0 0 - 0.

In the First Point, the differences between the wording in the Weymouth Ritual and that in use today are generally of little significance. "This Chapter" is referred to as "this Princely Council", "the earth quakes and the rocks are rent" is rendered as "an earthquake heaves its convulsive power", and there is no reference to "the despair and tribulation which sit heavily upon us". A series of amendments – "years", "months" – indicate some uncertainty about the length of the symbolic travel imposed upon the Candidate[582], and a few words in the Prelate's Prayer differ from today's usage. As originally written, the Ritual prescribed 'Music' during the seven perambulations, but a later hand has interpolated "In the absence of music The Prelate may read the 53rd Chap Isaiah" – this is the earliest reference in an English Ritual to the recitation of the 'Suffering Servant' verses, but it is probably an interpolation made after the Amendments authorised by the Supreme Council in

1873. With the exception that the Candidate has to pledge himself in his Obligation "without evasion or mental reservation of any kind", as in the Craft, the wording in the First Point is identical from this point on to that in use today[583].

After the final Prayer of the Prelate in the First Point, the Candidate, still wearing the Jewel of a Knight of the East and West, is invested with a black Apron. Three circuits of the room are made before the MWS leaves, and the Candidate is challenged on the Seventh. The Captain of the Guard then tells him that "This attire is not compatible with that humility which is necessary for those who wish to recover the lost word. Retire and clothe yourselves in dust and ashes, and I will then summon Raphael to your assistance". The Candidate retires to the Reception room, his jewels are removed, and the Marshal conducts him to the Chamber of Death where he is left to meditate while 'The Dead March in Saul' is played. Raphael comes to guide him, using words identical to those in the Ritual today[584], the 'Dead March' changing to 'Sound the loud Timbrel o'er Egypt's dark sea' as they enter the Red Room. In Raphael's announcement to the MWS he adds "the Valley of the Shadow of Death" to the dangers and difficulties through which the Candidate has passed, saying that he is now fortified by Faith, Hope and Charity. The MWS, having thus been told how the Candidate "came hither", asks what supported him, and receives the reply "The example of our Saviour's sufferings". The instruction to ascend the ladder has been variously amended, but in each case the ladder leads to "the Mansions of Glory and Perfection". The ascent takes place, with no Scriptural commentary on the words of the rungs, the last Initial being that of Judah, as in every earlier Ritual of the Degree. In congratulating the Candidate the MWS adds words taken from St. John[585], and the Word is then affixed "in its proper place".

The Candidates kneel to be Installed, after which each is first presented with a Rose, and then invested with the Collar and Jewel of the Order, finally being 'Sealed'. The wording is the same as that in use today, except that there is no explanation of any item of the Regalia[586]. The Signs are communicated in the familiar way[587], except that the 'O' Word (and not 'E....') is the first given in the Sign of the Good Shepherd, and that this sign incorporates that which is communicated today as the Second Sign. The Perfected Prince is then proclaimed ("with Trumpet sounds or Music") and takes his seat.

In the Third Point and in the Closing substantial amendments have been made to the original manuscript text, specifically those promulgated by the Supreme Council in 1873 to which reference will later be made. In its original form, however, the Brethren enter two-by-two, in reverse order of seniority and carrying white wands, processing seven times round the room while the choir sings "Behold how good and pleasant it is for Brethren to dwell together in Unity"[588]. The Circle is at once formed of all present without a separate admission of the new Prince. The 'Invitation' proceeds almost identically to that in use today[589] as does the 'consumption'[590], but when none of the 'elements' remain, the MWS says (in *English*) "All is consumed", the "Living Circle" is again formed, the Prelate gives his Commendation[591] and an Anthem is sung[592]. After this, the MWS 'rejoices' *before* requesting the Word to be consumed, but otherwise the language is identical with that used today (except that the Prelate pronounces "Consummatum est"), the 'Nunc Dimittis' is sung, and the Chapter closed with familiar words.[593]

The Amendments which have evidently been progressively made to the 'Weymouth' Ritual indicate the minor changes being made to the procedure before 1873. This is generally confirmed by a very similar manuscript Ritual copied for Invicta Chapter in 1864[594]. In this copy, the lengthy description of the rooms is identical to that in 'Weymouth', as is much of the ceremonial working, all of which therefore may be presumed to be copied from the Supreme Council 'official' Ritual presented to the Chapter. Some developments have, however, taken place. The instruction by the MWS for the Candidates to be presented with a black apron before withdrawing from the First Point is included, but enclosed in brackets, with the footnote "Note. That portion between [ ] is now omitted"[595]. In the Sign of the Good Shepherd, the 'O' word is no longer used, and it is now 'E' (rendered as 'I') which is exchanged with P.V. At the commencement of the Third Point, the "Living Circle" is initially formed excluding the new Prince, who is then admitted to the "*Loving* circle of our hearts". Finally, the Closing is given as in "Weymouth", but with the curious and unexplained note "Closing *[not now used]*."[596]

The principal interest of the 'Invicta' Ritual is that it contains several items not recorded earlier. These include the ceremony of the Installation (nowadays the Enthronement) of a MWS[597], that of the Consecration of a Rose Croix Chapter, and the full procedure for Affiliation. There are also copies of the "Constitutions & Bye Laws of the 33° relating to the Rose Croix Degree", and of a series of decisions of the Supreme Council concerning 'Rose Croix' Chapters for the period 29th June 1855–11th October 1859'. While the latter two have little bearing on the Ritual, much is of considerable historical interest[598].

On 16th July 1861 the Supreme Council approved the appointment of "William Hyde Pullen, S.P.R.S, as Secretary General as contradistinguished from the Illus. Grand Secretary", after which he maintained the Council's Minutes[599]. Since at least 1856 it had been the custom of the Supreme Council to present a copy of the 'Ritual of the Rose Croix' Degree to each newly Warranted Chapter[600]. It is uncertain by whom these were at first written, but by 1871, when the Supreme Council was established in its new headquarters in Golden Square, this task had been assigned to Pullen who wrote a beautiful schoolmasterly copper-plate hand. Several of his copies have survived, mostly bound in red leather.

The first of these which has been preserved is that copied for Sandeman Chapter[601] on 5th May 1871. It contains the detailed layout of the Rooms, the 'Directions' for conferring the Intermediate Degrees[602], a 'pro forma' Petition, and a list of Officers, the Director of Ceremonies being below the Organist and above only the Outer Guard. The ceremony is generally similar to that in the 'Invicta' Ritual, with the 'sword drill' being carefully indicated. There is no reference to the 'Suffering Servant' verses, which appears to indicate that they were not recited before 1873, the 'O' Word has disappeared, the 'I' Word is exchanged with 'P.V.', and at the appropriate point the MWS says "All is consumed"[603], after which the Prelate pronounces the 'Gloria' which is followed by the 'Anthem'. "Consummatum Est" is said by the Prelate after the consumption of the word, and before the 'Nunc Dimittis' which precedes the Closing. This takes place at "the first hour of the third day", although this was not promulgated by the Supreme Council until two years after the date of this Ritual. The Closing is as in the previous Ritual, as is the Installation (not yet Enthronement), but the Consecration of a new Chapter is not included.

On 11th February 1873 the Supreme Council approved a schedule of "Alterations to the Ritual of the 18°, Rose Croix". This contained sixteen items and a 'Note'[604]. The most important of these changes was the adjustment of the chronology by Opening a Chapter at "The Ninth Hour of the Day", and Closing it at "the First Hour of the Third Day, being the First day of the Week". The Prelate was authorised to read the relevant verses from the twenty-seventh Chapter of St. Matthew after the Opening, the 'Suffering Servant' verses during the perambulations[605], and the first seven verses of Mark XVI in the Closing, but none of these was mandatory. However, the 'Nunc Dimittis' was "to be sung after the words 'Consummatum Est'". In addition, the Degree was to be further divorced from that of Knights Templar by re-naming the Registrar the 'Recorder'.

These changes were circulated on a printed sheet which can be found stuck into several of the preceding Rituals. The changes were incorporated into the text of all subsequent copies made by Hyde Pullen, and, after him, by his son. These copies provide a uniform Ritual, although with occasional presumably scribal errors. For example, 'H.R.D.M.' is spelled out as 'Harodim' in the 'Antigua' Ritual of 30th April 1879[606], and this is perpetuated in the 'Hugh Sandeman' Ritual of 1895[607]. The latter has no drawings of the Tracing Boards, but the 'Preliminary Remarks' still state "In the centre of the room shd. be the tracing board..."[608].

It is not known for which Chapter the last manuscript Ritual was copied. By January 1899 the Supreme Council had taken the decision to have the Ritual printed for the first time. In January 1900 the Secretary to the Council (as he then was) replied to a request from a Recorder "Certainly you can have all the rituals you require", the first time such a request had not been denied with the response "it has to be made out in manuscript at the cost of great labour"[609].

Appendix A

The furnishing of the rooms necessary for the conferment of the Eighteenth Degree, from the 'Weymouth' Ritual, numbered '3' in the Supreme Council archives (1855/6).

This Degree requires three Chambers and if possible an outer or preparation room for the reception of Candidates when the preceding degrees to the 17th are to be given by name unless the same is done in extenso. The next is named the Black Room this should be hung with black, the floor covered with oil cloth representing a Mosaic Pavement in black and white squares or lozenges. In the East two Black curtains arranged so as to be drawn asunder entirely and sufficiently open to show the Altar, which should be raised on three steps, and covered with black with a white border, and on which silver or white swords are worked (vide 1st page) Behind and above the upper step or (*sic*) transparency on which are represented three crosses (vide 1st page) the Centre and highest cross should have the mystic rose (black) placed in the centre of the cross and surrounded by a Crown of Thorns. The other two crosses should have a skull and cross-bones depicted at their feet. Behind the curtain and at the foot of the Altar should be a triangular table covered with black cloth and a white fringe round the Edge on which must be placed three wax lights, a Bible Compasses, Square and triangle.

Beside the Altar there should be a couch for the M.W.S. to recline on. On the Altar, before the transparency at the foot of the cross should be placed a Rose made of black crape. In the centre of the room must be the tracing board (vide 1st page) and on the floor towards the West a painting of Seven circles in white on a black ground, and on the centre a rose. In the North, South and West there must be three pillars Six feet high, on the Capitals of which must be inscribed Faith Hope and Charity, or rather their Initials F. H. C. painted on a small tin or card, & suspended by a hook to each pillar. Each Column must be surmounted by eleven lights disposed in a box, having eleven holes thus

.

. .

. .
F
. .

. . . .

and the letter F. H. or C respectively in the centre.

If the black room be sufficiently large it may be divided into two by a second black curtain behind the Altar; at all events there must be a passage thence to the red room according to the position of the Apartments. From the Black room should open the Chamber of Death and thence the red room, but if this cannot be managed, the Candidates after being refused admittance in the second point of the Ceremony must be sent into the reception room, and the Black room transformed into the Chamber of death.

The Chamber of Death must have the Emblems of Mortality strewed about and sundry obstruction &c so placed that the Candidate may have some difficulty in groping his way to the black curtain, behind which a lamp of Spirits of Wine and Salt must be placed, the wick of the lamp also strewed with Salt, and two or three persons in winding sheets grouped around it as corpses. The Chamber of Death may be lighted by transparencies representing skulls, cross bones &c, or by Seven flambeaus fixed in Skulls & Cross bones.

The third chamber or red room must be brilliantly illuminated.
All the Brethren in their highest costumes ranged with their banners behind them. The room hung with red. In the centre the tracing board (vide 1st page). At the West end of the tracing board the representation of the mysterious ladder of seven steps.

On the Altar must be seven steps & thirty three lights behind a transparency representing the blazing star, with seven points in the Centre of which is the letter G. On the top step of the Altar must be the Cubic Stone, in the front of which a red rose opened with the letter G in the centre. The Altar must be profusely ornamented with roses and perfumed with Attar of roses. No cross should appear in this part of the degree, but the word when found can be suspended to a silk thread stretched across by small hooks behind each letter, and above the cubic Stone, when they can be easily removed previous to the word being burnt. The last part of the ceremony is given in the red room arranged as above; except the ladder is to be removed and a pedestal covered with a white cloth placed at the East end of the Tracing Board, on which are placed a

Salt Cellar, and a Salver of Biscuits or Passion Cakes, on each side a cup, one containing the loving mixture, the other Spirits of Wine with Chloride of Strontium in which to burn the word.

Appendix B

Anthem at the conclusion of the Third Point

Grateful Notes, and numbers bring,
While the Name of God we sing,
Holy, Holy, Holy Lord,
Be they Glorious Name adored.
Men on Earth, and Saints above,
Sing the Great Redeemer's love;
Lord thy Mercies never fail,
Hail, Hail, Celestial goodness hail.

While on Earth ordained to stay,
Guide our footsteps in the way,
Mortals raise your voices high,
Till they reach the Echoing sky.
Men on Earth, and Saints above,
Sing the Great Redeemer's love,
Lord thy Mercies never fail
Hail, Hail Celestial goodness hail.

Appendix C

ALTERATIONS in the RITUAL of the 18°, ROSE CROIX as approved at a meeting of the SUPREME COUNCIL, on Tuesday, 11th February, 1873.

AT PRESENT	FOR THE FUTURE
1. The Registrar of a Chapter to be called	1. The Recorder
2. The Report◆◆,◆◆,◆◆, ◆ (this is the Report of the 17∞)	2. To be ◆◆◆◆◆◆, ◆ This to be corrected throughout the Ritual
3. At opening, the First General's answer, instead of the "*Sixth or First Hour*".	3. To be "*The Ninth Hour of the Day*"
4. After the opening	4. The Prelate may read a portion of Scripture, Matthew XXVII v.45 to 54, both inclusive
5. At the description of the Jewels to be worn by the Candidates, instead of "*the Order of Knights Templar*"	5. Say "*belonging to orders not recognised by the Supreme Council*"
6. When the alarm is given, instead of "*Generals*"	6. Say "*General*" (this should be *Second* General)
7. For "*Give me the sign*"	7. Say "*Give me the Word*"
8. When the Candidates proceed on their travels	8. The Prelate may read Isaiah LIII (in absence of music)
9. On arriving at the Pillars in the North South and West	9. They take up the letter "F" at the *third* round, "H" at the *fifth* and "C" at the *seventh*
10.	10. After the Obligation the Candidates should be placed in the West
11. Before giving the Third Sign	11. The Casual sign should be explained

12. The business of the Chapter should be transacted after the Second Point
13. At the end of the Third Point, after the words "*Consummatum est*", the "*Nunc Dimittis*" to be sung and all retire to their seats
14. The Closing to be used on all occasions.

15. In Closing. Instead of *It is the Ninth or Last Hour*"	15. The Prelate's answer should be "*It is the First Hour of the Third Day, being the First Day of the Week, the Hour of a Perfect Mason.*"
16.	16. After the sentence ending "*to love one another*", the Prelate may read Mark XVI v. 1 to 7, the M∴W∴S∴ Concluding as usual.

Note – The Report of the 17° should be used by the Candidates until they have been perfected.
Approved
CHAS, JNO. VIGNE, 33
M∴P∴S∴G∴C∴

Appendix D

Tracing Boards

Soon after Stephen Morin returned to Dominique in 1763, he visited Jamaica. Here he met Henry Andrew Francken. Francken, who had been born in Holland in about 1720, and had lived in the Island since 1757, being naturalised a year later. He was a minor official of the local Admiralty Court.

Morin at once gave Francken high rank in the 25-Degree Rite which he was constructing ('Morin's Rite') and appointed him 'Deputy Grand Inspector General of all the Superior Degrees of Free and Accepted Masons in the West Indies'.

After Morin moved permanently to Jamaica in 1765, he worked closely with Francken until his own death in November 1771. Thereafter Francken took over the direction of the new Rite. He wrote a series of manuscripts setting out in each what he claimed to be 'The Grand Constitutions of 1762', together with the Rituals of the various Degrees of Morin's Rite which he claimed were governed by the 1762 'Constitutions'. Three of these manuscripts are known to survive, one in the archives of the Supreme Council of England etc., one in the Library of the Supreme Council of the Northern Masonic Jurisdiction of the U.S.A., and one in the Museum and Library of the United Grand Lodge of England. The following description of the Tracing Boards for the First and Second Points of the Eighteenth 'Rose Croix' Degree is taken from the third of these. It has been dated as 'before 1790'.

- - - - - - -

18th Degree
This Lodge must have two apartments, the first represents Mount Calvary & the 2nd represents the Tomb of the Son of the grt. Archt. Of the Universe, which show allegorically the death and Resurrection of Jesus Christ.

1st Apartment
The draft of the Lodge is an oblong square and figured like Mount Calvary with the Tools of Masonry according to the description here after.

The Lodge is marked by Trebble Lines, in which must be wrote between the extremities, *Strength*, *Wisdom & Beauty* in the Interior E : W : N : & South with a dropping curtain from a canopy in the East.

At the East and South angles are the Sun and Moon, the heavens spread with stars and some dark clouds.

In the East is an Eagle, Rising in the air a Symbol of the Supreme puissance, 2 squares in one, on each of 3 circles, allegorically to represent Mount Calvary – opposite is a Mount with a Cubic Stone, as if it were sweating blood & water, to represent Christ in that situation, and on the cubic stone, a Rose, a symbol of his sweetness with the Letter G in the center of the Rose, signifying great archt. or the Expiring Words. The spaces between the clouds to represent those on Earth at the Time of the Sacrifice.

Below are the Tools of Masonry and the columns broke in many pieces, with the pavement all broke, to demonstrate that all parts depending on the work of Masons is destroyed when the architect is dead, and cannot be carried on, all the work divided. Everything ceased to be by his death.

A little higher is the Veil or Curtain of the Temple, torn in two parts at that time, on the outside of the columns the Seven knots of union of perfect Masons.

2nd Apartment
The draft of the apartment must be an oblong square with quadruple Lines between which must be wrote in the Interior, Faith, hope & Charity, and East, South, North & West round the Border.

In the East part must be a Cross, surrounded with a glory filled with clouds and 7 cherubims, in the centre of the cross a Rose Expendended (*sic*) and in the center the letter G. Below the 3 squares on which there are three circles, and in the opposite sides a small mountain with 3 triangles Enclosed in each other, on the Top of a Square Cubic Stone which is allegorically the holy Mount where Christ suffered – above the hill must be a blazing star with 7 points, in the center of which is the letter G, which is the allegoric representation of the Son of Man risen in all his Glory,. In the South a pelican feeding its young in their nest with his blood; an Image of the eternal Tenderness. In the North an Eagle is rising in the air the Image of the Supreme puissance, and below is the tomb. In the Lower part of the said squares, in the middle line from the East to the West, is the Tressel board, Cubic stone, hammer two foot rule a Level; on the North side the Rough stone, mallet setting tool and plumb; in the Exterior of the East a white Dove and the 7 knots of union among Masons.

- - - - - -

In no known Ritual is there an 'Explanation' of these Tracing Boards as a part of the Ceremony of Perfection; the only description of them is in Francken's manuscripts. Their position in a Chapter is described in the 'Weymouth' Ritual of 1855/6 (to the East of the '7 Circles' and of the 'Ladder' in the First and Second Points respectively) so that they must have been in use in English Chapters at least by that date. When the Supreme Council made a Northern Tour of Inspection in January 1869, in the course of which they were to confer the 30th Degree KH, the Chapter at which this was to take place was given the instructions "The Palatine would leave their furniture just as it was removing only the three Pedestals with F H C & their two tracing Boards".

In the earlier manuscript Rituals issued by the Supreme Council there are careful drawings of the Tracing Boards, generally in accord with Francken's description, but in later ones, there are diagrams, apparently printed, stuck in to the early pages. There is no representation of the Tracing Boards in the 'Hugh Sandeman' Ritual of 1895, although the instruction for their disposition still appears in the 'Preliminary Directions'. However, in the first printed version of the Ritual "*Privately Printed for the Supreme Council 33°*" in 1899, while there are comprehensive drawings of the layout of each of the rooms, there is no representation of the Tracing Boards, and the reference to their position in the 'Preliminary Directions' has been omitted.

There is no reference in the Minutes of the Supreme Council to any decision to discard the Tracing Boards. However, in *Sketches for the Rose Croix Degree* which was circulated to all Chapters in April 1889, there is the note "The Tracing Boards shown in the Ritual are not now used, nor are they necessary". (See footnote 53.)

Appendix E

Affiliation of a Knight Rosae Crucis to the Ancient and Accepted Rite

(Transcript of procedure in 'Invicta' Ritual [S.C. 17(i)] dated 1864)

Affiliation

S.G.I.G. 33°

You will take the volume of the Holy Law in your hand and assure me that on the penalty of all your former obligations; on your word as a master Mason; and on your word as a gentlemen you are duly qualified to be affiliated to our Order *as a Sovereign Prince Rose Croix* under the Supreme Grand Council of England & Wales.

Prayer

Oh Almighty & Sovereign Architect of the Universe who penetratest into the most secret recesses of the hearts of men. Purify ours with the sacred fire of Thy Divine Love. Banish from this Holy Sanctuary the impious and profane, & grant that we, being solely occupied with the great work of our redemption, may be enabled to distinguish the precious metal from the dross, and may not be deceived in the choice of him we are now about to affiliate. And may the bond of our union be ever cemented by Peace Benevolence and good will. Now unto the King Eternal, Immortal, Invisible, the only true and Wise God be the kingdom, the honour and the Glory now and for Ever. Amen

I must now call upon you to take a solemn obligation

I - - - - - - - - being a Free & Accepted Mason regularly initiated, passed and raised in a warranted Lodge most solemnly promise and swear faithful Allegiance, Fealty and submission to the Decrees of the Most Puissant Sovereigns Grand Inspectors Generals of the 33°, lawfully and constitutionally established on the 26th October 1845, sitting in Grand & Supreme Council at their Grand East in London for England & Wales & the Dependencies of the British Crown. I do further promise to hold no Masonic fellowship intercourse, or communion whatever in any of the Ineffable and Sublime degrees of Ancient, Free & Accepted Masonry with any Mason or body of Masons which at any time have or hereafter may be established in Great Britain or its Dependencies by any Authorities whatever except with such as are, or may be duly recognised and acknowledged as lawful by the aforesaid Supreme Grand Council. And I do further declare that I will (after my affiliation) as soon as convenient opportunity shall occur, sign my name in the Roll of the Golden Book of the Order.

Salute the Sacred Volume   (*contd.*)

By virtue of the Power vested in me as S∴G∴I∴G∴ 33° I hereby affiliate you to our order as an Illustrious & Sovereign Prince Rose Croix under the Supreme Gd. Council of the 33° for England & Wales & the Dependencies of the British Crown.

N.B. Only a Member of the S.G.C. 33° can affiliate.

---

556 'and Wales' does not appear in the Patent. The Supreme Council soon added this to its title, followed a few years afterwards by '& the Dependencies of the British Crown'. This was done without consulting either its American sponsors or the Supreme Councils of Ireland (established 1826) and of Scotland (established 1846), each of which at that time, together with 'England & Wales' comprised 'Great Britain', and each of which might also be considered therefore to have a legitimate involvement with events in 'the Dependencies of the British Crown'.

557 Jackson says "According to Bayard, some documents were sent with the Patent and others followed, up to August of that year [*1846*]. These included the full Rituals of the 18° and of the 30° to 33°" (RC p.163.) Bayard, writing in 1938, appears to be the only, otherwise unsupported, authority for this statement. C.J.M.

558 'Affiliation' was a simple ceremony presided over only by a member of the Supreme Council in a set form of words which included an Obligation. See Appendix E.

559 For example, 'the Opening of the Seals' as worked in the Camp of Baldwyn at Bristol.

560 Even today the Marshal is instructed to "See that the castle gates are duly guarded", as in the Knights Templar opening Ritual, but evidently inappropriate to Princes Rose Croix who meet in a Chapter on the site of the Crucifixion, and later on that of the Resurrection, and not in a fortified stronghold. This is emphasised in the earliest Rituals of the Degree. For example, "*Arrangement of the Rooms.* The first represents Mount Calvary and the second the tomb of J.C. The two together are intended to represent allegorically the events of his death and his Resurrection." *Royal Art of the Knight of Rosecroix* (1770) Wolfstieg 35.724. [French translation by CJ.M.]

Similarly, the quotation from the First Epistle of St. Peter which concludes the exhortation at the end of the Enthronement Ceremony refers to a passage of Scripture familiar and appropriate to Knights Templar, but absent from all early 'Rose Croix' Rituals.

561 The information about early Eighteenth Degree ceremonies under the English Supreme Council is chiefly derived from Press reports which frequently do not make all the circumstances wholly clear. It is possible that on occasion the Supreme Council constituted itself into a Rose Croix Chapter to confer the Degree. The Supreme Council has always exercised the right to act as a Chapter itself – this is done today at every Consecration, and formerly it was

not uncommon for Brethren to be Perfected in the Supreme Council Chapter before a Consecration in order to qualify them to become not 'Founders' but 'Original Members' of the new Chapter.

562 "at Birmingham [Vernon, now No.5], at Bolton, at Manchester, at Liverpool [apparently Palatine Chapter, now No.7, was to be authorised to meet at each of these towns], at Axminster [originally Coryton, now Coryton and Rougemont No.2, meeting at Exeter] and at Weymouth [now Weymouth No.4]."

563 Ritual numbered '6' in the Supreme Council archives.

564 William Tucker was the first Grand Secretary General of the Supreme Council.

565 RC p.28.

566 In the earliest Chapters Warranted by the Supreme Council of England, the Princes' regalia consisted of a Sash, an Apron (with which the Candidate was invested in the 'Black Room'), and a Collar. Swords were worn, and drawn at various stages in the Ceremony, until they went out of fashion at about the time of the First World War. See A & A, pp.586-9

567 Possibly it is significant that Charles Kemeys Kemeys Tynte, the first 'Most Eminent and Supreme Grand Master' of the Grand Conclave of Knights Templar after its 'Revival', was a member of Coryton Chapter.

568 In fact the 'O word' is given in full in this and in almost every preceding Ritual, sometimes ingenuously concealed as 'Sneiro'.

569 These words are inappropriately said at this stage in many older Rituals, and to place them here was not an invention of the English Supreme Council. On the other hand, in the printed French Ritual of 1770 (Wolfstieg 35.724) these words are more appropriately said in the First Point after the recital of the calamities which have accompanied the loss of the Word.

570 Numbered '7' in the Supreme Council archives.

571 "During the time when the Council of the 33° (under which we now give this degree), was in abeyance in this country, which occurred when James the 2d. took the Supreme Grand Council to France with him, at the time of his abdication in 1686, this Degree was attached to that of Knight Templar, in order to preserve it in England, but when after some years the Supreme Grand Council of the 33° which had been transplanted from the Continent to America, resumed their power in London in the year 1845, they claimed the exclusive right of giving the 18th or Rose Croix degree ..."

572 With the exception of the 'chronology' in the Opening and Closing which was not amended until February 1873 (v. infra).

573 1st Epistle to the Corinthians, XIII, vv.4-10, but the second part of v.8, whether by accident or design, is omitted ("but whether there be prophecies ... it shall vanish away").

574 At this time, only the MWS was entrusted with the full Ritual of the Degree. He then prepared, or had prepared, 'Scripts' each setting out the words and actions of each of the individual Officers of the Chapter. That for the 'High Pontiff' of St. Peter and St. Paul Chapter in Bath is preserved in the archives of Supreme Council (No.29). It appears to be in the handwriting of Charles Vigne, and is initialled by him.

The somewhat extended Prayers may be the work of the first 'High Pontiff' of this Chapter, the Reverend George Bythesea, a High Churchman who was considerably concerned with the activities of the Supreme Council in its early days, and was the Chaplain of the 'High Grades Union'.

575 Numbered '3' in the Supreme Council archives. There is little doubt that it was used in Weymouth Chapter, for in the 'Opening' the MWS says "Very excellent and perfect Princes be pleased to assist me to open ... Chapter of the Princes of the Holy order of H.R.D.M." and before the word 'Chapter', 'this Weymouth' has been written in pencil. ('The' has also been crossed out, and 'Sovereign' substituted to read '... Chapter of Sovereign Princes of the ...')

This may be one of the earliest 'official' Rituals issued by the Supreme Council. Not only is there a blank space for a Chapter name to be inserted, but the fly-leaf bears a clear impression of the Supreme Council seal, authenticated by the initials of C.J.V.(igne) who was Grand Secretary General from November 1855 until Cox was appointed to that Office in 1857.

576 An insertion regarding the Collection of Alms is preceded by an insertion in pencil 'Note of Ill Bro T. Co. DIG S.D.' Thomas Coombs 32° was appointed Deputy (as the appointment was then called, strictly in accordance with the 'Grand Constitutions') Inspector General of the 'Southern District', of which Weymouth Chapter formed a part, and Advanced to the 33° in 1873; he resigned in 1875.

577 This is reminiscent of the procedure regarding the Knocks in Lodges of Mark Master Masons.

578 Appendix A.

579 Appendix D.

580 The Supreme Council amended this to 'The Ninth hour' on 11th February 1873 (v. infra).

581 For example, 'Most Excellent and Perfect Prelate' not 'E. & P. Prelate', 'very excellent and Perfect Princes', instead of just 'Princes'.

582 [It could be thought that the original 'thirty three years' might be the most appropriate in the present context. C.J.M.]

583 In the Pauline quotation 'whether there be prophecies etc.' is again omitted, and there are one or two minor differences in wording, for example in the exhortation of the MWS 'your happy return from your travels' is interposed before 'your having found... ' but there is nothing of any great significance.

584 The only difference is that today's 'Mansions of Light' were then 'Mansions of Bliss'.

585 "In the beginning was the Word, and the word was with God and the word was God. I am alpha and omega, the beginning and the ending saith the Lord, which was, and is, and is to come, the Almighty".

586 The newly Perfected Prince is only exhorted to "Be careful by the Exercise of Faith, Hope and Charity to continue to deserve these Emblems, which are symbols of hidden truths, known only to the Perfect Mason".

587 The First Sign is, however, still that of 'Admiration'.

588 The 133rd. Psalm.

589 Instead of 'perfection of Masonry', 'culminating point, or perfection of masonry'; instead of 'Princes, we now

invite you', 'Let us invite them'; instead of 'And let us invoke', 'invoking thereon'; instead of 'rising from the tomb we ascend', 'bursting from the tomb we rise'. 'Emmanuel *in the skies'* is added but 'Glorious' is omitted. It is difficult to regard these variations as other than trivial.

590 The point is stressed that two sharing Brethren 'dip the broken pieces at the same time', an evident piece of symbolism which Brethren might consider today. Unusually among early Rituals, the remains are not, for example 'cast on the fire', but "When all have participated the MWS proceeds if any is left to call the Tylers to finish it".

591 "Gloria in Excelsis Deo, et in terra pax, hominibus bona voluntas".

592 Appendix B.

593 As in the note regarding the Third Point, differences are trivial, for example 'dissipated' rather than 'dispersed'.

594 This Ritual, numbered '17 (i)' in the Supreme Council archives, was copied for Invicta Chapter (now No.10) by '*Matthew Cooke, (Capellarum Regiorum nuper et Alumnis)* 43 Acton Street, London W.C.Scripsit. 1864. *Organista et Amanuensis, quod re Clerum et Literarius.*' (The words here shown in Italics are printed on a label in Gothic script, with the address, 'scripsit' and date in holograph.)

595 The 'Weymouth Ritual' states that in the First Point the Princes wear "a black apron usually the reverse of the Rose +", and the 'Antigua' Ritual "a black apron & collar, usually the reverse of the Rose Croix", but there is no reference to this in the 'Hugh Sandeman' Ritual of 1895. There is no reference to the Candidate's investiture with a black apron in any manuscript Ritual subsequent to the 'Invicta', neither is there any reference to the newly Perfected Prince being presented at any stage with regalia other than a Collar and jewel. The Apron remains a minor mystery.

596 There is no indication of the source of this curious interpolation, but that it was evidently a practice not restricted to Invicta Chapter is indicated by Item 14 of the directions which the Supreme Council published in February 1873 (v.i.) "The Closing to be used on all occasions."

597 The wording of the Installation (Enthronement) Ritual used today is somewhat curtailed compared with that in the 'Invicta' Ritual (Inv. 'distinguished Office', 2004 'Office'; Inv. 'He is well skilled in our sublime mysteries and observant of the moral precepts of our forefathers and I have no doubt', 2004 'He is well skilled in our mysteries, and I have no doubt'; Inv. 'the great responsibility', 2004, 'the responsibility'; and so on). With these additions the wording of the 'Invicta' Ritual is almost the same as that worked today, save that no collarette nor jewel is presented, the MWS-Obligate receiving from his predecessor first the 'Charter', and then the Holy Bible (in the words used by the Prelate today) after which he is inducted into the Chair. He receives the same exhortation as given today, and appoints his Officers, followed by the 'Charge', identical to that today apart from some minor expansions ('...fervent piety, *which are constantly ascending from our altars..*', '... children of humility *and in our lives and conversations, as well as*

in our fraternal intercourse, so illustrate the beauty and excellence of our Order that, without comprehending our mysteries, the world may exclaim "How good and pleasant..." ' , etc.)

598 Some of these 'decisions', although dated in each case, are not recorded in the Supreme Council Minute Books.

599 W. Hyde Pullen was a schoolmaster in the Isle of Wight who for many years had also acted as confidential Masonic Secretary to Dr. Henry Beaumont Leeson who was Sovereign Grand Commander from 1851 to 1868.

600 For example, the 'Weymouth' Ritual authenticated by the seal of the Supreme Council, and by Vigne's initials. It was considered that one complete copy of the Ritual was adequate in each Chapter. For example, on 12th January 1883 Hugh Sandeman, the Grand Secretary General, wrote to the Recorder of St. Leonard Chapter No.39 at Blandford "The only Ritual of the 18º is the Manuscript one issued by this office for 25/- ... . . it is very unusual to issue copies of this Ritual to any but M.W.S's. of Chapters." A. & A, p.434.

601 Sandeman Chapter, now No.32, was originally Warranted on 10th May 1871 to meet in Calcutta, but removed to Bournemouth (England) in 1972. The Ritual is authenticated by *three* impressions of the Seal of the Supreme Council and is signed by 'Nathl. Geo. Philips, 33° Lt. Grand Commander'.

602 The Intermediate Degrees are now split into three groups as is done today – 'Grand Lodge of Perfection' (4th to 14th), 'Grand Lodge of Princes of Jerusalem' (15th and 16th) and 'Grand Lodge of Knights of the East and West' (17th).

603 In today's Ritual: "All have partaken".

604 Appendix C.

605 But only "(in the absence of music)".

606 This Ritual, numbered '19' in the Supreme Council archives, is transcribed in Hyde Pullen's customary immaculate copper-plate, but unusually the copy has been made into a smaller black-bound notebook. Antigua Chapter was Warranted in 1879. On the first page is written "The M.W. Sovereign 'Antigua' Chapter Rose Croix – April 1879. S.H.C.33°" and at the end of the main text, "Certified. Shadwell H. Clerke 33° Grand East London 30 April 79" below which is embossed the Seal of the Supreme Council. Antigua Chapter surrendered its Warrant in 1926, together with its 'certified' Ritual; and other documents. (Antigua Chapter No.884 is a successor Warranted in September 1980.)

607 Numbered '44' in the Supreme Council archives. (Hyde Pullen had retired in February 1881, and his son Edward Pullen was appointed 'Asst. Sec. to the Su.Co.' in his place. The text in this manuscript is written in copper-plate, but in a larger hand easily distinguishable from that of Hyde Pullen, and is, presumably, that of his son, Edward.) It is certified by 'Hugh D. Sandeman, 33°, Grd. Secy. Genl., 7 March 1895' below which is embossed the seal of the Supreme Council.'

There is no indication for which Chapter this copy was made. Possibly this was Salween Chapter No.131, Warranted in 1894 to meet in Maymyn and Mandalay, which surrendered and returned its

Warrant in 1930, conceivably including its book of
Ritual among its Chapter records. (See SCLB No.40,
p.856, Tower/Garett [last Recorder of 131],10th March
1930.)

608 A pamphlet dated 15th April 1889 entitled *Sketches
for the Rose Croix Degree* was circulated to all
Chapters over the signature of the Grand Secretary
General, Hugh Sandeman. The fly-leaf is marked
"*PRIVATE AND CONFIDENTIAL (To be retained
under lock and key, by the Recorder,* pro tem.)*" It
contains more detailed drawings of the furniture and
layout of the rooms for the 'Rose Croix' Degree
Ceremony than any that have been published before
or since, including one of the 'Shrouded Figure' in the
C. of D. The 'Explanation' is also very detailed – for
example the candlesticks on the Altar in the Red
Room "may be small white or rose-coloured china
candlesticks, or tin ones painted white", and "The
Mystic Ladder, lying on a white cloth in the middle of
the room, may be made of wood, to fold, or of red
braid, about two inches broad, sewn on one width of
white calico, and should be 8 or 9 feet long". The
description of the 'Seven Circles' ("painted in white on
a piece of American black oil cloth") says "in the
centre is the Pelican". After enumerating the
necessary "books for use in a Chapter", the statement
is made "The Tracing Boards shown in the Ritual are
not now used, nor are they necessary". (The
pamphlet also contains the full Ritual for the
Consecration of a Chapter.)

609 A & A, p.582.

Essay 17

The evolution of today's English Rose Croix Ritual
Part Two. Printed Rituals from 1899

When we are Initiated into Freemasonry, and whenever we subsequently acquire another Degree or enter another Order, there is a natural tendency to think that what we then experienced was the 'right' way to do it. It is easy to forget that the Ceremony has not always been conducted in precisely that way. Every Degree and Order has undergone continual adaptations over the years. It is doubtful if the Craft as a whole would have survived for so long if this had not been the case.

Jackson pointed out that the Eighteenth 'Rose Croix' Degree has probably preserved its original form more closely than any other in the Ancient and Accepted Rite – and that includes the three Symbolic Craft Degrees! The ceremony today is still recognisably the same as that recorded in the French Rituals of the 1760s. The lessons to be learnt have not altered. But even in the last hundred years or so there have been significant detailed changes in the Ritual authorised to be used in Chapters under 'The Supreme Council for England', as its Patent originally described it. Step by step it took the form with which we are familiar today. This Essay sets out to describe this process from the time that the Supreme Council first authorised an official printed Ritual in 1899.

There was an evident need for a standard Ritual when for the first time in 1852 the Supreme Council for 'England' granted 'Patents' or Warrants for Rose Croix Chapters to meet outside London. Three years later Weymouth Chapter was in possession of an 'official' Ritual authenticated by the Seal of the Supreme Council together with the initials of Charles Vigne, then the Grand Secretary General. For the next forty years the Supreme Council issued one copy[610] of an 'official' manuscript Ritual to each Chapter when it received its Warrant. Each was embossed with the Seal of the Supreme Council and signed by one or more of its Members. To make these copies in his immaculate copper-plate hand became one of the duties of Hyde Pullen who had been appointed "Secretary General as contradistinguished from the Illus. Grand Secretary". After Hyde Pullen retired in 1881, his son Edward Pullen, was appointed in his place and made the necessary copies[611].

In February 1873 the Supreme Council issued to each of its Chapters a printed sheet of amendments which were included in every subsequent manuscript copy of the Ritual. The careful copying of the Pullens, father and son, resulted in few alterations to the successive manuscript Rituals, which now included the 'Installation' (Enthronement) of a MWS in addition to the conferment of the Intermediate Degrees by name, and the work of the Eighteenth 'Rose Croix' Degree itself. There were, however, certain anomalies. Earlier 'official' Rituals had contained diagrams of the two Tracing Boards of the Eighteenth Degree, either carefully drawn, or pasted in[612]. By March 1895 these diagrams are omitted from the Manuscript Rituals, but in the description of the Black Room the 'Preliminary Remarks' still state "In the centre of the room shd. be the tracing board" although Tracing Boards seem to have fallen out of use in the Degree some years previously[613], and there is no mention of the second Tracing Board in the Red Room[614].

In 1898 the Supreme Council had apparently decided to approve the printing of the Ritual of the Eighteenth 'Rose Croix' Degree. There is nothing about this decision in the Council's Minutes until a brief entry on 16th January 1899 notes "The Revised Ritual with Sketches was submitted and approved". Evidently it met with a ready sale[615].

On its early pages this first printed Ritual illustrated in seven diagrams the layout of both Black Room and Red Room with details of the equipment which they contained. There is no longer "a couch for the MWS to recline on"; instead, perhaps more conventionally to modern eyes, "there should be, on the right, a Throne for the MWS, and one for the Prelate, on the left". There is no reference to Tracing Boards. There is, however, one considerable anomaly. The floor-cloth in the Black room is described in the 'Preliminary Directions' as "a painting of Seven Circles in white upon a black ground with a rose in the centre", as it had been in all the preceding manuscript Rituals. However, on the explanatory Diagram[616], there is not a Rose, but a Pelican. The Pillars in the Black Room had always earlier been specified to be 'six feet high', but this dimension was now omitted. "Sundry obstructions" are specified in the "Chamber of Death" as in earlier Rituals, together with "one or more persons in w....g s....s"[617], and it was to be illuminated by "seven flambeaux fixed in Skulls and

Cross-bones". In the Red Room, again as in earlier Rituals, there was to be upon the Altar, in front of the Cubic Stone, "a red rose opened with the letter G in the centre". For the 'Third Point', a coloured cloth is particularly specified for the 'pedestal' on which the consumables are placed, "biscuits or passion-cakes" being specified as they had been in all the previous English manuscripts. There is, however, no 'tasse'. Instead, a second cup is to be provided "in which to consume the Word". This is a tradition going back to the French Rituals of the 1760s.

The Opening is unchanged from that in the preceding manuscript Rituals. The "Very Excellent and Perfect Princes", with drawn swords, form lines in the North and South, and are commanded to 'Sheathe Swords' before being proved by the Generals by Sign and Word, while at the same time the Outer Guard enters the Chapter to give the Sign and Word to the Captain of the Guard who then reports to the Marshal "All is secure without". The Chapter is opened by the MWS, using words almost identical to those in the Ritual today, the only addition being that, after the Prelate's Prayer, the Princes give the Sign of what was still referred to as 'Admiration', six and one.

Even though there is no reference in the Minutes of the Supreme Council to any revision of the Ritual having been carried out, there are sufficient minor changes in the working to indicate that some such deliberate process had taken place. Before the Candidate(s) are admitted they have to sign not only a petition, but also an Obligation of Allegiance, much of the wording of which is the same as that in the Obligation formerly taken by 'Rosae Crucis' Brethren seeking affiliation. No reason is given for the introduction of this additional declaration. The Marshal presents the Petition to the MWS, who obtains the approval of the Princes, before the Marshal seeks to introduce the Candidates[618]. No longer is a Trumpet sounded on their admittance[619]. "The Princely Council" has become "The Princely Chapter", but, in the recital of the calamities which have overtaken them, still "an earthquake upheaves its convulsive power", and at "rent asunder" "here the curtains before the altar are drawn apart".[620] In the previous years there had been several changes in the symbolic time for which the Candidates travelled. The '1895' Ritual said "33 days"; this is now "33 months", during which perambulation the Prelate reads (and, no longer, simply "may read") the Fifty-third Chapter of Isaiah. Nothing else has changed, but it is curious that, in the reading from the Epistle to the Corinthians after the Obligation, the latter part of the 8th verse is omitted, as it has been in all previous Rituals in which the passage has been included.

As in earlier Rituals, the Candidates are now instructed to retire to prepare by meditation to resume their travels, before re-entering, apparently without any Report or Alarm, "clothed in their highest Masonic costume". In former years this used to be specified as that of 'Knights of the East and West', and any Templar Regalia was firmly prohibited, but there is now no guidance as to what is acceptable. Seven circuits are made, the MWS withdrawing to the Red Room on the third, other Brethren progressively leaving until the Captain of Guards prevents the entry of the Marshal and Candidates on the Seventh. Once more the Candidates retire to the Reception Room, this time for a Crape to be placed on their heads[621]. They enter the Chamber of Death, the 'Dead March' is played, Raphael comes to conduct them to the 'Mansions of Bliss', and as they enter the Red Room, the music changes to 'Sound the loud timbrel'. Raphael reports the perils through which they have passed, including, *before* the inquisition by the MWS, 'The Valley of the Shadow of Death', fortified by the three Virtues of Faith, Hope and Charity. As in previous Rituals, the answer to the question by the MWS "What supported you?" is "The example of our Saviour's sufferings". No Scriptural quotations were attached to the four last steps of the ladder, the last rung being 'Judah' as it had been from the earliest times of the Degree. Swords are drawn and pointed to the Word when it is affixed, before it is saluted. After the Accolade, as in earlier Rituals, it is a 'Perfected and Puissant' Prince of the Order of Rose Croix who is invited to rise. The Candidates are then invested, but there is no reference to an Apron, nor is any explanation of the regalia given. The Signs and Words are communicated almost exactly as they are today, after which the newly Perfected Princes are proclaimed.

There remains only the Third Point, the Princes no longer re-entering the Red Room two-by-two with white wands in their hands. Nor, while doing so, do they chant the hundred and thirty-third Psalm 'with the Gloria patri'. They are told that they have arrived at the 'culminating point' of masonry, first forming the "Living Circle" without the Candidates, and then admitting them to the "*loving* circle" of their hearts, "loving" as it had always distinctively been since this piece of ritual was first introduced. As heretofore the MWS looks forward to "bursting" rather than no more than "rising" from the tomb. When the elements have circulated, the MWS says "All is consumed", and the Prelate pronounces in Latin the 'Gloria'. The Anthem[622] is then sung. The MWS "rejoices to have united" *before* requesting the Prelate to remove the Sacred Word, the latter saying "Consummatum Est" after it is consumed. The 'Nunc Dimittis' is then chanted before the Brethren resume their seats. The closing is almost identical to today's Ritual[623]; no longer is the Prelate permitted to read St. Mark Chapter 16, Verses 1-7 as he was in 1895.

On Page 2 of this Ritual there is a list of 'Addenda et corrigenda', most of which are 'addenda', doing no more than to add references to the layout diagrams at appropriate points in the text. However, evidently a proof-reader has conscientiously assumed that, after forming the "living" circle, admitting the Candidates to the *loving* circle of our hearts, a charming expression which appears in the preceding manuscript Rituals, must be a printer's error for "living", and has so amended it. Regrettably this amendment has remained unaltered[624].

Early in 1902 the Supreme Council obtained estimates for printing a new Edition, and on 28th June authorised another 1000 copies to be printed by Warrington and Company instead of Kennings. The reprint contained only minor alterations apart from the 'Addenda et corrigenda' in the 1902 Edition. It still contains 'the anomaly of the Pelican', represented in the Diagram as such, but described in the text as a 'rose'. Less emphasis was laid on sword-drill[625]; swords were no longer to be drawn in the Opening, in which the "Thrice Excellent and Perfect Generals" have become "Very Excellent", and the "Most Reverend and Perfect Prelate" has similarly become "Very Reverend". The Candidates continue to take a separate 'Obligation of Allegiance' as well as submitting a Petition. In the Second Point, the letters of "the Word, when found, can be suspended to a silken thread stretched across above the Cubic Stone". In the Third Point, the Anthem is no longer mandatory, but "may be sung" – the words are no longer printed. Otherwise there appear to have been no alterations to the 1899 version.

In March 1905 the Supreme Council appointed a sub-committee[626] to look into the questions of a "sealed pattern" for the clothing of the Degree, and of amendments to its Ritual. Little time was wasted; on 10th July 2,000 copies of the new Ritual were ordered "to be printed, and a free copy of the same to be sent to every Chapter and Inspectors General of the several Districts". The Council expressed the wish that the revised Ritual should be brought into use as soon as possible.

The explanatory diagrams were redrawn, and for the first time the 'Preliminary Directions' include "Seven Circles ... with a Pelican in the centre" as depicted in the Diagram since 1899. "A red or purple cloth" is specifically prescribed for the pedestal in the Third Point, upon which there is no second Cup or other provision for consuming the Word. Since there are no directions as to how this should be done, it can only be assumed that this marks the start of the present-day procedure.

In the Opening none of the Officers are either "Most" or "Very" – all are "E. & P.". Nor is there any reference to Swords, although the Princes still stand in two lines to be proved – evidently there was a desire to do away with unnecessary formality. The Opening is unchanged, including the "Sign of A". "The Petition and Obligation of Allegiance" are combined into a single document which each Candidate signs.

Changes have been made in the Second Point. "The earth quakes" rather than "upheaves its convulsive power". Only four departing Circuits are made, "the MWS, Prelate, Supreme Council and Inspectors General" leaving on the first, and the Candidates' progress being halted on the fourth. On entry to the Red Room, the Candidates now reply that they were supported by "F., H and C." – the last allusion to the sufferings of Our Lord has been eliminated. In the Investiture there is still no reference to an Apron, nor any explanation of the Clothing. Neither in the Third Point nor in the Closing is there any reference to choral singing, except that after the 'Gloria' "an anthem may be sung", but no words are specified.

Anyone who has been concerned with the publication of a Masonic Ritual would agree that in spite of the most scrupulous care, it is well-nigh impossible to deal with every matter which some conscientious Brother may wish to query. The wide availability of the 1905 Ritual proved no exception to this. For example, the Council was asked at what Chapter the Bible should be opened, "who may be present at the arranging of room for the 3rd Point", and at what stage in the ceremony the Altar Candles should be lit[627]. However, when a further Edition was called for in 1909, the only addition of any significance to the wording was a brief elucidation of the withdrawal before the Third Point, the rubric now reading "After which all, except the 33°, none of whom join in the procession, retire while the room is prepared for the third point". Nor were any changes made when the Ritual was again reprinted in 1912. However, the Supreme Council were now seriously considering revising the working.

In various Rituals there is some inconsistency in at least the spelling of the word given with the First Sign. On 4th December 1913, the Council Minutes formally record "It was decided that the word in the first sign should be in future H******", that is to say the word in common use today[628]. This amendment was incorporated in the next Edition of the Ritual in 1917; evidently it was a novelty to some Brethren because the Supreme Council received letters querying it.

This was not the only change in this Edition. On 4th May 1916 the Minutes of the Supreme Council record "It was agreed to restore the fuller explanation of the steps of the ladder of the 18° Ritual", and on 26th April 1917 "Instructions for the Third Point were considered"[629].

The first elaboration in the revised Ritual is that in the First Point "here a gong is sounded" before the curtains in front of the Altar are drawn apart. The major innovation is the introduction of the Scriptural quotations after the last four steps of the ladder in the Second Point. But it is questionable whether this was, as the Council Minute stated, a "restoration". No such "explanation" of the steps has come to light in any earlier Ritual, English or Continental. In communicating the Signs and Words, that for the Word accompanying the First Sign is set out as "H...n.a." so that there can be no mistake. Then, for the first time, there is an explanation of the "clothing" – "This may be given as an Address" – which is identical to that given mandatorily today[630]. The "Instructions for the Third Point" which had been foreshadowed amounted only to the inclusion of:

The living circle is formed with arms outstretched (not crossed) the Candidate being outside the circle.

Evidently in some Chapters the Brethren regretted that various readings and chants were no longer included in the Ritual to which it was understood that the Supreme Council wished to have strict adherence without extraneous additions. The Council was, however, prepared to stretch a point for the benefit of long-established Chapters. Albert Edward No. 87 was one of these to which at first Tower had taken it on himself to write on 28th November 1917: "There is no reason why you should not sing Psalm 133 and the Nunc Dimittis", but he was not prepared to authorise the reading of additional pieces of Scripture. He referred to the Council the Chapter's request to read from the 27th Chapter of St. Matthew at the Opening, and from the 15th Chapter of St. John at the Closing. On 17th January 1918 the Supreme Council resolved "that deviations and additions to the Ritual were to be deprecated, but that the Supreme Council do not object to the above being an old custom of the Chapter."

The Ritual was reprinted in 1919; on 27th November the Supreme Council accepted an estimate for £141.10s. for 5,000 copies "without burnished edges". This appears to have been only a simple reprint without amendments. A further reprint was made in 1926, and some minor editing appears to have been carried out[631], and further rubrics added[632]. In particular the question about the Altar Candles is resolved by adding to the 'Preliminary Directions' "The Altar lights should be lighted for the 2nd and 3rd Points unless already done". In the previous Edition, there had been a footnote to the truncated reading from the Epistle to the Corinthians "In lieu of the following 1. Cor. 13. v.4-10, may be read by the Prelate". Now, for the first time, the full passage of Scripture is included in the printed Ritual. In the Second Point, the explanation of the Regalia is still only an optional Address.

The next printing of the Ritual was made in 1931[633]. The first amendment is a note to the list of Officers that an Assistant Recorder and an Assistant Director of Ceremonies may be appointed when the Chapter numbers over forty members[634]. The admonition about Candidates necessarily professing the Christian Faith (and the duty of the MWS so to inform them) is now printed immediately before the First Point. An alternative prayer is inserted at the end of the First Point[635]. The explanation of the Regalia remained optional[636].

A major revision took place before the Ritual was again reprinted in 1938[637]. For the first time since 1905, the explanatory diagrams of the Chapter fittings were re-drawn. The 'Preliminary Directions' were also re-drafted, but no changes were made to the disposition of the Rooms and their furniture. Many of the rubrics were clarified, and there was a general 'tidying up'. For example, when in the Opening the Generals receive the Word and the Sign from the Brethren, they now pass from East to West, so as to finish in their proper places instead of vice versa as heretofore; in addition, the MWS addresses his questions to the First General, and not to "the Generals". Before the Lodge of Perfection, the rubric states: *"The Candidate should not wear any Masonic Regalia"*, clarifying the situation and doing away with the old instruction that he should wear his "Highest Masonic Clothing". Single knocks are inserted for opening the 'Intermediate Lodges', and the Marshal is given the duty of opening and closing the Bible. Several changes are made to the Opening Prayer in the First Point[638], and thereafter the rubrics are made more explicit[639]. At the end of the First Point, the only Prayer specified is that given as an alternative in the previous Ritual.

Changes to clarify some of the rubrics in the Second Point are also made, but perhaps the most interesting introduction is that for the first time the first Sign is described as that of 'Adoration' and not of 'Admiration' as it has been since the earliest days of the Degree. The explanation of the Regalia was still permissive and not mandatory[640].

The War then intervened, and no revision or reprint was made until 1951 when the Supreme Council decided to carry out a major overhaul of the working. Before the revised version was printed, at the request of the Supreme Council the King Edward the Seventh Chapter of Improvement privately rehearsed the draft working, into which some of their suggestions were incorporated[641].

The result was a wholly new Book of Ritual[642], with the 'Plans' re-drawn, the 'Directions' re-written, and lists of furniture and equipment provided for each stage of the Ceremony. Even the type-face was updated. The list of Officers was unchanged, except that Stewards could now optionally be appointed. In the Black Room, the "Rose made of Black crape" at the foot of the Cross was omitted. The Opening was revised; although the 'Castle Gates' continued to be duly guarded, no longer did the Princes stand in two columns to communicate Sign and Word, but as soon as the MWS was assured by the Marshal that the Chapter was secure, all stood to Order, and the MWS proceeded with the Opening, and, after the Knocks, the Prelate opened the New Testament[643]. After the Prayer, the seven-fold 'Sign of Adoration' was omitted. The Intermediate Degrees were then conferred as in the preceding Ritual[644] . A short explanation of each of the three group of Degrees[645] was introduced. In the First Point, instead of standing in the West, the Candidate is taken to the Veil, which is not drawn at "rent in twain", although the gong is sounded. The changes to the first Prayer are retained, and the reading from Isaiah is set out in full[646]. To hand the letters to the MWS the Marshal "passes through the Veil" which is drawn when they have been received. The closing Prayer is the request for Faith, Hope and Charity, and not the one substituted in the previous Ritual. The Candidate does not then depart "to meditate", the MWS saying "Having found the three fundamental principles of our Order let us go forth in search of the lost Word".

The rubrics in the Second Point have been made very explicit, but the Ceremony is unchanged except in two particulars. The Candidate seeks to advance not to the "Mansions of Bliss", but to those of "Light", and there is for the first time a reference to the "Apron", the MWS saying "I invest you with the badge of the Order", and the explanation of the Regalia is mandatory. There is no change either in the Third Point or in the Closing, except that the rubrics are more detailed, and include the provision of a tasse which is lighted by the Prelate with a taper kindled from the Altar.

Even the Supreme Council could not escape the pitfalls which lie in wait for those who make major alterations to a Ritual. Soon after publication a sheet was issued setting out "Corrections for 18° Ritual (1951 Edition)" which were incorporated in a reprint in the following year, of which the most noticeable was the removal of the "gong"[647]. Further minor changes were made in editions published in 1958 and 1961, of which perhaps the most important in the latter were the instruction that when exchanging the Sign of the G.S. "you should never bow", and the substitution in the Third Point of "All have partaken" for "All is consumed". The Apron, however, was now optional. After the MWS says "I invest you with the badge of the Degree", there is now the rubric *The above words will be omitted if no apron is worn*".

The Supreme Council again reviewed the Ritual in 1966, but the new Edition contained only minor changes of wording. The quinquennial review in 1971 gave further instruction to the Brethren by introducing the schedule of the timing of lighting the candles and placing the Word on the Altar in the Red Room. In October 1973 the Grand Secretary General had to write to all Recorders to say that "The 1971 edition of the Ritual has sold out rapidly", enabling the typographical correction to be made – "after "Seal", add "engraved with a Rose". In consequence of this, the next formal revision did not take place until 1978, when again only minor changes were made, but by 1984 the Apron had been done away with, and the MWS no longer presented the newly Perfected Prince with the "badge of the Order"[648]. This Edition of the Ritual was reprinted in 1985 and 1989 without amendment.

The 1994 Edition contained two considerable changes. In the first place, it was considered that the interpretation of the fourth letter of the Word added nothing to the progression in the previous three, and that the Biblical quotation which had been attached to it increased the obscurity. "Jerusalem" was therefore substituted, to which a quotation could be attached more in keeping with the subject-matter of the Degree[649]. Secondly, "Consummatum Est" was removed from the Third Point, where it had always been inappropriate. In additional to these emendations, the representation of the Word on a prism was introduced.

Appendix A

The Anthem sung at the conclusion of the Third Point. This was mandatory until 1902, and thereafter permissive until 1917.

> Grateful notes and number bring,
> While the name of God we sing;
> Holy, Holy, Holy, Lord
> Be thy glorious name adored
>
> Men on earth, and Saints above,
> Sing the Great Redeemer's love;
> Lord, thy mercies never fail,
> Hail, Hail, Celestial Goodness, Hail!
>
> While on earth ordained to stay,
> Guide our footsteps in Thy way;
> Mortals, raise your voices high,
> Till they reach the echoing sky.
>
> Men on earth, and Saints above,
> Sing the Great Redeemer's love;
> Lord, Thy mercies never fail,
> Hail, Hail, Celestial Goodness, Hail!

Appendix B

The wearing of swords in Rose Croix Chapters

The custom of wearing Swords in Rose Croix Chapters seems to have been obsolescent by the end of the nineteenth century. On 11th July 1900, Captain W. Portlock Dadson, the Secretary to the Supreme Council (the Office of Grand Secretary General had been temporarily put in abeyance in 1895) wrote to the Treasurer of *Mount Calvary in the East* Chapter No.47 in Singapore:

> "The custom of wearing swords in the Chapter 18° has become obsolete here, occasionally a man wears one. For my own part I like to see them used in the Arch of Steel formed for Distinguished visitors; we always did it in my mother Chapter, the Invicta No.40, and now only one old member comes in his sword. All members of the 18° are entitled to them, see page 28 of the R & R and pages 29 – 30 for 30° and higher degrees."

On 26th July 1906, the Secretary, John Tower, (the Office of Grand Secretary General was not restored until 1908) wrote to Bro. G.T.Fillingham of *Himalaya* Chapter No.80 in India:

> "It is quite correct to wear swords, though they are generally omitted in London, and may very well be dispensed with. However, it is not incorrect to wear them."

On 15th June 1909, Tower, now Grand Secretary General, wrote to the Recorder of *Rose of Sharon* Chapter, No.35, in Malta, Bro. F.Hully 30°"

"With regard to your query as to the use of swords in the 18th degree, I beg to say that they are not usually worn in London, though they are worn in many Chapters in England and are quite correct."

Evidently swords were not wholly discarded. Indeed the instruction which Tower sent on 17th November 1913 to Thomas Parker, the Recorder of *Huyshe* Chapter No.38, reversed the recent trend:

"It would be quite in order to form two lines and to receive the Supreme Council under what is termed an Arch of Steel, for which purpose the brethren would require their swords."

As late as 1919, writing about the arrangements for the Consecration of *Londesborough* Chapter No.208, Tower wrote "By all means have an Arch of Steel if you desire it". That the use of swords in Chapters continued to be permissive is illustrated by a Minute of the The Supreme Council on 22nd May 1924:

"Letter dated 15th inst. from University Chapter No. 30 asking whether the S.C. would object to the abolition of swords, was read, and it was decided to reply that if swords are not worn no fault will be found."

In the 'Rules and Regulations' the 'Clothing, etc.' for the Eighteenth Degree still included
Sword. – Gilt grip and mountings, red leather scabbard
until 1955.

Appendix C

CORRECTIONS FOR 18° RITUAL (1951 EDITION)

PAGES 6, 7, 20, 22, 36	Delete all references to the gong.
PAGE 28	Penultimate line – delete "E. & P."
	Last line – add full stop after "loss" and delete "and"
	To read, "loss. May the ..."
PAGE 32	Lines 14 and 15 — Add full stop after "allegories" and delete "and".
PAGE 34	Line 1 — Instead of "answer this" read "reply"
PAGE 38	Third Paragraph, line 5 — For "upon" read "on".
PAGE 39	Line 7 — For "bear" read "bare".
PAGE 47	Line 7 of rubric — Amend to read *They rise and give the first sign with the word H ... a seven times"*
PAGE 51 Line 6	To read *"Prince to the West, place him between and slightly in front of the Generals and stand on either side of him facing East"*
	Delete lines 9 and 10.
	Line 12 — After "Her." insert "*(in the South West)*".
PAGE 53	Lines 23 and 24 – ("*The Prelate with a taper ...*)"transfer as 4th and 3rd lines from foot of page with the addition *"when convenient during the above"*.
PAGE 59	8th line from foot – for "and this" read "which"
PAGE 61	Line 1 – after "Princes" insert "of the ... Chapter Rose Croix".
	Para. 3, lines 1 and 2 – delete ", the fundamental principles of our Order,".

610 Requests from Chapters or individual Brethren for additional copies were denied with the typical response "it has to be made out in manuscript at the cost of great labour". It appears to have been the duty of the first MWS to make 'scripts; for his Officers setting out only the individual work of each'. One of those that survives is that prepared by Charles Vigne, then the first MWS of St. Peter and St. Paul Chapter at Bath, for his 'High Pontiff' (Prelate). The Reverend George Bythesea. (Supreme Council Archives, Ritual No.29.)

611 Hyde Pullen died early in 1887, and the Supreme Council resolved that his pension should be paid to his widow who, in the following year, was also elected "to the benefits of the R.M.B.I." at the head of the Poll.

612 The diagrams of the Tracing Boards in the early English manuscript Rituals were reasonably accurate pictorial illustrations of the descriptions included by Francken in his 'Manuscripts'.

613 The latest reference so far identified as to the use of Tracing Boards is in a letter from Nathaniel Philips to Wike, the 'Registrar' of Palatine Chapter, on 13th January 1869, instructing him, on the occasion of a visit to Manchester by the Supreme Council to confer the Thirtieth Degree, to "leave their furniture just as it was, removing only the three Pedestals with F H C & their two tracing boards." A & A, p.129.

614 Another anomaly is that the 'Preliminary Remarks' in the Ritual authenticated by Hugh Sandeman, the Grand Secretary General on 7th March 1895, still state that "the preceding degrees to the 17th inclusive, are to be given by name unless the same is done in extenso', although there is no record of the Intermediate Degrees being conferred otherwise than by name for many years before that date.

615 On 8th January 1902 the Secretary reported that the Edition of 1.000 Rituals, supplied in January 1899 for £25 was nearly exhausted, 889 copies having been sold at two shillings and sixpence each (twelve and a half pence.).

616 Diagram '3'.

617 There was, however, no diagram of this as there had been in the *Sketches for the Rose Croix Degree* which had been sent to Recorders over the signature of the Grand Secretary General, Hugh Sandeman, in April 1889.

618 The Princes of the Chapter are as always instructed to wear black aprons, but for the first time they are not required to have "white handks to hold to their faces".

619 The Ballot is taken when the Petition is presented, but when the Marshal then asks permission to introduce the Candidates, there is no longer the cautious further enquiry as in the earlier manuscript Rituals "Brethren are your suffrages still in favour of the Candidates?"

620 Among minor changes of wording *'it is well* that you have arrived ...' instead of 'we rejoice', 'the discovery of the *mysterious word*' has become 'the lost Word', 'Sovereign Chapter' in the Obligation has become 'Princely Chapter', 'about to close' becomes *'now about to close'*.

621 There is no mention of the Candidates removing 'their highest Masonic costume', which is always indicated in earlier Rituals.

622 Appendix A.

623 The only trivial points of interest are that the MWS unaccountably addresses the Princes as 'my excellent Companions', (in 1895 it was equally unaccountably 'Very Excellent Companions'), and at this time, while the word was always 'the Sacred Word', it is 'the light', rather than 'the true Light' which is restored to our eyes.

624 There was one other substantial correction. The instruction that behind the Altar in the Red Room there should be "a transparency representing the Blazing Star with seven points, in the centre of which the letter G", was removed.

625 See Appendix B.

626 The Grand Treasurer General, Frank Richardson; the Grand Prior, Canon (as he then was) John Brownrigg; and the Grand Chamberlain, James Matthews.

627 The answers were, respectively:
• At any suitable Chapter in the New Testament "For general convenience & to prepare for the Procession, it is better that all should retire except such as are required for arranging the room, and Members of the 33° who do not take part in the procession " A few months later, this was clarified by the Grand Secretary General, John Tower, who wrote "... it only means that members of the 33° do not take part in the procession at the commencement of the 3rd.Point, and does not mean that members of the 33° prepare the room for the 3rd Point which can be done by the Outer Guard or any brother". The Supreme Council have always emphasised that there is nothing esoteric about the preparation for the 3rd. Point; the exodus is simply to enable the procession, in which 'Thirty-thirds' do not take part, to be conveniently formed.

John Tower wrote "Strictly speaking, I think that the candles should be lighted for the opening of a Chapter, though the operation is usually postponed until the actual ceremony of perfection is commenced. The reason for this is the heat generated by the 33 candles is rather trying in a badly ventilated room." See A & A, pp.583/4.

628 The Word is spelled out in full in the Minute.

629 The 'Preliminary Directions' contained a note which, while not strictly part of the working, illustrates a matter which at this time was seriously concerning the Supreme Council:
N.B. – Article 39 of the Rules and Regulations
The 18th Degree may be conferred only on brethren professing the Christian faith. The MWS must, therefore previous to the reception of Candidates, fully explain to them the nature of the O.B. which they will be called upon to take, viz. I.T.N.O.T.H.A.U.T., in order that they may be aware of the qualification required.

630 The only difference is that the 'Address' includes that the points of the Compass are extended on the segment of a circle "to an angle of 60°".

631 For example: 'The Candidate gives the letters to the Marshal who presents them to the MWS' instead of 'The Candidate gives the letters to the Marshal by whom they are presented to the MWS', 'All stand during the accolade' instead of 'All rise during the accolade', 'The Marshal leading followed by the

Candidate' instead of 'The Marshal and Candidate first'.

A more major change is that the Craft wording 'without evasion, equivocation', etc. has now been omitted from the Obligation in the First Point.

632 For example 'The Marshal leads the Candidate to the altar and instructs him to kneel' , 'The Marshal conducts the Candidate to the West', 'R. Conducts the Candidate to the MWS standing in front of the Altar.'

633 There is a note in the 'File Copy' – "1931. 5,000 copies (82 over) £88.5.6".

634 In subsequent Editions 'Stewards' were added to the optional Officers, and the restriction to '40 members' was removed.

635 O Lord, who has taught us that all our doings without charity are nothing worth; send thy Holy Ghost, and pour into our hearts that most excellent gift of charity, the very bond of peace and of all virtues, without which whomsoever liveth is counted dead before Thee; Grant this for thine only Son, Jesus Christ's sake. Amen.

(Since 1920 the Grand Prior had been the Revd. Arnold Whitaker Oxford.)

636 'Here the Address on p.45 may be given'.

637 [Perhaps, on a personal note, I may be allowed to record my affectionate regard for this Ritual which was in current use when I was Perfected on 13th March 1948. C.J.M.]

638 'who doth penetrate', instead of the awkward 'penetratest'; 'grant that we, aided by the power of thy divine spirit', instead of 'being solely occupied with the work of our redemption'; and 'may our Order be ever adorned by service, goodwill and peace', instead of 'peace, benevolence and goodwill'.

639 For example, 'Marshal directs the Candidate to take up', instead of 'he takes up'. 'The Prelate adjusts S...d and C....s' (and also later removes them) is added, together with other useful minor instructions as 'Marshal and Candidate bow and retire'.

640 A minor addition was made to the wording in the Third Point – the words "at the same time" were inserted before "pledging to each other". There is no record of why this interposition was considered significant.

641 Edward Bentley 33°, Preceptor, Private Communication, January 2004.

642 Its comprehensive nature is emphasised by the booklet being entitled 'Directions and plans for the ceremonies of the Rose Cross of Heredom'.

643 This had never before been indicated, but there was still no guidance as to at what passage the opening should be made. In addition, the Prelate was no longer 'Reverend and Perfect', but 'Excellent and Perfect' as were all the other Officers.

644 The only change in wording was that the Candidate was told that "the position of a Prince Rose Croix to which you aspire *requires* that you have had conferred upon you seventeen degrees of the Ancient and Accepted Rite of Masonry", while formerly he was told that it "indicates". [This is only speculation, but it seems possible that "indicates" might be a relic of the days when 'Rosae Crucis' Knights Templar were affiliated as S.P.R.C., without taking the Intermediate Degrees, but were deemed to possess them. C.J.M.]

645 4th to 14th ('Ineffable'), 15th & 16th ('Historical') and 17th (The first of the 'Philosophical Degrees').

646 An example of the newly introduced detailed instructions is the rubric "N.B. The marshal should time the circuits to agree with the Sections of the Scripture".

647 See Appendix C.

648 It is part of the 'Collective Wisdom of the Tribe' that the Apron was removed from the Regalia in order to reduce the not inconsiderable cost of being admitted to the Order, and I have frequently been told this by members of the Ancient and Accepted Rite, most of whom deplored the change. However, I was informed by M∴Ill∴Bro. Ingham Clark, who was Grand Secretary General at the time, that the reason why Aprons were no longer worn in the Eighteenth Degree was because they were inappropriate for a Philosophical Degree.

649 Although this substitution considerably emphasises the nature of the Ceremony which is being enacted, it has come about in a curious fashion. 'Juda' or 'Judah' has been the interpretation of the fourth letter of the Word since the French Rituals of the 1760s, and no other is found in any Ritual, manuscript or printed. Scriptural quotations were introduced in 1917, but then only to the Ritual of the English Supreme Council. The introduction of these quotations gave the opportunity for their message to be made into a quasi-progressive narrative, whereupon the fourth letter of the Word has been changed to fit better into this.

PART THREE

THE ANCIENT AND ACCEPTED RITE IN ENGLAND – SELECTED TOPICS

Essay 18
The Supreme Council – Expansion Overseas

(Note. Even though Chapters were not formally assigned Numbers until 1880, the Numbers then assigned are inserted in the text even to Chapters Warranted before this date.)

The Patent dated 26th October 1845, which was sent to Thomas Crucefix by the Supreme Council of the Northern Masonic Jurisdiction of the United States of America, only authorised the establishment of a Supreme Council for 'England'. It was not unreasonable for this Supreme Council, shortly after its formation, to add 'and Wales' to its title, because the Principality, unlike Scotland and Ireland, had no national Grand Lodge, and was under the Masonic jurisdiction of the United Grand Lodge of England[650]. However, within two years the 'Supreme Council for England' had included not only the Principality but also 'the Dependencies of the British Crown' in its title[651]. This was a more questionable addition. It appeared to exclude not only Ireland, but also Scotland (with which England had been a conjoint Kingdom since the Act of Union) from any property in these Dependencies. It implicitly claimed that the Colonies of the British Crown were exclusively 'English', which was, indeed, probably how most Englishmen regarded them at the time[652]. Ten years later the Supreme Council proceeded to act on this assumption.

By 1857 it had given Patents[653] to no more than seven Chapters in England. Four (or possibly five) of these were specifically established to supersede the conferment of the 'Rosae Crucis' Degree in neighbouring Encampments of Knights Templar[654]. The Supreme Council had a considerable task ahead of it to persuade all 'Rosae Crucis' Knights to affiliate, and to persuade those English Knights Templar Encampments which had not already done so to surrender the right to confer that Degree. However, though this still lay ahead of the Council, in April 1857 it does not seem to have hesitated to widen its responsibilities when it gave Dr. Benjamin Kent the authority which he requested to establish the Ancient and Accepted Rite in South Australia[655]. On 25th March 1859, some months after his return to England, Kent reported to the Council[656] on his 'proceedings' in Australia. He said that he had received a Petition from certain duly qualified Brethren requesting permission to open a Rose Croix Chapter at Melbourne and that he had granted them a provisional Warrant to do so. In July the Supreme Council acceded to a formal request which was received from the Melbourne Brethren[657] for a Warrant for a Chapter Rose Croix, back-dating it to 12th April 1859. This was duly despatched, together with a manuscript Ritual and the answers to several questions which the Brethren had addressed to Dr. Kent[658].

On the same day as the authority was given to Dr. Kent for 'South Australia', a similar authorisation was given to Hugh Sandeman, the District Grand Master of Bengal under the United Grand Lodge of England[659]. In the following October the Supreme Council also received a Petition from Ill. Brother Charles Goolden 31°[660] and also granted him a Warrant to hold a Chapter in the Presidency of Bengal. Neither of these two essays seems to have borne fruit, and it was to be ten more years before a Chapter was opened in India. However, a precedent for Warranting Chapters outside England had been set, and in April 1861 the Supreme Council agreed to give a Warrant for a Chapter at Gibraltar[661]. As a result, Henry Vernon, the Grand Secretary General, visited the Rock where he Consecrated Europa[662] Chapter (later No.14) on 23rd August 1861.

At about the same time as Europa Chapter was Consecrated, Mark Shuttleworth[663] wrote to the Supreme Council to say that several Brethren in Canada were anxious to establish a Rose Croix Chapter there under its authority. Although the Supreme Council resolved to grant a Warrant if a Petition was presented in due form, no more was heard of this proposal. Perhaps this was fortunate, because to have Founded a Chapter without consulting the Supreme Councils in the United States would have been a questionable move, challenging the jurisdiction in North America of two of the oldest Supreme Councils[664].

In October 1863 Dr. Robert Hamilton[665], who had been the District Grand Master and District Grand Superintendent under the English Constitution in Jamaica since 1859, sought powers to establish the 17th and 18th Degrees in the island. 'Higher Degrees' of one sort and another had been known in Jamaica at least since Stephen Morin set up a 'Grand Chapter of Princes of the Royal Secret' a century earlier. The Supreme Council at once resolved to send Hamilton a Warrant for an 18th Degree Rose Croix Chapter, and to Advance him to the 31st Degree as their Representative in the island. But Hamilton was facing a confused situation. Not only were there Craft Lodges in the island under the Scottish Constitution as well as under that of England, but many of the most influential Brethren belonged to a 'Sir Knights' Degree which Hamilton considered to be similar to the 15th and 16th Degrees of the Irish Rite. Then, in 1865, there was an 'Insurrection' in the island. Hamilton raised the matter again in 1868 when affairs were stabilised, but the Supreme Council then resolved to be more cautious as "that Island was in all probability the seat of one of the oldest S.G.Councils".

By this time a Chapter under the English Supreme Council had been established in a more remote corner of the Empire. The Council had hesitated before giving a Warrant to Colonel Greenlaw for a Chapter in Rangoon, saying that before this was done, it wished some assurance of permanence. When it issued a Warrant dated 10th July 1866, it may have been swayed by Greenlaw shrewdly naming the Chapter 'Leeson' (later No.21) after the Sovereign Grand Commander! The Council need have had no misgivings. After a hiatus during the Second World War, the Chapter flourished[666] until 1971, when political conditions necessitated its removal to England[667].

By 1868, when there were still no more than 18 Chapters Warranted in England, further progress had been made both in Canada and in India. As long ago as 14th July 1863 the Supreme Council had agreed to give James Gibbs and Arthur Moore a Warrant for a Chapter in Bombay. For five years Gibbs had been unable to open the Chapter, but in the summer of 1868 he asked for the Warrant to be sent to him[668]. Gibbs acknowledged receipt of the Warrant in February 1869, when he promised that the Chapter would be opened shortly[669]. Another Chapter, Mount Calvary[670], was opened in Lahore in July of that year, and Coromandel[671] was opened in Madras in September. Communications with India were slow. When a letter was sent from London, it took four months for a reply to be received. In December, the Supreme Council decided that it needed a representative in the sub-continent. It was therefore agreed not only to confer the Thirty-third Degree on Gibbs, a Judge in the High Court in Bombay, and to appoint him "our deputy in British India", but also to seek from him the nomination of two further Brethren for the same Advancement so that together they could confer the Thirtieth Degree 'Kadosh'[672]. Then, eighteen months later, Hugh Sandeman was given a Warrant for a Chapter in Calcutta, the Council having withdrawn his earlier authorisation[673].

In the meantime the Supreme Council's scruples about Warranting a Chapter in Canada had been resolved after a letter had been received from Albert Pike, the Sovereign Grand Commander of the Supreme Council of the Southern Jurisdiction of the U.S.A., in October 1867. To this the Council had replied that the Provinces in Canada were 'Dependencies of the British Crown', and that it proposed to grant Warrants to Canadian applicants. This blunt declaration, which formally contravened 'The Grand Constitutions of 1786', was received with surprising equanimity. Not only this, but Colonel McLeod Moore, the Grand Prior for Canada under the English Grand Conclave of Knights Templar, and himself an Honorary Member of the Thirty-third Degree of the Supreme Council of the Northern Jurisdiction of the U.S.A., sought permission to establish the Rite in Canada under the English Supreme Council. His offer was accepted provided that he signed the Oath of Allegiance, and, after having done so, McLeod Moore was given a Patent for a Thirty-second Degree Consistory. Further Canadian Brethren were Advanced to the Thirty-third Degree[674], the Consistory was established, and several Rose Croix Chapters were Warranted in the Provinces which the Earl of Carnarvon was seeking to amalgamate into the Dominion of Canada.

The Canadian Colonists were as independent-minded as those further south had been a hundred years earlier, but the Supreme Council failed to appreciate this. The Canadian Brethren soon made it clear that they wished to govern their Chapters of the Ancient and Accepted Rite themselves, and not to submit to direction from a body on the other side of three thousand miles of ocean[675]. Matters became more complicated when in 1871 the Supreme Council of Scotland Warranted not only a Rose Croix Chapter but also a 'Council' of the Thirtieth Degree in New Brunswick. The English Supreme Council believed that the Thirtieth Degree was not being conferred there in the presence of three S.G.I.G.s. Poor relations between the two Supreme Councils were exacerbated when the Scottish New Brunswick Brethren tried to obtain recognition from the Supreme Council of the Northern Masonic Jurisdiction of the United States, the Scottish Grand Secretary General, Alex Stewart, claiming, with dubious accuracy, that a Chapter had been established in New Brunswick before any Chapter had been Warranted in Canada by the English Council.

Thomas Harington, the first Canadian Brother whom the English Council had Advanced to the Thirty-third Degree, was making strenuous efforts to contain the situation. He was progressively given considerable authority over the Canadian Rose Croix Chapters. The English Supreme Council failed fully to appreciate the situation which was developing until Dr. Hamilton made a lengthy visit to the North American mainland in the Summer of 1873[676]. Hamilton wrote a comprehensive Report for the English Council, making it clear that the majority of the Canadian Brethren would be content with nothing less than self-determination. At first it seemed possible that they would be satisfied with a 'Deliberative Council' under the Presidency of a Grand Representative of the Council in England, but the formation of the Dominion of Canada spurred them on to demand their own Supreme Council. By November 1873 the Supreme Council for England was seeking the views of other Supreme Councils on this proposal, and by the end of the year the decision had been taken to grant a Warrant for a Supreme Council for Canada if no opposition to the proposal were received. The Scottish Supreme Council agreed somewhat reluctantly, and approval was received from several other Supreme Councils[677]. The Chapters and Consistories of the Ancient and Accepted Rite in Canada all voted in favour of the proposal[678]. Not only was the Warrant establishing the Supreme Council of Canada signed by all the Members of the English Council, but it also bore the signature of its Grand Patron, the Prince of Wales[679]. The Supreme Council for Canada was Constituted by Albert Pike, Sovereign Grand Commander of the Supreme Council of the Southern Jurisdiction of the U.S.A., on 16th October 1874[680]. With this approval from 'The Mother Council of the World' there could be no doubt of its legitimacy, whatever the 'Grand Constitutions' might say.

Even after the secession of the Chapters in Canada, of the sixty Rose Croix Chapters on the Register of the Supreme Council in 1874, sixteen were overseas. Three more Chapters had been Warranted in the Indian sub-continent[681] including Morning Star No.33[682]. The membership of Chapters in India was largely composed of Civil Servants and Officers in the Army who were frequently posted to other Stations or were absent on Active Service[683]. Because of the disruption which this caused, of the 14 Chapters Warranted in India by the end of the nineteenth century, half had surrendered their Warrants by 1905. The constant comings and goings of the membership of its Chapters was not the only problem which the Supreme Council had to confront. As had happened in New Brunswick, the Supreme Council of Scotland was proposing to Warrant a Thirtieth Degree Chapter in Bombay where, in the view of the English Sovereign Grand Commander, Charles Vigne,"she has neither any jurisdiction nor the requisite number of Members of the 33° legally to confer the K.H. Degree". There was some unrest among the English brethren because the Supreme Council had not itself implemented arrangements for conferring the Thirtieth Degree in India, although three Brethren had been Advanced to the Thirty-third Degree. The Scottish 30th Degree Chapter was inevitably an attraction for English Brethren in India, even though to receive the K.H. Degree within it would involve breaking their Obligation of Allegiance. Correspondence with the Scottish Council failed to resolve the matter, but for the time being James Gibbs was instructed to take no action.

The progress of the Ancient and Accepted Rite in South Africa followed a course very different from that in India, even though the problem of conflicting jurisdictions had to be faced there also. The establishment of the Rite under the Supreme Council of England in British South Africa was largely due to the efforts of Richard Giddy, then 32°. On 8th June 1873, Giddy, then in London, was granted a Warrant for Adamanta Chapter to be opened at "Griqualand West, S.Africa"[684]. After his return to South Africa, Giddy requested several further Warrants. On 13th October 1874 the Council nominated Giddy to the Thirty-third Degree, and appointed him Deputy Inspector General for South Africa in recognition of "his active and energetic services in planting the A. & A. Rite in South Africa where he has founded Six Chapters Rose Croix[685] within the last twelve months".

The Supreme Council of Scotland was also Warranting Rose Croix Chapters in South Africa, and, moreover, proposing to confer the Thirtieth Degree as it had claimed the right to do in New Brunswick and in Bombay. At least the English Council was in correspondence with that in Scotland and the problem could be raised with it, however unsatisfactory the answers. But the Dutch 'Grand Chapter', which the English Supreme Council did not recognise, was also active in South Africa, and was presenting a more insoluble problem. Apart from the jurisdictional position, intervisitation with Chapters from an unrecognised Constitution was evidently impossible.

These problems did not deter the English Supreme Council from continuing to Warrant Chapters in far-flung corners of the British Dependencies, always provided that the United Grand Lodge of England had a presence there. Mount Calvary in the East Chapter[686] was Warranted in Singapore in May 1873. It was in abeyance for six years after 1880, but revived, and apart from an interruption during the Japanese occupation after 1942, is still flourishing. Half a world away Union Chapter[687] was Warranted in Georgetown, British Guiana in July 1874, and, like Mount Calvary, continues successfully to meet. On the other hand, ventures in the Far East were generally less successful. Cathay Chapter[688] had been Warranted to meet in the Treaty Port of Shanghai in 1869, but surrendered its Warrant in 1884 when its most active member, Henry Kingsmill, appears to have been transferred to Hong Kong[689]. In May 1877 the Supreme Council acceded to Kingsmill's Petition to open St. Mary Magdalene Chapter[690] in the Port[691]. This proved a more successful venture, and the Chapter still meets in Hong Kong today, surviving the reversion of the island to China after the expiry of the lease.

However, Brother J.S. Cox, a member of St. Mary Magdalene Chapter, had less lasting success when he sought a Warrant for a Chapter in Japan. His application was supported by Charles Dallas, the District Grand Master for Japan under the United Grand Lodge of England, upon whom the Supreme Council authorised Cox to confer the Eighteenth Degree. However, at the same time Cox was made aware that the Supreme Council of the Southern Jurisdiction of the U.S.A. had given 'Letters of Credence' to a Brother Stevens to confer in Japan the Degrees of the Ancient and Accepted Rite below the Thirty-second. In spite of this complication, the Supreme Council gave a Warrant for Chrysanthemum Chapter No.94 to meet in the Treaty Port of Yokohama. Not only was there lengthy and somewhat acrimonious correspondence between Dallas and Stevens[692], but in 1882 Albert Pike wrote to the Supreme Council alleging that it was interfering in territory under his jurisdiction. In spite of every effort of Supreme Council, opposition in Japan proved too strong for Chrysanthemum Chapter[693], and it had surrendered its Warrant by the end of the century. Nothing came of an attempt in 1886 to revive Cathay Chapter in Shanghai[694].

In May 1875 the Supreme Council extended its activities to New Zealand by granting a Warrant for Star of the South Chapter[695] at Greymouth[696]. The first complication with which the Supreme Council had to deal was that a spurious Egyptian body[697] had given a Dr. H.S.Loth a Warrant to form a so-called Supreme Council in Edinburgh, and he had promptly Warranted another in New Zealand. Loth even had the effrontery to challenge the legality of the Supreme Council of Scotland. The situation then became even more confused when the English Supreme Council was requested by a member of Loth's spurious Council, William Officer, itself to grant a Warrant for a Supreme Council 33° in New Zealand! The necessity to deal with the incongruous state of affairs which had developed was for many years the background to the Council's efforts to establish Chapters in New Zealand under its jurisdiction. Five more Chapters were Warranted by the end of the century[698], but at the same time the Supreme Council of Scotland was also extending its influence in the Islands. For half a dozen years after 1885 an uneasy truce developed between the various competing bodies. Then, towards the end of 1893, there was another attempt to establish spurious Chapters in New Zealand. The illegitimate American 'Gourgas Council' sent one of its Brethren, Renzy, as an 'Inspector General' to open both Chapters and Consistories. No sooner had his pretensions been dealt with than a Brother J.H.Pagni unsuccessfully attempted to obtain recognition in New Zealand for the Ancient and Primitive Rite of Misraim.

In spite of the problem of competing jurisdictions, and the difficulty of maintaining Chapters in sparsely populated localities, the Supreme Council continued to Warrant them. Antigua Chapter No.84 was Warranted in 1878, but had an uneasy existence of less than fifty years[699]. Further Chapters were Warranted in South Africa and in India, although many of these were short-lived[700]. A second Australian Chapter, Percy No.113, was Warranted in Adelaide in May 1889. Mount Olivet Chapter[701] in Perak survived for only 20 years, but Bermuda Chapter No.123, Warranted in 1892, was more successful and is still meeting, as is Adams Peak Chapter No.133 in Ceylon.

However, the matter of 'competing jurisdictions' as between the Supreme Councils of England, Scotland and Ireland could not be allowed to remain unresolved. There had always been harmonious relations between the English and Irish Councils, but the disagreement between those of England and Scotland, which had surfaced at the Congress in Lausanne in 1876, had to be resolved. It was not only in India, Australia and New Zealand that brethren from the two Constitutions found themselves at odds, but even in territories such as Gibraltar. It took nearly twenty years to devise a form of words which each Supreme Council could accept. To do so was made no easier because the Supreme Council of Ireland, which in fact had little wish to see overseas Irish Chapters, had delegated the superintendence of its Rose Croix Chapters to a 'Supreme Chapter of Prince Masons' over which it claimed to have no direct control. The wording of a Concordat to which each of the three Constitutions could agree was not finally settled until 15th February 1893[702], a Concordat which today still governs the relations overseas of the three 'Home' Supreme Councils. Perhaps the most important clause was the fourth:

> "That no chapter shall be founded in any place outside the British Isles where, or in the neighbourhood of which, there is already a Chapter working under a Sister Jurisdiction without communicating with that Jurisdiction with a view to obtaining their approval."

When the Concordat was at last signed there were several outstanding matters to be resolved between the English and Scottish jurisdictions in respect of their Chapters in the 'Dependencies of the British Crown', but by the end of the century the Concordat allowed all these to be settled. The two Grand Secretaries General, Hugh Sandeman and Lindsay Mackersey, established better relations than the two Supreme Councils had enjoyed for many years, relations which have, happily, continued ever since.

At the outbreak of the Great War in 1914, out of some one hundred and eighty Rose Croix Chapters under the jurisdiction of the Supreme Council for England, fifty-five were overseas. The administration of these was a considerable burden, even though the opening of the Suez Canal fifty years earlier, and the subsequent introduction of the Electric Telegraph, had considerably improved communications. In addition to this, in the Indian Empire, and in the larger of what were still 'colonial possessions', many Brethren had a growing desire for more local control of the Order. The appointment of 'Deputy Inspectors General' or 'District Inspectors' did not wholly satisfy this, and in Australia the Supreme Council was strangely reluctant even to appoint such representatives[703]. Even where these had been appointed, and there were three members of the Thirty-third Degree in a territory, the Supreme Council would not authorise the conferment of the Thirtieth Degree *in extenso*, but continued to confer it itself by Patent. It was 1921 before even a small concession was made for Brethren in the Union of South Africa where under the Scottish jurisdiction the Thirtieth Degree was regularly conferred. Charles Aburrow, the 'Grand Inspector General' in South Africa under the Supreme Council for England, was given a lengthy set of rules under which he was permitted to give an 'exposition' of the Thirtieth Degree to Brethren on whom it had already been conferred by Patent, but to give the accolade was strictly forbidden[704]. Then, in 1928, a Deputation[705] was given a formal Commission not only to confer the 'Kadosh' Degree in South Africa, but, before doing so, themselves to elect suitable brethren to the Degree[706]. The first meeting to Advance such Candidates was held on 16th September 1926. Finally, in October 1932, the Supreme Council "decided to grant permission to the Grand Inspectors General of the Southern and Northern Divisions of South Africa to work the 30° under conditions to be arranged in due course"[707], and the first Meeting under the Warrant later granted took place at Bloemfontein on 23rd April 1934. The South African Inspectors General were not given the freedom which had been accorded to the Deputation in 1928, and all recommendations for Advancement to the Degree had to be telegraphed to 10 Duke Street for confirmation.

The Supreme Council declined to make similar arrangements either for Australia or New Zealand. However, in 1937 Viscount Galway, the Council's Grand Marshal, was appointed Governor-General of New Zealand[708]. Early in 1938 Galway received permission to confer the 30th Degree in Sydney in the course of a visit to Australia, and on his return to New Zealand he again conferred the Degree on several Candidates at a Meeting in 1940[709].

After the Second World War these concessions were inadequate to satisfy many of the Brethren in what were now the 'British Dominions' – the Supreme Council had added 'the Dominions' to the 'Dependencies of the British Crown' in its title. Progress towards self-determination was slow. Before Supreme Councils could be erected in the Dominions, the Supreme Councils of England, Scotland and Ireland[710] had to assure themselves that the interests and wishes of the Chapters and Brethren under their respective jurisdictions would be respected. The Supreme Council for Australia was Patented in 1985. Of the 134 Chapters previously Warranted by the Supreme Council for 'England and the Dominions and Dependencies of the British Crown' only seven elected to remain under the jurisdiction of the English Council and formed a District which became the responsibility of an Inspector General[711]. Rather more of the Scottish Chapters elected to retain their Allegiance to the Scottish Supreme Council which then Warranted several further Chapters in Australia, a situation similar to that which obtained nine years later when a Supreme Council for New Zealand was Patented, but with only one Chapter electing to remain under English jurisdiction[712].

There were many long-established Chapters in South Africa under allegiance to one or other of the 'British' Supreme Councils but the same arrangement as that in Australia and in New Zealand was not possible. The Union was 'occupied territory' – there was already a Netherlands Supreme Council there, with the many Dutch Chapters under its jurisdiction. To establish a second Supreme Council would have contravened the 1786 'Constitutions'. To provide some measure of self-government for the English Chapters, a 'Branch Council', responsible to the Supreme Council in London, was established in 1992 under the presidency of a Chairman. The Inspectors General of each of the seven 'English' South African Districts are members of the Council. No such expedient was necessary in India, because by 1980 all the Chapters in the sub-continent had either surrendered their Warrants, or bowed to political pressures and transferred their meetings to England.

Two of these Chapters have, however, since been resuscitated, East India No. 347 at Calcutta in 1997, and Poona No.37 at Fort Mumbai in 2000.

Although there are now independent Supreme Councils for three of the former 'Dependencies of the British Crown'[713], what is today 'The Supreme Council of the Ancient and Accepted Rite for England and Wales and its Districts and Chapters Overseas' retains a world-wide responsibility for Chapters under its jurisdiction. Of the 886 Chapters shown to be on its Register in the Year-Book for 2003, no fewer than 134 were overseas[714].

Appendix A

Transcription of the 'Letters of Credence' given to Dr. Benjamin Archer Kent by the Supreme Council for 'England and Wales and the Dependencies of Great Britain' in April, 1857 for 'South Australia', amended 14th July, 1857 for 'Australia'.

From the East of the **Supreme Grand Council** of the Sovereign Grand Inspectors General of the 33rd degree of the Ancient and Accepted Rite of **FREEMASONRY** for England and Wales and the Dependencies of Great Britain under the C. C. of the Zenith near the B. B. answering to 51° 30' N.Lat. and 6° W. Meridian of Greenwich.

To our Illustrious Most Valiant and Sublime Princes of the Royal Secret Knights K. H., Illustrious Princes and Knights Grand Ineffable and Sublime, Free and Accepted Masons of all Degrees Ancient and Modern over the Surface of the Two Hemispheres. To All to whom these letters may come

HEALTH, STABILITY, POWER

Know Ye That the Sovereign Grand Inspectors General lawfully and constitutionally established at our **Grand East London** in Supreme Council of the 33rd and last degree of the Ancient and Accepted Rite of Freemasonry and duly congregated this 14th day Thamuz H ^{m} 5617 Anno Lucis 5861 which corresponds to the Fourteenth day of July Anno Christi 1857 A. Ords . . . . . and A.M. 5617 at our Grand Council Chamber a Sacred Asylum where reigns

UNION, CONTENTMENT, WISDOM

Do by these Presents declare that our Illustrious Brother **Benjamin Archer Kent** of London is Master and Past Master of all Symbolic Lodges, Secret Master, Perfect Master, Intimate Secretary, Provost and Judge, Intendant of the Buildings, Elected Knight of Nine, Illustrious Elected of Fifteen, Sublime Knight Elected, Grand Master Architect, Royal Arch Grand Elect, Perfect and Sublime Mason, Knight of the East or of the Sword, Knight of the East and West, Sovereign Prince Rose Croix of H. R. D. M., Grand Pontif, Grand Master of all Symbolic Lodges, Patriarch Noachite, Prince of Libanus, Chief of the Tabernacle, Knight of the Brazen Serpent, Prince of Mercy, Commander of the Temple, Knight of the Sun, Knight of St. Andrew, Grand Elect Knight K. H., Grand Inquisitor Commander with all Right Prerogatives and Immunities appertaining to that Eminent Degree and Official Dignity.

We Furthermore nominate and appoint our said Illustrious Brother **Benjamin Archer Kent** our Representative for ~~South~~ Australia with full Power and Authority to form, organise and establish in the said Colonies of ~~South~~ Australia according to the Grand Constitutions of the Ancient and Accepted Rite promulgated at Berlin in Prussia A.D. 1786 a *Grand Lodges of Perfection* with authority over the Degrees from the Fourth to the Fourteenth inclusive a *Grand Councils of Princes of Jerusalem* having Authority over the Fifteenth and Sixteenth Degrees and a *Sovereign Chapters Rose Croix of H. R. D. M.* to govern the

Seventeenth and Eighteenth Degrees always reserving to ourselves and our lawful successors, Supremacy over the said Grand Lodge, Grand Council and Sovereign Chapter and Strictly enjoining our said Illustrious Brother and Representatve to cause all who may be admitted to any Degrees of the Ancient and Accepted Rite under the authority hereby given to take and sign the Oath of Allegiance to our Supreme Council and to transmit from time to time to our Illustrious Grand Secretary, authentic lists of every one who may be admitted under the powers hereby delegated to our said Illustrious Brother.

H.B.Leeson M.P.S.G^D C ^R 33° R+HRDMKHSPRS

George Vernon Lt Com^r R+HRDMKHSPRS Chas. John Vigne R+HRDMKHSPRS
Ill.Gd Treas Genl H.E. 33°

John A.D.Cox   R+HRDMKHSPRS   John Stephen Robinson
Ill Gr. Sec.Gen   R+HRDMKHSPRS

John George Reeve de la Pole R+RDMKHSPRS   Matthew Dawes R+HRDMKHSPRS

Henry A. Bowyer   R+HRDMKHSPRS   G.B.Cole   R+HRDMKHSPRS

WAX
SEAL

EMBOSSED
SEAL OF THE
SUPREME
COUNCIL

Author's Note: My grateful thanks are due to Ill. Bro. Owen D.H.Burton 30° for supplying me with a photocopy and a transcription of Dr. Kent's 'Letters of Credence'. He points out the errors in the co-ordinates – instead of 51° 31' N, 0° 06'W, they are clearly given as 51° 31'N, 6° W.

N.B. All the additions and deletions are confirmed by the initials 'C.V.' (Charles Vigne, Grand Secretary General) in the left-hand margin.

Appendix B

The Concordat of 15th February 1893 between the three 'Home Councils'

The following concordat has been entered into between the Supreme Councils of England, Ireland and Scotland respecting the conferring of Degrees:

1. That no private Chapter under either Supreme Council shall confer the 18° for a fee of less than Three Guineas[715], or upon a Brother hailing from a Sister Jurisdiction, unless by special permission from the Supreme Council of the country to which his Craft Lodge belongs. Nor shall a Rose Croix Mason be affiliated to a Chapter belonging to a jurisdiction other than that in which he was perfected without the special permission of the Supreme Council of his allegiance. But any Brother who has affiliated into a Lodge belonging to another Constitution from that under which he was initiated, and has been recorded in the books of its Grand Lodge shall be at liberty to apply for perfection to a Sovereign Chapter of Princes Rose Croix belonging to the Constitution to which he has come to belong.

2. That the 30° (or higher Degree) shall not be conferred on any Brother unless he is specially elected thereto by the Supreme Council of his allegiance, and that no Consistory abroad shall be held except for the purpose of conferring the Degree on Brethren so elected, and under special authority from the said Supreme Council.

3. That a Brother having sworn Allegiance to either Supreme Council shall not receive any other Degree of the Ancient and Accepted Rite from any other Masonic Body without the permission of the Supreme Council to which he has originally given such allegiance.

4. That no Chapter shall be founded in any place outside the British Isles where, or in the neighbourhood of which, there is already a Chapter working under a Sister Jurisdiction without communicating with that Jurisdiction with a view to obtaining their approval. In the event of that Sister Jurisdiction objecting to that Chapter being founded, the third Jurisdiction may be asked to act as arbitrators and their decision shall be accepted as final[716].

Appendix C

Rules respecting the exposition of the 30° by the G.I.G. in South Africa. (15th Dec. 1921)

No brother to be admitted to the ceremony unless he has complied with the following rules:

1. He must have applied for the 30° on the regulation form.
2. The form must be sent to the G.I.G. for his recommendation and by him forwarded to the Supreme Council.
3. He must have been elected to the 30° by the Supreme Council.
4. He must sign the Obligation which would be sent to him after his election by the Supreme Council and such Obligation must be returned when signed to the Supreme Council with the fee of fifteen guineas on receipt of which a Certificate will be forwarded to him.
5. He must produce the above-mentioned Certificate.

The accolade must never be given as that is the prerogative of the Supreme Council only.

650 Formally, the Ancient and Accepted Rite consists of 33 Degrees, from that of the 1st Entered Apprentice Degree to that of the 33rd Sovereign Grand Inspector General, both inclusive. In many Jurisdictions, such as those of England, Scotland and Ireland, the Supreme Council disclaims the right to work the first three 'Symbolic' Degrees – those of E.A., F.C. & M.M. – which are conferred under a Grand Lodge of Ancient, Free and Accepted Masons such as the United Grand Lodge of England. However, without these three Degrees the Ancient and Accepted Rite is incomplete, 'The Grand Constitutions of 1786' make no provision for this situation. The position has therefore evolved that a Supreme Council which does not itself work the first three Degrees cannot be regularly established unless there is a Regular Grand Lodge in its territory from which the Supreme Council principally draws its Membership.

651 *The Freemasons' Quarterly Review* of 17th December 1847.

652 Not many years later, Henry Newbolt, praising the valour of the Gordon Highlanders, an undoubtedly Scottish Regiment, could unblushingly write:
"The happiest English heart to-day
(*Gay goes the Gordon to a fight*)
Is the heart of the Colonel, hide it as he may."

653 'Warrants'.

654 Metropolitan, Coryton, Mount Calvary and Palatine certainly, and St. Peter and St. Paul probably.

655 The original Warrant entitled Kent to confer only the Degrees 4th-17th, but in July the Supreme Council extended this document, now described as 'Letters of Credence', to cover all Australia and include the Degree of Rose Croix. See Transcript, Appendix A.

656 "The Ill. Grand Secretary reported that he had communicated with Ill. Bro. Dr. B.A. Kent 31st. referring to his proceedings under the warrrant granted him to establish Rose + Chapters in Australia, but that in consequence of his (Dr. K's.) absence from home and the recent death of his wife he had not yet received his report." (Supreme Council Minute of 11th January 1859.)

657 "the Ill. B.B. Edward Thomas Bradshaw, Alexander James Gibbs, Gd. Elect. Kts. K.H., S.P.R. + of H.R.D.M. and Joseph John Moody S.P.R. + of H.R.D.M."

658 George Cole, the MWS of Metropolitan Chapter in London, and recently elected to the Supreme Council was delegated to answer the Australian queries. The Warrant was made out for 'The Metropolitan Chapter *of Victoria'*, but there is no record of its ever having been referred to as other than 'Metropolitan Chapter' (not to be confused with 'Grand Metropolitan Chapter' in London).

659 Hugh Sandeman had been Initiated in Meerut in 1847, but in which Chapter he was Perfected has not been identified.

660 Charles Goolden was a member of Metropolitan Chapter in London.

661 The Warrant was made out in the name of Edward Taylor Warry 18°, an Officer in the Royal Artillery, with whom Dr. Leeson, the Sovereign Grand Commander, appears to have been in correspondence for some time. Warry's name does not appear in the 1859 list of Members of the A & A Rite, although it is included in the 1869 list, but not as a Member of any Chapter, not even Europa. Possibly he had earlier been affiliated, but had joined no Chapter. The matter is complicated, because according to the Report by Henry Vernon in the Minute Book of the Supreme Council, when he consecrated the Chapter he 'Installed' Warry as MWS, but according to a letter written nine years later by Vernon's successor, Nathaniel Philips, the name of Brother Alton had been substituted on the Warrant because "Br: Warry R.A. was ordered away on duty". 'Br. Rev. George Alton' appears as MWS of Europa in the 1869 list.

662 On 21st November 1887 the Chapter was given permission to style itself 'Royal Europa Chapter' and to assume a special badge in honour of having Perfected the Duke of Connaught some years earlier, and then HRH Prince Albert Victor of Wales on 1st June of that year.

663 Mark Hodson Shuttleworth is shown in the 1869 membership list as having resigned from Metropolitan Chapter in London.

664 Article V. of 'The Grand Constitutions of 1786' provided that "In the States and Provinces which compose North America, either on the mainland, or on its islands, there will be two Councils".These already existed in the Northern and Southern Masonic Jurisdictions of the U.S.A. and presumably under the 'Constitutions' one or other could claim jurisdiction over the Canadian Provinces.

665 Hamilton had taken the 15th, 16th and 17th Degrees of the Irish Rite in Dublin in 1857, and the 18th on a visit to England in 1862.

666 For example, in 1948 the Chapter had 38 subscribing members and 47 in 1955.

667 The Chapter continues to meet in the District of Middlesex as Leeson Chapter No.21.

668 He was informed that although the Warrant had been 'drawn out', it had not yet been signed by all the Members of the Council. The Warrant, for Bombay Council (later No.18) was back-dated to 14th July 1863.

669 Bombay Chapter No.18 had a large membership until it had to leave India in 1976, transferring its Warrant to the Masonic Centre at Sindlesham, Berkshire. The Year-Books show the Chapter to have had 97 subscribing Members in 1948 and a similar number in 1955.

670 Mount Calvary Chapter No.26 surrendered its Warrant in 1893.

671 Coromandel Chapter No.27 met in Madras, Ootacamund and Bangalore until 1972 when political conditions constrained it to move to Maldon in Essex. In India in the 'forties and 'fifties it had had a subscribing membership of more than 50, including the distinguished brother Sir George Boag K.C.I.E, C.S.I., 33° (1955).

672 On 11th December 1869 the Supreme Council resolved that "the degree of 33rd be conferred upon Br. Js. Gibbs (Bombay) with a view to his being our deputy in British India, and with power to nominate to this Supreme Council two other eligible Brn. to receive the 33° in order to facilitate the establishment of a Chapter K.H. for which a dispensation will be

granted to work for 12 months when, if deemed satisfactory, a Warrant will be granted", but nothing ever came of this, although the Brethren were nominated and Advanced to the 33°. See A & A pp.169 & 860.

673 In 1869, Nathaniel Philips 'tidied up' both the 'Rules and Regulations' of the Order, and the membership list, transferring many brethren of whom nothing had been heard for some time to the 'Retired' List. (Philips' copy of the 'Red Book' with his compendious manuscript emendations is in the Council's archives.) When in December 1869 Sandeman proposed to use his earlier authorisation to set up a Chapter in Calcutta, to his considerable irritation he found that he had been placed on the 'Retired' List, and he was only granted a Warrant after paying his back dues and surrendering his earlier 'patent'. The Warrant was granted for Hugh Sandeman Chapter (now No. 32) on 10th May 1871, but in 1972 this had to be transferred to England, the Chapter now meeting at Bournemouth.

674 The Canadian Brethren Advanced to the Thirty-third Degree included Thomas Douglas Harington and Thomas Bird Harris.

675 In 1855 the Canadian Lodges under the United Grand Lodge of England had broken away and formed a Grand Lodge of Canada. (The removal of the Canadian Lodges from the Register of the United Grand Lodge of England was the last occasion when Lodge numbers were 'closed up'.) In his Report in February 1872, Charles Vigne, the Sovereign Grand Commander, was sufficiently oblivious of the Canadian sentiments to write in his Annual Report "We have had much trouble with the Brethren in Canada respecting Fees &c., and a spirit of Independence. such as they evinced some time since in Craft Masonry, appears likely to cause annoyance, still, I hope, by firm and judicious management, the feeling may soon subside".

676 Hamilton had at last been able to secure a Warrant for a Chapter in Jamaica; Jamaica Chapter (later No.48) was Warranted on 15th May 1873.

677 Formal approval was received from, for example, the Supreme Councils of Belgium, Greece, France, Costa Rica and Lusitano, together with the acquiescence of Albert Pike, the Sovereign Grand Commander of the Supreme Council of the Southern Jurisdiction of the U,S,A,

678 The Moore Consistory, the Murton Lodge of Perfection, and the Hamilton, London (Ontario), Keith, McLeod Moore, Hochelaga and Toronto Chapters Rose Croix, together with the Scottish bodies in New Brunswick.

679 The covering letter to Harington, signed by Shadwell Clerke, the Grand Secretary General, and Lord Carnarvon, the Sovereign Grand Commander, which was enclosed with the Warrant, added in a Postscript "The Sup∴Co∴ has succeeded in obtaining the signature to your Warrant of H.R.H. The Prince of Wales K: G: &c. Grand Patron of the Order in England and Wales. An addition which, no doubt, will be highly appreciated by the Supreme Council of Canada."

680 For a fuller account of the short period of seven years from the Warranting of the first Rose Croix Chapter in

Canada under the Supreme Council of England to the Constitution of the Supreme Council of Canada, see A & A pp.155-168.

681 Morning Star No.33, 29th May 1872 (Warrant surrendered 16th February 1892), Poona No.37, 1871 (Warrant Surrendered 1884), Mooltan No.46, 1873 (Warrant surrendered 1881).

682 Morning Star Chapter No.33 had been Warranted to meet in the Punjaub (sic). For seven years it worked successfully, but then fell into arrears and was transferred to the 'Abeyance List' in November 1882. In April 1883 it was temporarily revived by Col. Boswell 30°, but by 1890 it was again in arrears with its dues, and its demise was reported on 21st December 1891 by Col. A.H.Turner 31° who returned its Warrant which was deposited in the archives of the Supreme Council in February 1892. In 1921 the Supreme Council decided that there should be what amounted to a private Rose Croix Chapter of which all Members of the Supreme Council should be members, the remaining membership being by their invitation. Having by chance in their archives a surrendered Warrant with the appropriate number '33', on 21st April 1921 the Members of the Supreme Council signed a Petition (to themselves!) "to resuscitate the Morning Star Chapter No.33 with permission to transfer the Warrant to 10 Duke Street, London" and at a meeting on 27th June 1921, the Sovereign Grand Commander (The Earl of Donoughmore) declared the Chapter "resuscitated and restored to the roll of the Chapters", after which he was Installed as MWS and proceeded to Perfect the Bishop of Birmingham and Viscount Cave. Except that Membership is determined by the Supreme Council, Morning Star is in all respects a normal Chapter, and, for example, should it be appropriate to change the date of a meeting, the Recorder (who is ex officio the Grand Secretary General) must apply to himself for a Dispensation. The present author has been unable to discover why, at some date before 1992, the wholly erroneous statement (which no longer appears) 'The only known travelling Warrant' had been entered under the name of the Chapter in the 'Red Book'.

683 For example, early in 1881 the Recorder of Poonah Chapter wrote to say that "there was no prospect of it resuming work until the return of the Southern Afghanistan Army", there being only one Member apart from himself in Poonah.

684 Exceptionally, Giddy was Enthroned as MWS of Adamanta Chapter at a Meeting of the "Grand and Supreme Chapter Rose Croix" at the Grand East of the Supreme Council at 33 Golden Square, London, on 21st October 1873. This was one of the rare occasions upon which the Supreme Council exercised its prerogative of constituting itself into an unwarranted Chapter Rose Croix for such a purpose. More frequently it does so in order to Consecrate a Chapter; but such occasions should not be confused with meetings since 1921 of Morning Star Chapter No.33 (vide supra).

685 Adamanta No.50, MacLear No.83 (Warrant surrendered 1928), Eastern Star No.57, St. Paul No.56 (Warrant surrendered 1883), Perseverance

No.58 and St.John No.59. These were soon followed by Spes Bona No.60 (November 1874), Natalia No.62 (May 1875) and Rising Star No.66 (July 1875 – in abeyance 1882–1911).

686 Later No.47.

687 Later No.55.

688 Cathay Chapter was given the Number '24' shortly before it ceased to exist.

689 On 31st October 1884 Brother R.S.Gundry visited Golden Square while on leave in England and told Hugh Sandeman, now the Grand Secretary General, that only two or three of the "old members" were then living in Shanghai. Gundry had brought with him the Warrant of Cathay Chapter which he then surrendered.

690 Later No.73.

691 Two months later the Supreme Council Advanced Kingsmill to the 31° "Surplus to establishment".

692 Sandeman established that Stevens had been Initiated in Lodge Nippon No.1344, a Lodge under the United Grand Lodge of England, and that he had been passed and raised in it.

693 Chrysanthemum Chapter was given the option of meeting in Tokyo or Yokohama, permission was given to confer the 18th Degree on Brethren of less than 12 months' standing, generous Advancements were given to both the 30th and 31st Degrees, and permission to intervisit with the (non-Christian) American Chapters was accorded. Even the Chapter's signal error in having its manuscript copy of the Ritual printed drew only a mild rebuke.

694 At first Hugh Sandeman was enthusiastic about this, pointing out that there should be sufficient candidates from among the Brethren of the three Craft Lodges under the English Constitution in Shanghai. However, there was now a Scottish Chapter in the Port, and it became evident that there was no room for two Rose Croix Chapters there.

695 Later No.65.

696 The Petition for this Chapter was received from a Brother Ancher who was "the only Rose + Mason in the locality". He was sent a Dispensation to Perfect three other Brethren, and with their assistance Star of the South Chapter was opened on 25th October 1875 when 11 Candidates were admitted into the Order.

697 The Egyptian Council had been Warranted by the 'Supreme Council of Palermo', itself spurious because it had been established by the irregular 'Supreme Council of Louisiana', and, in addition the Egyptian Council was also tainted by the Ancient and Primitive Rite of Misraim which all regular Supreme Councils abhorred.

698 Excelsior No.78 (March 1878) at Christchurch, Southern Cross No.88 (June 1881) at Auckland, Wellington No.91 (January 1882) at Wellington, Latham No.93 (March 1882) at Wanganui, and Beckett No.135 (October 1897) at Christchurch. The first Chapter Warranted in New Zealand, Star of the South No.65, surrendered its Warrant in 1885.

699 The Warrant of Antigua Chapter later numbered 84 was granted to the Attorney General of the Island, H.J.Burford Hancock in March 1879, but it surrendered it in 1889 and was in abeyance until it was revived in 1893. In 1926 the Chapter finally returned its Warrant, together with its original manuscript Ritual which is preserved in the Council's archives. The Warrant is the last one issued which does not incorporate the serial number of the Chapter. In 1980 the Supreme Council refused to re-issue the original Warrant, and a new 'Antigua Chapter' was consecrated, fortuitously as No.884.

700 Several survived until after 'partition', but subsequently had to leave the sub-continent, among them the Duke of Connaught and Strathearn Chapter No.100 (6 October 1884) which transferred to London in 1968, Rose of Lahore Chapter No.128, (11 July 1893), which transferred to Manchester in 1982, Bethlehem Chapter No.156 (10 July 1905), formerly meeting in Calcutta, which transferred to West Croydon in 1973, and McMahon Chapter No.161 (6 January 1908), formerly meeting in Quetta, but since 1958 at 10 Duke Street.

701 Mount Olivet Chapter No.120 was granted a Warrant in 1891, but surrendered it in 1922.

702 See Appendix B.

703 The first Appointment of an Inspector General in Australia was that of Alexander Corrie as D.I.G. for Queensland in January 1928, followed by that of the Revd. A.T.Holden for the District of 'South Australia', comprising Victoria, South Australia, New South Wales and Tasmania, in June 1929.

704 See Appendix C.

705 The Grand Secretary of the United Grand Lodge of England, Sir Philip Colville Smith 33°, the Grand Secretary of the Grand Lodge of Mark Master Masons, Major Thomas Lumley Smith 33°, and the Grand Chancellor of the Supreme Council, Lt.Col J.M.Wingfield 33°.

706 See A & A, Appendix XVIII, p.1098.

707 The Warrant for the conferment of the 30° in South Africa is set out in A & A, Appendix XIX, p.1099

708 Galway was allowed to retain his Supreme Council appointment during his absence.

709 A further concession was made to the Australian Brethren when on 31st March 1938 the Supreme Council agreed to give a Warrant for the Holden Chapter of Improvement "for the purpose of rehearsing the 18° and from time to time giving expositions of the Intermediate Degrees from the 4° to the 17°", something which the Supreme Council had refused to allow elsewhere other than for the King Edward VII Chapter of Improvement.

710 The Supreme Council of Ireland had given a Warrant to at least one overseas Chapter.

711 Fellowship No.349 (Warranted 1944, Adelaide, S.A.), Lower Murray No.499 (Murray Bridge, S.A. 1956), Bon Accord No.698 (Brighton, S.A. 1971), Simeon No.825 (Moss Vale, N.S.W. 1977), Payneham St. Aidan No.865 (Marden, S.A. 1979), Darwin Trinity No.880 (Darwin, N.T. 1980), Fleurieu No.889 (Victor Harbour, S.A. 1981). With responsibility for Chapters in the Northern Territories, New South Wales and South Australia, territorially the D.I.G.'s task was not an enviable one.

712 Te Awamutu No.471 (Auckland, 1954).

713 Canada, Australia and New Zealand.

714 Apart from the seven Chapters in the Channel Islands, and two in the Isle of Man!

715 This is now £10.00.

716 This now reads "... without communicating with the Supreme Council of that jurisdiction with a view to obtaining its approval. In the event of that Supreme Council objecting to the founding of such a Chapter, the Supreme Council of the third jurisdiction may be asked ..."

Essay 19
The Chapters in the West

Before the Supreme Council for 'England' received its Patent dated 26th October 1845 from the Supreme Council of the Northern Jurisdiction of the United States of America, most English Encampments of Knights Templar conferred the Degree of 'Rosae Crucis'. This Degree had much in common with the Eighteenth 'Rose Croix' Degree of the Ancient and Accepted Rite; indeed, after the establishment of the Supreme Council for 'England' it was deemed to be equivalent to it, provided that those who had been admitted as *Knights Rosae Crucis* took an Obligation of Allegiance to the Supreme Council.

The Encampments of Knights Templar in England acknowledged the authority of a Grand Conclave which, however, exercised little or no control over the Degrees which were conferred other than that of Knight Templar itself. In 1846 the Rulers of Grand Conclave seem to have accepted that the 'Rosae Crucis' or 'Rose Croix' Degree was properly the responsibility of the newly-Patented Supreme Council. No record has survived of any discussions to this effect nor of any formal agreement that it should be the case[717]. However, in the early years of the Supreme Council the many Members of the Ancient and Accepted Rite who held influential Office not only in the Grand Conclave itself but, more particularly, on its Executive Committee, cannot have failed to exercise a strong influence on its proceedings. Further, within a dozen years, seven of the 'Provincial Grand Commanders' of the Knights Templar in England were, or had been, members of the Supreme Council[718].

Several Officers of Grand Conclave were also members of two of the influential London Encampments, *Faith and Fidelity* and *Mount Calvary*, as were many of the early members of the Supreme Council itself. Each of these Encampments in turn made arrangements to separate their 'Rosae Crucis' Chapters from their Knights Templar Preceptories[719]. These Chapters then accepted 'Patents' or Warrants from the Supreme Council, as 'Metropolitan'[720] and 'Mount Calvary'[721] Chapters Rose Croix respectively. Something similar may have occurred in Dorset where the Holy Cross Encampment of Knights Templar had been founded in 1844 to meet at Coryton Park, the seat of William Tucker, the first Grand Almoner of the Supreme Council. The Founders of 'Holy Cross' included Colonel Charles Kemeys Tynte[722] who was shortly to succeed the Duke of Sussex as Grand Master of the Knights Templar. On 9th June 1852, William Tucker, who had been Provincial Grand Commander of Knights Templar in Dorset since 1847[723], was presented with a Warrant to hold a Rose Croix Chapter at Coryton, the earliest Warrant granted by the Supreme Council[724] other than the two in London. The Chapter could hardly have been established had there not been consent at the highest level, although Colonel Tynte himself does not appear ever to have become a member of the Ancient and Accepted Rite[725].

Even so, there appears still to have been uncertainty in the minds of some Brethren as to whether Installation as a Knight Templar should not continue to be the qualification for Perfection as a Sovereign Prince Rose Croix. Even as late as 1868 Nathaniel Philips, recently appointed Grand Secretary General, could write:

> "It is looked on by many as a matter of course & right their being advanced, whereas it is a matter of favour, and must only be conferred upon those who by *their social position*, zeal and ability prove themselves worthy of the honour. I think, if we insisted upon every Brother being a Templar before being a Rose Croix, it would give us a better class of candidate[726]."

Be that as it may, the Supreme Council was careful to grant Warrants for its early Chapters only at places where there was already a Knights Templar Encampment. There may have been several reasons for this. In the first place, it was certainly hoped that every Knight Templar who had received the 'Rosae Crucis' Degree would affiliate to the Supreme Council of the Ancient and Accepted Rite and join a Rose Croix Chapter. This would evidently be more conveniently achieved if there were a Chapter Rose Croix meeting near an Encampment which was accustomed to confer the 'Rosae Crucis' Degree. Secondly, newly Installed Templars in Encampments which had practised the Degree would not feel disadvantaged in comparison with their predecessors if they could locally proceed to the 'Rose Croix' Degree, deemed to be equivalent to that of 'Rosae Crucis', – especially since initially the Officers of the Chapter would frequently be the same Brethren as the Officers of the Encampment. It might also have appeared prudent to Warrant Chapters adjacent to newly founded Encampments which would have no long-standing tradition of conferring the 'Rosae Crucis' Degree. This was done both at Coryton and also at neighbouring Weymouth where a Warrant was granted for a Chapter at the same time[727]. The Warrant of Palatine Chapter, another of the four Chapters Warranted in 1852, "authorised the holding of a Sov. Chapter of Rose Croix at stated times at Bolton, at Manchester and at Liverpool"[728] and was given to Matthew Dawes, the 'Provincial Grand Commander' of Knights Templar in Lancashire. This followed the same pattern, as St. James of Jerusalem Encampment at Bolton, founded in 1819 under a Dispensation, had received a Warrant from the re-constituted Grand Conclave in 1849, and Jacques de Molay in Liverpool had been founded in 1850[729]. Similarly at the same time Colonel George Vernon was given a Warrant for the Chapter which bore his own name in Birmingham, where Howe-Beauceant Encampment had been founded in that year also[730].

The next Chapter, St. Peter and St. Paul, was Warranted to meet at Bath where Bladud Encampment had been founded in 1852[731]. Bladud was not the only Encampment of Knights Templar in that City. Bath was also the home of one of the earliest English Templar Encampments, Antiquity. The Camp of Antiquity had already been working when Thomas Dunckerley had set up Grand Conclave in 1791. Unlike the Camp of Baldwyn in Bristol, of which Dunckerley himself had been a member, Antiquity had not prospered in the first half of the nineteenth century. By 1810 it was dormant, a subsequent attempt to revive it failed, and then in 1854 it accepted a Warrant from the Camp of Baldwyn in Bristol which was refusing to acknowledge the authority of the re-constituted Grand Conclave[732]. Antiquity followed Baldwyn's lead in ignoring not only Grand Conclave, but also the Supreme Council, each of the two Encampments continuing to confer their own series of Degrees. By 1856 St. Peter and St. Paul Chapter was Perfecting several Candidates at each of its meetings, many of whom were Knights Templar from the Bladud Encampment. It may have been the success of St. Peter and St. Paul Chapter which persuaded the Camp of Antiquity to add the 'Rosae Crucis' Degree to its sequence. This seems to have been a popular move, for in September 1857 it conferred the 'Rosae Crucis' Degree on six of its Knights[733].

In 1852 Davyd Nash resigned his Office of Grand Secretary General of the Supreme Council and returned to his native city of Bristol[734]. He was then appointed both Deputy Provincial Grand Master of the Province of Bristol and also Deputy Grand Superintendent of the Camp of Baldwyn. In 1857 Nash succeeded Henry Shute as Grand Superintendent, an Office recognised neither by Grand Conclave nor by the Supreme Council. Indeed, his claim to be 'Most Excellent Grand Superintendent of the Camp of Baldwyn' brought him into direct conflict with the latter. Although he had retired from the Supreme Council, this did not absolve him from his Obligation of Allegiance to it, and this allegiance Nash was breaking by presiding over Degrees which the Supreme Council did not recognise. Nash aggravated the position by writing three letters which were published in *The Freemasons' Magazine* in June[735], July and August 1857. Dr. Leeson, the Sovereign Grand Commander, wrote to Nash on several occasions[736], and John Cox, the Grand Secretary General, tried to meet Nash to discuss the problem. Not only was all this to no avail, but Nash circulated a pamphlet defending his actions. On 12th July 1858 the Supreme Council decided to expel Nash from the Order, resolving "that a notice to that effect be transmitted to the several Chapters holding under this Supreme Council and also to the Supreme Councils of Ireland and America"[737]. This action was well received by several Chapters who wrote to the Supreme Council to express their approval. Nash regarded himself as very ill-used, setting out his views in yet another letter to *The Freemasons' Magazine*[738].

Then, at least for the time being, the Supreme Council appears to have ignored the 'Camp of Baldwyn', but Grand Conclave renewed its efforts to persuade its members to acknowledge its authority. This was an easier task than that which the Supreme Council would have faced. The 'Camp of Baldwyn' worked a progressive system of seven Degrees of which the highest was 'Knights of the Rose Croix of Mount Carmel'[739]. Grand Conclave wanted no more than an acknowledgement of its own authority over the Degree of Knights Templar, without being overly concerned with whatever additional Degrees were being worked, while the Supreme Council required a separation of the 'Rose Croix' Degree from the remainder. In 1862 a Treaty of Compact was signed between the 'Camp of Baldwyn' and Grand Conclave, by which the latter's authority was recognised, the Superintendent of the 'Camp of Baldwyn' became the 'Grand Commander' of a Province with but one Encampment, and Baldwyn took its place on the Roll of Grand Conclave as number 'C' with Time Immemorial status. The Encampment of Antiquity at Bath, a daughter of 'Baldwyn' by virtue of the Warrant which it had received in 1854, followed its stepmother into the fold of Grand Conclave, also being awarded 'Time Immemorial' status and receiving the number '1'.

The Supreme Council could now do little more than to try to persuade individual brethren who had proceeded to the 'Rose Croix' Degree in Baldwyn and in Antiquity to affiliate. Charles Vigne, the first MWS of St. Peter and St. Paul Chapter in Bath[740], did what he could to secure the allegiance of these Brethren. In July 1865 he reported that he had persuaded some Members of Antiquity to affiliate, but that "some difficulty had arisen respecting the admission of such affiliated brethren into St. Peter and St. Paul Chapter[741]". He was congratulated and requested to "continue his exertions", but before he could do so, another complication had arisen.

Since 1852 the Supreme Council had granted ten further Warrants for Chapters in England. These included not only the Royal Kent Chapter in Newcastle upon Tyne, another city where a variety of Degrees had been worked from 'Time Immemorial'[742], but also three Chapters in the South-West Royal Naval[743] at Portsmouth, Alfred[744] at Taunton and St. Aubyn[745] at Devonport. The latter had been consecrated by Dr. Leeson, assisted by Charles Vigne, in the spring of 1865. In October, Vigne told the Supreme Council that he had received a letter from Vincent Bird, the Recorder of St. Aubyn, in which he said that an illegal conference of the 'Rose Croix' Degree had been summoned by John Huyshe "under the assumed authority of the Knight's Templar Warrant".

The Reverend John Huyshe, the Provincial Grand Master of the Craft in Devonshire was a highly respected Mason in the South-West[746]. He was both Deputy Grand Master of Great Conclave, and also Provincial Prior for Devonshire. Colonel Henry Clerk, the Grand Chancellor, investigated the matter, and it appeared that Huyshe was being encouraged to establish Rose Croix Chapters in the south-western Counties under his Knights Templar Warrant without reference to the Supreme Council.

Dr. Leeson wrote to John Huyshe in April 1866 making a very generous offer. He told him that if he and other Brethren in his Province who had received the 'Rose Croix' Degree without the authority of the Supreme Council would be willing on certain concessions to place themselves under the Banner of the Ancient and Accepted Rite, all questions would be waived as to the authority of the "Ancient Templar Encampments" to confer the 'Rose Croix' Degree, and all Brethren in the Province who had so received the Degree would be accepted without fee if they signed the Obligation of Allegiance. Furthermore the Supreme Council would give Warrants for Chapters in any towns which Huyshe might designate, and it would confer upon him personally both the Thirtieth and Thirty-first Degrees. In May Huyshe replied courteously, but said that he could only reply fully after "consulting with some of the Chiefs among my Brethren".

In the meantime, Vigne had made considerable progress in Bath, and in July 1866 he was able to present a Petition for a Warrant "under the name of the Antiquity Chapter of the Rose Croix of H.R.D.M."[747] The Supreme Council not only resolved to grant the Petition but empowered Vigne to affiliate the Petitioners provided that they subscribed the Obligation of Allegiance. If they were prepared to do this, the Warrant and their Certificates would be given to them "free of all Fees and Expenses". In September 1866 Vigne affiliated the Brethren, presented the Warrant and Installed the MWS.

At first, there was no such success with the Devonshire Encampments. In October 1866 Huyshe replied that he and his Brethren were unable to accede to the generous conditions which they had been offered by Leeson. Further correspondence in the following spring did not result in any progress being made. Indeed, a year later there was a further set-back. The Supreme Council was informed that an attempt was being made to form "an opposition Council", and that Huyshe had been offered the command of it. Furthermore, this information had been confirmed by Huyshe himself, but he had very properly declined the offer.

In the spring of 1868 Nathaniel Philips replied to a letter from John Huyshe in which the latter had apparently suggested some form of Union between the Ancient and Accepted Rite and the Order of Knights Templar. On 18th April Philips replied:

"I do not see how the amalgamation could be managed, and in fact it would be at variance with the Constitutions under which we work. They certainly do in Ireland insist on a Brother being a Templar & a Knight of Malta before he can receive the Rose + Degree[748], but though that is the case they are not amalgamated any further & each has its own Grand Officers and is quite distinct from the other."

Philips added that on the day after the forthcoming Meeting of Grand Conclave there was to be a 'Grand Chapter' of the 'Rose Croix', which Huyshe might like to attend and take the opportunity of discussing the whole matter.

Huyshe's reply apparently encouraged Philips to believe that Huyshe now accepted the situation, for he wrote again saying that if Huyshe would attend the 'Grand Chapter Rose Croix' shortly to be held, the Council would be glad to affiliate him and to confer the 31st Degree upon him, and, moreover, would afterwards visit Devonshire to affiliate all Brethren "who are willing to come under our authority"[749]. But only a few days later, Philips had to write again, for Huyshe had evidently been somewhat taken aback by his earlier letter. So far from acquiescing in the wishes of the Supreme Council, Huyshe seems to have misunderstood what was being suggested[750]. Discussions took place when Huyshe visited London for the Meeting of Grand Conclave on 6th May 1868[751]. Substantial progress was made, for although Huyshe was still unprepared to take the Oath of Allegiance[752], Philips wrote to thank him "most sincerely for having consented not to confer the Degree of Rose Croix under your existing Templar Warrants"[753]. Encouraged by this, in December Philips wrote to one of his correspondents "I expect shortly to have the whole of the Devonshire Brethren (who were made by Huyshe in the Rougemont and other Encampments) under our banners", and in the following month he wrote to the Cornish Brother, the Reverend George Ross, that he was glad to hear that there was a possibility of the "Cornish Rougemont Brethren" affiliating.

With a *rapprochement* with the Brethren in the South-West apparently in sight, and Antiquity reconciled with the Supreme Council, a further attempt was now made to persuade the Baldwyn Brethren to affiliate. Nathaniel Philips discussed the matter with the Earl of Limerick, now Provincial Grand Master for Bristol under the United Grand Lodge, and in February 1870 he was instructed by the Supreme Council to write formally to the Earl to see if progress could be made, but nothing came of it.

Philips' optimism about 'the Rougemont Brethren' was considerably due to an initiative being taken by Charles Vigne. He had been Perfected in Coryton Chapter but in 1869 it now had only seven Members. Vigne's hand may well have been strengthened when he succeeded as Sovereign Grand Commander in March 1869. After lengthy negotiations it was agreed that Coryton Chapter should remove to Exeter and amalgamate with Rougemont Chapter. The Minutes of the Meeting of the Supreme Council on 13th May 1870 record that the "Warrant of the Coryton Rose Croix Chapter was transferred to the City of Exeter under the title and denomination of the Coryton and Rougemont Union Chapter" and the united body took its place on the Roll of Chapters immediately after Metropolitan Chapter. To mark the importance of the occasion, the Consecration on 7th June 1870 was attended by all the Members of the Supreme Council, bringing with them Hyde Pullen 33°, the 'Assistant Secretary' to ensure that "everything may go off satisfactorily". In the following month it was reported to the Supreme Council that the new Chapter was well established. The acceptance of the authority of the Supreme Council in the South-Western peninsula was soon consolidated by John Huyshe generously allowing his name to be taken by the Chapter Warranted in Devonport in December 1871[754]. This was followed by Cornwall Chapter in Truro being Warranted in December 1874[755].

It then became apparent that the matter of Antiquity was far from settled. The Recorder, Edmund White, was apparently acting on the assumption that the Chapter's Allegiance to the Council was little more than a matter of form, and that it could continue to conduct its business in its own fashion. This became sufficiently evident for Nathaniel Philips to write to White on 15th September 1870 that the Chapter's books should be sent to him for examination, as it was believed that irregularities had taken place. Nothing was sent, and the Chapter was informed that the Supreme Council proposed to pay it "an official state visit" to inspect its books and furnishings and to see a Candidate go through the Ceremony of Perfection. The MWS replied asking the Supreme Council to defer its visit until 24th November. When the Members then arrived in Bath they could find no sign of a Meeting of Antiquity Chapter taking place and the Temple was occupied by a meeting of the Bladud Encampment. According to the Council's Minutes, the "Most Puissant Sovereign Grand Commander determined to forgo the visit of inspection, and in lieu thereof he called this Council of Emergency". The charges alleged against Antiquity included making Brethren 'Rose Croix' Masons without due notice and contrary to the rules of the Order, refusing admission to a member of St. Peter and St. Paul Chapter, allowing an unqualified Brother not only to attend but to take the Chair, failing not only to make the appropriate returns after the admission of five Brethren but also paying no fees nor applying for Certificates for them, having no Treasurer's accounts and no Alms fund, and, finally, still claiming to work the 'Rose Croix' Degree under the Templar Warrant. The Supreme Council thereupon resolved to suspend the Chapter and demand the return of the Warrant, and confirmed this decision at its next regular Meeting, forbidding the members of Antiquity to be received in any other Chapter.

The suspension of the Chapter was followed by a somewhat undignified war of words. The members of St. Peter and St. Paul Chapter, while not seeking to defend the actions of Antiquity, regretted both the suspension and also Edmund White being banned from their own Chapter of which he was a member of long-standing[756]. The members of Antiquity were in no submissive mood, and in May 1871 they circulated a pamphlet in which they set out all their correspondence with the Supreme Council and attempted to justify their actions in, as they chose to put it, withdrawing from the Ancient and Accepted Rite. They did not, however, rebut the specific charges which the Supreme Council had made against them. Moreover, they claimed that "Whilst recognising the Supreme Council, the controlling influence in the Chapter nevertheless reserved all their ancient rights to confer the Christian degrees in the time honoured manner as under a Templar Warrant."[757]

The Supreme Council replied in kind, circulating its own five-page pamphlet, in which the charges against Antiquity were carefully rehearsed, adding the further accusation that the Warrant was never exhibited to new Members, but was "hidden away in the escritoire of Brother Wilton since he received it from the hands of the S.C."[758] This resulted in a storm of correspondence in *The Freemason*, the journal of which George Kenning, the Masonic outfitter, was the Editor. Although Kenning himself was a member of the Order, his Editorials tended to support the view of the many Brethren whose letters claimed that the Supreme Council acted in too high-handed a manner in this, and, indeed, in other respects.

This somewhat heated controversy made no easier the task which had been accepted by the Provincial Grand Master of Somerset, the Earl of Carnarvon, who had been elected to the Supreme Council on the 27th February 1871. At the request of the Supreme Council:

> "in consequence of a letter he had received from Br. Parfitt, the M.W.Sov. of the suspended Chapter, he was willing to act as Mediator provided both parties agreed to rely implicitly on his judgment and to abide by his decision"[759].

Carnarvon made no progress, although evidently he made some suggestion to Bro. Parfitt because the latter replied that he had no authority to make the proposition[760]. There were such strong feelings within the Order that John Montagu, the Grand Secretary General, had to make a lengthy defence of the Council's actions at the Meeting held to obtain approval for the purchase of the new headquarters at 33 Golden Square. The Council stood firm, and Antiquity Chapter remained suspended for a dozen years.

In 1874 Colonel Shadwell Clerke, now Grand Secretary General of the Supreme Council, was also Great Sub-Prior of England in the ill-fated Convent-General of the Order of the Temple. He used his position to attempt to reconcile the 'Camp of Baldwyn' to the authority of the Supreme Council. In February 1881, the year after Shadwell Clerk had been succeeded as Grand Secretary General by Hugh Sandeman, the Supreme Council received and approved a Paper setting out the "conditions proposed as a basis of negotiations with the Baldwin [*sic*] Ch' with a view to the said Ch' coming under the obedience of this Supreme Council". A copy had already been sent to William Powell, the Superintendent of the Camp of Baldwyn. On 10th May, the Supreme Council approved the draft of a 'Treaty' with Baldwyn. That same afternoon, the Treaty was signed, sealed and delivered and the 33rd Degree was conferred on Brother Powell "the 32°∴ & 31°∴ having been previously conferred by accolade". Other members of the Camp of Baldwin were advanced to the Thirtieth, Thirty-first and Thirty-second Degrees. Then, at a special Meeting of the Supreme Council at Bristol on 28th October 1881, Captain Philips, the Lieutenant Grand Commander[761], presented the Warrant[762].

By the 'Treaty', the Brethren of Baldwyn agreed to accept this Warrant[763] and thereafter abide by the rules and regulations of the Supreme Council, keeping the Templar and the 'Rose Croix' Degrees separate, "and not, as a rule, worked on the same evening"[764]. In exchange, the Supreme Council agreed that the Chapter could continue to use its own Ritual, but would not confer "Any degree of the A. & A. Rite beyond the Rose Croix", that it might have a Bye-Law providing that candidates for the 'Rose Croix' Degree must be Knights Templar, and that the Chapter should have a Superintendent chosen by its own Brethren, and not come under the District Inspector for the South West District[765].

It was hardly surprising that the reconciliation with Baldwyn should be followed by an approach from the suspended Brethren of Antiquity, of whom one, Frederick Goldney, had affiliated to the Rite under the Supreme Council three years earlier. A few months after matters with Baldwyn were finally settled, Goldney proposed to the Supreme Council that a Warrant, empowering Antuquity Chapter to confer the 'Rose Croix' Degree, should be granted free of charge, and that all the 18 existing members of the Chapter should not only be registered, also free of charge, but, as "an act of Grace" should have the Thirtieth Degree conferred upon them.

The Supreme Council made it clear that it was not prepared to make any such concessions as had been made to Baldwyn. Antiquity had been suspended for "acts of contumely" in the course of which members had broken their Obligations. The most that could be done would be to restore the Warrant and register the

Brethren without charge. In April Goldney forwarded to the Council a more seemly Petition, and was congratulated by Sandeman on his efforts which had resulted in "the ice being now completely broken", but it was not until February 1883 that Antiquity was admitted to the Roll of Chapters. Formal numbers had been allocated to Chapters in 1880, and, its original Warrant bearing no number, Antiquity was assigned the next available number, 95. In spite of several requests for a lower number to be assigned, the Supreme Council has consistently refused to do so. But, with this exception, the problem of the Chapters in the West was at last closed.

Appendix A

Members of The Supreme Council and other Brethren active in the Ancient and Accepted Rite who were Officers of Grand Conclave, 1847–1860

Provincial Grand Commanders
Officers of Grand Conclave of the Order of the Temple

1847	Grand Second Captain	H. Udall	(No record in the 'Proceedings')	
	Grand Chamberlain	M. Dawes		
	First Grand Standard Bearer	William Tucker		
	Grand Almoner	H. Emly		
	First Grand Aide-de-Camp	Capt. G.A. Vernon		
1848	Second Grand Captain	Dr. Leeson	Dorset	William Tucker
	Grand Registrar	J.A.D. Cox	Kent	Dr. Crucefix
	Grand Chamberlain	M. Dawes		
	Grand Almoner	H. Emly		
	First Grand Aide-de-Camp	Captain G.A. Vernon		
1849	Grand Registrar	J.A.D. Cox	Dorset	William Tucker
	Grand Chamberlain	M. Dawes	Kent	Dr.Crucefix
	Grand Almoner	H. Emly	East Lancs.	Matthew Dawes
	First Grand Aide-de-Camp	A.H. Royds	Staffs.	Col.G.A. Vernon
	2nd Gd. A-de-C,	(R.J. Spiers)		
1850	Grand Registrar	J.A.D. Cox	Dorset	William Tucker
	Grand Almoner	H. Emly	East Lancs.	Matthew Dawes
	Grand Organist	M. Costa	Staffs.	Col.G.A. Vernon
	2nd Gd. A,D,C,	(R.J. Spiers)		
1851	Grand Chancellor	H. Emly	Dorset	William Tucker
	Grand Registrar	J.A.D. Cox	East Lancs.	Matthew Dawes
	Second Grand Captain	(R.J. Spiers)	Staffs.	Col.G.A. Vernon
	Grand Organist	M. Costa		
1852	Grand Chancellor	H. Emly	Dorset	William Tucker
	Grand Registrar	J.A.D. Cox	East Lancs.	Matthew Dawes
	Grand Organist	M. Costa	Staffs	Col.G.A. Vernon
1853	Second Grand Captain	Capt.A.Q. Hopper	Dorset	William Tucker
	Grand Chancellor	H. Emly	Lancs.	Matthew Dawes
	Grand Registrar	J.A.D. Cox	Staffs.	Col.G.A. Vernon
	Grand Organist	M. Costa		

(1854 and 1855 not available)

1856	Second Grand Captain	Dr.Kent	Lancs	Matthew Dawes
	Grand Registrar	J.A.D. Cox	Staffs.	Col.G.A. Vernon
	First Grand Expert	G.B. Cole	Dorsets.	C.J. Vigne
	Second Captain of Lines (	R. Costa)	Worcs.	H. Vernon
			Oxon.	H.A. Bowyer
			Kent	(Dr.H.J. Hinxman)
1857	First Grand Captain	G.B. Cole	Lancs.	Matthew Dawes
	Grand Registrar	J.A.D. Cox	Staffs	Col.G.A. Vernon
	Second Grand Expert	(R. Costa)	Dorsets.	C.J. Vigne
	Second Grand Herald	(William Banister)	Worcs.	H. Vernon
			Oxon.	H.A. Bowyer
			Kent (	Dr.H.J. Hinxman)
			Australia	Dr.B.A. Kent
			Bengal	H.S. Sandeman
1858	Grand Registrar	J.A.D. Cox	Lancs	Matthew Dawes
			Staffs	Col.G.A. Vernon
			Dorsets.	C.J. Vigne
			Worcs.	H.J. Vernon
			Oxon.	H.A. Bowyer
			Kent	(Dr.H.J. Hinxman)
			Australia	B.A. Kent Esq (sic)
			Bengal E,I.	H.S. Sandeman.

1859	Grand Registrar	J.A.D. Cox	(Appts. as for 1858)
1860	Grand Registrar	J.A.D. Cox	(Appts. as for 1859)
	Second Grand Expert	Captain M. Dawes	
		Grand D. of C. (W.J. Meymot)	
		Grand Banner Bearer (W. Smith C.E.)	

Senior Members of the A & A Rite elected/appointed to the Grand Conclave Committee, (ex officio in brackets)

March	1847	H. Udall, Dr.Crucefix, J.A.D. Cox	
	1848	H. Udall, L. Wilson, Dr.Leeson, Dr.Crucefix J.A.D. Cox	
	1849	H. Udall, L. Wilson, Dr.Leeson, Dr.Crucefix, J.A.D. Cox	
	1850	H. Emly, H. Udall, J.A.D. Cox	(Prov.G.C.'s ex officio)
April	1851	J.A.D. Cox, H. Udall	(Prov.G.C.'s + Gd. Chanc. Emly ex officio)
May	1852	J.A.D. Cox, H. Udall	(..... ditto .....)
	1853	H. Udall	(Prov. G.C.'s ,+ G.Chan Emly, G.Reg.Cox ex officio)
May	1856	(H.J. Hinxman) H. Udall	(Prov.G.C.'s+G.Reg. Cox ex officio)
	1857	G.B. Cole	(......ditto......)
	1858 -		(.....ditto.....)
	1859	(W.J. Meymot)	(.....ditto.....)
	1860	(W.J. Meymot)	(......ditto......)

(Prominent Members of the A & A Rite never appointed to Supreme Council in brackets)

Appendix B

Letter of Davyd Nash published in *The Freemasons' Magazine*, Vol. 4, pages 167/8 (1858)

"I assert most distinctly that, at the time we formed the Supreme Council, there did not exist in the minds of Dr. Crucefix, myself or Dr. Leeson, the remotest idea that our obligations to the Supreme Council involved the necessity of withdrawing from other Masonic bodies practising the degrees included in the Ancient and Accepted Rite. I believe that Dr. Crucefix, the Sovereign Grand Commander of the Order, was, and continued to be, a member of the Order of Mizraim. I know that neither Bros. Leeson, Udall, Wilson or Tucker, withdrew from the Chapters Rose Croix, with which they were associated, on taking the obligation to the Supreme Council; and I know further, that though my connection with the high Degrees at Bristol was perfectly well know to all the Brethren above mentioned, that neither they required nor would I have permitted them to require that I should withdraw from that connection. For a period of from five to six years, this state of things lasted. On the death of Dr. Crucefix, Dr. Leeson was elected Sovereign Grand Commander; but for some years the real management of the Order was in the hand of Bro. Henry Udall."

Nash concluded his letter by saying:

"The Supreme Council has, in my opinion, illegally separated itself from me, the majority of its members being necessarily ignorant of the early career of the Order."

---

717 In Knights Templar Encampments the 'Kadosh' Degree was a progressive Degree from that of 'Rosae Crucis', and was frequently referred to as the *'Ne Plus Ultra'*. When Encampments ceased to work the 'Rosae Crucis' Degree, inevitably the 'Kadosh' Degree fell into desuetude there because then the Brother Knights had no means of becoming qualified to receive it. It took its rightful pace in the Ancient and Accepted Rite as the 30th Degree GEKKH, although here the considerable K.T. references in the Opening, Closing and the 'Cavern' present something of an anomaly. *'Ne Plus Ultra'* is a term which has given rise to considerable confusion. It is becoming apparent that there was never a specific Degree which was entitled *'Ne Plus Ultra'* per se. It means nothing more than it says "Than which there is nothing further", and when it appears in a variety of contexts it simply indicates the highest Degree in a sequence of progressive Degrees. Thus, in Rites where there was nothing beyond the 'Rose Croix' Degree, this is called *'Ne Plus Ultra'*. For example, the Cornish Mason John Knight refers to the last 'Rosycrucian' degree in his sequence of twenty-five plus one Degrees as such. The Twenty-fifth Degree SPRS can be found referred to as *'Ne Plus Ultra'* before the institution of the Ancient and Accepted Rite of Thirty-three Degrees. It is curious that the words are retained in the Thirtieth Degree of the Ancient and Accepted Rite when Brethren may well hope to

proceed to the Thirty-first Degree and beyond.

718 See Appendix A.

719 Matthew Christmas, *A Short Account of the Origins and Early History of the Grand Metropolitan Chapter*, p.4 (July 1996)
   Ewen McEwen, *The Mount Calvary Encampment*, pp.21-24 (undated-?1990).
   H.V. Wiles, *Mount Calvary Chapter Rose Croix No.3, 1848–1948*, pp.36/7 (1948).

720 Afterwards Grand Metropolitan Chapter No.1.

721 Mount Calvary Chapter No.3.

722 Charles Kemeys Kemeys Tynte was Installed as a Knight Templar on 15th March 1818 in the 'Chapter of the Observance of the Seven Degrees', which in 1868 became the T.I Encampment 'E', but was erased in 1888.

723 William Tucker was also both Provincial Grand Master and Provincial Grand Superintendent for the Province of Dorsetshire.

724 The 'Patent of Constitution', as it was then described, was dated 21st March 1852.

725 Tynte's name appears nowhere in the earliest Supreme Council Membership list (1858). (Colonel Tynte died in November 1860.)

726 A & A pp.134/135.

727 All Souls' Encampment No.31 at Weymouth had been Founded in 1847, three years after Holy Cross at Coryton.

728 A & A p.20.

729 St. James of Jerusalem No.33 and Jacques de Molay No.36 Encampments are still working. St. Joseph No.9 in Manchester, also still working, is an older foundation, with a Warrant dated 1806.

730 The Regulations of the Supreme Council provided that the formal ceremony of 'Affiliation' could only be conducted by one of its own Members. By April 1856 a Member of each of these four early Chapters had been elected to the Supreme Council, and Affiliation could therefore be conducted in each of them – William Tucker at Coryton had been a Member of the Supreme Council since 1846, George Vernon (Vernon, Birmingham) was elected in July 1853, Sir John de la Pole (All Souls', Weymouth) in November 1854, and Matthew Dawes (Palatine) in April 1856. Charles Vigne, the first MWS of the next Chapter to be Warranted, St. Peter and St. Paul at Bath, and also a member of Coryton, All Souls' and Vernon Chapters, was Elected to the Supreme Council in June 1855. Since several members of Metropolitan Chapter were also Members of the Supreme Council, these Elections may have been seen also to provide representation for the time being of the Brethren at the highest level of the Order. (Mount Calvary Chapter was dormant at this time, and it does not appear in the November 1858 Register of membership of the Order – see H.V.Wiles, *Mount Calvary Chapter Rose Croix No. 3, 1848–1948*, p.38 (Privately Printed, 1948)

731 The date on the Warrant of St. Peter and St. Paul Chapter No.6 was the same as that on those of Coryton, Weymouth, Vernon and Palatine Chapters, 21st March 1852. The reason for this is unknown, as an 'application' for a Warrant for the Chapter was not made until the following year, and it was not Consecrated (by William Tucker and George Vernon) until 25th October 1853.

732 During its brief independence, Baldwyn gave Warrants to six Encampments: Antiquity at Bath (since 1868, No.1), Ascalon at Birmingham (removed from the Roll,1867), Holy Rood at Warwick (No.55, erased 1894), Vale of Jehoshaphat at Highbridge, and Vale Royal at Salisbury, (each of which had ceased to meet by 1862), and Percy at Adelaide in South Australia (No.57, transferred in 1982 to the Great Priory of South Australia).

733 Gerald Bryant, *A History of the First 150 Years of St. Peter & St. Paul Rose Croix Chapter No.6*, p.22 (Fosseway Press, Radstock, Ltd, 2003).

734 Davyd Nash had been Initiated in 1832 in the Royal Sussex Lodge of Hospitality in Bristol, although he did not join the Lodge until 1838. He resigned and rejoined on two further occasions before finally retiring from the Lodge in 1858. RC p.170.

735 The letter from Davyd Nash published in *The Freemasons' Magazine* for 20th June 1857, in which he claimed that in Bristol the two Orders, Knights Templar and the Ancient and Accepted Rite, were separate and distinct was singularly unconvincing. Having started by saying that "The Templar K——h which if not the 30th Degree of the Ancient and Accepted Rite, is difficult to distinguish from it", he then wrote:

"They [*the members of the A & A Rite*] have no other connection with the Knights Templars than arises from their holding their meetings in the same hall, subscribing to a common fund for the maintenance of that hall, under the terms of a trust-deed, for the benefit of all Masonic bodies in the province of Bristol, and being placed under the authority of an Officer [*that is, Nash himself*] who unites in his person the Grand Mastership of the Knights Templar [*an appointment which the Grand Conclave did not recognise*] and the superintendency of the Degrees of the Ancient and Accepted Rite [*to which the Supreme Council had never appointed him*]."

736 At the Meeting of the Supreme Council on 14th July 1857, Leeson said that " for some years past he had in correspondence (which he would now lay before the Council) remonstrated with the late Illustrious Grand Secretary General H.E. D.W.Nash in regard to his holding Masonic Fellowship Intercourse or Communication in degrees of the Ancient and Accepted Rite more especially in the 18th degree with Masons or bodies of Masons not duly recognized or acknowledged by Supreme Council as lawful and regular". He went on to say that he had recently received various communications from senior members of the A and A Rite alleging that Nash had violated his Obligation in defiance of the Council, and specifically that he had granted Warrants to hold Rose Croix Chapters.

737 The sentence was carried by the method traditionally appropriate for the expulsion of a Sovereign Grand Inspector General from the Order, that is, to have the offender's "name exposed in red letters in the councils and lodges throughout the world". Nash's full names were printed in red capital letters on paper nearly three feet long, and nine inches wide, a copy of which is preserved in the archives of the Supreme Council at 10 Duke Street, London.

738 His letter, which contains several points of interest apart from his indignation, is transcribed in Appendix B.

739 The full sequence was that of the three Symbolic Craft Degrees, taken in a local Lodge using the 'Bristol Working', followed by the Royal Arch, including the ceremony of 'Passing the Veils'. Then followed three chivalric Degrees which Baldwyn had probably acquired from France early in the nineteenth century, the Nine Elected Masters, Scots Knight Grand Architect, including Scots Knights of Kilwinning, and Knights of the East, the Sword and the Eagle. Then came Knights of St. John of Jerusalem, Palestine Rhodes and Malta, and Knights Templar, incorporating both the Mediterranean Pass and the Knights of Malta, and finally the Baldwyn version of the 'Rose Croix'.

740 In 1862 Charles Vigne resigned as Lieutenant Grand Commander but retained his membership of the Supreme Council.

741 Supreme Council Minute Book – see A & A p.130.

742 Eighty years later, on 20th November 1941, the Supreme Council received a request from the Royal Kent Chapter for its members to continue to wear "Old French Regalia unorthodox", See A & A pp.915/6.

743 Now No.9.

744 Now No.13.

745 Now No.20.

746 John Huyshe had to take the Chair in Grand Lodge at the especial meeting on 2nd September 1874 after Lord Ripon announced his resignation as Grand Master. Alec Mellor, *The Roman Catholic Church and the Craft*, AQC, LXXXIX, p.65, 1976.

747 For further details, see Bryant, *op., cit.* pp.22/23.

748 Philips himself was originally an Irish member of the Order. At the Meeting of the Supreme Council on 13th October 1857 "Letters were read from Bro. Furnell and other members of the Supreme Council of Ireland, in favour of Captain Nathaniel Philips of the 47th Regt., who had taken the degree of Rose Croix under that Supreme Council, requesting the Supreme Council of England to confer the degree of Kt. K.H. upon Philips should they deem him worthy. It was unanimously agreed to accede to the request." A & A pp.40/41.

749 Philips said that Bowyer had instructed him to write to Huyshe

"to communicate with you about our meetings in May & to inform you, that if you can conveniently attend at the F. M. Tavern Great Queen Street at 3.15 P.M. the Council will be ready to receive and affiliate you; and at a later hour you will receive the 31st Degree with a few who have been nominated for it ... . . I shall leave it to you to fix a time most convenient to yourself and members of your Rose + Chapters, for some of the S.G.C. to come down to Devonshire and affiliate all those who are willing to come under our Authority, & I shall feel much obliged, if you would at your leisure furnish me with a requisition for the names of the Rose + Chaspters for whom you will require Warrants ... I should like to be furnished with a nominal Roll in Duplicate, of all those for whom Certificates will be required.

750 John Huyshe was about to rent a house in London, in the same road as that in which Philips was living, Philips expressing his pleasure that "we are so soon to have you as a near neighbour".

751 Huyshe was Deputy Grand Master of Grand Conclave from 1861 to 1872.

752 One of his reasons for refusing to do so was that affiliation to the Supreme Council would cut him off from Masonic intercourse with his many friends in the Encampment of Baldwyn.

753 Philips wrote – It is with extreme regret that the S.G.C. have heard your determination not to take the Ob. of Allegiance, for it is hoped, that after the full explanation which has been given to you, the only difficulty in the way of a perfect union between the two bodies which unhappily divide this country had been arranged.The S.G.C. still trusts that time may induce you to reconsider your determination which makes this the only Country in which perfect accord between all bodies of Masons does not exist".

(In making this stement at this time, Philips may be considered to have been somewhat economical with the truth! C.J.M.)

754 Huyshe Chapter No.38.

755 Cornwall Chapter No.61.

756 Bryant, *op. cit.,* p.24.

757 Norman Wilkins, *History of the Ancient and Accepted*

Rite in Somerset, pp. 32/33 (Privately printed, 2000)

758 A & A. p.132.

759 *Ibidem.*

760 A & A pp.133/134.

761 Lord Lathom, the Sovereign Grand Commander, could not be present at this or at the earlier ceremonial Meeting owing to the recent death of his sister.

762 For a more detailed account of these proceedings, see A & A pp.358—360.

763 "A Warrant of Confirmation", to be given to the Chapter *gratis*, "The Baldwyn Chapter retaining their original (time immemorial) position, and being placed at the top of the list of Chapter Rose Croix". No.1 of the Articles of Agreement.

764 No.5 of the Articles of Agreement.

765 The Articles of Agreement are set out in full in Appendix VI of A & A. pp.1078-1080.

Essay 20
The Rose Croix Brethren at Bottoms and Rochdale

In 1845 Dr. Robert Crucefix Petitioned the Supreme Council of the Northern Masonic Jurisdiction of the United States of America for a Patent to establish a Supreme Council of the Ancient and Accepted Rite in England. He intended that this Council should control all the thirty-three Degrees of the Rite in England other than those of Entered Apprentice, Fellow Craft and Master Mason which were under the jurisdiction of the United Grand Lodge. He considered that, if his Petition were not quickly acceded to, the Supreme Council of the Grand Orient of France, the regularity of which was at least questionable, might give a Patent for England to some other controlling body of the Rite. When Crucefix received the Patent dated 26th October 1845, he seems to have been unaware that there was already in Yorkshire a Council which esteemed itself to be an independent superior body of the Rite.

At the turn of the eighteenth century there was considerable Masonic activity in the North of Derbyshire, the South of Yorkshire, and the East of Lancashire. The Craft Lodges and Royal Arch Chapters in this area were on the Register of the Premier Grand Lodge, the Moderns, and of its Supreme Royal Arch Chapter, but, in spite of this, many of their Brethren and Companions were active in a variety of Degrees and Orders 'outside the Craft'. These activities took place independently of what might be happening in London, in Bristol and the West of England, and in Newcastle. There were two centres of this – the villages of Greenwood and Stansfield, near the Yorkshire town of Todmorden (this centre was more usually known by the undignified name of Bottoms), and Rochdale in Lancashire, some ten miles further West.

Among the early Masonic bodies meeting at Bottoms were 'The Lodge of Prince George'[766], the Warrant of which is dated 1796, and which had moved to Bottoms from Haworth in 1812, and its associated R.A.Chapter, 'Affability', Warranted in 1807, which had removed to Bottoms from Heptonstall at about the same time. There was also the 'Prince Edward Encampment of Knights Templar'[767], the original Warrant of which is dated 30th October 1811. In addition, there was an old Mark Lodge, also named 'Prince Edward'.[768]

Early in the nineteenth century the Lodge of Prince George issued annual calendars. In spite of the Lodge's allegiance to the 'Moderns', these set out the times and dates of meetings not only of the Craft Lodge and of its associated Royal Arch Chapter, but also of a variety of additional Orders and Degrees. These included, among others, two Degrees described respectively as the 'Rosa (or 'Rosey') Cross' and the *Ne Plus Ultra*'[769]. It is of passing interest that the energetic Masons who practised all these Degrees appear not to have been the local gentry or squirearchy. A letter from the W.M. of Prince George Lodge to the Deputy Provincial G.M. in 1829 informed him that its members were "of none but the labouring class", and in 1842 a similar letter stated "that our Lodge is principally composed of the working class".[770]

The Calendar-lists of meeting-dates indicate that the Degrees of Freemasonry in Bottoms were kept "separate and distinct", but it is more difficult to be certain of what the various Degrees consisted. The uncertain position of the 'Priestly Order' considerably contributes to the confusion. This was the *Ne Plus Ultra*'[771]; there is no mention of a 'Kadosh' Degree in the earlier local records. The 'Priestly Order' was a 'Pillars' Degree, but not derived from that then based in Newcastle[772], and to which it owed no allegiance, as is indicated by the Warrant given to establish a 'Band' in Bottoms in 1819. This states that "We the Pillars of the Second Lancashire Union Band[773] finding many worthy & deserving Knight Templar Priests amongst us, who are desirous of a Band amongst themselves, in Compliance with their requisition We the Pillars of the said Band think it expedient to empower the following Priest Members of Lodges No. 574, 517, 541" (here follow seven names) "to establish a Band to be known by the Name of the first Yorkshire Union Band to hold the same from time to time as they should think proper under Sanction of their respective Warrants"[774]. This Priestly Order appears to have been worked continuously under this Warrant at Bottoms, at least until May 1871, carrying out more than 100 'consecrations'.

It is not easy to disentangle the relationship between the various Christian degrees being worked at Bottoms. The 'Pillars' degree was regarded as the 'superior' Order, referred to as 'The Antient 33rd Degree' on several Certificates. Two of these refer to the 'Rosa' Croix Degree at Bottoms. One, dated 1st August 1846, records that John Greenwood "took the Rosa Croix degree at Bottoms".[775] The other, which bears the same date, has the heading "Supreme Grand Chapter of the Rosa Croix" and "Held under the Supreme Tabernacle of the Antient 33rd Degree at Head Quarters in the East, Bottoms"[776]. It was issued to Joshua, the brother of John Greenwood whose signature, among others, it bears[777].

The date of '1st August, 1846' on <u>each</u> of the Certificates may be misleading. That John Greenwood signed his brother's Certificate as 'G Chancellor' on the same day as his own Certificate was dated, may indicate no more than that this was the first occasion upon which Certificates had been issued, without relevance necessarily to the date on which either brother had actually taken the Degree. William Pilling signing the latter Certificate as Past G.H.P also indicates that some form of 'controlling' body had been in existence prior to August 1846. One can speculate that the Reports of the activities of the Supreme Council in London in *The Freemasons' Quarterly Review* in July 1846[778] had been read at Bottoms and that the self-styled "Supreme Grand Chapter of the Rosa Croix" was, so to say, putting down a marker to indicate its own priority.

In May 1848, Albert Hudson Royds[779], later to become the Provincial Grand Commander of the Knights Templar in Lancashire, was himself 'Consecrated' in the 'Priestly' (or 'Pillars') Order at Bottoms. In the following year, Royds became the first 'Eminent Commander' of the Knights Templar 'Encampment of Prince Albert No.34', the original meeting-place of which was the Masonic Rooms, Ann[780] Street, Rochdale. So prominent was Royds in Freemasonry in Lancashire that within a few years this Encampment, and also the Preceptory which it became, was known simply as 'the Albert'.[781]

In 1862 Royds, now Provincial Grand Commander of the Knights Templar in Lancashire, was proposed by Dr. Leeson for membership of the Supreme Council in London[782]. Ill health prevented Royds from then accepting the invitation. Six years later the Council was having to deal with the problem caused by the activities of John Yarker in the South of Lancashire where he was trying to establish the so-called 'Ancient and Primitive Rite'. Nathaniel Philips, the Grand Secretary General, then wrote to Henry Bowyer, who had taken Leeson's place as Sovereign Grand Commander, to say that he was anxious to have Royds as a member of the Supreme Council "to subdue any problems with Yarker in the North", because Royds was "such a universal favourite with the Lancashire lads". Accordingly Royds took his seat on the Council on 5th May 1868.

During these years the Chapter at Bottoms continued to confer the Degree of Prince Rose Croix of H.R.D.M., disregarded by, and disregarding, both Yarker and the Supreme Council in London. In 1864 the 'joining fee' for the Bottoms Chapter was one guinea[783], two years later this was increased to one and a half guineas and further increased to two guineas in 1869[784]. John Fingland 'joined' the Chapter in 1866 (his 'Declaration' was witnessed by Mitchell Helliwell (who had signed Joshua Greenwood's Certificate 20 years earlier as '2nd.Capt. Gen'), as did Thomas Croxton whose own Certificate was dated 24th June of that year. On 16th December 1866 the Certificate issued to John Copley was headed:

"Supreme Grand Chapter of the Rosa Croix

Held under the

Supreme Grand Tabernacle of the Antient 33rd Degree

AT HEAD QUARTERS IN THE EAST, BOTTOMS, STANSFIELD, YORKSHIRE"

The document goes on to certify that "our Illustrious Sir Knight Cousin *John Copley* having been previously been dubbed a Knight of the Royal Religious and Military Order of Masonic Knights Templar and created a Red Cross Knight of Babylon was this *16th* day of *December* A.D. *1866* A.L. *1833* received, admitted and constituted an Excellent and Perfect Prince Rose Croix of H.R.D.M., was also advanced to the degree of a Knight of the White Cross[785]". It bears the seal of the "Supreme Council of the Antient 33rd Degree", and the signatures of its Principal Officers[786], all of whose names, with the exception of that of Joseph Greenwood, appeared, but in different capacities, on the 1846 Certificates of the two Greenwood brothers[787]. On 5th December 1869, a similar Certificate was issued to William James Beck[788].

These Certificates[789] have several features of interest. That they were printed indicates, if confirmation were needed, that they were routinely issued by a body with a continuing existence, as does the progression of the Officers. That the 'Supreme Grand Chapter of the Rosa Croix' was held under the 'Supreme Grand Tabernacle of the Antient 33rd Degree' indicates that the 'Rosa Croix' was subject to the superior controlling body. The word 'Tabernacle', and the signature of the 'Most Wise Sovereign' being placed below that of an Officer denominated 'Grand High Priest', again indicates that this was a 'Pillars' Order.

The insertion of the 'White Cross Degree' after that of the 'Rosey Cross' is puzzling. Early in the nineteenth Century a 'White Cross' Degree appears in the 'Prince George' Annual Calendars, meeting on a different night from 'K.M.', which can hardly be anything other than 'Knight of Malta'. 'White Cross' can therefore not be identified with the 'Malta' Degree. Price has tentatively suggested that the Degree being worked was the 'White Cross of Torphichen', and that the sequence presided over at Bottoms was Red Cross Knight of Babylon, Rose or Rosey Cross, White Cross and 'Antient Thirtythird'[790]. As will be seen later, a 'Red Cross of Babylon' Degree was worked at Rochdale as a preliminary to the 'Rosey Croix' – the Candidates for the latter were introduced as 'Sir Knights Cousins' – but there is no mention of what might be thought to be the even more essential 17th Degree, 'Knight of the East and West'. The latter has much in common with the various Priestly Pillars Degrees, and its Jewel is a White Cross. It is therefore possible that this Degree had been transferred to a position *after* the 'Rosey Cross' as a suitable preliminary to the 'Antient Thirtythird or *Ne Plus Ultra*', if this, as appears probable, was a 'Pillars' Degree, similar to that now worked under the Grand College.

Eighteen months after the date on the 'Rose Croix' Certificate in the name of William James Beck, the members of the Supreme Council in London were somewhat startled by having brought to their attention a circular, signed by "William Ashworth, Chancellor pro tem". It announced that in a few days time a Meeting to confer the Thirtieth Degree was to be held in Rochdale by a body of which they had no previous knowledge[791]. John Montagu, the Grand Secretary General, was instructed to write a letter to Ashworth (to which he received no reply) and also to draft a letter for wide circulation on behalf of the Council[792].

Subsequent events, in so far as they concerned the Supreme Council, were reported to its Meeting on 10th May, 1871 by the Sovereign Grand Commander, Charles Vigne:

"In consequence of a Circular calling a Meeting at Rochdale by a spurious Body to confer the 30° and 32° having reached the Ill.˙.Lt.˙.G.Cr., Copies of the Letter before you were immediately prepared and within 24 hours, and before the Meeting at Rochdale assembled, they were posted to, and received by all of our Brethren in Lancashire, and a large number of Telegrams on the same subject were dispatched by the Ill.˙.Bro. Royds 33°, and I feel assured that the Circulation of this warning had a most excellent effect, not only in deterring Brethren from being present at the Meeting, but in proving the promptitude and activity of this Su.Co."

The second of these effects the 'warning' may well have had, but, so far as deterring Brethren from being present at the Meeting was concerned, Vigne was not only being unduly optimistic, but evidently had not read the Report in *The Freemason* for 25th February 1871[793]. This journal regularly included reports of Masonic Meetings in the various Orders. In this issue, under the heading 'Ancient and Accepted Rite', after a Report of a Meeting of the regularly Warranted Mount Calvary Chapter in London, it continued with a Report headed 'Rochdale Chapter' without any indication that there was anything out-of-the-ordinary about it. It reported the admission of John Fothergill as a member of the Order and the Installation of Bro. Prince as MWS for the ensuing year. It then went on to say that "after the convocation was closed ... several members formed themselves into a convocation of the Holy Order of K.H. etc."[794]. It would be interesting to know who were the "illustrious and distinguished princes of the order" who were reported to have been present, evidently undeterred by the exertions of Montagu and Royds. However, one might wonder how well the Chapter was attended by its own Members, because the new Knight, John Fothergill, was at once appointed Raphael, and the newly appointed Herald was a Past Sovereign, William Roberts, who had been a signatory of Copley's Certificate two years earlier as 1st Captain General of "The Antient 33rd. Degree".

This report in *The Freemason* was immediately followed by another under the heading "Holy Order of K.H. and Grand Elected Knights, or Ne Plus Ultra." which commenced "The inaugural ceremony of this convocation was held in the Masonic Rooms, Ann Street, Rochdale on Saturday last". The report went on to say that Ashworth read the letter which he had received from Montagu, as well as the Circular which the latter had despatched. The meeting agreed that their actions were no concern of the Supreme Council in London, after which "the ceremony was therefore proceeded with and several members of the Order of Rose Croix &c. duly admitted by ancient rites and ceremonies to the degrees &c."[795]. The report concludes "The officers were then appointed, invested, and installed for the ensuing twelve months, and the chapter was closed in due form, and with hearty good wishes for the Supreme Grand Council and other sister chapters[796]".

It was an unfortunate time for the Supreme Council in London to have the affairs in Rochdale brought to its notice. The Council was already under criticism for what several Brethren considered to be its unnecessarily harsh treatment of 'Antiquity' Chapter at Bath. It was being equally forthright in condemning the continuing attempts of John Yarker to establish his 'Rite of Mizraim' in Manchester. *The Freemason* had already published a lengthy letter from Yarker detailing his accusation that in several respects it was the Supreme Council which was acting irregularly and not him. The Council was not without its defenders. Yarker's allegations were strongly repudiated in a letter published in the same journal over a pseudonym[797], in which the writer supported the Council's views of Yarker's "evil example"[798].

The Editor of *The Freemason* was George Kenning, the Masonic outfitter for whose wares the journal never failed to carry a prominent advertisement. For several months the journal's editorial policy had been less than friendly to the Supreme Council, and in the following week the leading article condemned its actions in uncompromising language:

> "Unfortunately, however, the policy pursued by the Supreme Grand Council of late years, and especially since the retirement of Dr. Leeson from its head, has been retrogressive in its tendency and despotic in its operations. Masons who appreciate and admire many of the degrees of the Ancient and Accepted Rite are driven from its ranks by the glacial hauteur and extravagant pretensions of some members of the Council, who seem to fancy their peculiar mission is to make other people uncomfortable. The dissatisfaction which such a line of conduct has naturally created is not confined to the Bath Chapter, it is felt very strongly by influential metropolitan brethren – it exists in more than one provincial chapter; and unless conciliatory measures and a thorough reform of the present government of the Rite be speedily adopted, it is not difficult to foresee that the power of the Council will be shattered.[799]"

While this incendiary correspondence was in progress in the columns of *The Freemason*, the Installation Meeting of the 'Albert' Encampment of Knights Templar had taken place in Rochdale on Thursday 16th March. The 'Eminent Commander' was Clement Molyneaux Royds, the nephew of Albert Royds who, unusually, was absent on this occasion. There is no record in the Minutes or in other archives of the Supreme Council in London that Albert Royds corresponded with it about the Meetings of the Rochdale Rose Croix or Kadosh Chapters but he can hardly have been unaware of their proceedings. Royds, a Member of the Supreme Council in London, might have found it embarrassing to be present at the 'Albert Encampment' meeting, when James Holroyd, Enthroned as M.W.S. at the Rose Croix Meeting, was Installed as Eminent Commander, William Ashworth himself as 1st Captain, William Roberts as Registrar, John Fothergill, the Candidate at the Rose Croix meeting, as Captain of Lines and Robert Whitworth, 'Grand Chancellor' of the Rose Croix Chapter, as Almoner.[800]

The Degree of Red Cross Knight of Babylon, conferred on Knights Templar before that of 'Rose Croix', was also being routinely worked at Rochdale. John Fothergill had earlier been admitted as a 'Red Cross Knight of Babylon and Knight of the East and West', and, on the Saturday following the Installation Meeting of the 'Albert Encampment', three more Knights were installed[801] at a Meeting of the 'Rochdale Council of the Red Cross Knights of Babylon'[802].

William Ashworth wasted little time in replying to what he considered to be the calumnies made by *The Freemason's* anonymous correspondent. In a letter, which also appeared in the April 1st issue[803], he did not seek to defend Yarker, but challenged the contention that the latter had set an "evil example". He pointed out, correctly, that the 'Rochdale Chapter' had never owed allegiance to the Supreme Council in Golden Square, but he then went on to make the more contentious claim "and therefore they have no right whatever to dictate to us, as to what, how, when, or where, we may choose to confer the degrees which are so admirably worked at Rochdale", adding that "the authority to which we owe our allegiance dates much further back than that of the S.G.C. ... ... *Our authority*, which is much older than this, has never been questioned before, neither has it been termed a forgery". It was, however, the anonymous letter-writer's statement that the 'Higher Degrees' were conferred on candidates at Rochdale for 1s.6d. that excited Ashworth's greatest indignation, characterising this as "a barefaced fabrication on the part of your correspondent".

Ashworth concluded his long letter by again refusing to condemn Yarker, who was well known to many Rochdale brethren[804]. He considered that Yarker was doing as much for Freemasonry as was the Supreme

Council in London. "Is he alone," Ashworth asked, "in this quarrel with the S.G.C.?" In his last paragraph he indicated the basis of the unrest which he considered to exist, writing:

"We have no desire to interfere in any way with the quarrel between Bro. Yarker and the S.G.C. – supreme over its own chapters, not ours – but wish them and every other Council or body in Masonry, all the good and kind wishes it is possible to conceive, and hope the day may come when we shall all be united as one body, and when the executive will be elected, as in the Craft, by the voice and vote of the people in Masonry."

An 'emergency meeting' of the Rochdale Rose Croix Chapter, characterised in *The Freemason*, perhaps to rub salt in the wound, as "this prosperous chapter", was held on the 15th of April[805]. The meeting had been:

"summoned at the urgent request of several worthy and distinguished Sir Knights who were anxious to become members of this Illustrious and Princely Order. The chapter assembled at three o'clock, under the presidency of Ill. and Perfect Prince William Roberts, Past M.W.S., when Sir Kts. Cousins Ross and Bowers of Ashton; Sutcliffe of Burnley; and Burgess of Brighouse, being four of the Sir. Kts. who had requested the M.W.S. to convene the meeting, presented themselves and were duly constituted Illustrious princes of the Order."

The Rochdale Chapter was evidently attracting candidates from a wide area, all of whom, as 'Sir Kts. Cousins' had evidently taken the preliminary degree of the 'Red Cross of Babylon'.

The Supreme Council in London could not ignore the disquiet in several parts of the country. "A Grand and Supreme Chapter of Rose Croix" was summoned to meet on the 11th May 1871[806]. All the new measures which the Supreme Council was considering were laid before the assembled Members of the Order – its Incorporation, its Building programme at its 'Grand East' in Golden Square, its proposal to print the 'Constitutions of 1786', and the proposed Treaty with the other Masonic Orders. But before this was done, Montagu explained at length the reasons for the suspension of 'Antiquity' and for the condemnation of Yarker and his Rite of Misraim. Only the financial proposals attracted particular criticism with sometimes acrimonious debate. By the end of the day, the Supreme Council had received overwhelming support for its actions, and no one could say that it was now acting high-handedly.[807]

This passage of events seems to have persuaded the Rochdale Brethren that their position would be more secure if they were acting under the authority of a Warrant rather than relying only on 'Time Immemorial' status. Evidently the exercise in democracy which had taken place in London did not persuade them to transfer their allegiance to Golden Square. In any case a Warrant from the Council in London would not have permitted the Rochdale Chapter to confer the Higher Degrees, something which the former confined to itself. They therefore sent a Petition to Bottoms, in answer to which they received a Warrant as Rochdale Chapter No.1 from "The Supreme Grand Inspectors General of the Antient Thirtythird Degree and Grand High Priest of the said Grand Tabernacle". This conferred on them the power "to Perfect P.H.K.R.C. &c. in their several Degrees herein named", and granting them "such Powers, Privileges, Prerogatives and Immunities as do of ancient usage and Right belong to regular established Chapters and Noble Perfect Princes Harodim Kadosh Rose Croix ['and White Cross' *added in superscript*] of the said Order".[808]

It is extraordinary that Albert Royds reported none of this to the Supreme Council of which he was a Member[809]. He can hardly have been unaware of a Chapter which met in the same Masonic Rooms as the Encampment which he so regularly attended. There is no indication that Royds ever curbed the activities of the Rochdale Brethren other than by despatching telegrams at the behest of Montagu.

The Chapter at Bottoms, possibly already calling itself 'High Greenwood' Chapter, was as anxious as any other Masonic controlling body to make sure it received the appropriate fees. On 3rd September, two months after the Warrant was granted to Rochdale Chapter, its Minutes record:

"It was decided to submit an account to the Rochdale Chapter for the Warrant and Dispensation granted to P.P. Henry Prince, of Broadfield, Rochdale, and others and that the Chapter be requested to make a return of the Princes perfected by the Chapter since the issue of the Dispensation, and to pay the fees due in respect of the same.[810]"

However, after 1871 there are few records of the 'Rose Croix' Brethren either at Rochdale or at Bottoms[811], although Chapters may have continued to meet. The Brethren at Rochdale appear to have considered transferring their allegiance to the Council in London, for the Minutes of the Supreme Council on 8th October 1872, under the heading "Rochdale Brethren", record:

> "Letter from Brother Brockbank read. Resolved that upon these brethren petitioning, they may be affiliated upon the distinct understanding that they go through the ceremony on the first convenient occasion."

There is no reference to a body of Rochdale Brethren affiliating[812], still less to a Chapter being Warranted in Rochdale[813].

It was to be another twenty years before the Brethren at Bottoms decided to surrender their independence. On 12th July 1892 the Supreme Council approved and adopted a recommendation of its Committee:

> "That a Warrant be granted to Ill∴Bro. John Marshall 30°[814] and others to hold a Chr. at Eastwood near Todmorden in Yorkshire under the name of the 'High Greenwood' Chr., and that the same be granted free of charge in considersation of an old Chapter, unconnected with this Sup: Co., having existed in that place from Time Immemorial[815]."

A Warrant for High Greenwood Chapter No.124 was issued on the same day[816], but for sixty years there was no Chapter in Rochdale under the Supreme Council in London until Rochdale St. Chad No.494 was Warranted on 12th January 1956.

Appendix A

The Warrant of "The first Yorkshire Union Band" is preserved in the custody of the Lodge of Prince George No.308 in its meeting-place at the Masonic Rooms at Bottoms.
The full (manuscript) text reads:

> "We the Pillars of the Second Lancashire
> Union Band finding many worthy
> & deserving Knight Templar Priests amongst
> us, who are desirous of a Band amongst them-
> selves, in Compliance with their requisition
> We the Pillars of the said Band think it ex-
> pedient to empower the following Priest Mem-
> bers of Lodges No. 574, 517, 541, William Utley
> James Holt, William Ackroyd, William Shotton,
> William Smith, John Sutcliffe, Abraham
> Barker & others of their Successors to establish
> a Band to be known by the Name of the first York-
> shire Union Band to hold the same from time
> to time as they should think proper under Sanc-
> tion of their respective Warrants, to make such
> Worthy Knights Templars as they think proper

In Testimony whereof we have affixed the
Seal of our Band and Signatures. Given
in our Temple at Bottoms in Stansfield, Yorkshire this Ninth Day of May 1819 and of
Masonry 5819 and of the priesthood 1786

        Lodge 574 James North 1st Pillar
        Do. 574 John Holdsworth 2nd Do.
(Seal   Do 70 Thomas Brown 3rd Do.
of   Do 655 James Atkin 4th Do.
Band)   Do 574 Squire Barker 5th Do.
        Do 209 John Whitehead 6th Do.
        Do 209 Samuel Riley(?) 7th Do."

It may be noted that the 'Year of Masonry' is that obtained by adding 'the traditional Masonic 4000' to the Anno Domini, and not the 'Bishop Ussher 4004', as was the case, for example, in John Knight's datings in Cornwall, and that the 'Year of the Priesthood' is derived by subtracting '33', the traditional date of the Crucifixion, from the Anno Domini.

Appendix B

Note on the whereabouts of Warrants and Certificates to which reference is made

- 9th May 1819. Warrant from 'Second Lancashire Union Band', Bury to establish a 'Band' at Bottoms. Original in the custody of Prince George Lodge No.308 at Bottoms, Eastwood. (Also photocopy in Matthews, *op. cit.*) (Transcribed in Appendix A.)

- 1st August 1846. 'Rosa Croix' Certificate of Joshua (or Joseph) Greenwood. Photocopy in the Library of the Hallamshire College, S.R.I.A., Tipton Hall, Sheffield. (Quoted by Hewitt, *op. cit.*)

- 24th June 1866, 'Rosa Croix' Certificate of Thomas Croxton, original in Library of Hallamshire College (*v.s.*) (Quoted by Hewitt, *op.cit.*)

- 16th December 1866. 'Rosa Croix' Certificate of John Copley. Photocopy in Matthews, *op. cit.*

- 5th December 1869. 'Rosa Croix' Certificate of William James Beck. Original, photocopy, and hand-drawn copy in the Archives of the Supreme Council at 10 Duke Street, London. Presented to the Museum of the Supreme Council by Ill.'.Brother C Gardner 31°, January 1973. This Certificate is similar to those earlier issued to Greenwood and Croxton. (Hewitt, *op.cit.*)

- 1st July 1871. Warrant issued to 'Rochdale Chapter Number 1' by the 'Supreme Grand Council of the Antient Thirtythird Degree of England and Wales and the Dependencies of the British Crown etc.' at 'Station House, Bottoms, Stansfield'. Original in the Archives of the Supreme Council at 10 Duke Street, London. (Transcribed in Appendix C.)

Appendix C

In the name of the Great Architect
Of the Universe
Station House, Bottoms, Stansfield

A Place full of Light Wherein Reigneth Silence and Peace, But the Darkness
comprehended it not

To those whom it may concern

Greeting

And more particularly to the Illustrious Sovereign Grand Inspectors General and All those Most Valiant and
Sublime Princes of the Supreme Grand Council of the Antient Thirtythird Degree of England and Wales and
the Dependencies of the British Crown &c.

H. K. P. P. R. C. Health Peace and Goodwill

Know *Ye that We the Supreme Grand Inspectors General of the Antient* Thirtythird Degree, and Grand High
Priest of the said Grand Tabernacle, have received a Petition from Perfect Princes William Roberts, John
Knight, John Barker, William Henry Prince and James Holroyd, residing at Rochdale in the County
Palantine (*sic*) of Lancaster requesting us to Grant them our Patent of Constitution to open and form and
from Time to time hold a Chapter or Convocation in Lancashire to be called the Rochdale Chapter Number
1. at the Masonic Temple, Ann's Street, Rochdale, having duly taken the same into our consideration We do
hereby Grant to the above named Petitioners and their Successors, full power and Authority to Assemble
and to hold a Chapter or Convocation on the third Saturday in February and on the third Thursday in
October in each year at the Masonic Temple Ann's Street, Rochdale and from time to time at such other
places and times as they and their successors with our Consent shall be found necessary to Perfect P. H. K.
R. C. &c. in the several Degrees herein named **And** we do hereby appoint Perfect Prince John Barker, First
Most Wise Sovereign, Perfect Prince William Henry Prince, First Captain General, Perfect Prince James
Holroyd, Second Captain General, P. M. W. S. William Roberts, First Raphael, P. M. W. S. John Knight,
First Grand Marshall with such Powers, Privileges, Prerogatives and Immunities as do of ancient usage and
Right belong to regular established Chapters and Noble Perfect

and White Cross

Princes Harodim Kadosh Rose Croix ^ (*sic*) of the said Order Subject nevertheless to the Antient Statutes
and Orders of our Predecessors, and such as may be hereafter enacted by us or our successors in our Grand
and Holy Tabernacle of the Antient Thirtythird Degree.

Given at Head Quarters Station House Bottoms Stansfield near Todmorden the *First* day of *July* A.D. 1871,
A.L. 5875, A.O. 753, A.C. 557

William Shackleton

R + H, K, P, P, R,C

Sovereign Grand Commander

R,+, H, K, P, P, R, C. *James Lord*
Secretary General

William Pilling

<u>R + H, K, P, P, R, C</u>

Grand High Priest

766 Now No.308 under the United Grand Lodge of England.

767 Now No.18 under the Great Priory of England etc.

768 According to John E. Craven *An historical sketch of Freemasonry at Bottoms, Eastwood* (John Heywood, 1886) "At the time of the formation of the Grand Mark Lodge it was a disappointment to Prince Edward that it was not given No.1 on the list of Grand Mark Lodges, as it had been led to expect such a distinction."

769 The Annual Calendars included 'Craft Lodge, Craft Lodge Lecture, Holy Royal Arch, Holy Royal Arch Lecture, Knight Templar, Rosy Croix, Ne Plus Ultra, Knight Templar Lecture, Priestly Order, Red Cross of Babylon, Mediterranean Pass, Knights of Malta.' However, according to Craven (*op. cit.*, p.8) "Bottoms also conferred the degrees of Mark, Ark, and Link, Veils with Royal Arch, Rosy Croix, Old Mark, St. Lawrence, Mediterranean Pass, Knights of Malta, Eleven Ineffable Degrees, Priestly Order, or Old 33rd, Red Cross of Babylon, White Cross Knight, Knight of Constantinople, Ark Mariners".

770 Craven, *op. cit.*, p.65.

771 '*Ne Plus Ultra*' is not the name of a specific Degree. It is the term used in various Degree-sequences, both in England and in America and on the Continent of Europe, to indicate the highest Degree in a sequence – 'than which there is nothing further' . To refer to the 30th GEKKH as such under the Supreme Council of the Ancient and Accepted Rite for England is something of an anomaly. Cf Yves Hivert-Messeca "Ces systèmes se terminent le plus souvent par le grade de *Kadosh*, par celui de *Chevalier de Soleil* ou par celui de *Rose-Croix*, considérés selon les systèmes, comme le *ne plus ultra* de la maçonnerie." *Deux Siècles de Rite Écossais Ancien Accepté en France*, p.25 (Éditions Dervy, Paris, 2004)

772 Now 'The Grand College of The Holy Royal Arch Knight Templar Priests or Order of Holy Wisdom', with its Headquarters in York.

773 A 'Union Band' was a body composed of members of more than one Craft Lodge.

774 See Appendix A.

775 R. D. Matthews, "*Some Masonic degrees worked at Bottoms, Stansfield, near Halifax, during the nineteenth century*" p.18. (A paper read before the Chapter of Affability, No.308, on 5th December 1931.)

776 A.R. Hewitt,' NOTES ON THE ROSE CROIX AS 'WORKED' AT BOTTOMS, Yorks., 19th Century'; type-written summary (three copies) in archives of S.C., 10 Duke Street.

777 The certificate is signed by:
   John Knight Grand High Priest
   William Pilling Past G.H.P.
   Thomas Schofield M.W.S.
   William Roberts 1st. Capt. Gen.
   Mitchell Helliwell 2nd. Capt. Gen.
   John Watson Grand Scribe
   John Greenwood Grand Chancellor.

778 *Freemasons' Quarterly Review*, Volume 13, pp.367/8, 1846.

779 Of Brown Hill, Rochdale.

780 Or 'Anne' Street.

781 For example, in a report of a Meeting of the Encampment held on 26th September 1872, at which was recorded Royd's absence because of his daughter's wedding on that day, the report goes on to say "That this day may ever be remembered with pleasure by the P(rovincial) G(rand) C(ommander) is the wish of every Sir Knight of the Encampment which bears his honoured name."
   It continued to be known simply as such for more than a century, even appearing in the lists in the official 'Liber Ordinis Templi' (for example, that of 1958), as 'Albert Preceptory, No.34' until the original name on the Warrant was revived at the Preceptory's hundred-and-fiftieth anniversary in October 1999.

782 Royds was present as a 30º at the 'Convocation of the Higher Degrees of the Order' in London on 10th February 1854. In November 1858 he was shown in the list of members as S.P.R.S., 32º and a member of Palatine Chapter (Warranted 21st March 1852). He may well have taken the 'Rose Croix' Degree at Bottoms, and then affiliated in Palatine Chapter, for there is no record of his earlier career in the Ancient and Accepted Rite.

783 The earliest extant Minutes of "High Greenwood Chapter of Sovereign Princes Rose Croix" are dated 6th March 1864, when two Candidates, Samuel Simpson and Joseph Gledhill were Perfected. John Culpan, *A History of High Greenwood Chapter of Princes Rose Croix of H.R.D.M.*, p.6. (privately printed, 1992).

784 Matthew, *op. cit.*, p.18.

785 The Certificate is a printed form upon which the date and the name of he newly constituted Knight are entered in manuscript.

786 Wiliam Pilling, Grand High Priest; Mitchell Helliwell, Past Grand High Priest; Thomas Schofield, Most Wise Sovereign; William Roberts 1st Captain General; Joseph Greenwood, 2nd Captain General; John Watson, Grand Scribe; John Knight, Grand Chancellor.

787 In 1846 William Pilling appears on the Certificate as 'Past G.H.P.', Mitchell Helliwell as '2nd Capt.Gen.', Thomas Schofield as 'M.W.S.', William Roberts as '1st Capt.Gen.', John Watson is in the same Office as 'Grand Scribe', and John Knight was 'Grand High Priest'.

788 On this second Certificate, William Pilling again signs as 'G.H.P', and Thomas Schofield as 'M.W.S.', but the 'Past G.H.P.' is now Joseph Greenwood, John Watson is now '1st Capt.Gen., the 'Grand Scribe' is James Lord, and the G. Grand Chancellor is William Shackleton.

789 Beck's Certificate is in the archives of the Supreme Council, having been presented to the Council in 1973.

790 Brian W. Price, O.B.E., Private Communication,16th August 2000. See also Brian W. Price, *Metamorphosis. The Evolution of Prince Edward Council G*, (privately printed 31 Dec 2003) *passim*

791 "Masonic Temple, Main Street, Rochdale
   February 11th 1871
Dear Sir Knight,
By command of the Royal Commander of the Holy Order of Kadosh and 30 and 32 Degrees, a Convocation will be held in the Above Temple, on

Saturday next, the 18th Instant, at Six o'clock prompt, to create all Knights who present themselves and are found worthy of that distinction. We shall be happy to receive your name as a candidate on that occasion.
Yours fraternally
William Ashworth
Chancellor pro tem
All letters to be addressed to 21 Ann Street."

792 "Dear Sir and Brother,
The following circular purporting to call a convocation to be held on Saturday, the 18th inst., for the purpose of conferring the degrees Knight Kadosh 30th and 32nd having just reached us – [*here Montagu inserted a copy of Ashworth's Circular*] – we think it our duty to warn you against this illegal attempt to bestow degrees that we alone have a right to grant, according to our warrant and the Statutes of the A. and A. Rite (see Ancient Constitution) and to remind you that according to your O. B. you cannot even visit this or any other illegal body."

793 Volume IV, p.119.

794 **Rochdale Chapter**
"'The annual convocation of this chapter was held in the Masonic Rooms, Rochdale, on Saturday last, the 18th inst., Bro. William Roberts, P.M.W.Sov., in the Chair, in the unavoidable absence of the Most Wise Sov. Bro John Barker. The chapter was opened at 3.30, in the presence of illustrious and distinguished princes of the order, who honoured the chapter by accepting an invitation to be present. The minutes of the previous convocation having been read and confirmed, the muster-roll called, and other business transacted, Bro. John Fothergill, Red Cross Knight of Babylon and Knight of the East and West, was received, regularly exalted, and admitted a member of the Order according to ancient rites and ceremonies. After the ceremony, which was very efficiently performed by the respective officers, Bro. Prince, 1st Gen., was installed M.W.S. of the chapter for the ensuing twelve months, and appointed as his officers the following, Richard Hankinson, H.P., James Holroyd, 1st Gen; William Ashworth, 2nd Gen.; Robert Butterworth, Grand Marshal; John Fothergill, Raphael; Robert Whitworth, Grand Chancellor; William Roberts, P.M.W.S., Herald; William Briggs, Organist; Benjamin Toulson, Captain of Guard. The ceremony being ended, the convocation was closed, after having disposed of several matters which had been brought before the members, when several members formed themselves into a convocation of the Holy Order of K.H. etc."

795 "The inaugural ceremony of this convocation was held in the Masonic Rooms, Ann Street, Rochdale, on Saturday last, the 18th Inst. The convocation was formed at 6.30 when the Grand Chancellor *pro tem* read a letter he had received dated '33, Golden Square, London. Feb. 16th' and signed 'J.M.P. Montagu, 33°, Gd. Sec. Gen.', also several letters and telegrams that had been sent to him and other brethren in reference thereto – [*here follows a copy of Montagu's Circular Letter*].
"It was then unanimously agreed to proceed with the ceremony. The Supreme Grand Council having no authority whatever to assume to themselves alone the right to grant or confer those degrees, or to interfere with those who having had these rites handed down to them, as having been conferred from time immemorial, the ceremony was therefore proceeded with, and several members of the Order of Rose Croix &c. duly admitted by ancient rites and ceremonies to the degrees &c."

796 A fine piece of impertinence! The Report concludes "The brethren afterwards adjourned to a banquet provided by Bro. Butterworth of the Golden Fleece Hotel, in his usual *recherché* style, which was most heartily discussed (*sic*) and enjoyed. The cloth having been removed, the usual loyal and Masonic toasts were duly proposed and responded to by the several brethren. The visitors and sister chapters were severally responded to by the distinguished visitors."
This further confirms the probability that Montagu's efforts had not been uniformly successful. In view of the subsequent correspondence quoted below, it is not impossible that some of the visitors came from Palatine Chapter in Manchester.

797 'A MASON WHO BELIEVES IN HIS OBLIGATION', *The Freemason*, Vol.IV, p.169, 18th March 1871.

798 The anonymous writer concluded by saying:
"I am sorry to see the force of evil example is soon felt, and that some of the members of the Rochdale Chapter of Rose Croix, have held a meeting for the purpose of conferring the 30° and 32° which they have no more right to give than the *M.A.* or *D.D.* of Oxford or Cambridge. The Craft in general must have a very good idea of what these so-called degrees are worth when I inform my brethren that I have learnt, on very good authority, that the sum charged to such candidates as may be gulled will not exceed 1s. 6d."

799 *The Freemason* Vol. IV, p.184, 25th March 1871.

800 *The Freemason* Volume IV, 1st April 1871. In the Report of the Meeting, the wrong derivation of the name of the Encampment is again repeated; after the Installation of his successor, "The immediate P.E.C., Sir Kt. Royds, presented the Encampment with £5. 5s. to purchase a vote for the Boys' School, in commemoration of his having sat as E.C. in the encampment named after his uncle, Sir Kt. Royds, the Grand Commander for Lancashire ..."

801 J.S. Ross, John Ashworth, jun. (the 2nd Herald in the Encampment), and Thomas Burgess. The Degree may have differed little from that later adopted by the Grand Council of the Allied Masonic Degrees. Those Installed were addressed as 'Sir Knight Cousin'. Some may recollect that the victor in the debate is told "thou shalt sit next to me and shalt be called my cousin".

802 *The Freemason* Vol. IV, 1st April 1871.

803 *The Freemason*, Vol. IV, p.202, 1st April 1871.

804 For example, on 17th March 1870, John Yarker had been present when Clement Molineux Royds was Installed as Eminent Commander of the 'Albert' Encampment of Knights Templar. *The Freemason*, Vol III p.145, 26 March 1870.

805 Ibid, 22nd April 1871.

806 That the importance of the meeting was well recognised is demonstrated by the attendance of Brethren from many parts of the country – for example, Emra Holmes from Essex, the Revd.

Charles Spencer-Stanhope from his Parish at Crowton in Cheshire, and Lord Eliot from Cornwall.

807 John Mandleberg, *Ancient and Accepted*, pp.86-89, QCCC Ltd.,1995.

808 See full transcript in Appendix C.

809 Albert Royds was still alive up to 1890, when his death was reported to the Supreme Council.

810 Matthews, *loc. cit.,* p.18.

811 One of the last records of a "33rd Degree" meeting at Bottoms appears in the earliest Minute Book of the Prince Edward Council which had recently accepted the jurisdiction of the newly formed Council of the Allied Masonic Degrees:
"Station House, Bottoms, Stansfield May 7th 1871 This being a regular Meeting Convened by Circular the Holy Tabernacle of the Antient 33 was opened in the presence of

William Roberts	P.G.H.P.
Joseph Greenwood	F – P
John Knight	S – P
Thomas Schofield	Th – P
Mitchell Helliwell	Four – P
James Lord	
John Watson	
William Shackleton	

When C. Sir Kts. Frederick Whitaker and George Normanton were regularly prepared and admitted Friends & Pillars of our H. Temple." Price, *op. cit.,* p.47.

812 It is possible that Brother Brockbank affiliated; a 'G.P.Brockbank, of whose Advancement to the Thirtieth Degree there is no record, was further Advanced to the 31° by the Supreme Council on 12th February 1873.

813 In view of the Masonic activity in Rochdale – for example, it was also the home of 'The Grand Lodge of St. Lawrence the Martyr', a constituent Founder of the Grand Council of the Allied Masonic Degrees – it is remarkable that the Supreme Council in London received no Petition for a Rose Croix Chapter in Rochdale until that for Rochdale St. Chad Chapter, Warranted as No.494, in January 1956.

It is, however, curious, that, in December 1872, William Ashworth, the 'Grand Chancellor' considered it appropriate to write to the Supreme Council in London seeking a dispensation to allow members of the A & A Rite to appear in their regalia at a 'Royal Masonic Ball' which was to be held in Rochdale. Montagu, the Grand Secretary General, replied courteously that the Supreme Council had always considered that the permission of the P.G.M. of the Craft Province in which a Ball was to take place was quite sufficient to justify the members of the A & A Rite appearing in their distinctive regalia.

814 John Marshall was Initiated in Philanthropic Lodge No.304 before 1861. He was Perfected as a Prince 'Rosa Croix' at Bottoms in 1873. He did not apparently affiliate, but was again Perfected in Prince of Wales Chapter No.69 at Huddersfield under the Supreme Council on 6th January 1878, and Advanced as a GEKKH 30° in London on 26th March 1884.

Marshall was particularly active in the Allied Masonic Degrees, obtaining the Warrant for Prince Edward Council ('G') in 1892 and being appointed Grand Senior Deacon in the same year, and also in the OSM (Grand Guide, 1897).

I am indebted to Ill.˙.Bro. Brian Price, OBE, 30° for these biographical details.

815 Several Degrees were worked at Bottoms in addition to the 'Rosa Croix', and, generally speaking, the same Brethren were involved in all of them. On 11th May 1892 some of these Brethren, among them John Marshall, received from the Earl of Euston a Warrant for which they had Petitioned for the Prince Edward Council of the Allied Masonic Degrees (now 'Letter G'). It is hardly conceivable that the decision to Petition the Supreme Council for a Warrant was unconnected with this move. See Price, *op.cit.,* p.51 *et seq.*

816 (a) It is sometimes not appreciated that 'Time Immemorial' is a precise Masonic term implying that the body concerned was in existence before the erection of the controlling body to which it gives its allegiance. The Supreme Council thereby recognised the authenticity of the Chapter which had worked at Bottoms before the Council itself received its Patent.
(b) On 24th July 1893 the Supreme Council signed a Concordat with the Grand Council of the Allied Masonic Degrees, in which the former disclaimed any authority over the Degree of 'The Red Cross of Babylon' and the latter over the 15th, 16th and 17th Degrees of the Ancient and Accepted Rite, "being the Red Cross of Babylon", adding with characteristic Masonic casuistry "that these Degrees, although in some respects similar, are not identical but separate and distinct".
(c) The importance of the occasion was recognised by High Greenwood Chapter being consecrated at Eastwood by the Sovereign Grand Commander, the Earl of Lathom, the Lieutenant Grand Commander, Captain Nathaniel Philips, and the Grand Secretary General, Hugh Sandeman, attended by Charles Banister, the Inspector General for the North-Eastern District. Two months later the Chapter presented the Supreme Council with a copy of the book *Freemasonry at Bottoms, Eastwood*. In 1896 the Chapter received the Council's permission to change its place of Meeting to the Masonic Rooms, Hebden Bridge. In 1992 the Chapter celebrated its Centenary, but, apart from this, since accepting its Warrant 1892, its communications with the Supreme Council in London have not been other than routine.

Essay 21
The Supreme Council of England, etc., 1845-2004 – an overview

Unlike the position of the United Grand Lodge of England in the Craft, the Supreme Council of England and Wales and its Districts and Chapters Overseas is not 'The Mother Council of the World' – that privilege belongs to the Supreme Council of the Southern Jurisdiction of the United States of America. It has, however, gained considerable International respect by its adherence both to the principles of 'The Grand Constitutions of 1786' and to the precepts of United Grand Lodge. In particular, it rejects involvement in religious and political affairs, topics which in some countries are less narrowly defined, and national interests are seen as proper matters for both the Craft and the Ancient and Accepted Rite to propagate[817].

It would be naïve to deny that from time to time the Supreme Council of England has encountered difficulties both within its own jurisdiction, and in its dealings with the outside world. In 1845 Dr. Crucefix made his urgent request for a Patent to the Supreme Council of the Northern Jurisdiction of the U.S.A. in order to forestall the possible actions of a French body deemed by many to be irregular, in particular by the Supreme Councils in the U.S.A. Dr. Leeson's insistence on maintaining formal relations with the Supreme Council of the Grand Orient of France then caused the Council's American sponsors to withdraw recognition for half a dozen years until relations were restored through the efforts of Henry Udall. Meanwhile, within the English Jurisdiction the establishment of the Council had been well received by the governing body of the Order which this most affected – the Grand Conclave of the Religious and Military Order of the Knights Templar, which was explicitly not only Christian but Trinitarian. For many years, Knights Templar had progressed in their Encampments to the Degrees of 'Rosae Crucis' and 'Kadosh', Degrees which, after 1846, the Grand Conclave surrendered to the newly established Supreme Council. None of those concerned in this transfer had any doubt that under the Supreme Council the 'Rose Croix' Degree would similarly promulgate Trinitarian Christian principles[818]. Even so, the transfer was not at once accepted by all Knights Templar Encampments, especially those in the West and South-West of England.

In England, both the Craft and the majority of the Orders outside it are at least ostensibly democratic – the Rulers, supreme and subordinate, are openly elected by those of its Members who are qualified to do so. A Supreme Council, on the other hand, is a 'self-perpetuating oligarchy' – a new Member is elected by the unanimous vote of those already on the Council in accordance with the provisions of 'The Grand Constitutions of 1786' which govern the conduct of all Supreme Councils. Furthermore, there is no provision in the 'Grand Constitutions' for any periodic assembly similar to the *Quarterly Communication* of Grand Lodge. In 1870 this failure to communicate was leading to much unfavourable comment in the Masonic press.

There were two principal reasons for this. First, the Knights Templar in Bath had accepted the guidance of the Grand Conclave of the Order and had petitioned the Supreme Council for a Warrant for a Rose Croix Chapter, Antiquity[819]. The Supreme Council considered that, having obtained this Warrant, the Chapter then ignored the Council's Rules and Regulations. After a wordy exchange of correspondence, the Chapter and its Members were suspended. Many Brethren who were unaware of the full facts of the case were persuaded that this was an unmerited and high-handed action.

At the same time, the Supreme Council was having problems with another Order which was seeking to establish itself in England. Early in the nineteenth century two somewhat similar 'Orders' had surfaced, that of 'Memphis' in Egypt and that of 'Misraim' in Italy. The latter had been brought to France in about 1810 at about the same time as the Rite of Memphis also appeared there. For a time each of these two Rites seem to have been given a measure of recognition by the French Masonic authorities. The Rite of Misraim attracted sufficient Candidates in England for the Grand Secretary of the United Grand Lodge to send a circular in 1856 to all Lodges under its jurisdiction condemning the Order, and prohibiting English Brethren from associating with it.[820]

Both Memphis and Misraim were cumbersome Orders with a multitude of Degrees. Early in the second half of the nineteenth century they were together condensed in America into a single Rite of Thirty-three Degrees, possibly as a competitor to the Ancient and Accepted Rite. To become a member of this so-called *Ancient and*

Primitive Rite would violate the Obligation taken by each Prince Rose Croix. In spite of this, a Brother from Lancashire, John Yarker, vigorously propagated the 'Order', even though he himself had been through the Chair of a Rose Croix Chapter. The Supreme Councils of the two Jurisdictions in the U.S.A. concurred with the English Council in condemning the Rite as spurious, the more so when Yarker, having by this time been expelled from the Ancient and Accepted Rite, set up a 'Council of Rites' claiming authority over a variety of Degrees including the 'Rose Croix'.

By 1871 the Supreme Council was, however, sufficiently well established to wish to make several major changes in its organisation of the Rite. It had purchased permanent Headquarters at Number 33 Golden Square in 1868, and now wished to extend these by using its accumulated funds to buy a neighbouring property where a Masonic Hall could be built. It was further considered that it would be appropriate to Register the Supreme Council under the Companies Act. In addition, an alliance with other Orders was being considered. Mindful of the criticisms about its high-handedness, the Supreme Council convened "A Grand Supreme Chapter of Rose Croix" in May 1871 where these matters were discussed. The Meeting was well attended by Brethren from all parts of the country. John Montagu, the Grand Secretary General, took the opportunity to explain at length the Council's actions in respect of both 'Antiquity' and John Yarker. 'The Grand Supreme Chapter' accepted these explanations and also endorsed the other proposed actions, although there was a vigorous debate about the custody of the Funds of the Order, which resulted two years later in the appointment of a professional Accountant to prepare an Annual Statement. In spite of the success of this Meeting, the Supreme Council did not again find it necessary to enlist the support of the Membership in this way.

The Supreme Council was wasting no time in proceeding with the Treaty with the other Orders. This had in fact been signed in draft two months before the 'Supreme Grand Chapter' had been told about it. The parties to the 'Tripartite Treaty' were the Grand Lodge of Mark Master Masons, the Grand Conclave of the Knights Templar and the Supreme Council of the Ancient and Accepted Rite. The intention was to secure unanimity between the three principal recognised Orders outside the Craft on two matters in particular – on the one hand the recognition of other Orders, and on the other that a Brother expelled for a Masonic offence by any one of the three should be deemed to be expelled by the other two. Provision was made for a 'Judicial Committee' to which Appeals against Expulsion could be made. The Mark Grand Lodge was the last of the three to ratify the Treaty on 6th June 1871. Within two years the Treaty effectively ended the threat posed by Yarker's 'Council of Rites'. Yarker continued his activities for several years, but failed to attract sufficient followers to cause more than an irritation to the established Orders.

The recognition of the status of the Supreme Council was underlined when in 1874 the Earl of Carnarvon, one of the leading Statesmen of the day, accepted the Office of Sovereign Grand Commander. Not only this, but in December of that year, the Prince of Wales, already a Past Grand Master of the United Grand Lodge, agreed to become the Grand Patron of the Order. At a well-attended Meeting on 12th December 1874, the Degrees from the Fourth to the Thirty-second were conferred by name on the Prince. He then went through the full Ceremony of the Thirty-third Degree, before briefly taking the throne of the Sovereign Grand Commander and addressing the gathering, after he had been duly proclaimed and his Banner displayed[821].

Although the Patent for the Supreme Council from the Northern Jurisdiction of the United States of America described it only as 'for England', within half a dozen years it had described itself as 'for England and Wales and the Dependencies of the British Crown'. This implicitly denied any involvement of the Supreme Council of Scotland in the Ancient and Accepted Rite in what were still known as the 'British Colonies' overseas. As early as 1857, when only a few Chapters had been Warranted in England, the Supreme Council was taking steps to establish the Rite under its own jurisdiction as far afield as Australia and India. By 1861 there was a Chapter in Gibraltar, by 1868 several Chapters had been Warranted in Canada, and there was a Chapter in Malta in 1871.

The Supreme Council of Scotland did not accept its exclusion from the British Dependencies, particularly those in which there were Craft Lodges Warranted by the Grand Lodge of Scotland. Within the Craft there is no restriction on more than one jurisdiction Warranting Lodges in territories where there is no Grand Lodge established – the United Grand Lodge claims only to be that of *England*. The position in the Ancient and Accepted Rite, governed by 'The Grand Constitutions of 1786', is different. The relevant provisions assert that there can only be one Supreme Council in each European Kingdom *and its Empire*. When a Supreme Council is so established, the 'Kingdom and its Empire' are deemed 'Occupied Territory', and no other Council may Warrant a subsidiary body of the Rite therein. The anomaly of there being three Supreme Councils in the British Isles was tactfully overlooked both at home and abroad. But by styling itself 'of England and Wales and the Dependencies of the British Crown', the Supreme Council was implicitly claiming that the 'British Empire' was for all practical purposes the 'English Empire', a sentiment in which many contemporary Englishmen would almost certainly have concurred. The Scots thought otherwise, and claimed as much right as the English Supreme Council to Warrant Chapters in the British Dependencies, where the English Council considered these to be illegal interlopers.

The Scots also claimed to have established Consistories overseas in which to confer the Thirtieth 'Kadosh' Degree. The English Council doubted whether this was being conferred therein in the presence of three S.G.I.G.s of the Thirty-third Degree, as was mandated in 'The Grand Constitutions of 1786'. More importantly, there was the real prospect of English Princes Rose Croix seeking to be Advanced in these Scottish bodies contrary to their Obligations to their own Supreme Council, which only conferred the Degree *in extenso* at its Grand East in England. Matters were only resolved in Canada, where the Scottish Supreme Council had established Chapters in New Brunswick, when the Canadian Brethren made it clear that they were no longer prepared to be subordinate to a Supreme Council three thousand miles distant across the Atlantic Ocean. After protracted negotiations, the English Council gave a Patent for a Supreme Council for Canada which absorbed both the English and the Scottish Chapters[822].

While affairs were being concluded in Canada there had been a realignment of the United Orders of the Temple and Hospital in Britain. Less than a year after the Tripartite Treaty had been ratified by all three parties, an attempt was made to unite the three independent Great Priories of England, Scotland and Ireland into a single body, a Convent General with the Prince of Wales as its Grand Master. The Great Priory of Scotland foresaw the problems to which this might give rise, and withdrew from the discussions. However, in December 1873 those of England and Ireland were united under a new Constitution.

The three English governing bodies did not appreciate the consequences of the Tripartite Treaty which they had just signed until a Brother exercised his right to appeal to the Judicial Committee[823]. The Supreme Council then concluded "that the Tripartite Treaty had been, ipso facto, terminated by the Order of the Temple ceasing to be a Supreme Body on the formation of the Convent General"[824]. Considerable legalistic argument took place with no resolution of the problem becoming immediately apparent while the Supreme Council became involved with more pressing matters.

Since its inception the Supreme Council of England had maintained friendly relations with many overseas Supreme Councils[825], but had shown little enthusiasm for International Conferences. However, in 1875 it considered that several outstanding matters could be settled at a major gathering to be held in Lausanne. Its concern was mainly with 'Jurisdiction' – which existing Supreme Councils were properly constituted, and where they could regularly be established in future – and then to secure agreement on the prohibition of 'encroachment' by one Supreme Council on another's territory. In addition, perhaps the time had now come to review the provisions of 'The Grand Constitutions of 1786', specifically the need for three 'Thirty-thirds' to be present in person at the conferment of the 'Kadosh' Degree[826]. All this, it was suggested, could be embodied in a 'Universal Treaty'. The sponsor of the Council was Albert Pike, and although his Council was to send no representatives to Lausanne, he wished to see an International Governing Body of the Ancient and Accepted Rite exercising considerable powers to be embodied in a written Constitution.

The Conference was well attended even though no American representatives were present. It was well known that Albert Pike had long held the view that Membership of the Ancient and Accepted Rite, like that of Craft Masonry, could include those who, while expressing a belief in the G.A.O.T.U., professed Faiths other than Trinitarian Christianity. In other words, Pike considered that the Rite was as 'Universal' as Craft Masonry[827]. For this the English Delegation[828] would surely have been prepared, but its Members were evidently taken unawares by European anti-clericalism. The first topic discussed was the fundamental basis of recognised Freemasonry world-wide – the characterisation of, and the expression of belief in, the Creator of the Universe. Many French 'Intellectuals' were neither deists nor theists. They were agnostics, who, while accepting that there was a Creative Principle, denied that It was a Person Who manifested Himself by revelation[829].

To reconcile these views so that the Conference could get down to what the English Delegation considered was its real business, the latter, perhaps naïvely[830], accepted the formula "Principe Créateur" as a synonym for the G.A.O.T.U.[831] It is possible that the Supreme Council of Scotland was more aware of European ideology than were their confréres in England. Lindsay Mackersey, the Scottish Grand Secretary General, who was the only Scottish representative at the Conference, had wished to discuss forthcoming events before it took place, but in the current climate of relations with the Scottish Council, the English Council had been unwilling to do so. As soon as Mackersey learnt of the adoption of the ambiguous definition, he declined to accept this casuistry. He left Lausanne, leaving a letter with the Congress in which he set out the views of his own Council:

"As Masonic Principles have been understood and practiced (*sic*) in this country from time immemorial no one could, or can, be admitted to the First Degree of our Order who does no openly profess his belief in the existence of a God, and that in words which admit of no doubtful meaning."

Ignoring this timely reminder, the English Delegation enthusiastically participated in the work of the Congress, and three documents were accepted by its final plenary session. These were a 'Declaration' which included the ambiguous words 'Creative Principle', a revision of 'The Grand Constitutions of 1786' which included most of the jurisdictional alterations which were the particular English concern, and a 'Treaty of Alliance' which defined the "intimate Union and confederation between the Supreme Councils of the Ancient and Accepted Scottish Rite" which Albert Pike was anxious to see[832].

The Supreme Council for England ratified the work of its Delegates on 12th October 1875, and agreed to join the Confederation. It immediately acted on the agreed definition of Jurisdiction, its Circular sent to its overseas Chapters announcing this being greatly resented by the Scottish Council[833]. The latter wrote indignantly to the 'Secretariat' of the Conference in Switzerland, complaining about both the jurisdictional decision and the inclusion of the words 'Creative Principle' in the Declaration, sending a copy to the English Council and also to Albert Pike. The English Supreme Council defended the decisions on the grounds that if Mackersey did not like them he should not have withdrawn from the Conference, and insisting that the words 'Creative Principle' were inclusive of a belief in a Personal God. Pike refused to accept this; to him the concept introduced 'a new paganism'[834]. Certainly that was far from the minds of the God-fearing gentlemen who had comprised the English Delegation, and Montagu wrote a long Memoir to refute any such idea. This was printed and circulated in May 1876.

While this dispute was in progress, the Supreme Council had been informed that the Grand Lodge of Mark Master Masons had abrogated the Tripartite Treaty, but was still anxious to have a similar alliance. It proposed that representatives should meet and draw up a new Treaty. It is not, perhaps, surprising that while dealing with the aftermath of the Lausanne Congress, the Supreme Council should respond by writing that "it did not consider any advantage would be gained, at present, in forming a new Treaty".

At meetings with the Scottish Lieutenant Grand Commander, Lord Rosslyn, the English Council made strenuous efforts to resolve the jurisdictional problem, but to no avail. The French Council was equally intransigent about the 'Creative Principle'. In November 1877 the English Supreme Council withdrew recognition from that of Scotland. In the following year it was proposed to hold an International Conference of the Federation envisaged at Lausanne. In the meantime the Grand Orient of France explicitly rejected the idea of the G.A.O.T.U. as a Personal God, and the Supreme Council quickly followed the lead of United Grand Lodge in severing relations with it. The new Conference fell by the wayside. The English Council received no satisfactory reply to its request to each member of the 'Confederation' that its Council should confirm unequivocally the necessity of a belief in a Personal God[835]. It thereupon withdrew from the Confederation[836].

The Supreme Councils of England and Scotland remained estranged for a further ten years. However, in 1889, Hugh Sandeman was corresponding informally with a member of the Scottish Council, Sir Henry Morland[837]. In August Sandeman gave Morland a draft of three basic conditions which might lead to a reconciliation, emphasising that these were no more than 'suggestions'[838]. In laying these before the Supreme Council Sandeman pointed out that to adhere to "exclusive Jurisdiction" would prevent any compromise ever being reached. A Meeting was held in Edinburgh[839] at which Sandeman's 'suggestions' were considerably amended. The wishes of neither Supreme Council were wholly satisfied; for example, the English Supreme Council had to abandon its claim to "exclusive Jurisdiction" in the Colonies and Dependencies of the British Crown. But, in the interests of unity, in October 1889 each of the three 'Home' Supreme Councils signed and sealed the Concordat[840] which, updated from time to time, today still harmoniously governs the relations between them[841].

In the summer of 1894 the Convent General was, in the words of Frederick Smyth, about to take its "last shuddering breath"[842]. It had been popular with few, and had neither "lived respected" nor "died regretted". With the dispute with the Supreme Council of Scotland happily concluded, the English Council sought to revive the Tripartite Treaty. The principal objective of the earlier Treaty had been to ensure that a Brother expelled from one of the three Orders should be, *ipso facto*, deemed also to be expelled by each of the other two. In July 1894, after a lengthy discussion, it was concluded that this could be more easily be achieved by each governing body making such a provision in its own Rules and Regulations without the need for a formal Treaty. However, nothing had been said about the recognition of other Masonic Orders outside the Craft. In the preceding year the Supreme Council had been confronted with a problem arising out of this. In 1880 a Grand Council of the Allied Masonic Degrees had been set up to take "under its protection the Orders of Grand High Priest, St. Laurence the Martyr, Red Cross of Babylon and Knights of Constantinople"[843]. At the time this had attracted no particular attention from the Supreme Council, some of whose Members were already Members of one or other of these Orders. Indeed, in 1893 the Grand Master was the Earl of Euston, himself a member of the Supreme Council.

However, in June 1893 it became apparent that the Degree of the Red Cross of Babylon had much in common with the Fifteenth, Sixteenth and Seventeenth Degrees of the Ancient and Accepted Rite. The matter was resolved at a meeting between Members of the Supreme Council and of the Allied Grand Council. Since all present were Members of the Higher Degrees of the Ancient and Accepted Rite, it is perhaps not surprising that the meeting was able to come to a satisfactory conclusion, even if there is an element of Masonic casuistry in the statement in which this is set out[844].

These questions of inter-relationship having been settled, the Supreme Council was able to devote more time to the administration of the Order itself. In 1899 it broke with its custom of the preceding half century. Hitherto, a single manuscript copy of the Ritual was issued, together with its Warrant, to each new Chapter. In 1899 the Supreme Council authorised the printing of an official Ritual which could be purchased by any Brother of the Order. By the end of the twentieth century 17 further editions had been printed, some with minor amendments, and others with major additions such as the insertion in 1917 of Scriptural passages after the last four steps of the ladder.

In 1910 the Council sold its premises at 33 Golden Square, and purchased its present 'Grand East' at Number 10 Duke Street, where the existing house was demolished and re-built. On 1st December 1910 the Foundation Stone was laid by the Sovereign Grand Commander, the Earl of Dartrey, with all due Masonic Ceremonial, but no Opening Ceremony is recorded. The Minutes of the Meeting of the Council on 18th September 1911 are simply headed "10 Duke Street S.W." without further comment. The Council occupied the whole building until 1994, when the Grand Temple was refurbished, and, in the face of increasing costs, part of the premises was converted to be let off for office accommodation. A major part of this operation was financed by the generosity of the Brethren of the Order, Chapters which had contributed appropriately being allowed to wear a silver Rose on the collar of the MWS.

At the outbreak of the Great War in 1914, there were 166 Chapters under the jurisdiction of the Supreme Council, of which 56 were overseas. Its finances, however, were under some strain as a result of the acquisition of No.10 Duke Street. For nearly five years the administration of the Order was conducted by the Grand Secretary General, John Tower, often virtually single-handed[845]. However, during these War years, not only were fifteen new Chapters Warranted[846], but the Council's financial position was restored.

For many years the Supreme Council had from time to time constituted itself into "The Supreme Council Chapter Rose Croix"[847]. In 1921 it was considered that it would be convenient if the Supreme Council had also a regularly Warranted Chapter. The Warrant of Morning Star Chapter[848], fortuitously with the Number '33', having been surrendered in 1892, the Supreme Council petitioned itself to transfer the Warrant to 10 Duke Street. Not surprisingly, the Petition was acceded to, and the resuscitated Chapter was opened on 27th July 1921 with the Sovereign Grand Commander, the Earl of Donoughmore, in the Chair[849].

On 11th February 1921 two of the sons of King George the Fifth, the Prince of Wales[850] and the Duke of York[851], had been Perfected in United Chapter No.169. In 1932 each agreed to accept Advancement to the Thirty-third Degree. Even for such eminent Brethren this could not be done until each had been placed in the Chair of a Chapter[852]. At an Emergency Meeting the Duke of York was Installed as MWS of 'Morning Star', while the Prince of Wales was Installed as MWS of the Supreme Council Chapter[853]. Both were then Advanced to the 33° and elected Honorary Members of the Supreme Council[854].

The Ancient and Accepted Rite in England survived the Second World War with the same stoicism as it had weathered the First. A minor departure from former practice was the engagement for the first time of two ladies to assist with the clerical work[855]. Because of the danger from air-raids, the Library was removed to the home of the Sovereign Grand Commander, Lord Donoughmore, at Chelwood Beacon. On the evening of 23rd February 1944 10 Duke Street was severely damaged "by blast from Bombs on the top of London Library and at the junction of Duke Street and King Street", the caretaker and his wife fortunately escaping injury.

In 1960 the Supreme Council Warranted a Chapter in Finland, and by 1976 there were eighteen Chapters under its jurisdiction there. Evidently it was then appropriate to grant a Patent for an independent Supreme Council for Finland and this was duly done. Within the Commonwealth, each of the Scottish and English Supreme Councils had Warranted several Chapters in both Australia and New Zealand, many of the Brethren of which were also anxious to achieve self-determination. A Supreme Council for Australia, formed from both Scottish and English Chapters, was Patented in 1985, 151 of the latter subscribing to the new Supreme Council, although seven elected to remain under the English Council. Several of the Scottish Chapters also failed to join the Australian Supreme Council, and others were Warranted by the Scottish Council after its erection. The resulting situation has not been altogether satisfactory. When the Supreme Council for New Zealand was Patented in 1994, only one of the fifty 'English' Chapters retained its attachment to 10 Duke Street. Because of the prior formation of the 'Supreme Council of South Africa' by the Dutch Chapters in the territory, it has been impossible to act in a similar way in South Africa, but in 1992 much of the government of the English Chapters there has been ceded to a 'Branch Council', presiding over seven Districts with a total of 58 Chapters.

In the Year-Book for 2003, the Supreme Council for 'England' is shown as presiding over 886 Chapters, of which now only 129 are overseas[856].

Appendix A

CONCORDAT
WITH
IRELAND AND SCOTLAND
(See Rule 8)

The following concordat has been entered into between the Supreme Councils of England, Ireland and Scotland respecting the conferring of Degrees:

(a) That no private Chapter under either Supreme Council shall confer the 18th Degree for a fee of less than £10.00, or upon a Brother hailing from a Sister Jurisdiction, unless by special permission from the Supreme Council of the country to which his Craft Lodge belongs. Nor shall a Rose Croix Mason be affiliated to a Chapter belonging to a jurisdiction other than that in which he was perfected without the special permission of the Supreme Council of his allegiance. But any Brother who has affiliated into a Lodge belonging to another Constitution from that under which he was initiated, and has been recorded in the books of its Grand Lodge, shall be at liberty to apply for perfection to a Sovereign Chapter of Princes Rose Croix belonging to the Constitution to which he has come to belong.

(b) That the 30th degree (or Higher Degree) shall not be conferred on any Brother unless he is specially elected thereto by the Supreme Council of his allegiance, and that no Consistory abroad shall be held except for the purpose of conferring the Degree on Brethren so elected, and under special authority from the said Supreme Council.

(c) That a Brother having sworn allegiance to either Supreme Council shall not receive any other degree of the Ancient and Accepted Rite from any other masonic body without the permission of the Supreme Council to which he has originally given such allegiance.

(d) That no Chapter shall be founded in any place outside the British Isles where, or in the neighbourhood of which, there is already a Chapter working under a Sister Jurisdiction without communicating with the Supreme Council of that Jurisdiction with a view to obtaining its approval. In the event of that Supreme Council objecting to the founding of such Chapter, the Supreme Council of the third jurisdiction may be asked to act as arbitrator and its decision shall be accepted as final.

(The Rules of the Supreme Council 33° of the Ancient and Accepted Rite for England and Wales and its Districts and Chapters Overseas)

Appendix B

The definition of *The Degree of the Red Cross of Babylon*

The meeting to consider the status of *The Red Cross of Babylon* was held on the 18th July 1893, and was attended by:

On behalf of the Supreme Council of the Ancient and Accepted Rite

Captain Nathaniel Philips 33°, Lieutenant Grand Commander
The Earl of Limerick 33°, Grand Chancellor
Frank Richardson 33°, Grand Treasurer General

On behalf of the Grand Council of the Allied Masonic Degrees

The Earl of Euston 33°, Grand Master
Charles Matier 32°, Grand Secretary
W. J. Hughan, Hon. 32°

The following memorandum was subsequently signed by Captain Philips, on behalf of the Supreme Council, and by the Earl of Euston, on behalf of the Grand Council of the Allied Masonic Degrees.

It has been mutually and formally resolved and agreed between the Supreme Council of the 33° for England and Wales and the Colonies and Dependencies of the British Crown on the one part, and the Grand Council of the Allied Masonic Degrees on the other part.

1. The Supreme Council 33°∴ waive any right, authority or jurisdiction over the Degree denominated the "Red Cross of Babylon" which is conferred by authority of the Grand Council of the Allied Masonic Degrees to enable English Knights Templar to gain admission to Masonic Bodies of that Order in America and elsewhere.
2. The said Grand Council of the Allied Masonic Degrees disclaim any right, authority or jurisdiction over the 15°∴, 16°∴, and 17°∴ of the Ancient and Accepted Rite called respectively Knights of the Sword or East, Princes of Jerusalem, and Knights of the East and West, being the Red Cross of Babylon.
3. To prevent misunderstanding in the future it is declared that these degrees, although in some respects similar, are not identical but separate and distinct.

Given at London this twenty fourth day of July, One thousand eight hundred and ninety-three.

Appendix C

Freemasons' Hall
London
24th October 1859

Dear Sir and W.Master,

I am directed to inform you that it has come to the knowledge of the Board of General Purposes that there are at present existing in London and elsewhere in the country, spurious lodges claiming to be Freemasons.

I herewith furnish you with a copy of a certificate issued by a Lodge calling itself 'The Reformed Masonic Order of Memphis, or Rite of the Grand Lodge of Philadelphia', and holding its meetings at Stratford in Essex.

I am directed to caution you to be especially careful that no member of such body be permitted, under any circumstances, to have access to your lodge; and that you will remind the brethren that they can hold no communication with irregular lodges, without incurring the penalty of expulsion from the Order, and of liability to be proceeded against under Act 39, George III for taking part in meetings of illegal secret societies.

I am further to request that you will cause this letter to be read in open lodge, and the copy of this certificate to be preserved for future reference in case of necessity.

I remain, dear Sir and Brother

Yours fraternally

(signed)

WM. GRAY CLARKE, G.S.

---

817 For example, when Gheorge Comanescu, the Grand Master of the (unrecognised) National Grand Lodge of Romania met the Prime Minister, Radu Vasile, on 26th April 1998, the Press Report in the Bucharest daily newspaper *Currentul in Societate* stated that the Grand Master had "offered its support to the present Government, especially to bring some foreign investment into Romania".

818 At the level of the governing bodies, this transition was undoubtedly facilitated by the extensive common membership of the Supreme Council and the Grand Conclave.

819 Antiquity Chapter was later given the number 60.

820 See Appendix C.

821 This Banner is today on the First Floor landing of No. 10 Duke Street.

822 To establish a third Supreme Council in North America was apparently in violation of 'The Grand Constitutions of 1786', but it received the blessing of the 'Mother Council of the World', the Supreme Council of the Southern Jurisdiction of the U.S.A., whose Sovereign Grand Commander Albert Pike, constituted the Supreme Council for Canada on 16th October 1874.

823 Ill. Bro. Major Burgess, 31° who 'retired from the Order' in May 1874.

824 A & A, p.501.

825 Apart from its relations with its sponsor, the Supreme Council of the Northern Masonic Jurisdiction of the U.S.A., and its evident desire to receive the approval of the Supreme Council of Ireland for its early Meetings, as early as 1848 the Supreme Council welcomed representatives of that of 'the Brazils' to a meeting. A & A, p.15.

826 This requirement posed a particularly difficult problem for the Supreme Council in India where even if there were three 'Thirty-thirds' somewhere in the sub-continent, distances made it difficult for them to meet. The English Council wished an amendment to 'The Grand Constitutions' by which only one S.G.I.G. needed to be present, provided that he had the written consent of two others.

827 That the Ancient and Accepted Rite, and specifically the 18th 'Rose Croix' Degree, can be 'Universal' comes as a surprise even today to many English Brethren. This 'Universality' is, in fact, the case in the great majority of Supreme Councils throughout the world. The three virtues, Faith, Hope and Charity are regarded in these Councils not as Pauline but as universal virtues without which progress cannot be made towards a better world and the amelioration of man's condition. The Cross is considered only as a figure formed by twelve right-angles, which refer both to the Twelve Signs of the Zodiac, and to the twelve months of the year. The Degree is esteemed to convey a message of Hope, of Revival, of the certainty of the annual springtime regeneration, which is in itself a symbol of the hoped-for regeneration of mankind. The letters INRI, though quoted in some 'Universal' Rituals as an aside with the meanings attached to them in our Chapters, are stated to stand either for "Igne Natura Renovatur Integra' , 'Fire renews the whole of Nature', an interpretation ascribed to the old philosophers, or for "Indefesso Nisu Repellamus Ignorantiam", "We must banish Ignorance by unwearied efforts". For a detailed historical discussion of this, see Pierre Mollier, *Deux Siècles de Rite Écossais Ancien Accepté en France*, pp.171 *et seq.*, Éditions Dervy, 2004. The only Supreme Councils in which their subordinate Chapters work the 18th 'Rose Croix' Degree as Trinitarian Christian are those of the three 'Home Councils', England, Scotland and Ireland (at home and overseas in each case), Australia, New Zealand, Iceland (where the Rite comes under the National Grand Lodge of Iceland), Finland, and the Nordic Countries where the Rite forms part of a wide-embracing Christian Masonic system. The Supreme Council of England is in amity with various 'Universal' Supreme Councils, for example those of the Southern and Northern Jurisdictions of the U.S.A., Argentina, Brazil, France (the Supreme Council recognised by the GLNF, but *not* that of the Grand Orient) the Netherlands, Portugal and Switzerland, between which inter-visitation is freely permitted (2004), but the Year-Book and the Grand Secretary General should be consulted before it is undertaken.

828 John Montagu, Dr. Robert Hamilton and Hugh Sandeman.

829 The term 'agnostic' had been coined by Thomas Huxley six years before the Lausanne Conference was convened. It was intended to indicate a person who, while accepting that there was a First Cause of Creation, believed that man could only obtain knowledge of the Universe from perceptible material objects. Therefore, the nature of an imperceptible First Cause, and, *a fortiori*, Its Personality, were, by definition, unknowable. An agnostic therefore discounted both Revelation, the mainspring alike of Judaism, Christianity and Islam, and also the personal God whom these faiths believed to be its author. On the other hand, Universal Freemasonry, as proclaimed by all Regular Grand Lodges from Time Immemorial, was rooted in the belief that the G.A.O.T.U. was a personal Being Whose revealed will was recorded in the V.S.L.

830 Or, as the then Sovereign Grand Commander of the English Supreme Council M.˙.Ill.˙.Bro. Sir Trevor Matthews, wrote seventy-five years later in a letter to the Grand Secretary General, Ernest Dunn, "our representatives were not as wide awake as were those of Scotland". A & A, p.273.

831 It has even been suggested, though without any real evidence, that Montagu invented this formula so that discussions could start on the matters with which the English Delegation was primarily concerned.

832 Initially the "Union and confederation" could include only those Supreme Councils which were represented at the Conference – those of England and Wales, Belgium, Colon (for Cuba), France, Hungary, Italy (Turin), Peru, Portugal and Switzerland. The Conference intended that these should be joined by the Supreme Councils of Chile, Canada, those of the Northern and Southern Jurisdictions of the U.S.A., and of the Argentine Republic, Central America (Costa Rica), Mexico, Greece, New Granada (Colombia), Uruguay and Venezuela.

833 The definition of Jurisdiction was equally resented by the Supreme Council of the Southern Jurisdiction of the U.S.A. which was already in dispute with that of France about American Chapters in the (then) French Colony of the Sandwich Isles (Hawaii).

834 Pike was surprised that the reply of the Supreme Council had been signed by Lord Carnarvon. He said that "if we were to adopt the phrase, our sanctuaries would be abandoned, and our rituals would be annihilated". He contemptuously dismissed the views of the Belgian Bro. Riche who wrote that in Europe to profess belief in a personal God was possible, but that to impose such a belief was not, Pike replying that to reject a Personal God was to cease to be a Mason.

835 The formula put forward by Hugh Sandeman, the Grand Secretary General, was "La Francmaçonnerie proclame, comme elle a proclamé dès son origine, l'existence de Dieu, le Grand Architecte de l'Univers, et l'immortalité de l'âme."

836 The matter of the Congress of Lausanne is dealt with at length in A & A, pp.269-309, and also in C. John Mandleberg, *The Lausanne Congress of 1875*, Heredom, Vol.6, pp.83-111, (1997).

837 Both Sandeman and Morland had been District Grand Masters in the Craft in India, Sandeman under the English Constitution, and Morland under the Scottish.

838 Sandeman's 'suggestions' were:

 1. That no private Chapter under either Sup: Council should confer the 18° for a fee of less than £3.3.0, or upon a brother hailing from a Sister Jurisdiction unless by special permission from the Sup.˙.Co.˙. of the Country to which his Craft Lodge belongs.

 2. That the 30th or higher degrees be conferred by each Sup.˙.Co.˙. on Brn: abroad by Patent only, and that no Consistory or Tribunal be allowed to work outside the Grand East of each Sup.˙.Co.˙..

 3. That a Brother having sworn Allegiance to either Sup.˙.Co.˙. shall not receive any other degree of the A. and A. Rite from any other masonic Body without the permission of the Sup.˙.Co.˙. to which he has given Allegiance.

839 At the Meeting which took place in August 1889 the

English Council was represented by Nathaniel Philips and Hugh Sandeman, and that of Scotland by Sir Henry Morland and Lindsay Mackersey.

840 There was one dissentient voice on the English Supreme Council. Major-General Henry Clerk, the Grand Treasurer General resigned from the Council rather than assent to the terms of the Concordat.

841 See Appendix A.

842 Frederick Smyth, *Brethren in Chivalry, 1791-1991*, p.62, Lewis Masonic, London, 1991.

843 Harold Prestige, *The Order of the Allied Masonic Degrees*, p.14, Second Edition by Frederick Smyth, 1998.

844 See Appendix B.

845 In January 1919 Tower wrote to the Recorder of Percy Chapter No.113 in Australia, Bro. Gurr:
   "This year I have had to type them [*the forms for the annual Chapter returns*] myself as I am working practically single-handed; my Clerk having been called up". A & A p.543.

846 Three of these were overseas – Lukis No.188 (Delhi), Hawkes Bay No.199 (New Zealand), and Lily of Kasauli No.200 (India).

847 In its earliest days this had been done for the purpose of affiliating 'Rosae Crucis' Brethren. The Chapter was also convened from time to time to Perfect Brethren of particular distinction, for example, The Earl of Shrewsbury and Lord Lathom on 17th March 1875, and Lord Suffield and Francis Knollys, the Private Secretary to the Prince of Wales, on 8th February 1881. Before 1870 a Prince Rose Croix could Advance to the 30th Degree without having served as MWS of a Chapter, and on 10th October 1877 there had been a "Special Meeting of the Supreme Council Chapter Rose Croix" to Install in the Chair Dr. Hamilton 33°, a member of the Supreme Council, who had not previously been so Installed. At Consecrations of new Chapters at the present day the proceedings start by formally opening "The Supreme Council Chapter". A & A pp.333/4.

848 Morning Star Chapter was Warranted to work at Dera Ishmail in the Punjaub (sic) in 1872, apparently primarily for members of the Punjaub Frontier Force. The Warrant was returned from Kohat on 16th February 1892 and deposited in the archives of the Supreme Council. A & A, pp.378/9.

849 In some recent years it was stated in the 'Red Book' that Morning Star Chapter No.33 possessed "The only known travelling Warrant". This error was corrected in 2002, the Petition granted by the Supreme Council was only for "a change of Meeting place". The Supreme Council itself controls the membership of the Chapter, the Grand Secretary General for the time being acting as Recorder and the Grand Treasurer General generally being its Treasurer.

850 Afterwards King Edward VIII.

851 Afterwards King George VI.

852 It should, however, be noted that no such arrangement had been made when the then Prince of Wales (later king Edward VII) had been Advanced through all the Degrees, Fourth to Thirty-third, before becoming Grand patron.

853 Evidently two Brethren cannot be MWS of the same Chapter at the same time.

854 The Minutes of the Meeting of the Supreme Council on 10th March 1932 record "It was reported that H.R.H. The Prince of Wales K.G. and H.R.H. The Duke of York K.G. were installed as M.W.S's of the Supreme Council and Morning Star Chapters respectively, and subsequently received the 30°, 31°, 32°, and 33° at a meeting held here on Tuesday 8th Inst. and both were elected Honorary Members of the Supreme Council". John Tower, the Grand Secretary General, forwarded the Certificates of the two Royal Brethren, writing to Admiral Sir Lionel Halsey, the Private Secretary of the Prince of Wales "I have the pleasure to inform you that H.R.H. the Duke of York, Most Wise Sovereign of the Morning Star Chapter No.33 appointed you to the office of first General of that Chapter to which you have been elected a joining member". A & A, p.909.

855 Evidently in 1914 it had not been thought appropriate for female assistants to be employed in Masonic premises even in war-time. Probably John Tower, still Grand Secretary General in 1939 (he died in office in September 1942), at his advanced age was not prepared again to administer the Order single-handedly. At all events, Tower engaged Mrs. Main at £3/week in October 1939, and a year later she was joined by Miss Buckle.

856 To avoid any misapprehension, the 129 'Overseas' Chapters do not include those in the Isle of Man and the Channel Islands – nor in the Isle of Wight!

Bibliography

'Amblaine, Henri' (Alain Bernheim), *Masonic Catechisms and Exposures,* AQC, CVI, 141, 1993

Anderson, James, *The Constitutions of Freemasonry, 1723*

Anon. *Art Royal du Chevalier de Rosecroix*, Wolfstieg 35.724, ?1770

Asprey, Robert B., *Frederick the Great, the Magnificent Enigma*, (Revised Edition) Book-of-the-Month Inc., New York, 1999.

Barbier, *Le Journal de l'Avocat Barbier,* Vol. II, Paris, 1737

Batham, C.N., *Chevalier Ramsay, a new appreciation,* AQC LXXXI, 280, 1981

Baynard, S.H.Jr., *History of the Scottish Rite of Freemasonry*, New York, 1938

Benimeli, Fr. José A. Ferrer, *Masoneria Inglesia e Illustracion*, Vol.i, Madrid, 1982

Bernheim, Alain, *Avatars of the Knight Kadosh in France and in Charleston,* Heredom, Vol.6 p.162, 1997

Bernheim, Alain, *Did early 'High' or Écossais Degrees originate in France?*, Heredom. Vol.5 p.100, 1996

Bernheim, Alain, *Notes on Early Freemasonry in Bordeaux (1732-1769)*, AQC, CI, 33, 1988

Bernheim, Alain, *The* Mémoire Justificatif *of La Chaussée and Freemasonry in Paris until 1773*, AQC, CIV, 95, 1991

Boerenbeker, E.A., *The Relations between Dutch and English Freemasonry from 1734 to 1771*, AQC, LXXXIII, 149, 1970

Brodsky, Michel, *Les mythes et les légendes de la Grande Loge Unie d'Angleterre*, Renaissance Traditionelle, No.129 p.133 (January 2002)

Bryant, Gerald, *A History of the First 150 Years of St. Peter & St. Paul Chapter, No.6*, Fosseway Press, Radstock, Ltd., 2003

Carlile, Richard, *Manual of Freemasonry*, Reeves and Turner, London, ?1845

Carr, Harry, *The Early French Exposures*, QCCC, London, 1971

Carr, Harry, *The Conjoint Theory*, AQC, LXVI, p.44 (1953)

Chain of Union, The, (American Edition), l'Institut Maçonnique de France.

Choumitzky, Reputed transcription presented to Grand Lodge Library by Quatuor Coronati Lodge No. 2076 of *Etienne Morin*, Bulletin de la Grande Loge Nationale et Régulière Loge Saint Claudius, No.21, 1927 (Original not available in Grand Lodge Library)

Christmas, Matthew, *A Short Account of the Origins and Early History of the Grand Metropolitan Chapter,* privately printed, 1996

Cooper, F.J., *R.W. Bro. William Tucker, Prov. Grand Master of Dorsetshire, 1846-1853*, AQC LXXXIII, p.124, 1970

Craven, John E., *An Historical Sketch of Freemasonry at Bottoms, Eastwood, Near Todmorden, Yorkshire*, John Heywood, Manchester, 1886

Cryer, The Revd. N. Barker, *A Fresh Look at the Harodim*, AQC XCI, 116, 1978

Culpan, John, *A History of High Greenwood Chapter of Princes Rose Croix of H.R.D.M.*, privately printed, 1992

Dalcho, Frederick, *Orations of the Illus. Brother Frederick Dalcho Esqre. M.D.*, John King Westmorland, Dublin, 1808

Daniel, J.W., *Pure – and Accepted Masonry. The Craft and the Extra-Craft Degrees, 1843-1901*, AQC CVI, 68, 1993

Dermott, Lawrence, *Ahiman Rezon,* 1756 Edition

Fairbairn Smith, J., *The Rise of the Ecossais Degrees*, Chapter of Research of the Grand Chapter of R.A.Masons of Ohio, Vol. 10, 1965

Freemasons' Magazine, The

Freemasons' Quarterly Review, The

Grand Constitutions of the Ancient-Accepted Rite of the Year 1786, The, (Albert Pike's translation), The Supreme Council for England and Wales and Dependencies of the British Crown, 1859

Hamill, John, *A Third Francken MS of the Rite of Perfection*, AQC, XCVII, p.200, 1984

Hamill, John, *The Jacobite Conspiracy,* AQC, CXIII, 97, 2000

Harris, Ray Baker, *Eleven Gentlemen of Charleston*, Washington, D.C., 1959

Hewitt, A.R., *Another Francken Manuscript rediscovered*, AQC, LXXXIX, p.208, 1976

Hivert-Messeca, Yves, *"De Generalissimi Magni Episcopi Vagentes"*, Deux Siècles de Rite Écossais Ancien Accepté en France, 1804-2004, p.59, Éditions Dervy, Paris, 2004

Howe, Ellic, *The Rite of Memphis in France and England 1838-70*, AQC XCII p.1, 1979

Jackson, A.C.F., *Freemasonry in Jersey*, AQC LXXXVI, p.177, 1973

Jackson, A.C.F., *Joseph Glock*, AQC XCIV p.43, 1981

Jackson, A.C.F., *Rose Croix*, Revised and Enlarged Edition, Lewis Masonic, 1987

Jackson, A.C.F., *The Authorship of the 1762 Constitutions of the Ancient and Accepted Rite,* AQC, XCVII, p.176, 1984

James, P.R., *The Crucefix Oliver Affair*, AQC LXXIV, p.53, 1961

James, P.R., *The Union and After, 1813 to 1917*, Grand Lodge, 1717-1967, Oxford University Press, 1967

James, P.R., *The Grand-Mastership of H.R.H. the Duke of Sussex 1813-43*, The Collected Prestonian Lectures 1961-1974, (Vol 2), p. 11, Lewis Masonic, London, 1983

Jones, Bernard E., *A Freemason's Guide and Compendium*, Harrap & Co., London, 1950

Kahler, Lisa, *Andrew Michael Ramsay and his Masonic Oration*, Heredom, 1, 19, 1992

Kervalla, André, & Lestienne, Philippe, *Un haut-grade templier dans les milieux jacobites en 1750: l'Ordre Sublime des Chevaliers Elus aux sources de la Stricte Observance*, Renaissance Traditionelle, No.112, 229, October 1997

Knoop, D., Jones, G.P., & Hamer, D. *Early Masonic Catechisms*, Revised Edition, QCCC, London, 1963

Knoop, D., Jones, G.P., & Hamer, D., *Early Masonic Pamphlets*, reprinted edition, QCCC, London, 1975

Lane, John, *Masonic Records*, 2nd. Edition, London, 1895

Lassalle, Jean Pierre, *Des Constitutions et Règlements de 1762 aux Grandes Constitutions de 1786*, Celebration du Bicentenaire des Grandes Constitutions de 1786, p.9, Suprême Conseil pour la France, 1986

Lindsay, Robert S. (Ed. A.J.B.Milburn) *The Royal Order of Scotland*, Wm. Culross & Son, Coupar Angus, 1971

Litvine, Jacques, *Anti-Masonry: A Neglected Source,* AQC CIV, 121, 1991

MacDonough, Giles, *Frederick the Great, a Life in Deed and Letters,* St. Martin's Press, New York, 1999

Mandleberg, C. John, *The Lausanne Conference of 1875,* Heredom Vol.6 p.83, 1997

Mandleberg, John, *Ancient and Accepted,* QCCC Ltd., London, 2000

Mandleberg, John, *The Secrets of the Craft,* AQC, CXIII, 14, 2000

Matthews, R.D., *Some Masonic degrees worked at Bottoms, Stansfield, near Halifax, during the nineteenth century* (A paper read before the Chapter of Affability, No. 308, on the 5th December, 1931, and published by the Chapter)

McEwen, Ewen, *The Mount Calvary Encampment*, (Undated - ?1990)

Mellor, Alec, *The Roman Catholic Church and the Craft*, AQC, LXXXIX, p.60, 1976

Mollier, Pierre, *Le grade maçonnique et le christianisme: enjeux et pouvoirs des symboles*, Deux Siècles de Rite Écossais Ancien Accepté en France, 1804-2004, p.171, Éditions Dervy, Paris, 2004

Mollier, Pierre, *Nouvelles lumières sur la Patente Morin et le Rite de Perfection,* Deux Siècles de Rite Écossais Ancien Accepté en France, 1804-2004, p.31, Éditions Dervy, Paris, 2004

Naudon, Paul, *Histoire, Rituels et Tuilleur des Hauts Grades Maçonniques*, 3rd. Edition, refondue et augmentée, Dervy-Livres, Paris, 1978

Poll, Michael, *The philalethes*, June 2001

Price, Brian W., *Metamorphosis. The Evolution of Prince Edward Council G* (Allied Masonic Degrees), privately printed, 2003

Rickard, F.M., *William Finch, Part 2*, AQC LV, 163, 1944

Rylands, Harry W, (Ed.) *The Records of the Lodge Original No.1, now Lodge of Antiquity No.2*, 2nd Edition Revised, privately printed by Harrison and Sons for the Lodge of Antiquity, 1928

Sandbach, R.S.E., *Priest and Freemason*, (Revd. Edition) Lewis Masonic, London, 1993

Smyth, Frederick, *Brethren in Chivalry, 1791-1991*, Lewis Masonic, London, 1991

Speth, G.W., *The English Lodge at Bordeaux*, AQC, XII, 6, 1899

Stephenson, R.L., *Kidnapped*

Thorp, John T., (Edited Vibert, L.), *French Prisoners' Lodges*, (2nd. Edition, augmented) The Lodge of Research No. 2429, Freemasons' Hall, Leicester, 1935

Tuckett, J.E.S., *The Origin of Additional Degrees*, AQC, XXXII, 5, 1919

Tunbridge, Paul, *The Climate of English Freemasonry, 1730 to 1750,* AQC LXXXI, 88, 1981

Valette, Th.G.G., *The Island of St. Eustatius and its Lodges*, AQC, XLIV, 57, 1931

Vibert, Lionel, *Some early Elu manuscripts, AQC*, XLIV, 171, 1931

Voorhis, Harold Van Buren, *The Story of the Scottish Rite*, Henry Emerson, New York, 1965

Waite, A.E.W., *A New Encyclopaedia of Freemasonry,* Combined Edition, Wings Books, New Jersey, 1994

Waples, W., *An Introduction to the Harodim*, AQC LX, 118, 1947

Ward, Eric, *Early Masters' Lodges and their relation to Degrees, AQC*, LXXV, Part I, p.124, Part II p.155, 1962

BIBLIOGRAPHY

Whitney, Geoffrey, *A Choice of Emblemes and other divises*, Leyden, 1586

Wiles, H.V., *Mount Calvary Chapter Rose Croix No.3, 1848-1948*, 1948

Wilkins, Norman, *History of the Ancient and Accepted Rite in Somerset*, privately printed, 2000.

Wonnacott, William, *The Rite of Seven Degrees in London*, AQC XXXIX, p.63, 1926

Yates, Frances A., *The Occult Philosophy in the Elizabethan Age*, Routledge & Kegan Paul, London, 1979

Yates, Frances A., *The Rosicrucian Enlightenment*, Paladin Edition, Granada Publishing Ltd., 1975

Index

Holmes, Emra 186

Holroyd, James 184, 186

Holt, James 182

Holy Land 16-17

Holy Wisdom degrees 57

Holy Royal Arch, The, degree 14, 20, 46, 53

Honis, Samuel 65, 67

Hopper, Capt. Arthur Quinn 83, 95
  Howe, Ellic 67

Hoyte, Ald. 88

Hughan, W. J. 32? 194

Hully, F. 149

Husenbeth 74

Huxley, Thomas 196

Huyshe, John 169, 176

Illuminism 40

Ingham Clark, Alastair 151

Intermediate degrees 121-122, 124-125, 130-131, 133, 143, 147, 150-151

Installation ceremony 20, 143

International conferences 190-191

Irish College of Rites 64, 69

Irish Rite 156, 163

Isaiah 116

Jackson, A. C. F. 32, 36, 41, 66, 107, 112, 114, 119, 127, 130, 139; Grand Constitutions 51; *Rose Croix* (revised 1987) 9, 14, 18, 21-22, 27, 51, 59, 66

Jacobites 14-15

Jahan, Joseph 43

James, P. R. *The Grand-Mastership of HRH the Duke of Sussex* (1983) 73-74; *The Crucefix Oliver Affair* (1961) 74

James Stewart, the Old Pretender 15

James, Lord Steward of Scotland, 15-16, 59

Jewels and insignia 128-130, 132

Jocelyn, Hon. A. F. 88

John Coombe Masonic Library, Hayle 60, 73

Jolly 123

Joly, Alice *Un Mystique Lyonnais et les Secrets de la Franc-Maçonnerie 1730-1824* (1938) 112

Jones, Bernard E. *A Freemason's Guide and Compendium* (1950) 58-59

Jones, F. W. 63

Jones, G. P. 18, 58

Jonville, Chaillon de 24, 27, 29-31
  Journal de l'Avocat Barbier, Le (1737) 15, 18

'Kadosh' degree 23-24, 43-44, 65, 67, 69, 73, 76, 81-82, 90, 95, 109, 113, 121, 127, 156, 174, 177, 186, 188; in South Africa 159, 190

Kahler, Lisa *Andrew Michael Ramsey and his Masonic Oration* (1992) 18

Kelly, Maj. Joseph 66

Kelly, Martin 25

Kenning, George 171, 180

Kent, Dr. Benjamin Archer 124, 155, 160-161, 163

Kent, Duke of 60-61

Kervalla, André *Un haute-grade templier dans les milieux jacobites en 1750* (1997) 26

Kilwinning, Scots Knight of, 73, 175

Kingsmill, Henry 158, 165

Kipling, Rudyard 116

Knight, John 60, 69, 112, 174, 184-185

Knights of Constantinople 60

Knights of Malta 58, 60, 69, 73, 121, 169, 175, 179

Knights of Palestine 175

Knights of Rhodes 175

Knights of St. Andrew 69, 79, 107, 114

Knights of St John of Jerusalem 16-17, 58, 175

Knights of the Eagle 29, 31, 69, 73, 107, 114, 175

Knights of the East 24, 27, 29-30, 36, 38, 43, 73-74, 79, 81, 122, 175, 194

Knights of the East and West 50, 122, 125, 127-128, 131-132, 144, 179, 194

Knights of the Pelican 69, 107, 114

Knights of the Rose Croix 47, 73, 84;
  Mount Carmel 168

Knights of the Sword 22, 24, 29, 73, 79, 122, 175, 194

Knights Templar 22, 54-57, 61, 65, 68-69, 71, 76, 78, 81, 88, 95, 109, 110, 128, 130, 151, 169, 175-6, 178; Templar Order's destruction (1313) 22, 28; in Cornwall 60; in Ireland 63; in Lancashire 168, 178; Grand Conclave 65, 70-71, 81-83, 121, 140, 156, 167, 189; early records lost 73; Bath 188; Bristol 102; Rituals 118, 139. See also under Encampments, Knights Templar

Knollys, Francis 197

Knoop, Douglas 18, 58

Lacorne, Jacques 24, 27, 29-30
  death in 1762 24

Lahore library 32

Lassalle, Jean-Pierre 43, 45; *Des Constitutions et Règlements de 1762 aux Grandes Constitutions de 1786* 44, 51

Lathom, Lord 176, 187, 197

Laurent, Pierre 69

Lausanne Congress, 1876 158, 191, 196

Lechangeur 65

Leeson, Dr. Henry Beaumont 60, 71, 73-84, 87, 89-93, 95-98, 100-101, 103, 110, 113, 122-123, 130, 141, 161, 163, 168-169, 174-175, 178, 180, 188

Leigh, Lord 87

Leinster, Duke of 63-64, 67, 75, 77, 111, 122

Lestienne, Philippe *Un haute-grade templier dans les milieux jacobites en 1750* (1997) 26

Leszczynska, Maria (Queen of France) 14

Letter from the Grand Mistress (1724) 58

Levy, Moses Clava 45

Liebem, Israel de 45

Lillie, Col. Sir John Scott 66

Limerick, Earl of 33? 170, 194

Lindsay, Robert Strathearn 41, 54; *The Royal Order of Scotland* (1971) 59

Link degree 60

Litvine, Jacques *Anti-Masonry: A Neglected Source* (1991) 26-27

Liverpool, Palatine Chapter could be held in, 168

Lodges
  Albany, 'Ineffable Lodge of the City of' 33
  Antiquity, now No. 2, U.G. L. E. 58
  'Bear at Bath', see Royal Cumberland
  Berlin, Lodge first opened by Bielfield 42
  Bordeaux 'Lodge of Perfection' 29, 36, 38
  'Brilliant', London (Shireff) 121
  Burlington, now No. 96 U. G. L. E. 70, 75
  Charleston 'Lodge of Perfection' 38, 44
  Dresden, Lodges of Rectified Scottish Rite 39, 44
  'Enfants de Mars et de Neptune', Abergavenny 74
  Honour, Lodge of Bath, now No. 379 U. G. L. E. 88
  Horn Lodge 54
  'John Coustos' Lodge 15, 29
  Le Contrat Social, adds to its title 'Mère Loge du Rite Ecossais à l'Orient de Paris' 39
  Loge d'Ecosse ou des Elus parfaits (Bordeaux) 23
  Loge La Candeur 39
  Loge La Française 20
  Loge La Parfaite Harmonie, Dominique 31
  Loge La Sainte Trinité, Paris 24
  Loge La Vèrité, Cap François 44
  Loge L'Amitié 21
  Loge L'Anglaise, now No. 204, *G. O. de France* 20
  Loge Parfaite Harmonie 21
  Loge Saint-Jean de Jerusalem, Paris (Lodge of the Grand Master of the Grand Lodge of France) 26
  Marseilles, 'Mother Lodge' of 44
  Metz, Lodge presided over by Meunier de Précourt, 24, 29, 73
  Murton Lodge of Perfection 164
  Nippon, Japan, U. G. L. E. No 1344 (Warrant surrendered) 165
  Peace and Harmony, Lodge of London) Now No. 60 U. G. L. E. 74-75
  Perfect Observance No. 1 ('Grand Lodge of the South of the Trent'), (previously 'St. Georges de l'Observance') presided over by de Lintot 56
  Philanthropic, Leeds, now No. 304 U. G. L. E. 187
  Philanthropic, Abergavenny, then No. 658, Warrant surrendered, re-founded as St. John's Lodge No. 818 U. G. L. E. 74